BU
UNIVE

Last Stop: Duisburg
A family's escape from Pogroms and the Holocaust

Candace

Rechtschaffen-Gillhoolley

europe books

ISBN 9791220125734
First edition: July 2022
Edited by Stella Fusca

Last Stop: Duisburg
A family's escape from Pogroms and the Holocaust

To my parents,

for an unlikely love story between a noble elephant and a lovely leggy giraffe.

In middle school the principal remarked that I was dramatic, friendly and an average student. Visibly upset, my dad stood up and replied, "there's nothing average about my Candi. She'll be outstanding with her family behind her." His un-wavering devotion taught me more than how to work hard but how to live my life.

My mom taught me to be fiercely independent from a young age. She demanded I have a career and be in control of my own destiny. Her dreams are my milestones and I share all my success with her. She is my best friend, my advocate, and the voice in my head that wants me to be brave. I will never falter nor want for anything in the world or beyond with a mother as devoted as mine. I did it for you mom. xoxo

To all the survivors who got out. What you endured enabled future generations to thrive.

ACKNOWLEDGEMENTS

I want to thank the team at Europe Books for their support. Ginevra Picani, Alicia Guinot, Elisa Giuliani, and Stella Fusca managed all my expectations as a debut novelist and expressed themselves with grace and candor bringing my dream into a reality.

The Rechtschaffens. We number in the thousands and live on every continent of the world except Antarctica. When we trace our lineage to western Ukraine and southern Poland, we all become one family collective. Most notably, a thank you to David Rechtschaffen, my Canadian cousin whose extensive research was critical to the backbone of this novel. He introduced me to *The Yizkor Project: Rozniatow. A testimonial* written by the survivors of the Holocaust to reclaim what The Nazis tried to erase.

Yizkor Book in Memory of Rozniatow, Perehinsko, Broszniow, Swaryczow, and Environs Hardcover – April 5, 2013, by Shimon Kane (Editor), Thomas F. Weiss (Editor) JewishGen, Inc.; Illustrated edition (April 5, 2013)

There are a few friends in particular whose endless support and friendship have shaped me into the person I am today.

Nikki Vines, Nicole Beaulieu, Heather Martin, Rachel Weber, Erin Twohey, Jessica Hamermesh-Nathanson, Jess Bloch-Whitehall, Kira Willig, Diana Gooljar, Phil Gooljar, Mike Mikowski, Alison Pressman-Goldenberg, Rona Sinclair, Sean Dennis, Raquel Lobaton, Jen Silverman and Girlie Polignon.

Kim Miller Shurie, my own extraordinary person. Your strength, wisdom, and compassion make life bearable in the harsher moments. With you I know I'm never without support. You took my manuscript, brazenly tore it apart, and patched it back together with insightful comments and prompts. I love you.

Edi Vermass, a friend from Holland, who sought me out in 2005 and supplied documentation Which took the story from black and white in my mind and turned it into full color.

Blake Shepard. Your love of family speaks deeply to me. You are a constant light and source of warmth. I'm better for having you as part of my life and family.

Julie Gillhoolley. You came into my life when my father died. Your sweetness and casual nature allowed me to heal from the greatest tragedy of my life and grow into new loving relationships. You're my family, my friend and occupy significant residency in my heart.

Grandma Barbara Kaliff, you are my lucky charm sitting in heaven next to Dad and keeping him company. For months in the hospital, you held me as a sick newborn, loving and protecting me. My own fairy godmother, in some ways, I imprinted upon you. I craved to be the person you saw within me. Sophisticated and luxurious, you maintained gloriously until 101 years old. I know you're witnessing my achievement. You never stopped believing in me. You cherished family and your loyalty was legendary. I hope to carry that torch. This was my first step.

Dad, you are the inspiration for this novel and the smartest person I ever met. The universe chose to testify to your ancestry, survival, and innovation. Pledging your life to mom, raising your family, and observing Judaism were your pillars of happiness. Honest, pious, brilliant, and sensitive to the harshness of the world, you raised me to study hard, think visually and love passionately. You taught me to see that my Dyslexia was merely the jump off point not the destination. If I worked hard enough, I'd see the gift within. You always said, stay sweet. You didn't get a chance to see me become an adult, but I did. I love you and wish I could still remember the sound of your voice. I hope you like the book.

Mom, you are always in my corner. Your undying love and support crafted me into an amazingly capable and nurturing woman. I'm honoured for the world to know how much I love, respect, and need you in my life. You boost me up and are essential to my health and wellness. Your drive makes me stronger. Sharing my life with you as an adult and witnessing your joy in my success makes the reward even more valuable.

Tommy, my brother, my first idol and the standard to which my achievements were measured. From early on you made it safe for me to be my most authentic self. I never fit the mold and you nurtured those characteristics enabling my wellness and growth. You are the only one who understands what it was like growing up in our house. I still idolize you and forever love you.

Ronin, my son, you are my head. My first great achievement, you empower me to push beyond my self-imposed limitations. An enigmatic leader whose compassion, strength, and intelligence leaves me in awe. Find the voice of reason within and listen more. The silent cues will protect, guide, and take you farther. The amount of love and respect I have for you is immeasurable.

Autumn, my daughter, you are my heart. I'm your advocate and champion for as long as you need me. Your existence drives me to achieve ultimate health and wellness. Your humor, observation and beauty leave me in awe. I take our trust and love very seriously and know how lucky I am to have created you. I lava you.

Sean Gillhoolley. You are the greatest gift the universe chose to bestow upon me. With you by my side, I'm unconquerable. You show me love, wonder, adventure, and fulfilment. You nurtured and taught me to take notice, demand respect and love myself. Endlessly protective of my heart; you show me every day what love can create when you dare to believe.

Candace M Gillhoolley

Candace.novelist@gmail.com
FB: @CandaceTheNovelist
TW: @gillhoolleyc
www.candacegillhoolley.com

*When something seems impossible,
do it every day until you master it.*

Dr. Rudolph N. Rechtschaffen

The Rechtschaffen's family tree

PROLOGUE
I May 1939, Berlin, Germany age 7
Manfred Rechtschaffen

The Gestapo came for Abba (father) last night. He warned me this could happen. In my neighbourhood, others have disappeared. Those left behind wept. Their misery is uglier than their gruesome reality. Abba isn't returning.

In the pit of my stomach, a hardened scab remains of the wound created by his absence. I climb into my baby brother, Rudy's crib. His gurgling breaths alleviate the itch.

Exhausted, I drift to sleep, holding Rudy, and try to forgive Abba for leaving us. On the weekends, Abba and I made breakfast sandwiches together.

His speciality was fluffy whipped eggs with minced onion seasoned with salt and pepper between toasted buttered rye bread. First, he taught me how to toast the bread.

Next, I practised cracking eggs and then whipping them up in a bowl. When you cook eggs, he says, the pan must be hot enough to see the slab of butter sizzle. He taught me how to hold and use a knife and how not to chop off my fingers. The secret, Abba says, is to tuck your fingers underneath at the knuckle when slicing an onion.

Abba used Ima's (mother) porcelain bowl from the shelf and beat the eggs into a frothy yellow batter. He poured the eggs and onions into the skillet. After the toaster popped, Abba folded the eggs upon themselves. We ate our delicious breakfast creations together. He wasn't fussy about manners and often spoke with his mouth full of food.

Breakfast concluded with the same sentiment every time, "A new day brings a fresh start."

This morning the aroma of coffee draws me from bed.

I untangle myself from Rudy and skulk into the kitchen. Yesterday was awful. Just when I didn't think it could get any worse, I was proven wrong again.

Craving a fresh start, I squeeze Ima around her waist then run across the kitchen. The pressure building inside of me is keeping pace with the drum beat in my ears.

I can't hear anything else. Even shrieking couldn't unleash this terror coursing through my body. Ima reaches out and pulls me towards her. Her embrace deactivates my alarm.

She smells like cinnamon and butter.

I want to protect her, but I don't know how.

Offhandedly she asks, "Can you get Rudy for me?"

"Of course," I say.

I walk away and hear the fork clanging against the porcelain bowl. The sound reminds me of Abba. If I start to cry, Rudy will notice, and I'll have to explain away my tears.

I'm incapable of finding adequate words. Rudy toddles over to Ima. With a fistful of her apron, Rudy's toothy grin brightens the room. She coaxes Rudy into the highchair, and I add bread to the toaster. While she salts the eggs, I set the table. Our choreographed ballet of breakfast preparation is complete. Rudy eats with his hands and misses his mouth more often than he succeeds. His joy invigorates me.

Ima confesses to exhaustion. Her bloodshot eyes hurt to glance at; normally emerald-green, their pallor is closer to moss. Ima pulls on her fingers when she's nervous.

Normally controlled, her intensity concerns me. If I distract her just enough, she'll stop pulling at her fingers. My mind races through ideas and nothing seems worth the effort.

She talks to herself and answers incongruous questions, like, "yes, it's warm enough," and "the cream does smell strange." A twister of thoughts whirls through my mind.

Ima wants to open the store for the day. I'm not sure either of us will be able to focus. She unlocks the front door, turns the sign from closed to open, and exhales.

Ima is not one to run, when faced with the choice, she'll fight. I'll help her today, and tomorrow, and for every day after that until she doesn't need me anymore. She'll greet the customers and I'll make the tea.

Her "speciality customers" could arrive at any moment. In private Ima mocks these Nazi wives and calls them "the Hens."

She addresses them with a disingenuous smile. Warning me at every turn how stupid poultry is. Rudy and I come back to the apartment for his mid-morning nap.

Ima prefers I stay close by in case Rudy wakes up early.

He never does, and I tell her this daily, but today I choose not to remind her. I want to be alone. The skin underneath my eyes feels paper thin like a matchbook. My eyelids burn on the insides. Closing them momentarily alleviates the awful sensation but it doesn't completely solve the problem.

After Rudy nods off, I enter my parent's bedroom and bury my nose deep in my father's pillowcase. His forgotten imprint still smells like him.

A motorcycle brigade roars past our store. Ima wobbles. With trembling hands, she locks the store's front door, flips the signage, and pulls down the blind. Without completing her usual close down procedure, she scoops up Rudy, and rushes home. The air in our home is musty and it makes my heart ache. I'm annoyed. My stomach growls for warm chicken soup and rice. To distract myself, I protectively lock the front door and the windows for the night. That was Abba's job. I look at Ima with slumped shoulders and dark smudges under her eyes. I suggest a family nap the way Abba used to when Ima was tired from being up with baby Rudy the night before. Her face floods with relief. My help made her feel better. A warm yellow glow sweeps itself over my body. We pile into her bed and we're asleep within minutes. As the sun sets, Ima wordlessly prepares supper. My thoughts remain suspended before me.

Too many are building up like hot kernels of popcorn popping on the stovetop. Silence around our dinner table is awkward, like an itchy wool winter blanket. She pushes her mashed potatoes around the plate. I clench my teeth and swallow a tasteless lump of food.

A key shakes the lock above the door handle. Abba installed that extra lock before baby Rudy was born. Maybe it was Herman's idea? Without realizing it I rush towards the front door and nearly collide with a savagely beaten version of Abba. I don't even recall standing up and leaving the dinner table. Instead, I collide with a savagely beaten version of Abba. Enclosing my arms around his midriff, I'm as effective as a woodpecker trying to hold up a bull. He falters and we slide to the floor.

"No. My. Left," he pleads in anguish.

His voice is almost unrecognizable but not nearly as much as his sweet soft face. His right eye is swollen shut and all of his blood in his body looks uncontained beneath his skin.

"Can I help?" I ask. My heart pounds in my ears.

He terrifies me.

"Not now, Manfred, we have to wash Abba," instructs Ima.

I fetch the sacramental water basin.

"I love you," he says to Ima.

"Kiss me." They kiss and I don't look away.

Abba's hands are covered in minor scrapes and bruises. He paws at her face tenderly. Tears stream from her eyes and he clumsily kisses them. Her hands move tenderly.

I'm covered in goosebumps. Abbas' face is misshapen to resemble someone else. His fair hair is pasted oddly on the top of his head. Ima dips a cloth into our Passover basin, twists and squeezes the excess water and mercifully tends to Abbas' wounds.

They speak and I occupy Rudy.

Rudy squeals, "Abbabbaba!" The mood lightens.

The stress of the day rolls over me like a tank trampling wildflower. Rudy and I climb into my bed to give our parents their alone time.

My windows rattle behind my curtains from motorcycles thundering past our apartment. Terrified of the Gestapo's return, like a shot from a gun, I ran into my parents' room. Abba offers me a sleepy grin. He stands before me holding a sledgehammer with his one good hand.

"What is going on in there?" I ask.

"I had to wait for the motorcycles to cover the sound," he explains.

"Why?" I ask.

Unbothered by the commotion, Ima stands by the window, like an owl, examining the street for food, from the shadows.

"I'm preparing a hole in our wardrobe for you to hide in," says Abba.

Tears streak his cheeks as he builds our sanctuary. His bruised arms never quit.

"The adrenaline in my body is holding back the pain," he interprets.

"My body is in shock from the arrest, Manfred. Once I stop moving, the suffering will overwhelm my body. This is how the body mends itself."

Sawing away the closet walls, he says, "The hole will be big enough for you, Rudy, and your Ima."

"What about you?" I ask.

"I need a place to hide you and Rudy from the Nazis. They're going to come back and we're not going to have enough time to run away. I can't go and buy lumber right now or paint. Crafting a fake door is unthinkable. The best I can manage is to conserve extra plaster from the closet as we dig this hole."

Feverishly, he works and stops talking. Abba removes part of an architectural support beam to increase the space.

He splits the timber to shreds unfazed by the splinters.

A ghastly pain fills my gut, and my mouth begins to water. Shuddering, my back is slick with sweat. To preserve my hands, I wear thick wool socks while scooping out the rubble from inside the closet.

Periodically, I creep inside the widening hole to test our progress. I crush my frustration into small, tiny fists. My chest feels like a motor overheating.

My Ima says, "Manfred, the Gestapo will return. It is your job to grab your brother and hide."

******

Rudy and Abba feast upon a smorgasbord of milk, eggs, toast, pancakes, and coffee. Ima smells of freshly baked challah. Ima moves throughout the apartment and Abba track her every step. We spend the day inside and listen to the radio. Abba is stiff, and when he moves, he winces. He favours his left hand and arm. Ima brings him tea and honey cake.

I tell Rudy, "If someone knocks on the door, you run to the hole. Do you understand?" Rudy nods his head.

We practice racing to the closet and climbing inside. Rudy struggles to close the false door from the inside. With each undertaking, he gets faster. Every night, the Gestapo patrol our neighbourhood. Abba calls their behaviour a death of one thousand cuts. The Nazis' foot is always on the Jews' neck. The torture is relentless, and the stress builds to a point where a strong person would break. When dad returned from prison, his nightly routine changed.

After our parents put us to bed, Abba goes into their bedroom and spends time with Ima.

When I hear the hinges on my door groan against his body weight, I know he's finished his patrol around the apartment. The doors and windows have been doublechecked and re-locked, his baseball bat is in hand, and my burning eyes succumb to exhaustion because he is vigilant outside my door.

******

Heavy jackboots shake the walls. Vomit rises in my throat. With sweaty palms, I gather Rudy in his favourite soft blue blanket. We climb inside our hideaway. I give Rudy my lucky rabbit's foot. His hazel eyes open wide.

"Remain here until I come back. No sound," I urge.

I place my finger to my lips in a familiar gesture and lean over to kiss him. Once I secure the fake door for Rudy, I enter the living room. I sit down in the center of the room and start playing jacks.

The German Shepherds bark angrily. The Police keep them hungry on purpose. I swallow the lump in my throat.

The pounding of impending jackboots intensifies. The boots stop. The door handle shakes but remains closed. I count ten, nine, eight, seven-the front door breaks open, bumping on its hinges. I miss the ball with my right hand but seize a fist full of jacks with my left. The cool metal distracts me long

25

enough to catch my breath. Squeezing the jacks harder focuses me. The ball rolls under the table. A giant officer looms over me. My heart is beating quicker than ever.

I wonder, can my heart explode?

"Where is your father?" booms the towering man.

His wide nostrils flare as they smell something unpleasant. His eyes are obscured by the shadow of his cap.

The brass buttons shine against the dullness of the muddy pea colour of the uniforms. His belt and straps are made from brown leather.

Using my best German, I stutter, "H-h-he is n-not here."

I tear my focus away from his beak.

"Where is your mother?" The Nazi demands.

What should I say? She is not here, and I'm annoyed.

Surprised by my resentment, my body overheats. My anger comforts me.

"Where is your mother?" The Nazi screams.

I will not crumble.

"She is with my brother," I reply within a heartbeat.

He pushes me aside and four new men file in behind him. His breath is rotten, and his teeth are stained yellow.

I remain fixated on my opposition. The men rummage around the room upturning drawers and spilling their contents on the floor. A vase is carelessly mishandled and shatters against or living room floor.

Dishes are broken and the fresh apples on the counter are eaten.

The Nazi barks, "Manfred, Would you like a bicycle? Boys your age, get a modern bicycle to navigate Berlin with from Hitler." His expression softens.

Does he not realize that we are Jewish?

"Yes." I replied. If I said anymore, I might throw up.

"Excellent. Come outside with us and choose your bicycle. We'll return with it tomorrow."

He clicks his heels, and I do my best not to jump, but I fail. He's pleased to see my fear. I hate him even more.

Ima says it's important not to let hate live inside of you. The anger builds and doesn't have anywhere to go. It corrodes until it controls you.

Once he steps back, the other men follow suit. I'm supposed to pursue him but I'm not going to. My feet remain cemented to the ground. I squeeze the jacks in my hand hard enough to pierce my flesh and remain vigilant.

That's what I did to defy the Nazis.

"I cannot leave without my brother," I answered. One officer laughs and punches the other on the shoulder. They're grinning at my expense. I'm not naïve.

My anger makes me brazen.

"Come with us downstairs. You'll pick a bicycle, and we'll return tomorrow," says the laughing man.

His gnarled hand reaches out for me. If I scream, Rudy might come out from hiding. It is my job to protect my brother. From the moment he was born, Ima said he belonged to me. He is my responsibility.

Abba said, "Never leave with them. You'll not return."

"Not without my brother. I cannot go without my brother," one officer turns to another and argues.

"If you don't come now..." the sound of howling dogs interrupts him. There is a high-pitched whining noise. One soldier leaves. The dogs bark frenetically. Another soldier hurries out, saying, "Get ready, Manfred. When we come back, we'll bring a red wagon for your baby brother."

Two soldiers and the officer remain. The officer steps forward and places his hands on my shoulders. His fingers are long and bony. He reminds me of a skeleton.

If a skeleton man's hands touch me, will I become a skeleton? "There will be no further pardons" declares the skeleton man. He glances at his timepiece. I wish he would leave. The dogs bark louder now. I count silently to regulate my breathing. I beg Hashem to have the beasts keep yapping. Bark! Bark! I scream inside my head. I'm astonished they cannot hear me. The dogs bark more. The men appear flustered. The skeleton man and one of the soldiers leave the apartment and argue outside the door. The soldier runs down the corridor.

The skeleton man returns and directs the last soldier.

"Go outside and find out what is keeping everyone? This is taking too long."

The skeleton man smiles wickedly at me. He clicks his heels, but I don't jump. His authority is not power over me. He's petty. I detest him. I loathe every Nazi.

The skeleton man leaves and adds, "until tomorrow."

I open my parents' door and head straight for the closet. The false wall is intact. Rudy didn't open it. He listened.

I remove the wall and see Rudy sucking his thumb and rubbing the rabbit's foot against his nose. I climb in and replace the false door.

Chapter 1
September 1868 Rozniatow, Galicia, age 8
Tzizel Rechtschaffen

Mist hovers over the wet dewy grass waiting for daybreak to burn it away. The bottoms of Abba's trousers will be soaked unless he remains on the dirt path to the synagogue. Before dawn we see wild hares run under shrubs, birds gathering seeds for their young, and squirrels chasing each other. A nervous squirrel who senses danger sounds like a bird. But once you see a squirrel make that sound you could never forget it. When the sun washes over the Carpathian Mountains, Abba's in the synagogue, donning his tallis and tefillin. His battle armour, Ima calls it. My parents like to tease each other. He says love is shown in the little gestures and the side comments. He's told me on numerous occasions that Ima's laugh is contagious.

"The first time I heard it, I knew I would marry that woman." Ima says, "Abba is most at home inside the synagogue."

His friends, Wolf Hoffmann, Shaye Frieldler, and David Axelrad are there within moments of his arrival. If anyone is missing it is because they are gravely ill. Ima says they congregate before the morning minyan (group of ten men) quietly preparing themselves for the day. They've been doing this since their bar mitzvahs. They stand around a wooden table in the back of the sanctuary. Their velvet bags are engraved with their Hebrew name sewn in a gold-coloured thread. Each bag, a precious gift from their parents in the preparation of their bar mitzvah, contains their tefillin.

Lately, my brothers Yakkov and Mordechia join Abba and I in the mornings' prayers. The boys learned how to pray in school, but the girls don't get to attend school because everything a good little Jewish girl needs to know can be taught to her by her mother in preparation for marriage parenthood. Abba taught me to pray because he found illiteracy lazy.

He believed no one had the right to deny anyone their personal time with Hashem. That's exactly what prayer is; your own time is now.

Bar'chi nafshi et Adonai, Adonai Elohai, gadalta m'od, hod v'hadar lavashta. Oteh or kasalmah, noteh shamayim kay'riah

Bless, Adonai, O my soul!
Adonai my God, how great You are.
You are robed in glory and majesty,
wrapping Yourself in light as in a garment,
spreading forth the heavens like a curtain.

"Strong communities are built around a singular ideal," Abba explains.

"My father brought the Torah to our community. The synagogue is Hashem's house."

Abba saw the synagogue as a home away from home. I learned how to read, write, and pray there.

My brothers Shalom, Shimshon, Mordecai, Binyamin, and Yaacov never fuss when they're in the synagogue.

My father, Hersch Tzvi Rechtschaffen, is the wisest man in Rozniatow. He smells like soap and sunshine. He taught me to approach life as one small task to accomplish at a time. Everything can be managed if you can break it up into bitesize pieces.

The steady flow of his wisdom trained me to stow away the advice for a later day. He enforced this behaviour by asking me to repeat certain nuggets back to him. I didn't like parroting, it made me feel small. He never spoke to my brothers in the same way. It's as if they were born with more knowledge than me. But I can sew a button, mend a sock, add, and subtract faster than most of them.

During the service, esteemed representatives of the congregation perform an Aliyah (calling a congregant up to the Bimah (an altar) for a section of the Torah reading.)

These blessings are both physical and spiritual. Ascension to the bimah completes the hallowed rite of the blessing.

My favourite Aliyah is when they lift the Torah for the congregation to behold. The unfurled Torah reveals the inner secret scroll. No one touches the inner scroll with their uncovered hands. Not even the rabbi. Only the strongest men can carry the unfurled Torah with their arms outreached. Young bar mitzvah boys carry the Torah close to their chests. They fear dropping it because that dishonour would not only fall on him but his entire family. The older men can hold the scroll shoulder-width apart.

But if they hold on for too long their faces always look like tomatoes. They lack the proper strength in their stomachs. Abba plants his feet on the ground, unwraps the scroll as far apart as his arms can part, and lifts the Torah towards the heavens. Cultured, charitable, simple, hard-working, we are all well rooted Jews. Our congregation lauds Abba's spiritual and physical strength.

After Maariv (The Jewish evening prayer recited after sunset) I join Abba before the fire. I sit on his lap and look up into his wiry beard. The skin looks pale and tender. Resting my cheek upon his chest I hear his heart thump against his ribs.

Chapter 2
February 1869 The Hague, Holland Age 19.
Sophia Annaliesse

"Sophia Annaliese, it's time to wake up," signals mom. The outline of my mother's hourglass figure is backlit by the sunlight streaming through my window. I rub my eyelids to wipe away the exhaustion. The fragile skin beneath my eyes ache. When I'm this tired my eyelid twitches all day.

My body is warning me. Instinctively meeting my needs, my mother presses a cold cloth to my forehead. The headache brewing behind my eyes cannot escalate. She hands me a warm cloth this time to wash the slumber from my eyes.

"I stayed up late agonizing over the bodice."

The wrinkles between her eyebrows deepens as worry registers on her face. A remarkable lady born at the wrong time wasn't shown any opportunity. No one nurtured her artistic talents and sensitive eyes. Mom learned to clean houses. When she married my father. He delighted in her imagination. They had little, but he bought her oil paints and brushes of every size. She transformed our home into her canvas, each surface another masterpiece. My nursery became a jungle vines and branches held smiling monkeys, rainbow feathered toucans, sloths hanging upside down by their tails, and rabbits with big floppy ears.

I fastened fabrics and fashioned old textiles into fresh garments. I took apart old pillows and learned the cross stitch: useful for decoration but not for blouses and dresses.

Mom deconstructed baby clothes and worn-out fabric, and I mastered invisible seams for dresses and skirts. The whipstitch was hard to master. My parents encouraged my exploration. Mom painted on the discarded fabrics and breathed new life into textiles. Dad was in awe.

"When have you committed the bodice for Eva Weintraub?" While she is talking, I make my bed. A small habit I started young. Making my bed in the morning is a habit of an organized person with a clear mind. At night after a long hard day clambering back into a neatly made bed is a small pleasure, I give myself.

"Not until next week, but motivation shows up unannounced," I start.

"At midnight, I prepared a cup of tea and I fell asleep before I could rinse out the teacup. My dreams frustrated me. When I woke, the light was so dim, I couldn't thread a needle."

"Did you figure it out?"

"The problem? Yes, I figured that out. Eva has different measurements; she has a wider abdomen than bust and slender arms. The fabric did not lay on her body the way I wanted."

"How frustrating," my mother muses. She is my inspiration. Her dedication to preserving her appearance is admirable. My mother is a proud woman, neither ostentatious nor a martyr. She holds herself in high regard and expects others to present themselves with the same level of excellence.

She maintains, a small scoop of vanity helps maintain one's vitality.

"It was," I admit.

She turns, "what changed?"

"The leftover tea left a textured design in the teacup's bottom. The layers inspired me to gather up the fabric and create new lines to display her assets." I brush at my tangled hair.

"I will not make a garment that is not exquisite."

"You don't rest enough. The body and mind require nourishment. Inspiration occurs at the most awkward moments."

She hands me a fresh cup of tea. Her smile comforts me. My father knocks on the door and doesn't wait for an answer.

"Your mother and I have bought a small retail shop in the center of downtown. Street traffic and visitors coming from the train station will bring new clients every day," he declares.

"Your God-given talent deserves a greater audience."

He crosses the room and kisses me on top of the head.

"Sophia, real estate in the downtown's heart lends credibility to your business. You will prevail in the luxury textiles."

My father reaches for my mother and wraps his arms around her. He kisses her and his lips linger. Feigning annoyance she pushes him away playfully.

"We picked a store with a picturesque display window."

He interrupts, "You can choose what to feature, the vision is yours." He's so excited his words smile.

"I might have suggestions if you don't mind."

"I can only imagine your list of ideas. Go ahead." I grab a leather-bound notebook on the table and sit poised, ready.

"Your display window can feature exotic fabrics imported from Asia," she begins.

"Perhaps we feature a display that highlights the beautiful long-legged birds of the Netherlands like storks and egrets." I envision the store window, and a rush of excitement rolls over me.

"I could change the scene in the display window every two weeks. Mannequins dressed for the holidays and occasions like weddings, baptisms, or graduations."

I locate a pencil. Great ideas spin around in my head. My parents gave me life. They raised me with love and protected me. Now they are giving me a future.

******

Six months later, my family's retail shop, Annaliese, is profitable. We design custom clothes for ladies from all over the Netherlands. We have return-customers from as far as Antwerp. I work behind a three-way mirror in the dressing room. Half mannequins create a makeshift wall to separate my workspace from the dressing room.

Mother keeps small satchels of dried flowers in every nook of our store and keeps the store filled with fresh tulips for color and national Dutch pride. Our brand is luxury.

Mom works behind the register when she isn't attending to the customers. Our store is small. She concerns herself with the flow of our customers. If they crowd the store, then good customers will leave. Our store's success is personal to her. A well-dressed man enters. He asks for the designer, and my mother calls me to the shop floor. His muscular frame and honey golden tan steals my breath away. His clean-shaven face highlights stormy sea-green eyes and weathered crow's feet. A friendly smile brings you in, and his voice is robust but disarming. He smells of lemons and sea salt. My mother sits on a chair behind the register while I introduce myself. He half bows to me.

"I need a new suit. Your fabric in the window is unique. I am a well-travelled man. A seafarer. Others call me a pirate."

He stops and laughs. My mother clears her throat. He removes a velvet sack of coins from his pocket and places it on the shop counter.

"Mademoiselle, you tell me how much it will cost to make the suit. I will pay you double to have it made within the week."

I swallow.

"Your offer is generous, but alas, my specialty is women's garments, not men's suits. Men's suits have unfamiliar patterns and lines to master."

"I didn't know. Can you do it?"

"Yes. I make them for my family."

"Your attention to detail inspires me. Your vision is romantic. Choose the textiles and make me look one-of-a-kind," says the stranger.

"To meet your deadline, I would have to drop other projects. Relationships mean everything. Retaining clients in conjunction with a solid reputation and a valuable product has made our store successful. I nurture all of our clients which builds trust. Which allows me to use my own vision to create something custom and beautiful. Which I know they'll be happy with."

But I am intrigued by what he asks. I must juggle a few things. He says bashfully, "I don't want to cause you any inconvenience."

"It's going to be busy, but not an impossibility," I want to explain why his request is impossible for me to fulfill.

But I am intrigued by what he asks I can check on a few things.

"Madame," he gestures to my mother, "the gold within should cover the cost of the fabric. I'll bring more tomorrow for the cost of labor."

My mom handles the sac and nods to me.

"Sophia-Annalisse, there is enough to get started," says my mother.

"Mom, can you come over here?" I turned back to him.

"She will take your order, while I get my papers together to write measurements."

My mother introduces herself.

He says, "My name is Zac Verbelte. As you may have heard, I am a seafarer."

"Hello, Mr. Verbelte," says my mother. She removes a small scale from a shelf below her workstation. She weighs the sack, and he regards her gesture with a grin.

"Take the entire sack. There will be alterations. It will be easier to keep track of that. I love how you communicate with your daughter with your eyes. The two of you are close."

My mother smiles at his observation but continues with business.

"Our featured textiles are expensive. As a brand-new customer and self-identified pirate, we cannot extend you credit - we will need to charge you upfront. Once we cut the fabrics, we cannot reallocate them. I am sure you understand. But you will be pleased. A man of respect needs a Sophia Annaliese custom-designed suit."

I interrupted her sales talk, "We can start with your measurements, sir."

"Honor me and call me by my given name, Zac."

I extend my hand. He takes mine in his.

"May I call you Sophia?" he asks.

Intense heat rises from my neck to my forehead. I must be blushing.

"Yes, you may."

My hand sweats before he lets go. The next night, he returns an hour before closing and asks to see my progress. I show him my paper templates. I break down what I do and how I think. Cutting is precise, and mistakes are unforgiving. Sewing is a craft where flaws can't remain unnoticed.

The following day, Zac arrives in the late afternoon with a carafe of wine and pastries.

"I love sweets," he says.

"I have a flavor in mind. It took four bakeries, but I found it."

"That kind of habit is dangerous."

He laughs, "You are right. I can't let my waistline change after you've created a masterpiece."

Zac asks me what drew me to fabrics over others. Talking to him is light and fun.

"Tell me the story of the piano in your shop window. Do you play?"

I sit on the piano bench, blow on my hands, and rub them together. My fingers land on middle C and I play a short, simple tune every child learns before their first recital. I want to impress him. I want him to come back every night and ask me questions. He is interesting.

His stories of the sea scare me and excite me.

The sun sets. Our time together incinerates like a freshly struck match. Caught up in the early stages of adoration, I grow sullen knowing we've run out of time.

Shadows fall upon Zac's face, darkening him.

"Sophia, my dear, what is wrong? Your whole demeanor changed. Like a deflated balloon before my eyes."

Dad arrives to walk me home from the store. He shakes Zac's hand and asks him how his day was. Zac bows his head out of respect to Vader.

"Sir, the weather did not disappoint, and my body is strong and healthy."

Zac shares the progress I have made on the garment and how impressed he is with the quality of our textiles. They speak for another ten minutes while I close the store.

By then, Moeder is ready to join us on our walk home. She smiles when she sees Zac by my side. When I am ready to leave, mom and dad suggest Zac walk me home.

At our home, he waits for me to go inside and lock the door behind me. Once inside, I place my hands on the door.

Zac stirs a passion deep inside my body. He respects me and is a gentleman, but I am ready for him to stop being polite and surprise me with a kiss. I have never felt more alive, and I want to taste his mouth.

He returns to the store every night except for Shabbat. I use the extra time to work on some of my other projects.

The time that I spend on his suit is more pleasure than work. I sew while I daydream.

When the kids last night I had to stand up on my tippy toes. Each stitch filled with eagerness.

Waiting until we see each other again.

"You please me. You appreciate me as much as I admire you," he says.

My feelings are growing for him faster than I imagined possible. Each time the bell rings, I look up, hoping to see his face. His lips and eyes capture me.

He has long, thick black lashes. He confides in me.

A need for his attention grows. I finished his suit later that week, and we began the detailed fitting.

"Sophia, while you work on the alterations, you can teach me how to play the piano."

"Zac, teaching you the piano will take a long time."

"I plan on it taking as long as it takes."

I cannot stop from blushing.

Chapter 3
April 1881 Harstenhoekweg Holland Age 8
Amalia Verbelte

"Amalia," shouts my father, "you must listen. This is your job as part of this family."

His face is red, and I'm scared. He's never scared me before. I want him to stop.

"I don't want to smell like farm animals!"

I look into his eyes and fill my chest with air and courage, screaming, "I am in control of my life!"

My father doesn't understand, and he never will. Smokey gray clouds churn in the Sapphire sky. Their hypnotic swirl undulates to a primal song I can't hear. As the streaks of mist transform into pulsating sprites, their dance intensifies. Their arms and legs flail in opposing directions while arching their backs. Their limbs appear limitless with their extended spindly fingers and pointed toes.

The choreography drips with intent. As the wind picks up, the formation of vapor changes. Small sparks of lightning tickle the center of the clouds. Streaks of the slate segment the sky. Thunder beats in the distance like tribal drums. If the delicate balance of electricity shifts, a full-blown thunderstorm will erupt. The wind is the maestro, and a slow strong breeze can blow out the embers in the sky. A solid gust will ignite a downpour that can soak my clothes within seconds. I consider my options. I run to the gate and onto the street, the harder my feet pound into the dirt the stronger and more righteous I feel. Running faster than ever before, I ignore his pleas to come back. I don't wait for his reaction. He can't yell at me if I am out of earshot. Winding behind neighbors' homes and shops, I use my secret route. I can get to the sandy beach or hide in the forest. There is a bench where you can see the water, a historic windmill in the far distance, and play in the thick green unmanicured grass. Ducks swim and birds fly back and forth in the trees. I've seen chipmunks, moles, field mice and tiny orange salamanders on the rocks at the edge of the smaller ponds off the larger ocean.

The modest brook behind my home is my sacred spot. No one is here.

I shout, "HELP ME," into a void.

My released frustration emboldens me. I throw myself onto the ground in a baby's tantrum while pounding my fists into the soil.

Hot, angry tears stream down my full cheeks.

"It's his fault! He's stupid and insensitive."

A small voice interrupts me.

"Who are you talking to?"

I jump, and scream.

Grabbing my heart, I holler, "You scared me."

I hadn't noticed anyone coming down Duck Pond Road.

"Who are you?"

"I'm Dora."

A small girl, smaller than me, with brown hair, a narrow nose, and ears that stick straight out from her head.

"I'm Amalia. Do you live near here?"

My fingers are buried in mocha-colored earth.

"I do. I live down the lane, across the pond from the duck-lings. I'm near the boardwalk."

"I know where that is."

We talk and she asks me why I was crying and screaming.

"I lost my temper. I yelled at my father."

Dora's eyes widen into large saucers.

"If I wailed at my dad, he would strike me."

My father would never hit me. Dora looks miserable after her confession. Her eggshell skin is riddled with pink rashes that look itchy and angry.

"Let me help you. The pond's water will soothe and refresh you. Follow me. We'll walk in as deep as we can."

With Dora beside me, we wade in too far and start to swim. Laughter replaces my tears and she's no longer dour.

"My father doesn't care about my opinion," I say.

"Everyone deserves respect," Dora says.

"You should stop doubting yourself. That was the last time."

Sensitive, smart, and modest, she removes a peach from her bag and gives it to me.

"Take it," she waves me off, "I have another."

Sticky juice drips down her fingers and she talks with her mouth open. She licks her fingers and washes them off in the water. Then dries her face on the back of her sleeve.

"A good crisp apple is my second favorite fruit, after a peach." I opine.

"Yellow, green, red, no matter the color or tartness level, apples never mislead."

She giggles and declares me funny. I stick out my tongue. She crosses her eyes.

"I love yellow. It always makes me happy. Sunshine, butter-cups, squash flowers, I could go on and on."

"I love sunflowers. Tall, fat sunflowers," I say.

"In the early mornings in the summertime, the meadow is flooded with dew. The tall grass leaves my legs wet. At dawn, the sunshine is not powerful enough to warm up the air. The air smells fragrant, and the earthiness tickles my nose."

"I love that smell," says Dora.

"Once the sun warms up, the aroma evaporates."

We spent hours together devising myths about the locals in our community. Our elaborate stories grew complex.

I would confuse the truth with fiction. We pretended to own an exotic animal farm. We knew all the local wild animals because we fed them leftover stale challah.

Staring into the bluest of skies I say, "It's nice to have someone to talk to."

She giggles at my sincerity. I'd be offended if I knew she didn't actually care. That's her way. When you get too close to her heart she freezes up. Dora loves rabbits. She doesn't like what her father does to their rabbits after they're born. I don't ask for an explanation. Her father lets her keep a runt from every litter. She can talk the afternoon away if she's talking about rabbits. She understands a lot. Dora might be the smartest person I know aside from my dad.

"My father says milking the cows is my job and I don't have a choice."

My body shivers at the wretched thought. The texture of their utters makes me want to curl up into a ball.

"There is always a choice," says Dora.

"Hashem says what separates us from animals is our ability to choose. That's our freedom. That's what makes us human."

"I do plenty on the farm," I whine.

Embarrassed for myself, I put my hand over my mouth.

Smiling, she says, "I am sure you do, but adults do not listen to children."

"After I feed the chickens, I wash off their faces because they are messy eaters. No one ever told me to do that. I came up with that myself. Once their faces are clean, I collect the eggs and bring them inside. At night, I sing for the chickens. My songs help them make delicious eggs."

"Makes sense to me. You should teach me your songs and I can sing to my rabbits."

The next thing we do is march around the pond after a duck and sing my chicken songs. Dora takes a pebble and tosses it across the water. Watching it slip beneath the surface brings me peace. Laying down in the dirt, I lose myself in the shifting clouds. They transform from a bear into a dog into a sailboat into a girl with a pretty hat. When the sun sets, there is a moment when the sky's still blue, but the moon is a bright shining globe. The in-between moments of day and night are my favorite. The moon is brighter than the sun.

"I love living here," says Dora from beside me.

"I was born in Antwerp and shortly thereafter, we moved to Scheveningen. My parents came here for their honeymoon. It's considered a popular vacation destination for Jewish people."

She sounds like a mother.

I say, "My father says it's nice living in a place where there is already a synagogue. It means folks are less likely to run us off."

"My father says the Jewish community here does very well for themselves. Living here is the best of both worlds. We are The Hague's most beautiful fishing village and resort, but we can walk downtown if needed."

Having someone my age to share my thoughts and feelings with helps temper me. During the summer months, the two of us are inseparable. Our parents have no idea that we tell each other everything. I tell her when my parents fight.

She shows me her bitten fingernails. One year during Yom Kippur Dora and I did not fast. We ate all day. I don't even know why we did it, but after we felt bonded to each other forever.

Chapter 4
May 1876 Przemyśl, Poland
Mozes Meijer Eisner

The Harbor Master's bellowed orders infiltrate my dreams. The citizens of Przemyśl awake to seagulls' caw hours before sunrise. The San River is navigable here and weaves itself through Przemyśl, a popular nexus for trade routes importing Slavonia silks, Croatian hemp, licorice, and Hungarian wheat. Other goods are harder to come by: Estonian timber, Belgium chicory, and endive. The seaport is as much my home as my parents' house. My earliest memories of my father are our walks to the seaport.

Rubbing the last remnants of slumber from my eyes, I wake up slowly. Abba is notably silent. I brace for one of his short all-knowing speeches. He will reveal something about me, he thinks I don't know.

All the signs are there: he clears his throat, prepares his words carefully and I'm a captive audience.

"Mozes, accept who you are and what you need. Sleep is vital to your mind. Sleep well and you are in noble spirits; otherwise, you are rough. You are like me." Father chuckles. He taught me never to make an important decision when tired or hungry. The mind needs the energy to think, and rest, to digest important issues. His laugh is deep, and his voice reverberates in my chest when he speaks. His confidence is infectious. His face is kind, but he does not offer his smile easily. My father is a calm man. He is a teacher by nature, and a good one. I learn easily from him.

He does not talk down to me. Smart and disciplined, his day begins hours before everyone else.

He shares with me, "I like to work by the light of the stars. Hashem begins the day at sunset. The echoes of paradise are closest to me then. I embrace this life."

He explains, "My Tefillin and my Tallis are how I choose to begin my day. We choose a good Jewish life. There are fourteen prayers to praise Hashem for your life. They include the ability to see, use our bodies, get dressed, feed ourselves, and love. We have the power of opportunity. Hashem shows us how to conduct a life filled with a mitzvah."

Upon our arrival at the docks, Father finds a small patch of shade to spend the day. His long biceps flex and contract as he unrolls a woven mat big enough for the two of us. It is surprising how he can fold himself up. He is tall and long like a rail. When he holds my hand in his, he dwarfs me. I am struck by his thick manicured fingers. His thumbs are wide and square-shaped.

A tall thin man should have long spindly fingers. I am shorter and stouter. His hands belong to my body. Dad says I will see a big change around my Bar Mitzvah.

Escaping the direct sunlight is vital to finishing the entire day at the port in one spot. We are both fair-skinned. In fact, we move from pale to sunburnt with nothing in between. We try to sit as close to the vendors as possible, noting how they conduct their trade. Once we settle, Father removes his muddied boots with worn soles and leans back on his bony elbows.

As the ship's anchor, the pace shifts. Young shirtless men run up and down the long wooden planks and move barrels of fish. Their chiseled stomachs and flat hollow pecs are incongruous. Men open their stalls and unpack inventory. These creatures of habit set themselves up the same way every day. They're superstitious and limited in attempting to stem the chaos. Their rigidity holds them back. Other merchants choose their spots by chance. Mood, weather, availability, even emotion can dictate the location. These vendors are happier. They see the skyline of fairy tales before us. Watching people makes me happy for hours. We craft tales of wonder and intrigue out of strangers' lives. Women with silver in their ears collect supplies to prepare food for the workers. Their bronze skin is the color of burnt butter.

They build small fires and the air fills with spices like black pepper, cumin, and paprika.

What meals do they eat? My father places a sprig of mint in my breast pocket.

"Smacking the mint leaves releases a soothing mint scent. The taste calms your stomach when the stink of fish guts is crushing," he says.

He points to Baron, a fixture at the harbor with his plump belly, short legs, and enormous hands, practically too big for his frame. His hands can carry several wicker baskets at a time. He is normally a talkative man who sweats profusely. On a muggy summer day, his shirt is sweat-stained down his spine and under his arms.

Surprisingly, his personal scent reminds me of tart green apples and late-season tree-honey.

Before Baron's stall fills with patrons, he says, "Mozes, quick, catch this," and lobs a red apple my way.

"Thank you," I said to Baron.

He takes great care of his rapeseed flower stall. Ripe red apples overflow from hand woven fruit baskets. Dried aromatic

49

flowers tied from the walls of the stall add to his welcoming display. Baron wipes his brow with a red bandana.

"Tell me about Baron and his merchandise," Father instructs. "Paint me a picture. Listen to Baron and his patrons. Does he sound happy?"

No, he is not happy. His stall is not joyful. Customers leave in a hurry. Baron winces as he hands a woman a small basket of apples.

"His service is slow, and his customers wait too long. It was not like this yesterday. He usually smiles."

One spring, when the sludge was thick, Father injured his back while struggling to lift his foot out of a sinkhole. Hunched over and frowning, Mother encouraged him to stretch his arms to the sky to push his back to unknot. Pressing his palms against the door frame with labored breathing, he remained like this until his muscles relaxed.

I never saw Father unfit before that day.

Baron's grimace reminds me of Father in the door frame.

"What's wrong with him?" inquires Father.

"He is using the table to support his weight. His back hurts and he cannot hold himself upright. He lifted a massive crate yesterday. Baron lifts crates like that regularly, but you pointed out he did not lift the crate properly. You mentioned that he would surely regret doing that."

My voice breaks with my confusion.

"What is upsetting you, Mozes?"

"The inconsistency upsets me. It is not sensible. I want rules, Father."

"When you are young, you heal fast. Once you hit thirty, your body punishes you for not appreciating your limits.

What would you do if you were him?"

"I'm not sure. He needs to sell to eat. The day is a waste for him in this state."

"His inventory could expire if he does not sell it today," observes Father.

"I didn't think about the expiration of the goods."

"That is a significant consideration."

"But he isn't making a good impression," I say.

"You are correct, Mozes. People prefer their desires satisfied. When you feel good, you spend more. The momentum of the sale is critical."

Baron does not finish the day. After lunch, he tosses me a few more apples. My father smiles as I attack one apple after another. My reward for good observation is the option to choose the next vendor to investigate. Stalls that cause my nose to tingle in a good way are my favorite. Drawn to spices like cumin, marsala, and ginger. Their colors remind me of the sunrise — oranges, reds, rust, browns, and golds. These are the magnificent colors of my morning strolls to the seaport.

******

The next season and every season afterward, I visit the harbor without Father. I examine how men clean fish, sell lemons, bake bread, and fix shoes. One day, a man named Matheo hands me a fish, a blade, and a pail. He wears a white shirt, stained with perspiration, and a blue scarf around his neck. His hair is the color of oil. It laid flat on top of his head. I gut the fish, pull out the innards, and place the fish back in another bucket filled with cool water.

I learned how to say bok (hello), and ugodan dan (have a nice day.) Sardine is sardina and riba means fish. Beyond those simple words, I do not understand a word he says. My family speaks Polish, German, Yiddish, and Hebrew.

The ability to speak multiple languages opens doors, so I will learn Matheo's language too.

He moves his hands and shows me what to do. I gut the riba, remove the kosti (bones), and clean the ribljeg crijeva (guts.) Before suppertime, Matheo's wife Anita hands me a sardine sandwich and two coins. A yellow and orange scarf keeps her short brown hair off her face. Her eyes are light brown, and she has a freckle inside her left eye. She is a slight woman, but her hands are strong. She marinates the sardines in fresh lemon juice and then fire-grills them. The sandwich is fresh and simple. When the saltiness of the sardines combines with the smoke from the grill, the taste is exceptional. Adding the sour zest of lemon juice makes me ache for more. My fingers sting as I lick them clean, revealing the many invisible cuts from my day's work. Clutching a coin in each hand, my chest swelled with pride, I showed Father my earnings. At the next sunrise, I stand in front of Matheo's sardine stall. When he arrives, he hands me a fish, a knife, and a bucket. Anita prepares a grilled sandwich for breakfast and lunch. Matheo pays me again, two coins. And my summer days are filled with work and learning.

My days at the port end as the school year resumes at the Alte synagogue. Inside the dank classroom, my heart races as my hair grows damp on my head. My hands itch and I long for the aroma of fish, salt, and mint. I'm more comfortable among men who labor with their hands than the Jewish scholars. They yell and punish me because I cannot sit still. Rabbis call me stupid. I hate them. Each day, I wake with a twisted stomach. The Rabbis speak my name with disdain. Samuel, the Rabbi's son, snickers like he is better than me. He calls me a rabid animal. I show restraint when I send the desk sailing out a window instead of him. I walk out of school with more conviction than I have ever felt, never to return.

I ran to the port without stopping. Every step away from school makes me bolder. My anxiety melts away. I scream,

"The Rabbis aren't better than me, they're better at being Jewish than me."

Running through the crowds at the port, I spot Anita. She opens her arms and I bury myself in her embrace. My fury fades as she kisses my cheeks and pulls me towards Matheo. He strolls over and places his hand on my head.

Matheo introduces me to Jan, a short fat man with thick hands.

"Jan needs someone to carry boxes and crates."

He nods and smiles.

"Mozes has worked for me for months. He is strong like a bull."

"Good. Let us get started," says Jan.

We meet incoming ships together and I assist him with the inventory. I am good at math, and he pays me three coins a day and unlimited fish soup. I run errands for Jan and move throughout the entire port with purpose. I know almost everyone. Older ladies my mother's age chase after me to feed me. I never say no to food. When I work with Jan, I am quiet and serious. He instructs me not to speak during transactions with unknown captains. My role is to be a spy. I gather information and report back to Jan. When a new captain's crew meanders through the port, I follow behind. Once they settle, I listen. Does the crew grouse? Is the captain respected? How does the crew speak to one another when the captain is not present? The more precise the information, the nicer the reward Jan gives.

Never hesitant to act, I keep busy and earn good wages. I pretend for weeks to my parents that I still attend school. One night, I fell asleep at dinner. The next morning, Father hands me a new bucket and cloth. He instructs me to never lie to him again, and to wash better after working all day in the sun. We never speak of school again. I stop hiding my earnings and hand them over to Father. He places them in a mason jar on the shelf in the kitchen.

"Be what you want, Mozes. My papa only told me what I could not be because I am a Jew. You will be afraid; we are all afraid, but we can choose not to show fear and to act boldly," says Father.

One day, a cobbler needs an extra set of hands.

"I am precise," I explain, and he teaches me to resole shoes, hundreds of shoes; he can chalk and measure by eye. Tedious work, but I am paid by the sole.

A Slovakian named Peter shows interest in my quick hands and attention to detail. He sells textiles. The merchandise is rare and expensive; exotic silks are sold by the yard.

His trade does not hire inexperienced hands. One must wear cotton gloves when handling luxurious fabrics. Sweat or oil from fingertips stains the fabric.

Peter displays his fabrics and asks me, "What are the differences you see between the fabrics?"

I study the texture, color, and weight of each fabric.

I explain these differences with Peter in his native tongue. My analysis earns me five coins.

"We start on inventory," Peter explains.

I log his merchandise in a book and measure the fabrics cut each day. I collect all the scraps and place them in a woven basket on the counter at the end of the day.

Peter says, "Take those to your mother and let her use them." Waste costs Peter's money. He teaches me how to master measurements and cut rare fabrics. These high-demand lustrous silks are fashioned into hats, shirts, skirts, and jackets. No two customers want the same cut. Merchants in crisp white button shirts and clean pants speak to Peter. Their hands are soft, and young boys race after them carrying their goods.

Peter dresses me to look like these boys. He is very generous. After a year of working for Peter, he plans my first trip away from home. The trip will last one week.

Peter explains, "Local small markets will give you the best return. The silks will impress young women. Their mothers will buy them by the yard to make their daughters new clothes."

"But I am an outsider," I start to explain when Peter cuts me off.

"You speak more languages than anyone I have ever met in all my years of working. You have a young face with a man's strength. People will trust you."

Being calm makes me approachable. Always respectful, I discover people will talk with me. I listen to their needs and recognize which products will be in demand.

Father had told me, "All sale transactions are the same. An apple is an apple. All language is part of a larger tapestry. Interpreting body gestures helps when communicating with anyone, no matter their spoken language. The spoken word will come and that will be your talent. Communicating and getting along with all kinds of people will carve out your destiny. My papa never gave me that consideration."

As I travel, I sleep in my wagon and guard my inventory.

I like my own company and the solitude of the road gives me time to think without distraction. At night, after I catch a few fish, I eat under the moon. To be a traveling merchant is a young man's game. When I am hungry enough, I catch and skin a squirrel or rabbit and roast it on an open fire. Using my hands to kill my dinner terrifies me until it does not. The insatiable hunger within, quelled by the kill. Invigorated by my self-reliance, I see the world in a new way. What did those small-minded Rabbis know? They do not have the skills to live a life of adventure. Could they leave their mothers before Bar Mitzvah and sell Bulgarian tobacco? Each time I travel,

I make more money for Peter. He sends me out with a full load, and I never come back until I exhaust my inventory. The farms of Romanians, Hungarians, and Bohemians are like my backyard. My perception of the world has changed. It no longer seems enormous. The world is conquerable.

"What did you learn this time, Mozes?"

Peter asks as he pours fresh fish soup into a bowl.

"Eat first," he instructs.

A quick sip calms the growling inside my stomach. The melded flavors of fish, onions, and carrots slide down my throat and warm my body.

"Albanian honey is in demand. When I head west, I want to bring an extra two crates. I never seem to have enough honey or blackberry jam. Figs are popular. You can roast, stew, or pickle Bulgarian sugar beets," I ramble on, spilling details and a patchwork of observations.

Peter smiles and leans forward, taking in every word. My insights are valuable. I finish the soup, and he hands me a plate of chicken, potatoes, and roasted carrots. We speak for hours. I walk home with enough coins to fill four mason jars and a fresh trout for my parent's dinner.

I gain experience and stay away longer and travel farther with each trip. When I turn fifteen, I bought a horse, a wagon, and a bedroll. I stocked my wagon with honey, olives, figs, spices, and plum brandy from Serbia. I will be a success on my own now.

Chapter 5
June 1880 Perehinske, Galicia
Naftali Herzl

Rebbe Hersch Rechtschaffen arrives in Perehinske to considerable fanfare. Two beautiful black stallions lead his custom carriage. A mountain of a fellow, his character is one of hospitality and philanthropy. Wary of his sharp-wit, esteemed men never approach without a prepared D'var Torah (Torah portion for the week.) His charity doesn't extend to his valuable time. His life is ruled by Torah, and he donates to schools and other educational endeavors. Before he commits to any new projects, he asks himself, will this bring food to my Shabbat table? His charity doesn't extend to his valuable time.

From villages to townships Rebbe Hersch, his four brothers, his cousin Efriam and good friends like Shabtai Tanne, Hersch Halsband, and Izzy Zucker built homes, synagogues, schools, and mills to bolster their neighborhoods. Once a town grew beyond its borders, they formed another one. Right before Shabbat, Rebbe Hersch Tzvi Rechtschaffen approaches, my mouth runs dry. I look at the sky and nearly blind myself from the sunshine. Townsfolk mill around, however, no one approaches or interrupts. A man of power demands respect without saying a word. He has nothing to prove. As he comes closer, he says "Naftali Herzl, your Rebbe spoke of you."

Without a pause I say, "If the Rebbe says it, who am I to argue?"

He leans forward and pats me on the back.

Stroking his thick white beard he says, "your Rebbe told me you are never without a book in your hand, Naftali Herzl. Why is that?"

"I couldn't read as a child. My father said read every day until you master it. If you quit on yourself, the only one who fails is you. There will be no one else to blame. Learning is a gift. If it's meaningful, it's never easy. Identify your greatest weakness and work on it until it becomes muscle memory. Make the body remember what the mind cannot."

"Your father was wise," he concludes.

"What else did he teach you?"

"He explained simple machines. How to take them apart and reassemble them. His approach to living was basic - figure out the puzzle. He encouraged my intelligence."

"What a blessing."

We walk slowly together. He is disarming.

"Abba said I must work harder because I'm bigger."

He cracks a smile.

"It's true. I share this problem."

He clears his throat.

"Naftali, will you pray beside me on Shabbat?"

He leans in, "I'm used to having my children around me. You would honor me by sitting beside me."

"You honor me with your request." We shake hands.

This Shabbat is important. On my way home, I pass by Rebbe David and almost walk right past him.

"Good Shabbos, Naftali."

Rebbe David is a good man whose outstretched hand was there for anyone.

"Good Shabbos," I say.

"I won't keep you for even a moment. This weekend is very important. I'm sure you understand why."

"Yes, I understand."

"I would never suggest something I didn't feel was right in my heart. You need this family as much as this family needs you. Rebbe Rechtschaffen is traditional and conducts his affairs with dignity. Known to be one of the best prayer leaders, during the high holidays his services extend well into the late afternoon. Your soul will be shaken when you hear his rendition of Neila during Yom Kippur. When he implores Hashem for forgiveness the heavens open up."

******

Before the Kabbalat Shabbat (a sequence of Psalms called Welcoming the Sabbath), Rebbe Rechtschaffen sits down in the front row of the temple, a position of reverence within the synagogue, usually held by town elders and Gabbai (the men who run the synagogue and aids the rabbi.)

I didn't ask but he explains, "Once I enter the synagogue, I'm free of the outside world. I sit in the front row to be in front of Hashem."

Every seat in the synagogue is before Hashem.

"Hashem doesn't care where you sit. Your devotion is enough." I say.

Rebbe Rechtschaffen nods. "Hashem gives us choice."

As the service unfolds, the Rebbe's impassioned prayers are indisputable. His melodic voice drowns out the Cantor, the leader of the service. Lebish Margolis and his brother Nachum look at our guest admirably. Those brothers have an impressive standing in our community. By the Amidah,

Rebbe Rechtschaffen wrangles the congregation to his will. Rabbi David whispers to his friend Motka Zolkin.

******

On Saturday morning, I arrive earlier than I ever have before. I wanted to be here before Rebbe Rechtschaffen arrived.

My intention to arrive before my honoured guest was calculated. Understanding that kind of behaviour is deemed respectable by men like Rebbe Rechtschaffen.

He greets me with a flash of white teeth. He laughs and claps his hands.

"I am rarely surprised, young man. Arriving before the masses sets the mood for the day."

He reveals, "My relationship with Hashem is personal."

"Today, Rebbe Rechtschaffen, I want to be sure Hashem hears me. I'll sit in the front row."

He chuckles at the inside joke.

"Roznaitow started as a land lease, did you know that? A man named Groner, and his brother-inlaw turned potatoes into alcohol, and built homes for the Jews they employed. Good family men flocked, and a new township was born. It hasn't all been easy as the Ukrainians don't always like the Poles, and when times are tough, and food is scarce everybody hates the Jews."

After the Amidah, Rebbe Rechtschaffen says, "You may call me Rebbe Hersch."

Today's sermon is about a fire and the choice two brothers must make. Rabbi Hersch listens intently to Rabbi David—a charitable and practical man who is revered by all.

Rebbe Rechtschaffen reflects, "investing your Shabbat with me means a lot. It's my favorite day of the week. It's more than a day of the week—it's a life experience. A man like you will cherish my daughter. Your reputation precedes you. Continue to be kind and soft-spoken—it will charm my daughter, Tzizel. She is my youngest and my jewel. She likes to read and sit in the sunshine. At dawn, I will head back to my wife, Etel."

He leans in, "will you come and visit us in two weeks?"

A lump forms in my throat that suffocates my words.

"Thank you. You honor me."

"Let me present you to your destiny. Do you need transport?"

"No, sir. I have a horse and cart."

"Even better. We can't compromise a man who takes care of his own business," says Rebbe Rechtschaffen.

Chapter 6
October 1880 Perehinske, Galicia
Naftali Herzl

I met Tzizel by the ancient wells of Rozniatow. Her father says she spends hours picking wildflowers: including sunflowers, lilies, and irises. There are fields of bright silky yellow buttercups, purple flowers with honey yellow interiors, and tall white wildflowers.

I chose the most colorful batch I could find and fashioned a handle out of my handkerchief.

A girl comes into focus with long chestnut brown hair tied in a braid as thick as an angler's rope. Effortlessly pretty, her features are delicate, hickory brown almond-shaped eyes, a small pert nose, and deep pink lips shaped in a tidy bow. Her smile brightens her face.

"I called your name. Were you lost in thought? My name is Tzizel." Her mellifluous voice carries me away.

"Yes, I'm Naftali Herzl."

I extend my clumsy bouquet. She's petite and beautiful. She could have any man. My mind is riddled with insecurity. "Good day, Tzizel."

She says, "It's nice to meet you, Naftali. The flowers are exquisite."

Her eyes sparkle when she's happy.

"My father said you were thoughtful."

"Thank you, Tzizel."

"My father is a great judge of character," says Tzizel.

Her eyes close and she lifts the flowers to her nose.

"He mentioned you like flowers."

I playback what I said and think I sound stupid.

"I'm lucky to meet you."

Taking in a breath, I close my eyes.

My mind clears like a cerulean sky.

"The flowers are lovely. Did you know there are hundreds of different wildflowers in these hills and valleys? What made you choose these flowers? Was it their smell? Color?"

As the sunlight filters through the leaves, Tzizel's face is cast in shadow. She moves in slow motion before my eyes, lifting the bouquet to her nose. Her eyes close and her lips part. I have witnessed something I will always cherish. I do not think I have ever seen anything more beautiful in my life. I want to know everything there is to know about her. What makes her laugh? What does she dream about?

"Which is your favorite kind of flower?" she asks.

"The periwinkle ones with a lemon-yellow center. Some of those are in the bouquet. The hue is pale, not vibrant, almost washed out by the sun's intense rays."

She regards her hands and grimaces, wiping her palms on her apron. She tilts her head up to the sky.

"I could draw for you if I had my pencils and papers. Close your eyes."

I do not. She giggles.

"Trust me and close your eyes. Can you picture fresh raspberries growing on a bush?"

"Of course, I've seen raspberries growing on a raspberry bush," I answer playfully.

"Have you seen the tiny green stems that connect the raspberry to the bush? If you grab a bunch of raspberries by those green stems, hold them together, like this very bouquet, and flip them upside down, that is what the Muscari Blu plant looks like."

Her hands dance as she speaks.

"I can see the flower in my mind. Your description was enchanting."

"Did Abba tell you which flowers to pick?"

"He didn't tell me which kind you liked."

"My father has never asked me."

"Now I know something very important to you – Muscari Blu." Knowledge excites me.

I try to remember - don't stop breathing; when you stop, you can't think. A horde of bees protecting their honeycomb buzzes inside my stomach. Tzizel confidently holds my gaze. The scent of pine trees fills the air. We walk in silence. Tzizel tells me about her town. Her ancestors collected hundreds of books including the Talmud and Code of Jewish Law. Their community is based upon reading, learning and teaching. The surrounding towns call the citizens of Rozniatow, "the book people." Rozniatow was established in the 17th century. When most Jews, at the time, didn't use last names, the Rechtschaffens did. They can trace their family's line back into the early sixteen hundreds. The town began as a clearing surrounded by the woods. The Rechtschaffen brothers dug into the earth for weeks and created a lake. The men built a mill, an administration center and a synagogue to worship. More people came to the town filling roles like cook, craftsman, carpentry, banker, and apothecary. When she speaks of her ancestry her passion is tangible. Her liquid brown eyes captivate me. her love of family is what defines her.

"Isn't it fascinating to watch the birth of a town? Being a founding member fosters ownership.What do you think?"

Lost in your eyes I don't hear what she's saying.

"Can you hear me? Embarrassed, I blush from head to toe.

"I'm sorry, what did you ask me?"

She leans in, "I would rather know more about what you were thinking about."

"Honestly."

"Yes," she says and her lips pout.

"When I was young, Father took me to the mountainside and taught me how to pick mushrooms. He identified ten different kinds that day and only two were edible. The following day we chose a new patch. We brought home all the edible varieties. A man can live his whole life eating mushrooms and drinking fresh water from the book. My father identified ten different mushrooms. Only two were edible. The following day, he chose a new patch. We brought home all the edible varieties. A man can live their whole life eating mushrooms and drinking fresh water from the brook. It's important to know what will sustain you."

"My big brother did the same thing, but with red and purple berries. I love berries. I love strawberries, raspberries, blueberries, and blackberries. I could eat berries all day long. My brother taught me which berries I could eat in nature, and which could hurt me. Our Uncle Lieb taught him, and he said it was his responsibility to make sure I understood." When he left and moved to Israel the whole family missed him.

"I don't know berries. Would you be willing to teach me?" I ask.

"My father said you love to learn. He said you are the smartest person he has ever met. I thought nobody could be smarter than my father. Does that sound childish?"

"Not to me."

"It's important to be inquisitive. I ask questions until I understand something. That can frustrate other people. I do not care. If I do not understand, then the other person should determine an alternative way to communicate. I must know what is happening around me. I cannot be afraid. Circumstances will change. No one should be able to take advantage of me."

She places her hands on her hips. It could be an aggressive stance, but not in the way she does it. She is building up the courage to ask something.

"Are you used to being the smartest person in the room?"

She intrigues me with her implied familiarity.

Tzizel laughs and calls members of the town her family.

I am not from a large family. The people she weaves into hers make me jealous. Such security in a young woman shows how well her family raised her. How can I want to be part of her life already?

"Have you ever gone ice-skating? My parents made each one of us skates. Once the ice was thick enough, we skated the winter away. The family rule was father goes first. If the ice withstood his weight, it was safe for us."

"That sounds exciting. I've never been on skates," I admit.

"That's a shame. This winter, I'll teach you."

"I should make a list."

She laughs out loud and covers her mouth.

"Do not stop that enchanting sound," I begged her. "Your laugh is lovely."

Tzizel steps closer. "Thank you."

She turns and sees an older man.

"Reb David, please meet Naftali Hertz from Przemysl."

A tall man with a thick unruly black beard presents himself. I shake his hand and he smiles.

His easy-going nature should make him a wonderful Melamdim (teacher of the Hebrew language.)

We exchange a few more pleasantries and he says goodbye. "He taught my brothers, Shalom and Shimshon at the Cheder."

"If I had a teacher like that, I might never have left school." A sadness casts a shadow in her eyes.

"Not everybody gets everything in life. Had I grown-up here your father would never have come to find me."

We continue walking and I can sense the tension between us. "What makes you the happiest?"

Her eyes sparkle.

"Swimming is my elixir. My mom says it's important to be happy."

She explains as a child she would enjoy the fresh water in the pond. The wooden wheel from the flower mill kept the water circulating and also provided power to the rest of their business.

Children swam in balmy weather and openly enjoyed themselves. Once you become a married adult it's not considered proper to swim in public anymore.

I am moved by her words. When I am sad, I want to float weightlessly. Stretch my arms and legs out and drift away. Floating provides a sense of calm and peace that I need.

"There are cool, azure private ponds in Przemyśl. There is one right next to my farm."

"That sounds lovely."

"You could swim there whenever the weather allowed. It's ours." My voice trails off. Her whimsy is infectious.

I whisper, "the water heals."

My mouth goes dry. I do not want to stop talking to her.

"I would swim the weekends away."

She slides the flyaway hairs from her braid behind her ear with her delicate long fingers. Her hands move in a mesmerizing dance. Before my father passed away, he told me the moment I met the love of my life I would feel it in my body and in my bones. I listen to him but never having been in love, I didn't know what he meant. Now I do. She's enraptured me. The air smells sweeter around her. The sun's warmth cradles our skin.

"Let us walk up the brag."

Tzizel throws her shoulders back.

"What's a brag?"

"That's the hill that rises at the base of the pond. It overlooks the groves filled with trees in bloom."

"Show me more."

The scenic beauty of the town can be seen from on top of the highest hill. We walked along an exotic street nestled between small rivers and navigated by quaint bridges.

"Can you see the courthouse?" She asks.

"I'm humbled by its size."

She points to another building where streams of young children come running out.

"That is our elementary school where Poles, Ukrainians, and Jewish children grow and learn together."

"If everyone in life starts with the same advantages, the world can only get better."

"Naftali, the life you live sounds wonderful."

Under a tree at the top of the brag, we overlook the Ringplatz.

She points to a house and says, "over there is Chana Weismann house."

They were in a hotel, restaurant, and the tavern popular location for local weddings.

At night, the mountains are deep blue, and the pine green forest creates a beautiful horizon.

"I enjoy how much you love your hometown."

Her head tilts to the right.

"Our community feels like one big family. My father's cousin Pinkas and Mr. Schwartz run the town bank. After Doctor Diamand marries Clara, they'll stay at my father's house. If my father wasn't a rabbi, he would've been a doctor."

He said that was his greatest dream. He believes doctors are the smartest people in the room, and since they can save lives, they were the closest to God. Dr. Diamand will practice medicine out of my father's house until they save up enough money to have their own home.

We turn our heads toward one another. It is the most intimate we can be. My hands are by my side, and I stare at her hands. I ache to touch her fingers.

"How do you know when you meet the right person?"

"I will know it."

She places her hand on her heart.

"Here. My heart has never failed me."

"You're so confident."

Afraid I might have insulted her, I say, "I only mean you respect." She laughs and shoves me.

My skin is branded by her touch.

"Did I shock you?"

"You did shock me. But I'm a quick learner."

"Tell me more about Rozniatow."

"There is a big synagogue, which differs from the small one. We also have a Besh Hamedrash. Our synagogue is as strong as a fortress. It provides shelter for the neighborhood. My family has been in Galicia for nearly two hundred years."

"Tzizel, your family history is enviable."

"Father says the Jewish people don't get to settle. It is impossible to preserve a Jewish family's history. I love my home. The security of knowing a place on earth that lives and breathes Rechtschaffen."

"You are truly fortunate. Would you ever leave here?"

"I wouldn't," she says, and my heart sinks.

My home is amongst tree merchants and landowners. We are not as busy as Rozniatow. I need quiet.

She steps too close to me. Too close. The heat from her mouth warms my cheek.

"If I met the right person, someone who understood me, and liked me visiting my home whenever I wanted to, I could live anywhere with that man."

"Tzizel, I've met no one like you."

"I'm one of a kind," she says with a sneaky smile.

"My father raised me to think for myself. I could read and write by five years old. I'm as fast as any of my brothers."

"And modest?" She smiles and blushes.

A man runs towards us and nearly knocks another man on his bicycle over.

"That's Philip Ferscht, the town's barber on the bicycle. The man running towards us is my uncle Efraim, who owns the flour mill."

"Tzizel," he bellows, "you lost track of time! You need to head home."

The fire in her eyes dims.

"Yes, I have to head home."

She runs towards Efraim. She turns and says, "I will see you at the synagogue on Shabbat. After lunch, we can take a Shabbat walk together."

The service will seem endless, waiting for my chance to have another walk with her. Her entire family will watch me, judging my piety. Hasidim pray three times a day.

I do not. I hope it is not important to her that I pray three times a day.

"Tzizel, is it important for you to pray three times a day?"

"No. As long as you pray, you pray for the right things."

Chapter 7
July 1888 Przemysl, Poland age 35
Isaac Eisner

Mozes walks through the door, grumbling. Covered in sweat, he doesn't smell as ripe as I would suspect.

My thirteen-year-old son is heftier than me. Last year, we shared the same waist size. For the high holidays, I offered him a jacket I wore when I first married his mother, but the jacket strained across his back. Last month, Mother produced a brand-new wardrobe. He has already outgrown his pants. Young, energetic, and saturated with limitless stamina, he's worked alongside the men in the village since he was nine. I am glad he is a hard worker. My son's voice is deeper than mine but still cracks at the oddest times.

"Father, the days are ruthless. The work is arduous, and I ache to the bone, but it strengthens me. I've met everybody from the municipality. The older more experienced men serve as the masons and carpenters. Because I don't have any experience I dig and dig all day. The master-builder is in charge," says Mozes.

"I could be a master builder one day," I ask, "Can Jews be master builders?"

The sweet fragrance of sticky amber sap emanates from my son's clothing.

Mozes says, "I don't see why not; it's not a government position or a military post. It makes the city better."

Mozes tears a piece of challah from the loaf. He gorges himself on fresh yellow challah. Relishing the soft inside piece over the crust with poppy seeds. He scoops another helping into his hand. Barely swallowing his first portion he shoves the next piece of Challah into his mouth. He wipes the crumbs from his face with the back of his hand and then cleans his hand off on the leg of his pants. Holding a mason jar of seltzer in his hand he drains the contents in one gulp.

"Przemyśl could be a defensive gem. Fifteen other fortresses are under construction. Our fortress is one of the larger projects. The master-builder estimates it will be completed in five years."

Mozes is happiest after a hard day of physical labor. Sweat glistens on his skin and his shoulders relax. He is not built to study Talmud. His temperament is active. His mind needs more activity.

"The steady work is preferable to your mother. It keeps you close to home. She worries less in the spring and summer. Once fall arrives, the sky is dark before dinner and her imagination runs wild," I say, studying his face.

I lean back. "Laying stone is not enough for you. Neither is digging holes."

Mozes collects his thoughts. His response is precise.

"The carpenters have the hardest jobs. But I want more. I work beside boys whose fathers' built fortresses for Austrians. Some talk and others work in silence. I prefer the talkers. The stories they tell keep me entertained."

"What fascinates you, the anecdotes, or the destinations?"

"The people. Each one has a tale, a set of accomplishments, and dreams. Dad, I would love to travel more. I enjoy meeting new people."

"Manual labor is a waste of your mind. Your happiness is important. Dream beyond Przemyśl."

"Emperors and kings appreciate how desirable Przemyśl is. Mountains on one side and lowlands along the San River. And the Russian Empire disturbs everyone," warns my son. "During the Crimean conflict, Austria built fifteen kilometers of the fortress to keep the Russians at bay. They are a different breed. Harsh and ferocious."

"Father, what did you do for the Austrians?"

"As a carpenter, I learned how to handle, cut, cleave, and puncture wood with iron nails. You must honor the wood to make it bend to your will."

I smile, remembering those past days.

"The leaves from the trees are like small gifts. When they change color, nature announces autumn's arrival. Jumping into a pile of leaves is as much fun now as it was when I was three. Knotholes in trees tell a story. Each one is unique. My mother created new beehives by placing a small piece of honeycomb into a new knothole."

Chapter 8
1890 Harstenhoekweg, Holland
Amalia Verbelte

"If you'll indulge me, sir, I would like to tell you a story."
Mozes Meijer began. My father stands back and allows the
man entry into our home. My father leads the way to our
sitting room, sits down in his favourite chair, leans back and
listens. A tall, sinewy man with thick chicory colored hair
and hazel eyes stands before my father. He has a small
brown mole above his lip on the left side of his face and a
matching mole on his neck above his collared shirt.
"My name is Mozes Meijer Eisner. Today I came upon a
harvest market around lunchtime. A young woman negotiated with a fishmonger. The vendor sought to take advantage of her youthfulness. Your daughter, a beauty, came
to the market prepared; her confidence put her in control."
"What else did you notice?" I ask. The man turns around
abruptly. His eyes make me lose my breath. I swallow.
"I saw my future." He says simply. The room goes silent.
I'm not sure what to do. My father looks at me and then
looks at the stranger.

"You startled my daughter with your intention. I like that you speak plainly. It says a lot about you. You aren't boastful. Honesty is essential in my home. My daughter was raised to be smarter than any man around her." I smile at my father. I walk over to him and sit down next to him.

I explain to my father and the strange gentleman the buying habits in our community.

"The fishmonger, Levi, knows everyone. That's what happens when you're the main source of fish here. But he's sneaky and when he can do a quick little jab, he will. Locals can eyeball a portion without a scale, but once Levi adds up different pieces of fish, his sums are inaccurate. He's a no-goodnik. He cheats." My father roars in laughter, slapping his thighs and clapping his hands.

"She tells a good story," says my father.

Every weekend he returns. Arriving before Shabbat. He turns away business for our shabbats together.

Tonight, after dinner, Mozes Meijer whispers to me, "I count down the days until you will be mine."

My knees weaken. The small hairs on my neck react to his breath. On our fourth Shabbat walk, he asks me, "do I still make you nervous?"

"In the best way," I reply. I'm practically panting for air. When he's near me my body buzzes. Our engagement lasts six weeks. Mozes and I marry at sunset under the stars. Our chuppah, made of wildflowers, is spectacular.

Chapter 9
September 1868 Rozniatów, Galicia, age 8
Tzizel Rechtschaffen

Naftali says, "Walker can't sit still, Tzizel. A wild stallion who charges from one task to another has nothing on Walker." I snicker because it is true; the best humor is. He's mischievous. I lean into Naftali's shoulder and my hair cascades out of my headscarf. I pinned it up hastily this morning. Naftali takes a section of my hair between his fingers and tugs on it. His tenderness makes me blush.

"My Walker is compelled to roam. His energy will shape his course. Impulsive and eagerly distracted, his unrelenting energy doesn't bother me."

We proceed in silence until we encounter an aged man stranded by a lame horse. Naftali and Walker work, while Aron speaks quietly to the horse with his hand on her nose. His gesture establishes a trust with the animal. He is effective. I must remember to tell Naftali about this tonight after dinner.

Tonight, Walker helps me prepare dinner. I enjoy cooking with him. When I capture his focus he is unstoppable until the project is complete. The trick is to find something that I need done that will interest him enough to get started.

Because once he starts he will feel compelled to finish. He chops the onions and garlic for the Shabbat cholent (meat casserole), and I shuck fresh peas. I season the beef with paprika and green herbs, he tosses the potatoes into the boiling water, and I chop the celery into two-inch cubes.

"Be careful, Walker, it's not fresh onions that burn you, it's the small cuts on your lips and fingers. It's garlic and lemons you need to be mindful of." Naftali directs Walker to wash his hands.

"Tzizel, your father requested to talk to me."

Concerned, I ask, "About what?"

"Shalom's dedication to Zionism. His favor will cause a shortcoming in his life."

"Naftali, Dad understands only one way to live. Family and Hashem drive every decision he makes. Worldly concerns confound him. Shalom's priorities upset your father."

"For those who do not worship Hashem with the same zeal, Zionism offers an alternate path towards enlightenment."

"Why must Shalom rock the boat? My father is a Hasidic Jew. For centuries, our family lived one way. My father cannot see Shalom's perspective."

"Your frustration with Shalom astonishes me, Tzizel. We elected to live differently from your household. Doesn't he deserve the same freedoms?"

"My father is rigid, but he's always been right."

"Shalom told me, 'Zionism is a sapling tree. The roots represent the devotion the Jewish people have for Hashem. Zionists love being Jewish, and their passion creates an insatiable thirst to move to Palestine and live free amongst other Jews. The trunk is education, teaching youngsters to learn Jewish rituals passed from generation to generation, advocating through love, devotion, and sacrifice. Embracing our songs, dances, and traditions. Zionism brings the generations together. The branches are the various sects that practice their faith through their actions. Their tactics vary, some raise money to buy back Palestine, and others would use force to take back Palestine. A Jewish homeland is universally appealing. A shared tenet of both Zionism and Hasidism is the singular focus on the education of children."

"He and Shalom should work together. I dream of them spreading the love of Judaism side by side. The path taken is unimportant. The destination is to love Hashem." Tzizel says.

"Rebbe Hersch must accept that Shalom is his own man."

"Boundaries are not my father's strength," I explain.

"He appreciates the life we have created, Tzizel. We have balance."

Chapter 10
1903 The Hague, Holland
Amalia Eisner

The Yentas work overtime to keep up with our world-wind courtship. Mother confides, "small-minded townsfolk consume themselves with the lives of others. Their obsession can ravage whatever they hold dear. Let the gossip blow away in the wind like a whisper." My Holland is the most beautiful place in the world. When you live by the water you enjoy the bouquet of the sea all day long. No matter if you're an urban dwelling or country living, various modes of transportation from boats and ferries to trolleys and cars made commuting and expansion accessible.

The Dutch are sociable and outdoorsy. I never see anyone walking alone. If they are, it's because they haven't met up with a friend who's around the corner. A Dutch person is constantly in motion. They're either riding a bike, pushing a cart full of little children, or boating on the water. The tulip personifies the people. Tall and fragrant, the people and the flowers are bright and colorful. Their petals are thick and silky. Strong enough to withstand an intense April downpour or gusty day in May. Dutch families live authentically. Community standing in Holland comes with its own reward.

Volunteering and providing for all around you is currency. Mozes has that kind of capital in Dobromyl.

Our lifestyle is unlike anyone else's in our village. Mozes is a merchant and brilliant at forming connections. His small empire expanded throughout eastern and western Europe. He is meant for more and while others are satisfied to conduct business locally, he plans for a future not simply tomorrow.

He's built a life, owns his home, travels extensively, and provides for the community. Mozes promises fields of wildflowers, surrounded by thick effervescent trees where birds take refuge and raise their own families. I didn't believe him, but I believed in him. In the fall, I plant as many tulips as I can get my hands on. After making it through an arduous winter, the tulips are a welcome harbinger of spring. In Dobromyl, wildflowers of every shape, size and color overrun the terrain preparing the land for wild berries, raspberries, and strawberries. Come summertime yellow peaches which are firm yet soft burst in your mouth when you bite greedily into the orange flesh.

Once the snow arrives its newness blankets everything. A stillness covers the earth. Glistening snowflakes create a brightness that can blind. Once the snow arrives it doesn't melt until March. It was perilous to keep warm. Mozes admired my mettle. If the cold wasn't going to kill me the isolation would. Glacial Dobromyl winters meant bone clattering, shuddering, and blue lips. As an interloper in Dobromyl, emotional security outside of Mozes was unattainable. Insulated by the climate, once the snow thaws, I venture out, push past the seclusion, and elect to hope.

Leaving everything you know because you fall in love with a man who wants to show you the world is as exciting as it is terrifying. Taking that leap of faith is courageous. But if you risk nothing you might risk everything. I listen to the women in the village. Practising their inflections at home in front of the mirror. Trying to adapt to their vocabulary. Transforming the Dutch me into a woman of Dobromyl.

My need to belong in some small way—makes me doubt myself. I listen to the women speak to each other and watch their mannerisms. When they lean in and whisper or when they laugh out loud exposing bad teeth.

The Polish language feels clumsy in my mouth. I don't know where to place my tongue to pronounce certain words. I chip away at the Dutch me and transform into a lady of Dobromyl. My need to belong in some small way was as intense as a craving. However, that same weakness fills me with self-doubt. Occasionally, I see someone from my childhood. My heart leaps into my throat and bubbles of excitement course through my veins. Emotionally, I'm soaring. Then something in my head clicks and I understand that it's an impossibility. I'm not going to walk down the street and see anyone that I grew up with. It's an uncommon practice to migrate from Poland to Holland. People don't go from Holland to Poland. They go the other way. Yet I still hold on to hope that a childhood friend would move here. When I put down my guard and relax, somebody exposes me and I feel like I'm an imposter. They all ask the same thing, "you're not from here, are you?"

Their accusations stain my assurance. Laughing through the internal damage I respond with courtesy.

I wasn't home. My history wasn't around every corner. In a strange land, it's hard to propel myself forward and be a wonderful mother and wife to a good man when I'm alone. I wish someone would invite me over for tea or a Shabbat luncheon. The nights are the longest when he's away on a business trip. Once my husband is home his personality and devotion fill my world and every inch of oxygen in our home. The children and I will stay up all night visualising his tales, opening our presents, and listening to the plans for his next trip abroad. All the excitement finally drains the children and they pass out all over the family room. We leave them where they are and cover them with blankets. Tiptoeing back into our bedroom to reconnect we giggle like newlyweds. My husband is the only one who can fill the void.

Within four years I gave birth to Maurice, Francois, and Gideon. Once Cyla arrived, I absorbed what I liked and dismissed what disinterested me. I had friends who taught me recipes and local customs. The longer I stayed here the more substantial some of my relationships became. I learned local customs and preferences. The loneliness stopped. My heart was full with love for my family and my community.

Chapter 11
September 17, 1905, Dobromyl, Poland
Amalia Eisner

Our three boys: Maurice, Francois, and Gideon devour my energy. Maurice, my serious one, is ten and mirrors my spouse, Mozes, with wide shoulders and thick legs. Francois is seven and the same height as Maurice, but thin as a rail. Gideon, my youngest son, is five. He hugs everyone.

My boys have chestnut brown hair and warm cinnamon brown eyes. Cyla, my little sweetness, is three. Born with caramel colored hair and olive eyes, she's the quiet in the storm of the boys. Cyla favours Maurice, he's pure in her eyes—a champion. Her affinity with him makes Gideon jealous. Francois notices but isn't disturbed.

Francois is independent and doesn't care what anyone thinks. He is passionate without logic and his loyalty to Maurice honours us. Francois imprinted on Maurice since birth; his eyes only tracked Maurice.

Maurice's recommendation to him is commensurate with Hashem. Gideon's alliances have not been identified.

While Mozes works, Maurice remains within earshot. He hovers like a newlywed, letting his worry consume him.

Maurice and Mozes are self-sufficient. Their impenetrable morality makes for a hearty constitution.

I have a headache and I'm lying down on the couch in the middle of the day. Our routine has been disrupted and that upsets the children. Agitated, Maurice orders François to mind Gideon and Cyla. Gideon plays with wooden blocks as Cyla toddles over to me.

Cyla kisses me clumsily on the head.

"Ima, I want a little girl."

"Cyla," scolds Francois, "Don't speak to Ima that way." Gideon forgets his blocks and his eyes widen with fear. Francois's quick-tempered, leap-without-hesitation persona surprises Cyla and enrages Maurice.

Maurice admonishes François, "She's a baby. She doesn't realise what she's saying."

"Stop yelling at me, Maurice, you don't know everything!" Francois insists. Gideon walks over to Cyla and pats her sienna curls. He picks her up and hugs her. The two of them play and topple over one another in fits of cackles.

Calming the children, I reply, "It's alright, François. Cyla has forgotten."

There is too much upheaval. Preparing lunch for them moves me to tears. I cannot stand steadily as my feet grow numb.

"I'm starving," demands Cyla.

I throw my legs over the side of the bed and stand. Grunting, I dig my fists into my lower back to alleviate a spasm. To ease the ball of knots, I need to lean against the door frame. Maurice pleads with me, "Go back to bed. It hurts to watch you move."

His intentions are pure, as he wants to take care of me but doesn't know-how. I need Mozes.

"You are being mean to her," says François.

"He doesn't mean it that way, sweetie," I say, defending Maurice. Maurice and François go to the kitchen and prepare egg sandwiches on challah. My stomach rumbles. The warm challah calls to me. I cannot recall the last time I ate.

Cyla screams and something breaks. Gideon cries.

"Is he hurt?" I say no to no one in particular.

"Gideon? Where are you? I can't see you."

Gideon hollers, "I didn't mean to break it. It's Cyla's fault." His flushed face says more than his words. is flushed. Gideon ploughs into my belly with his wooden horse. A cramp seizes my left side; knocks the wind from me.

"Play with me," demands Gideon.

Sweet thing. I want to sleep. I close my eyes. Cyla is crying and I hear Maurice in the other room comforting her.

"Go find Maurice," I instruct François in a whisper.

He runs out of the room. A pillow cradles my collar, and my spine relaxes.

These contractions are splitting me apart. As a new one rolls over me, the pain in my back radiates outward. Washed in anguish, I need it to stop. I can't catch my breath. There's not enough air to fill my lungs. My other births were easier.

Maurice returns with François, panting.

"What do you need?"

"Bring me Bubbe. Aunt Sadie too." Biting the inside of my lip to attain poise, I draw blood.

"Take Cyla with you." If the children could leave, I would scream to release the pressure.

"She will slow me down," whines Maurice.

"You are right," I agree.

"François, you take Cyla with you to fetch them."

He adores Cyla and would not wish to agitate her.

"There's no rush, but take her and go," I pleaded.

François grabs Cyla and dashes from the room.

Gideon mumbles, "He is a superb listener."

His devilish tongue keeps me in stitches.

"Gideon, bring me the coldest wet cloth you can. Ring it out and try not to drip water all over the floors."

"Is the baby moving, Mama?" asks Gideon.

"Yes, the baby is moving." Gideon smiles. He hands me a soaking wet cloth. Maurice takes the cloth and invites Gideon into the kitchen and learns by doing. Maurice is an excellent teacher. He is intuitive enough to recognize how Gideon learns. When something breaks, he puts it back together. He trusts what he can see and feel with his own hands. Maurice lays a cool cloth upon my aching shoulders.

"Gideon, help me."

Gideon chirps, "What do you need?"

"Go outside. Leave the door open. Grandma and Aunt Sadie will be here shortly. Look for them. You greet Bubbe and Sadie and bring them here."

"What a marvellous idea, Maurice. You're growing into a man."

Maurice has a traditional soul. He is caring but is still autonomous.

"Maurice, I'm closing my eyes for a spell."

******

The pain abates, allowing me to catch my breath. Becoming a parent is petrifying. With each birth, I would throw away my life for my unborn child. My mother is my midwife and knows how to protect me. She brought my babies and my sister, Sadies' babies into the world. Three generations are intertwined. She is a virtuoso and conducts my orchestra of children with finesse and elegance.

My mother speaks to my babies and the boys groan. Sadie ushers them outside, she's a wonderful mother and an even better sister. She is the smallest, but the strongest in our family. Her hands especially. She has six children of her own. Right now, her oldest, Anna, is corralling the rest of them into submission. She offers to prepare snacks.

I grab her arm.

"Stay," I choke.

My mother replies, "Sadie, go feed the babies."

I surrender to the extraordinary pain.

"Where does it hurt, Amalia?"

Rolling onto my left side, I gasp, "my back."

She uses the heel of her palm and digs it into the center of my back above my tailbone. The circular motion of her massage releases pent-up pressure. Her hands move over my hips. Mom walks in and instructs me to identify the intensity of the pain on a scale of one to ten. The contractions are an eight and a half, but my discomforts never drop below a five.

"Pick a color, Amalia."

The first time she taught me this, I never imagined it would work. Mind over matter, she explained. Women for centuries give birth over and over until they can no longer conceive. Red.

"Fish guts on the seashore are red. My contractions are red."

"Let us pick something else, Amalia. Not blood. Picture a wildfire."

"A flickering flame is orange and yellow," I say.

"Describe it to me."

"The matchstick strikes and the flare soars. It incinerates the enveloping air."

"Amalia, a settled flame is plump."

"I want orange."

As the pain recedes, my protracted stomach undulates like a wave washing up on the shore. Sand slips between my toes and I'm dragged towards the sea. My balance fails and salty foam covers me. Another surge crashes and bubbles pop on my belly button. I mold the lather into a large ball—and the globe rises from my abdomen to my rib cage. My chest contracts; and invades my throat. Sadie washes my face, hands, and feet. The coolness on my toes brings me back to the present.

"Amalia, you need to stay awake. The time is upon us," commands my mother.

"Gravity can help. Let me walk around."

The blankets slip onto the floor, and I shiver.

"I'm so cold."

Mother says, "It won't be much longer."

Sadie holds my hand. Her fingers are cool to the touch.

I dream of water, lost in the drift of orange and froth. Mother, honey-colored, directs me through and out of my torrent of pain.

Jewish history tells us that Mozes had an older brother named Aron and a younger sister named Marjem.

Mozes guided the Jews through the desert for forty years. Marjem had an exceptional capacity to identify underground reservoirs along their path. Marjem sustained an entire tribe for over forty years in the desert.

A wave of effervescent bubbles delivers my Marjem.

כומע אלל שהו תהירסת תהערע חס שאתע ר

Come all who thirst there is water.

Chapter 12
July 1906 Rozniatów, Galicia
Hersch Rechtschaffen

I'm the youngest of five sons. We live by the laws of Torah and Hashem. We're taught to honour our parents and bring them great nachas (pride) by marrying strong and intelligent women. My father, Schulim and my mother, Blima Hartman attended my wedding to Etel in the city of Skole, L'viv. Within three years we had Benjamin, Szymson, and Sheinze. Benny adores Sheinze whom he nicknamed Charlette. My brother, Lieb, went to Antwerp then to America. Now he is in Palestine. My friend, Jeremiasz, wants his children, Eidel, and Edna to go to Palestine. Stroking his flames is a fair hair beauty named Shifra.

She teaches the children songs from our ancestors on Shabbat afternoons.

Rechtschaffens are resolute and deliberate. Each morning when I thank Hashem for another day of breath, I urge him to watch over my family near and far. The desire to live in spiritual utopia where Jews thrive and praise Hashem. When doves soar in aromatic air their days begin at sunrise when the light is bright, but the hot weather has not yet baked itself into the earth. All commerce and education cease. Entire families return home for naps. Work and school commence once the sun is on the other side heading to the west.

Supper is not served till after nine o'clock when the sunlight finally fades.

My friend Dovid Hausler lives on a kibbutz along with other families from Rozniatow like the Nussbaums and the Friedlers. The bountiful landscape supports its population. He stood in front of the caves of Abraham and paddled in the Dead Sea. His family sleeps in a tent beneath more stars in the sky than Rozniatow.

Unlike my brothers, Winter is my favorite season. The crunchy sound of snow beneath my boots satisfies me, while the brisk air invigorates me. The snow sparkles with flecks of ice mixed into softer snow. The fresh snow cages the chaos which lies beneath.

My brother Judah needed to curl up in front of the fireplace to fall asleep. The brutal chill of winter depressed him and darkened his mind. A travelling merchant at the docks told Judah about Argentina, where thousands of Jews from South America immigrated from Spain and France. In the cheerful sunshine, Jews thrived. Judah kissed our mother, hugged my father, and left for Argentina. He apologised for disappointing them. He wasn't interested in defending his position and affirmed he knew best.

The Argentinian government is anti-Semitic yet nurtures successful Jews. After a month, Judah bought himself an ostrich farm. We knew what an Ostrich was, but none of us had ever seen one. Native to Argentina, these enormous birds with long necks, small heads, and skinny legs are fast and stupid. Their value is in their feathers. It took him two weeks to catch his first dumb bird. Argentina is the source of exotic feathers. Beautiful feathers accentuate fashion, and we can use misshapen ones in pillows and mattresses. European demand grows daily.

Tzizel husband Naftali is clever and unafraid of real-world issues. His perspective helps me. He is a good father to Walker and little Aron. The last time he and Tzizel visited us, I spent time in quiet prayer late into the night by candlelight. Naftali joined me while Tzizel put Walker and little Aron to bed.

I placed my hand on his knee and said, "I have been thinking about Walker. Such a beautiful boy. Tall and strong."

"Let us say a prayer together. We don't want the evil eye to see him."

I believe this, to me the prayer means a lot.

"Naftali, he doesn't look Jewish. This will help him."

"Sad, but it's true."

"The time has come. He needs to leave."

"Tzizel and I have spoken about it. We have been preparing for him. He works hard on the farm and is sturdy," says Naftali.

"He's smart and should have plenty of opportunities," I state flatly.

Sending away our best young men is not a way to build a strong community. We need the youth to sustain us.

"Will being Jewish always hold us back?"

"Yes," I confess.

Naftali's voice rises, "The Russians. It's always the Russians. Peasants are restless and starving; frightened of the unknown, suspicious, and untrusting. The political unrest, the strikes, the instability of the military. Our children deserve better. All freethinkers deserve better than Russian control." He stops.

The room is silent. I clear my throat and Etel walks in.

"Naftali, it is not just the Russians. It is anyone more power-ful than the Jews. Murderers of foreign descent have invaded

Galicia for centuries. A Jewish life holds no value." My father-in-law gave me his name, like his own son.

His covenant.

My wife Etel appeared in the doorway.

"Not every non-Jew is bad. The powerless struggle while the powerful bleed their kingdoms dry of good men's lives."

"The Russians are evil. They would make Walker a soldier. Stick him on the front lines. That's how they treat an expendable Jew."

Naftali whispers, "He is still too young."

"The elders in the synagogue want several boys to go together. Travelling together will make them all feel safer. Some will stay in Germany; others will go as far east as Prague. Walker will go to England. I want him off this continent. As far away from the Russians as possible."

I must be strong, but it breaks my heart to send my grandson away.

Naftali clears his throat. "Tzizel will need time to prepare."

"He's running out of time," I say.

My younger brother, Judah, married Peshe, to no one's surprise. Her mother and mine have been planning that marriage since the birth of both the children.

Our community is tightly knit with neighbors and distant cousins intermarried. For centuries, the Rechtschaffens have lived this way. Judah, my youngest brother moved to Austria with Zosia. Two years afterward, Zosia, Judah, and his twins Samuel and Simcha arrived in Palestine. Yidel went to Argentina.

Chapter 13
June 1880 Perehinske, Galicia
Aron Rechtschaffen

My thighs and shins cramp from the cold. Jumping up and down on the balls of my feet didn't help. My attempt to shake off the glacial weather is a failure. I blow into my hands. The tips of my fingers grow damp from my breath but refuse to warm. Ima left me a pair of socks and a clean shirt on the mantle. Under the cloak of darkness, I roam the perimeter of our property, checking on our fence, fixing broken wooden slats, and loose wires. I clear away tangled branches and form piles: one for firewood and one for junk. As my firewood pile rises, I examine how long it will take me to break it down. Abba says you can never have enough firewood available.

He survived severe winters when others perished. Winter has no patience for the feeble and youthful.

Objects glow in the bluish hue cast by the lingering sun trickling through the clouds. A twilight underlit effect emerges when the sun sets below the mist. The air is stuffy. Any colder and it will snow. The first coat of snow is my favorite. The illumination of snowflakes redeems the displeasure associated with a Dobromyl winter. Rozniatow is run by my mother's family. Uncle Efraim owns and operates the flour mill. He and Zayeh Hersch built our township. There are three temples and one church. Each synagogue attracts a particular congregation.

The Kloiz welcomes butchers, leatherworkers, farmers, and beekeepers. The great house of learning for the Jews of Rozniatow is the Beis Midrash. Tailors, artisans, exporters, and moneylenders daven there. Intellectuals, the Rebbe's household, and visiting guests will circulate throughout the buildings but will be the most comfortable in the Big Synagogue. It sits between the Beis Midrash and the Kloiz.

The Big Synagogue is majestic. A legion of white-roofed ramshackle cottages and houses crowd the gaps in between the other buildings and stalls in the Ringplatz. The rest of the Ringplatz has accommodation for visiting wagons and stalls. Zayed Hersch devoted a year to build his own brick house. He knew a brick house retains heat in the bitter winter and keeps cool in the summer.

My grandparents shared what they had; Abba keeps the embers lit in the fireplace for anyone seeking warmth, and Bubbe Etel leaves the rear kitchen door accessible to the hungry with a pot of potato and leek or chicken soup with Kreplach. She's also a medicine woman. Blending local herbs and plants to make a paste that can soothe rashes and cool down high fevers. Basswood trees are the basis of existence here in Rozniatow.

They make the air smell sweet, earthy, sour, and pungent. We cook the sap and use the bark in tea.

Bubbe Etel's treasured secrets belong to her daughters. In springtime, green buds burst from brown scaled branches, and small butter-yellow flowers strew the fields. The congestion from the pollen prevents him from sleeping soundly. Yet he remains in the bed, next to mom, blowing his nose in a futile attempt to clear it. His nose doesn't clear because it's swollen, not stuffed.

Ima can't sleep when Abba is unhappy. She explains, "It's easier to get out of bed and make him a fresh cup of tea tree. Once he drinks the tea, he can breathe, and everybody can go back to sleep."

Chapter 14
January 1908 Dobromyl, Poland
Amalia Eisner

On Mozes' latest trip abroad, he ran into his Uncle Karl in Przemyśl. Their business prospered because they elevated each other. Karl is a ready, aim, fire kind of guy. Ruled by his instincts there is no data in his calculations.

He is a hustler. He sees an opportunity and he goes for it. Mozes' abilities run narrow but deep. He persuades people to do things they never would've imagined—which improves their lives. He brings out the best in others.

He's incomparable. People crave his attention, and they want to please him.

When Mozes first saw the craftsmanship from the islands, he teamed up with Karl. He finds a way into whichever inner circle he needs to be a part of. New connections and trading partners were contracted. Karl is the shining light in the family. His family took the biggest leap of faith and landed solidly.

Unexpectedly one evening he shows up at my door.

"Amalia," says Karl "your family is beautiful."

Karl's adaptable nature makes him the best kind of guest. He cherishes family as much as a fine bottle of wine.

Mozes says, "Amalia keeps me busy."

The men snicker like silly children. Mozes' laugh keeps me in love with him. His sparkling personality is childish and infectious. Being within earshot of his voice makes you feel like you're in on the joke. Maurice runs into the room distracting everyone.

Karl boasts, "Mozes, you made a handsome man."

Maurice acknowledges the compliment, and blushes through a smile. Karl walks towards Maurice and shakes his hand. Gideon runs in, followed by Francois. I can't hear myself over the noise the two of them create. Karl can't get enough of our commotion.

"You wait, Karl. This chaos will come to you," I say kindly. We consider removing the children to get down to business, but he insists their joy feeds his soul. Once they fall asleep. Karl's family has their own story of running from the Russians. Karl's father witnessed his older brother untimely murder. The next day the remainder of his family left for Belgium. Plenty of boys like me were dragged from our warm beds and whisked away to lands unknown. The synagogues in Belgium opened their doors to me. Karl explained that living there was like an alternate universe. A place where religion doesn't define you and your talents and dreams matter.

Mozes says, "In Germany, Jews live that way. For hundreds of years, the Germans have understood what's important, which is education and scholarship. They nurture talent no matter where it comes from. A great pianist like Mendelson or a great thinker like Einstein have opportunities in Germany."

Karl says, "I'm lucky. I met a man named Jonathan Varnovick, a man in his thirties who paints apartments. He needed an assistant and plenty of work came our way. After that I helped older Jewish widows with household chores and deliveries." Karl is a popular guy and is happy when surrounded by commotion and laughter.

"Holland is my dream," I confess.

Mozes moves across the room and places his hand on my knee. He squeezes it and kisses me on the cheek.

He whispers, "I will bring you back home one day. All in good time, my bride. I promised you an adventure first."

He turns from me and tells Karl, "Berlin is my dream. Poor and rich Jews access the highest levels of education. If you're driven enough, opportunity abounds."

Karl says, "Who doesn't love Germany?" Mozes nods.

I tease, "the women in Holland are more your type, Karl. Ruddy, strong, and impossibly tall. They're waiting for you, around every corner."

"I have an opportunity back in New York," proclaims Karl.

Mozes screams in excitement. Karl and Mozes spoke feverishly for a while. Mozes replies, "On my recent trip down south, I met a man. His people come from the West Indies. Island folks who dress immodestly but aren't vulgar. Poor by European standards, you wouldn't understand their happiness. They're good community loving people."

Mozes shows Karl some exotic crafts.

"The textiles are unlike anything I've seen in Europe. Each object has a story. I find it difficult to determine which pieces have a market."

Karl says, "when I came across spices from Asia, I wasn't aware of their value."

"How did you figure it out?" I ask.

"Amalia, it wasn't easy. Dried seaweed was my first loss."

"What happened?"

"The market I had access to was uninterested. The blame

rested solely on my head. The product was delicious. The problem was educating the market. The issue was time, there wasn't enough time to even make a dent in the mindset of the community. People don't like change. Integrating seaweed with other more common foods might've made all the difference."

"What did you try after seaweed?" asks Mozes.

"Fish flakes."

"Fish flakes?"

"Jews like salt. I went after the balabusta's (strong community women.) They eat capers, gefilte fish, and whitefish salad. Little pops of salt. If you get the balabustas you get the entire town. The same way the Italians like anchovies— I wanted fish flakes— to be used as commonly. I set up a sample tray. Meats, vegetables, and starch sprinkled with fish flakes."

"You have an eye for what will sell," says Mozes.

"Sell what captivates your attention or solves a problem."

Karl spends a few more days and devises a plan with Mozes.

They talk about New York and Berlin. They imagine the possibilities. Mozes loves the idea. He wants to leave Dobromyl. The night before Karl leaves, he speaks to me in the kitchen.

"You must push him to move to Berlin. He'll do whatever you want. You have way more influence in this relationship than you realize. Make him think it is your idea."

By the end of the conversation with Karl, I felt handled and manipulated. Undoubtedly Karl was right, and Berlin was our future. But I'm not the kind of wife that plays games with her husband, her children or her life.

Karl went back to Belgium and the business grew each month. The profits ticked up and Mozes took some time off when our daughter Marjem arrived. Her birth was a hard recovery for me. Bedridden for weeks, my impatience intensified. Mozes never wavered. He hired a doctor and Karl hired a Romanian apothecary for my rehabilitation. I wore oatmeal on my breasts to soothe tenderness and bathed in lavender to reduce swelling and bleeding.

We considered moving back to Holland. But going backwards felt wrong. In Berlin, new schools for Jewish children opened up. He stopped talking about Berlin and I focused on the children. That's his way of digesting a change. He's quiet and thoughtful and then he bounces.

Chapter 15
May 1909 London, UK
Walker Rechtschaffen

Dear Abba,

The overbooked passenger ship was as lively as the Ring-platz before Rosh Hashana. I travelled in steerage to work off the cost of my ticket. The dank smell challenged me. Too many unwashed people, pinched, in sustained dread, radiating a stench I'd never smelled before.

I hoped everyone learned the basics from their parents. Leaving home made me appreciative. Ima took exceptional dignity in a clean home. She coached me in manners. Even the saltiness of the sea air tasted stale and filthy.

The captain asked my age. I said seventeen. He chuckled at my expense. I accepted his terms. My job was janitorial. I had to keep an attentive eye on seasick passengers and clean up any mess. One night, two sisters' green pallor alerted me. I pushed them towards the ship's railing and held their hair as they threw up overboard. Comforting them the way Ima consoled me when I was sick with the spotted fever. Rubbing their backs helped. After they were sick, they would feel better. The choppy waves affected women and children more than men. On the second evening, I noticed a woman with strawberry blonde hair. She wore it wavy to her shoulders.

She kept to herself, but she engaged me in a small discussion. I wasn't comfortable at first. I pointed out how London was my destination. She grinned. It felt different from how the captain roared at my expense. She whispered, "We're all going to London, dear."

She valued my privacy. It was nice to not be alone. She wore a fitted tweed suit and a huge hat with a great fringe. Her fox shawl fastened around her shoulders with a cameo pin. I sauntered up to the top deck and sat on an empty bench. With Ima's blanket wrapped around my shoulders, I stared into the night sky. My hunger made me tired. The blonde woman approached and handed me her extra bread and milk. I ate, and she told me a story. The cadence of her voice was motherly. Her name is Pearla. Her mother believed a sea king presented her in a clamshell on the day she was born. Pearla fell in love with a tall prince at fifteen. They married two years later and had a son, Harry. Her tale was sweet — nothing extraordinary. The Russians raided her home and assassinated her partner and boy. London is her fresh start. My only accomplishments are languages and brute strength. Pearla Shapira became my shadow for the rest of the trip. We ate our meals together on the top deck. She said there's nothing more extravagant than eating beneath the evening stars.

She's amusing in a curious, quirky way.

Every night, I'm guaranteed a small loaf of stale brown bread and watery soup with potato and an unidentifiable protein. Every night, Pearla offers me half of her meal. I decline. When she's finished, half a plate of bread remains.

Pearla shames me into eating better. Watching me eat makes her joyous.

Pearla says life is tougher when you are alone. She said I was brave. I appreciate her interpretation of me.

After our pilgrimage, she called for a porter. I offered myself up for the position. She gladly accepted and told me she intended to hire me within 30 minutes of meeting me. Her home is magnificent; clean and sparsely decorated. After the brief tour of her living room, master bedroom, and the den. She approached the last room, tentatively. Pearla caressed the door as if it was

a child's face. Her lips quivered, and my heart ached.

"This was my son's room." She presented me with a fresh set of linens and towels.

"Relax and take a bath. I will provide our supper, and then you can write to your parents."

Pearla and I are learning English together. I sent a letter off to Uncle Judah in Argentina and Uncle Lieb in Palestine. Uncle Judah assigned me to research the ostrich feather trade from London.

Cutler Street is the core of the ostrich industry. Dozens of stalls display the plumes for consumers. They transfer the feathers in massive wooden crates, thousands at a turn. A wealthy ostrich merchant required a linguist. I turned into his runner. Rich ladies pay three or four pounds for one plume!

London is a whole unknown world. Tall black men with British accents are the most anomalous to me. I've never met a black person before. Plump Indian women who smell of Paprika and Coriander. They resemble my aunt Blima and her friends from Rozniatow. Children running wild in the streets like abandoned dogs and young poor mothers working as maids in rich men's homes. Some people have the capital to squander. Others don't have two coins to rub together.

You taught me to be open-minded and I'm grateful for you both. Meeting people without prejudice allows me a level of the comfort others lack. Accents don't bother me and using broken language makes sense to me. I trust people's intentions. What I know to be true is you and Ima adore me. You sent me away to save me from the Russians. If you could've found a way for me to stay, I'd still be there. You prepared me for life when I wasn't paying attention. Ima taught me to cook. You made me fish, hunt, and travel as a young man. I can mend my own socks and speak in six Languages. Hashem guided me to Pearla Shapira. There is no need to worry. She cares about me. Her son was murdered. I can't replace him, but we can help each other. She says Ima is courageous. She praises you for delivering me to her.

I miss you.

Love, Walker

Chapter 16
October 1910 Dobromyl, Poland
Marjem Eisner

The high holidays mark the transition from summer to fall. Mama takes out the extra heavy quilts, threadbare from years of use. She washes and hangs them on the line to dry in the lazy afternoon breeze. The shorter days herald the wintry weather to come as the humidity is now absent from the air. At night, remaining awake once the lanterns are extinguished is challenging. Waiting for my turn to be tucked in, I stand on my tippy toes to hug my Papa.

Wrapping my arms around his neck, I leap and curl my legs around his torso like a spider monkey. He hugs me back and feigns shock. Mama, always conscious to protect her husband, reminds me to be mindful of Papa's back. Impulsively I promise her I will, but I don't know what she's talking about. Gittel and Henie are in their night dresses with their hair in braids. They cuddle waiting for story time. Their bond is strong. Gittel sleeps better when baby Henie sleeps beside her. Mama pats her lap, her signal for us to quiet down.

Papa hands Mama the cracked leather bound storybook and she lays it down upon her skirt. Mama reads two stories. Before she begins the second story, everyone is tucked into their beds. Their blankets covering them up to their noses. My blanket smells of bliss and sunlight. The sunbeam scent lingers for a full week. Beneath the surface, I stretch and flex my toes and feet. Gittel and Henie's soft snores make Mama's voice fade in the distance. Paradise surrounds me as I slip into sleep effortlessly.

By morning the air around me is crisp but not too cold. Rubbing my bare legs against my quilt is irresistible. Closing my eyes against the morning sun has me seeing orange through my eyelids. The sun's intensity makes my eyes tear. Saturday mornings are my time to spend with my papa. My brothers don't walk with him because he leaves the house just past sunrise. All my sisters accompany mama and therefore won't be at the service until at least ten o'clock in the morning. He tells me what it was like when he was a child. We sing gospels and he tells me old folk stories. The sound of his heels against the cobblestones sound like a donkey walking down a boulevard. He called it the Shabbat Pony. Papa asks me about school and my dreams at night. The rest of the world melts away and it's just the two of us. If I would have stayed in bed, I'd miss out on our time together.

The Shabbat service is special to me. The morning prayers set the pace for the rest of the day. Arriving late disrupts the evolution of the service. That's what Papa says. While I recite my prayers, he maps out the fundamental components of the service. We begin with the Adon Olam, a prayer and poem written in Spain by Sh'lomo ibn Gavriol. Afterward, the Yidal prayer is a lead and response song. Next is The Kaddish, the prayer for the dead. Papa says some call it the orphans' prayer, it's recited by those who have lost a parent. Hashem understands the significance of that loss. Losing a parent, no matter your age, orphans you. Your foundation crumbles and those left behind must rebuild and heal.

The smallest fissure in your foundation causes irreparable harm. Distracted by Mama's hushed whispers, I regain my composure before I begin the Ein Kamocha.

When she whispers in that way it means important adult information is being relayed from woman to woman. When it's not for everyone to hear, it's especially fascinating. My ears naturally perk up. Adult conversation has its own cadence and tone.

"...We have three girls, ...our religious beliefs prevent the boys..." Her friends nod their heads.

"Amalia, where will you go?"

"Nowhere. He travels far. It's nice to dream, no?"

Hanging on every word she says, ladies lean into her space. Their bodies are tightly coiled in anticipation of her next move. Is she oblivious to their interest? Genuine issues like freedom, education, and my future are discussed without the consideration of the men. Up here in the world of women, Mama is a queen.

After the Kaddish, Mama and Papa walk home in front of Gittel, Henie, and me. Maurice and Gideon burn off their energy after services by racing ahead of all of us. Sitting quietly for long stretches is hard on them. Francois manages the inactivity better. He prefers to walk beside Gittel and hold her hand. She's a funny little girl. Henie yanks my arm aggressively to get my attention. I turn to scold her.

As I open my mouth she says, "Marjem, don't walk so fast."

"I don't want anyone knowing when!" Papa insists to Ima in a tone I've haven't heard before. He sounds serious and angry. Papa's words hurt her. Her face flushed in embarrassment. He cherishes her, why would he make her feel bad? She says she feels like a newlywed, but I don't see the adoration now. They are locked inside a deep discussion. There's more going on here than I understand. The conversation in the rafters was important.

Mama pleads, "Mozes, can't I say goodbye?"

The way she asks permission makes my stomach twist in pain. She sounds small, and there's nothing insignificant about her. She is generous, likeable, and intelligent.

When she responds, her voice cracks. She reconsiders her words. Twenty minutes earlier, she was a queen. This is a different version of her. The air grows thin. I take a deep breath.

"Where are we going?" hushed whispers distract me.

My ears perk up. Her tone is one used for adult conversation only.

"...We have three girls, ...our religious beliefs prevent the boys..." Her friends nod their heads.

"Amalia, where will you go?"

"Nowhere. He travels far. It's nice to dream, no?"

Hanging on every word she says, I hold my breath.

Tightly coiled in anticipation of what her next move will be, the other ladies lean into her space. Is she oblivious to their interest? Are they not important enough to her? Genuine issues like freedom, education, and my future are discussed without men.

Up here in the world of women, Mother is a queen.

After the Kaddish, Mother and Papa walk home in front of Gittel, Henie, and me. Maurice and Gideon run ahead to burn off energy after services. Sitting quietly for long stretches is hard on them. Francois manages the inactivity better. He walks beside Gittel and holds her hand, the same way I do with Henie. She's a funny little girl who's uninterested in anything not about her. But she loves to hold my hand.

"Marjem, don't walk so fast," scolds Henie as she pulls me backward. Cyla picks her up and ends her whining.

I want to catch up to Papa.

"I don't want anyone knowing when!" Papa says to Ima.

He sounds angry. Papa's words hurt her. He cherishes Mother. She says she feels like a newlywed, but I don't see the adoration now. They are locked inside a deep discussion. There's more going on here than I understand. The conversation in the rafters was important.

Mother pleads, "Mozes, can't I say goodbye?"

The way she asks permission sickens me. She sounds small, and there's nothing insignificant about Mother.

She is generous and intelligent. But when she opens her mouth her voice cracks. She reconsiders her words. Twenty minutes earlier, she was a queen. This is a different version of her. I relish in her strength, not this version of her. The air grows thin. I take a deep breath, but I cannot get enough air. The edges of things become fuzzy. I am dizzy.

Where are we going?

Chapter 17
1911 London, UK
Walker Rechtschaffen

Dear Abba,

In London, ostrich feathers are valued against diamonds. The extraordinary demand has achieved a frenzied pitch. I'm trying harder than ever to establish a name for myself. To unwind from the day, Pearla and I play card games like ginrummy, poker, and crazy eights. Pearla says men who gamble away their income aren't men who share my values. It's not a Jewish man's game, however, we play it with tea crackers. It's a life skill and Pearla believes I should be prepared for any situation. I told her you would agree.

She makes delicious almond cookies and blueberry waffles. Once a week we eat breakfast for supper in our pyjamas and slippers while listening to the radio. Pearla says Kings and Queens eat breakfast for dinner regularly. Her knowledge is extensive. She worries about me too. She reminds me to cry when I'm scared by something I've seen in the street. I can't be hard all the time.

My friend Max believes everything is up for the picking. He's not a criminal. He was raised without a lot and knows how hunger can begin at night and continue on into the next day. He never wants to be hungry again. When Max focuses his attention on you, the rest of the world falls away.

He's engaging, fluent in English, and trustworthy. Fluency is essential to success here in London. Many different cultures can speak the same language but they're intonation changes the comprehension. The Irish, Scots, and Welsh speak the same Queen's English, but it resonates differently. If you communicate using Yiddish, no matter what country you're from, you can be understood. Having that singular unifier helps the Jews to continuously succeed.

Jews in Britain are the merchant middle class. Their bellies are full, and they sleep on feather mattresses with pillows at night. They have tenured positions in teaching, law, and engineering. Most Jews divert income specifically for upward mobility. These Jews have assimilated and live life with a higher purpose. Political rumblings of imminent war keep everybody on alert. The Russians have earned their malicious reputation globally.

Many Eastern Europeans families succumbs from torture at the hands of the Russians. Migrating to London in fear of total annihilation, they worked hard and made a good life for themselves.

It's simple. The Russians have an abject hatred for Jewish people because the Jewish faith believes in something greater than mankind. The state prohibits worship, which costs them nothing.

But the Russians' pettiness breeds contempt. Their hardships, horrific in nature, change them. You wouldn't think survival, breathing free air, finding love and making a family, can feel like torture.

Certain wounds never mend.

Guilt is as deadly as a bullet to the heart.
I fear for Aron. I see it differently now. He's tall—so tall and
strong, like an ox. Send him abroad this summer. Give him a
cart and a donkey. See what he can learn.

Love, Walker

Chapter 18
May 1912 Dobromyl, Poland
Amalia Eisner

The magnitude of Mozes's worries eclipses his usual talka-tive nature. I'll spot him reading and realise he hasn't turned the page in at least ten minutes. He falls asleep wearing a fur-rowed brow on his face. On his last trip south, he attended a few burials. Barbarians destroyed centuries-old gravestones in ancestral cemeteries. The townsfolk on the Baltic Sea were ransacked. Their homes torched; their families ripped apart by death or displacement, the ravage was ineffable. Whatever they could plunder, they took, and what remained, they set on fire. Upon his return, his dreams are violent and steal his sleep. The restlessness strips the sheets from our bed. He awakens, gasping for air, and cannot slip back into sleep. Mozes's morning gaze lacks focus, and he's preoccupied.

"The sickly stench of fear is soaked into the air."

He's in a dark place. The fear makes him angry. The women gossip in the markets and men in the temples. There is no secret to survival—it comes down to luck.

"Put the desperation away, Mozes."

I may have expressed too much. Boundaries help take care of the unknown. I scribble down my reflections and store them in a crate. When I close the lid, I stop speculating.

"Mozes, the impending invasion of the Russians dominates every conversation."

"Can I say goodbye?"

"I'm sorry, Amalia, no one can know."

Chapter 19
March 1913 Perehinske, Galicia
Aron Rechtschaffen

Abba isn't taking me into Rozniatow today. Rather, I must clean the barn before Pesach. He'd never ask Walker to remain home and clean because he preferred his company. It's hard not to notice how much Abba misses Walker.

I'm nothing like him. Skillful, strapping, and smart—I don't fill the void Walker created. He's my best friend and the only person who understands me. He confessed that Ima favors me. My protests were empty. Ima says she loves us equally, but I know she prefers me.

Before daybreak, Ima and I take a walk. A thicket lies ahead with a winding path.

"This is my special place. I happened upon it when pregnant with Walker," says Ima.

A canopy of saplings obscures the sky. Raised roots litter the terrain. Unseen birds warble in their burrows to their newborns.

"My mind shuts off and my body takes over. Being here brings me comfort."

"Do I bring you peace?"

"In so many ways. As a baby, when you were hungry, you'd alert me to your needs by rubbing your little lips against your sweet little fists. You and I never needed words to communicate. After I fed you, I patted you on the back and helped you digest your meal. You gave me comfort because I could easily soothe you. I held you over my left shoulder and your legs sprung up like a frog. Those moments are mine."

She's never been the same since they sent Walker away. We don't talk about it much but we all miss him. At first my parents worried about him night and day waiting for any type of correspondence to come from him proving that they had made the right choice. Eventually those letters did arrive and the cloak of worry disappeared.

"Ima, he's healthy in London. Safer than here in Poland." Her silence says enough.

I don't recall trudging back to the barn to remove the light blankets from the horses. Abba insists the horses don't require the blankets.

But Ima says, "if they stay dry, they stay calm. Ima has taught me everything I know about horses. The horses can't endure direct wind or rainfall."

Abba walks in and runs his hands over the horses, checking for bruises, scrapes, or puncture wounds.

"Come here, Aron." I stop shoveling.

"Check her eyes," he adds.

"They aren't runny. Her nose is fine."

I check her hooves for cracks or loose shoes.

"She's healthy."

"Scrub out the water troughs and the feed bucket," says Abba. The gunk that builds upon the sides is gross. Touching slime puckers my skin.

"After the stall, I'll do that."

"Alright. Whichever you prefer," he says unfazed. I sigh.

"Do you want me to clean the troughs first, Abba?"

"Before I head to the Ringplatz, I want the horses to be clean and fed."

"Alone?"

"Ima suggested you help me. But you have chores. Scrubbing the barn will take the entire day."

Since Walker left, this task is mine. The scrubbing cracks the tender skin around my nails. The cracks take weeks to heal. Ima rubs honey on my fingers when they're sore.

"I can work late, after we come back, Abba."

I can't contain myself. I love the Ringplatz. The tumult of swarthy men shouting and exotic women balancing their wares on their heads. Thursdays are the best day.

"Alright. Let's settle the horses and get started."

I fly through my chores and we head into town.

"Why don't we live closer to Rozniatow?"

"Being a founding member of a community where I can immerse myself in nature and praise Hashem, is a life worth living." He clears his throat and trains his eyes forward.

"What are the three pillars of Perehinske?"

"Righteousness, charity, and scholarship," I say.

"What does that mean to you?"

"We surround ourselves with people who care about one another," I answer.

Abba says, "living here lets me focus on what's important. I prefer a slow-moving lifestyle."

"You love the farm, Abba" I murmured.

"More than me. I wish I liked it more."

Not seeing his reaction emboldens me.

"I wish we lived closer to Grandmother Etel."

The strain between my shoulders relaxes. A huge weight has been lifted that I didn't realise I was carrying.

"A grown man must own his words."

He reaches for my thigh and squeezes it. He smiles.

"When I married your mother, I could work with whoever I wanted. Zeyde Efraim at the flour mill and Uncle Hersh needed more help with the oil press."

"Both those options sound way better to me than shovelling dirty hay and cleaning out slimy water troughs."

"Grandpa Hersch left Rozniatow to find me. He believed new family members strengthen the bloodline."

Abba continues, "When I saw your mother, my heart stopped beating. Her big hazel eyes and long chestnut coloured hair mesmerise me instantly."

He clears his throat and his cheeks flush.

"How did you convince Grandpa?"

"I'm a quiet man, but I pray loudly to Hashem. I'm no better than anyone else, but I want Hashem to hear me, to understand me. I told Rebbe Hersch I'd make my world about Tzizel. I wasn't afraid of hard work. I ran my farm and traded in timber. He took me to the synagogue and prayed beside me."

The wagon bumps over a large rock in the track. We passed my friend Ludovic's family farm. He is working in the fields with his father and four brothers. From a distance, it is hard to distinguish Ludo from his father. I don't want Ludo to recognize me.

"There's a new pond down the road from the mill. The water's so clear you can see straight to the bottom."

"Is it true?"

"Is what true?"

"Is the water that clear?" He stares into my eyes.

"Yes," I say.

"One day you'll take me. There's nothing wrong with taking a break after a hard day of work. You're right. Farm life makes me happy."

"Did you want to be a farmer?"

"I'm not sure I ever asked myself? Working with the hot sun on my back takes a toll. What's important to me is that you have a choice."

"Do I have a choice?" I ask.

"Life is more than what's right in front of you."

"I know that." My grin is cheeky, and my father gives me a mock frown before he clucks to the horses.

"Why do you like Judaism?" I want to thoughtfully answer. "I enjoy how Jews celebrate the Sabbath here. When my voice blends with the congregation, our united devotion is magnified. I love hearing everyone sing Lecha Dodi. Buzzing from evening prayers with the Carpathian Mountains behind me I know I am meant to be exactly where I am."

He begins to hum, and the sound is deep and robust. I close my eyes and listen.

Chapter 20
June 1913 London, UK age 15
Walker Rechtschaffen

Dear Abba,

England is an impressive place. From sunrise to sunset people come, go, buy, and sell. On any given day, the most improbable assortment of individuals interact.

Well-dressed men in suits stand next to destitute orphans with dirty faces and hair infested with lice. Mothers escort young adolescents to school. Large groups of boys run through the boulevards while others attend neighborhood schools. People move purposefully.

Living in a sizable city can be impersonal. Pearla helps and provides me with balance. Having this time, on my own, has enabled me to turn into the person I want to be. Other boys my age are homeless and sleeping in abandoned warehouses. They wash in public restrooms and eat garbage behind cafes. I come home to a warm dinner, a soft bed, and a peaceful place to rest my head.

I've mentioned Max to you before. He moves decisively like a cobra, never wasting his time, money or his ideas on the unworthy. Originally from South America, he came here with his father, Nick. Max's mom stayed behind with the other five children. Last year, Max's mama became sick, and his father went back to South America. After she died, Nick stayed in South America. His father works on an ostrich farm owned by an old blind man. The ostriches of South America have the most colorful feathers: natural blues, purples, greens with yellow and orange tips. Nick ships the feathers from Argentina to us, which eliminates the need for a middleman. We outsource the cleaning because the apparatus is expensive, and the work is dangerous.

In extreme cases, men lose fingers and are burned. The workers are Italian, Jewish, or Irish. We have a good thing going here. Which reminds me, did you hear about Uncle Judah?

A dangerous illness swept through his ostrich farm and damaged most of his livestock. To save the ostriches, he sold them to a neighbor. Uncle Judah now specialises in beef.

I met a girl named Rosie. She's enchanting. She works as a curler in the ostrich trade. Her sister's also a curler—she needs fine fingers, sharp eyes, and patience for the work. They take damaged plumes and revolutionise them into exotic treasures. An apprentice curler earns good money. Rosie It's generous and tender hearted. I hope to tell you more about her in my next letter.

I love you all,

Walker

Chapter 21
September 1913 Dobromyl, Poland
Amalia Eisner

Dobromyl's allure unfolds when the seasons transition. Once the weather hovers above freezing, it takes another month for the intolerant snow to vanish. The viscous mud is pungent and loaded with minerals. Farmers lose their galoshes walking through the fields. Within a month, the rolling plains flourish. By early September, the air chills without caution, surrendering its moisture, shocking the apples with sweetness. The low-lying sunsets red and yellow leaves ablaze against an azure sky. Squirrels, rabbits, and an occasional fox sprint in the exploration of food for hibernation. The sunsets are earlier now. Bitter cold seeps beneath our wooden farm door and through the hairline fissures in the door jamb. My thick wool clothing offers little shelter, even with the extra cotton lining. Everyone dresses in multiple layers. Galician winters are endless. Mozes left early this morning to prepare for our next journey. I left Maurice in charge of the children. They remain at home, warming by the fire. He will deputise Francois and Gideon. Cyla will help Maurice and demand to be placed in charge of the girls. Between the four of them, they can handle Marjem, Henie, and Gittel. The youngest two need the most attention. The children are in capable hands. Today I can be alone with my thoughts.

Ignoring the tears freezing on my face, I plod through the snow to the market. Our horses' bray, shaking off the chill. The biting wind blows my eyes dry.

We are moving away without warning and this will be my last chance to see everyone that I care for.

I must visit Tamar's honey stand. Butter Blonde, blue eyed, with rosy apple cheeks, she married Steven the town administrator, her beautiful locks are now covered in respect for their marriage. His ability with numbers is unparalleled. His silly sense of humor disarms any foe. Her envious high cheekbones and rosy lips make her natural beauty enchanting. Tamar, a mother of three, is high energy. Her smart and spirited children are well-mannered.

She is a wonderful mother and cherishes the family that she created for herself.

My friend, Rachel, meets me at the market entrance, her hair a mass of charcoal curls tied back with a blue scarf. A single grey streak of hair whimsically strays from her bandana. Her big amber eyes draw you in from the minute you meet her. There's a lot going on behind those eyes. Sometimes they're filled with compassion and love when you need her support and friendship. Other times they're distracted and brooding. That's when you know she has a great idea and she's creating something in her mind. Her bubbly personality extenuates her allure. Spending time with her is a treat. When I first met Rachel, she was already married to Matthew. Artistic and unconventional, her studious husband enjoyed her flair.

When she doesn't understand something, she finds a book and reads it voraciously. She studied medicine and helped the town's apothecary when needed. A midwife and a valued member of our community, she understands what it's like to be a daughter, mother and a wife.

Rachel adores her husband Matthew and her children Anne and Leo. When we first met, she gave me a painting. I've never received such a gift. I took it home and hung it in our living room. She painted a mural in our synagogue depicting Noah's ark and all the creatures in the universe walking two-by-two. Her daughter Anne has the same artistic flair. She looks just like her beautiful mother down to the eyes and beautiful lips. Her son Leo is the serious one and resembles her husband Matthew. Leo blows the shofar at the synagogue because his ability is majestic.

"Amalia, the sun is bright, the sky is blue, it's good to be alive," Rachel says.

Trailing her is Leo. He spends his days talking up Jessica Weiss' daughter, Sadie.

Leo asks, "Mrs. Eisner, do you want your usual order?"

"Yes, I do. Thank you, Leo."

While he prepares two hens and two dozen eggs, Rachel and I kibitz. We amble away from her stall and into the market arm-in-arm.

"Amalia, a short line has formed at my stall. I must go back to work." We embrace.

My silent farewell is a kiss on Rachel's cheek. My lips quiver. I might give myself away. Once we leave Dobromyl, there is no going back.

I came here as an unknown. I met lovely women like Rachel, Tamar and Girty.

Tamar and Rachel will be mad at me. It will take time, but they will understand what I did. Rachel buys a cinnamon roll from our friend, Girty. I reach for Rachel, but I miss her. She never glances back.

Drawn to the sweet aroma of cinnamon-infused butter, I walk up to Girty's stall. Girty and Alexie bake yellow cinnamon raisin Challah, spiced raisin buns, and sweet cakes. Girty's secret is blending cinnamon into the butter. I have tried, but without precise measurements, it doesn't taste the same. Girty befriended me the moment I moved here. It's easy to feel lonely and slip between the cracks when you don't have family around you to check in on you. That's what Girty became for me. My check in, a touchstone in Dobromyl.

Two challahs and six spice buns later I make my way to Ursula's stall to buy apples and cider. A milling crowd of people holding glass jars, silver cups, and goblets surround Ursula. She is a queen holding court. I hand her a jar of homemade apple-berry compote from my larder.

"I used your compote on brown bread and in my rabbit stew, Amalia. You are thoughtful to share with me. Today's special is the small red sweet apples. They are perfect for pies, even with the skin on. Scrape the skin off for compotes and apple sauce."

"I'm baking two pies," I inform Ursula.

Ursula eats a slice of apple with her paring knife and wipes the blade on her apron before placing it back into her pocket. She turns, stirs a large pot of fresh cider, and reaches for my silver goblet.

"Eat an apple every day to stay healthy," she advises as she pours the hot apple cider.

My stomach growls and my mouth waters in anticipation. She is an apple expert. Ask her which apples to use for which meals and she knows.

"I eat more than an apple a day," I say, patting my stomach. "I brought the largest cup I could find for your cider today." The aroma of apples, cloves, and cinnamon encircles me. If I sip too soon, I'll burn my lips. As an eager eater with little self-control, I count to ten and blow on the surface. I lift the cider to my lips. Ursula sees my troubled expression, hands me a piece of apple, the perfect salve for my burnt lips. I turn to see Leo, who grabs my overflowing burlap sack of apples for my home delivery.

I wish to say goodbye to my friends, but in Dobromyl, whispers become truths in a few dozen retellings. Mozes is a leader in our community. He contributes his time, energy, and financial resources to those in need. His generous spirit drew me to him. Dobromyl loves him and by extension me. His loss will be felt. Dobromyl is too remote for Mozes's expanding business.

On his last trip to the Baltic Sea, he made a new friend; a craftsman from Latvia who specialises in amber gemstones and silver bangle bracelets. In Paris, Mozes's contact Michel identified a burgeoning interest in London for costume and non-precious jewellery. Berlin would be the best place to set up residency. Cobblestone streets, buildings three stories high with picturesque windows occupying all the stores on the bottom floor. This is the lifestyle he wants for us. Luxury items, baked goods, clothing stores, and private Jewish children's schools are in the neighborhood. Mozes will escort our three sons to high-end men's barbers and haberdasheries. The local patrons of Jewish-owned bookstores, groceries, butchers, and bakeries will be our friends. Berlin means wearing white leather Edwardian day gloves in the finest tea shops along the Under der Linden. My daughters, Cyla, Marjem, Gittel, and Henie will attend premiere schools and meander through local museums. Mozes's connections throughout Eastern Europe will feed Western Europe's demand. Mozes taught me nothing in life is given, but if you are brave, you can take it.

Chapter 22
August 1914 London, UK
Walker Rechtschaffen

Dear Abba,

Pearla helped organise a beautiful wedding for Rosie and me. We wed at the courthouse. Rosie held a bouquet of giant yellow and white trumpet daffodils. Her sister, Teena, and Pearla witnessed our ceremony. Afterward, we drank champagne and ate strawberries. Pearla insisted Rosie move into our flat, as our apartment is big enough. Teena visits often. Pearla enjoys the increased commotion of our extended family. Nine months after our wedding, Rosie gave birth to Michael Patrick and Julie Ellen.

We were not expecting twins but whoever is? A week after the birth Rosie became ill. A fever overwhelmed her. Pearla nearly drowned Rosie's fever with chicken soup and matzo balls. Within two weeks Rosie was back on her feet.

With the war afoot, communities are tightening their belts and budgets. The state launched a luxury tax on imported goods, which has handicapped the entire feather trade. Max and Nick negotiated a new contract with our wholesalers, but we are not seeing the level of traffic we saw five years ago. When Aron made it to Minsk last summer, he identified a new market. Romanians understand feathers are not an extravagance, they are fundamental to maintain warmth. People living in wintry climates need feathers for beds, pillows, or duvets. From Berlin, Aron will lead our expansion east. The banks of Galicia are fertile ground for our trade.

I'll keep my family safe here and you remain safe there. No matter where we're located in Europe, invades the whispers of war.

Love, Walker

Chapter 23
March 1915 Perehinske, Galicia
Aron Rechtschaffen

Burlap is an essential tool in the Polish timber trade. Jewish artisans had a surplus of burlap but couldn't afford Polish timber to heat their homes. My easy-going nature allowed me to weave my way within Polish and Ukrainian communities. My religion gave me access to the Jewish community. I was an ideal nexus point. The protection of youth made me approachable and oddly trustworthy. Trading regular polish timber for Jewish burlap, I peddled the timber at a lower cost, which the Jewish people could afford. I used that money, and I bought a colt and a wagon.

Papa's eyes looked tempestuous, and he moved frenetically. The late-night moon glowed high in the sky casting ominous shadows across his face. This was not my Papa. Something was very, very wrong, and I couldn't place my finger on it until I realised my horse and cart were gone.

A bolder-sized ache filled my gut. My hands itched and I felt my fingers swelling.

"Aron, the Russians are coming, which is bad for everyone." He takes a deep breath.

"The Ukrainians are strong, and a community led people, but they get nervous when the Russians get too close."

"We all get nervous, don't we?"

"You're very wise for being so young. And that's going to help you. There is a beautiful world waiting for you beyond the confines of Galicia."

"My friend says that the Russians ship Jews off to Siberia to relocate their own citizens further south."

"The Russians squander the lives of good people. They suffer and lose over and over again. To them Jewish souls are expendable. They need our bodies to throw away on the front line."

Here it begins, the rationalisation. He needn't explain himself why he sold my horse and wagon.

"Bubbe Etel received a postcard. The rumors upset Zayde Hersch."

"What did the postcard say?"

"Aron, the elders conferred. The Jewish people have no clear protection from either the state or the community around them. Everywhere we go, we're outnumbered. Over the generations there's been intermarriages. The Jews find that abhorrent while others turn the other cheek."

"Would you disown me I'd I married a non-Jew?"

"Aron, I want you to live."

He explains how the Polish do not want to organise mass deportations. He questions if we can bribe local officials to simply look the other way when the Russians come for me? In this situation, hiding would be noble. But more likely ineffective.

Pity eclipses his eyes. "I can't stop them from taking you."

"I know. You need to protect Mama. It's my lucky day to show you what I'm made of."

My humour falls flat. He tells me a terrible story about another town in Poland where the Russians drag the Rabbi out into the central plaza by his beard. They'll demand he select one hundred men to volunteer for their army. The next day, they petition for five hundred more men.

As we travel through the night, his right hand clutches my knee. Stories of his childhood spill from his lips; like a damn overflowing after the winter melt. There will be no other time. I'm leaving home forever.

"When you speak to a man, look directly in the eyes. Shake his hand solidly. Be confident. Your size makes you an admirable rival."

"Yes, sir."

"Never mumble. Don't depend on the first agreeable person you encounter. Keep your own company. If I would make someone my friend, then you make them yours."

"Most people won't pass your test."

"Exactly," he says, and smiles.

The timbre of his voice and the smell of earth occupy my senses. We arrived at the train station.

"Be the man your mother raised you to be." Abba's voice trails off.

"Thank you, Abba." My arms encircle his skinny shoulders. He puts a hand-sewn silk embroidered sack with a zipper in my lap.

"It's exquisite," I say. It is stuffed with coins.

"The gold is yours. Gold's the only true standard. Don't depend on paper capital, it never holds value. Better to barter. Establish yourself first."

He hands me a basket clearly prepared by Mama. He peppers me with last-minute wisdom.

"When you get there, send me a postcard. Pick a picture of something I've never seen. Tell me stories. What Berliners are like. The food you eat."

"I will, Abba."

"It's alright to be alone, to depend on yourself. You will never be lonely because you have a family."

******

As the train rolls out of the depot, I open the basket. A brown paper-wrapped package is held together with a single red ribbon. I bring it to my face and breathe in, hoping to smell Mama one last time.

The package contained the whitest handkerchiefs—pressed and folded with sharp corners with my initials "AR" stitched into each one. Ima said a proper man carries a crisp handkerchief.

Chapter 24
June 1915 NYC, New York
Kalman Karl Eisner

Dear Cousin Mozes,

Moving away from home was the hardest thing I've ever done. My sense of adventure took over after I left Poland and landed in Belgium. Belgium treated me well. The work was good, the women were lovely, and the food was delicious. Even within Belgium, I'm defined by my Judaism. Escaping conscription in Poland empowered me. Other young men ventured forth to England and others to America.
I will be an American. Being an American means having power, control, and a greater purpose. I will always be the goofy Jewish boy from Dobromyl but in New York, I'm a serious man. I get up before dawn and study the city inch-by-inch. The metropolis is my new forest. An underground train worms itself through the earth beneath the city. It's called a subway. It cuts traffic to minutes instead of hours. There are buses, streetcars, and more people than I have ever seen. Work by the docks is easy to come but I didn't come all the way here to be a fishmonger. Without regular work, keeping

a schedule is problematic but fundamental to prosperity. A keen eye will see opportunity around every corner. Mastering English will lead to better employment. The language is complicated. Every day I write down new words I've learned and practise them at night. I write down everything that doesn't make sense to me including people's names and addresses.

Americans love sports. In the springtime, the frenzy for baseball takes shape. It is a leisurely sport with men dashing around in a diamond, hitting a ball with the bat, and tossing the ball from participant to participant. They eat hotdogs and drink beer outside at public games. Americans enjoy their families, their friends, and their free time.

The entire country celebrates together on the Fourth of July and Thanksgiving. Families travel across the country to their grandparents' house and eat gigantic feasts of turkey or goose with mashed potatoes, bread stuffing, cranberry, and yams with a sugary white gooey topping called marshmallows. Watching the family celebrate makes me miss home.

My goal is to own a store. Making friends is easy. But making quality friends takes time. I need to find the right community where I can thrive. People need people. I leave you with that message, my sweet cousin.

Love,

Cousin Karl Eisner

Chapter 25
November 1915 London, UK
Walker Rechtschaffen

Dear Abba,

I was drafted. The military doesn't care that I'm Jewish. I'm an able-bodied man who excelled at a battery of tests one afternoon. My aptitude test ranked me in the top five percent at math. They verified my physical reflexes and my health, and I reported for a swim test.

I told them, "all Jews learn how to swim in childhood. Our God requires this life skill."

My agility training intensified daily. After another three weeks of drilling, I'll be deployed. I avoided conscription by the Polish and the Russians, but now I fight for Britain. They trained me on the best equipment. Training means a lot of things, but most importantly, it means running. Running when you eat, running when you brush your teeth, running while you dress, even running when you eliminate. A lot of men in the army were just like me, displaced as teenagers, running away from evils we had no control over.

Abba, I'm surrounded by good men, men who I trust with my life. It takes character to serve a goal bigger than what you can see in front of you. Some enlist because the military is considered a family business. Their fathers served, and their fathers before them. Those men believe the first tour you sign up for is in honour of your family. Every tour afterwards is in honour of the men you serve with. In Boot Camp you learn— a brother by your side means you're never alone. That must be how grandfather felt about God. I understand it better now than I ever did before. The true belief in something greater than you provides an unbreakable foundation.

I climb towers many stories high, and at the top, the instructors put a harness around my hips and groin. The towers get higher, and we keep jumping. I jump and plunge towards the ground. My stomach lifts into my throat and I'm exhilarated. They call it jump training. It's unfair to call it training when it's so much fun. I learned airplane construction, cockpit controls, armory, and machine-gun operation. The ground school classes are my favorite, learning to operate in a wooden frame, being tossed here and there, is thrilling. The ground crewmen are the strongest workers. They're the smartest men in the unit. They service the airplanes and take care of us. Building planes and taking them apart has freed my mind to machinery. The first time we went up into the sky the commander had complete control. He flew us around and explained what we should do in case we lose our bearings. We practised this several times. On my first solo flight, my adrenaline took over until I found myself hovering weightless in the sky amidst the clouds. The privilege to see the world from a bird's perspective mesmerised me.

I'm always in motion. This part of my personality unnerves many people. I've come to realise it's not something I can control. My compulsive need to move isn't out of disrespect, it's a force within me that's more compelling than any other force out there. The same drive to move plagues me at night when I sleep. I awake trapped in the twisted remains of my cover and bedsheets.

In the bluest skies hovering in the cloud, calmness washed over me, and I recognized my purpose. God is all around me. He is the sky and the clouds. He is the man in my unit who stands beside me. He is you and Ima. He is Pearla and Rosie. I will write again as soon as I can.
Enclosed is a picture of my family.

Love, Walker

Chapter 26
May 1916 Perehinske, Galicia
Naftali Herzl

Dear Aron,

Your timing was impeccable. The Russians unleashed an unseen bloodlust through Lithuania, their hatred trained on the Jews. Villages burned to the ground. Tsar Nicholas II declared Poland independent. Poland is a new country under its own control. Jews are free but not protected.

They drafted Walker. Ima is inconsolable. We toiled to preserve you both from induction. Walker asked Rosie's sister to move into the apartment with Pearla. Pearla helps care for the twins when Rosie and her sister have shift work in the munitions factory. In Britain, opportunities opened for women to work and support the war effort while men fought on the battlefields.

The Rozniatow Rechtschaffens are an exciting bunch. Your uncle Shalom became an ardent Zionist. The organisation educates teenagers and young children about Jewish civilization, ceremony, and language. Their teachers are men and women in their twenties. The younger the educator, the more effective they are at converting teenagers into avid Zionists. Their mission is pure. As you know, Jews love to learn. Being able to spread the love of Judaism is, to me, the greatest mitzvah one can do.

Last week, youngsters like you amassed all the children together to sing songs, wave flags, and dance in big circles. The Zionists take charge of their lives and spread the gospel they believe in. This summer, your uncle is going to establish a camp for young Jewish children to attend. They are learning about Judaism, outdoor survival techniques, and socialising with their peers. Your grandfather is rigid. He is digging in his heels when it is unnecessary.

Different is not wrong. Change is not bad. We can all love God in any way we choose to.

Eretz Yisroel, as a devoted Jewish state, is appealing.

I am glad you are there. Being a good person can be overshadowed by religion. Heading east for a better life where you are not limited by religion is the way of the future. Yetta's son is moving to Austria next week. Austria is not far from Germany. You should reach out to him. Tell him what it is like to be on your own in a strange place. Uncle Mordechai is emigrating to Australia. Uncle Zacharia is going with him. I have never heard of Australia. Mordechai and Sosa want to live where it is never cold.

I am proud of you and anticipate your next letter,

Abba

Chapter 27
September 1917 Berlin, Germany
Aron Rechtschaffen

Dear Abba and Ima,

My sleep in Berlin is fitful. Nature is far away, and it's hard to find calmness. The stillness of the farm suffocated me as a child; now, sleeping outside among the rustling leaves and staring into thousands of stars sounds blissful.

On the farm, I knew it was March because the birds began their full-throated birdsong at four in the morning on the cusp of sunrise. Ignoring the call and repeat of the birds was impossible. With my eyes closed, distinguishing the different species outside my window in the morning eased me into the day. The sounds of the city never cease which makes harbingers of Pesach hard to hear.

Showering after work helps calm me from the tumult of the day and there is plenty of hot water.

In the mornings, I go to the corner breakfast shop. I love the smell of eggs on the grill, buttered toast, sausage, bacon, and hash browns. Daily, I buy an egg sandwich. Seth, the line cook, knows my order by heart—scrambled eggs with chopped onions and green peppers. The sandwiches are easy and inexpensive. There is a restaurant run by the incomparable Kimberly Miller. She serves dinner out of her living room. It's her own business, it's cash under the table, the food is outstanding, and the company is entertaining. Two dining room tables run the length of her apartment. Several linen tablecloths adorn the tables. The chairs are mismatched, as are the plates, utensils, glasses, and linen napkins. It is all quite charming. The food tastes like home. I stopped losing weight after I started eating at Kimberly's. She introduced me to grapes. She has a mane of wild curly white hair and a wrinkle-free face. The pictures on her mantle show a teenage buxom blonde with a cute, pert nose and a mischievous smile.

Baskets of bread overflow on the tables for everyone to enjoy. Customers bring their own bottles of wine. Our infamous hostess never turns down a glass of wine offered by a guest. It's like living on a kibbutz with better food. Last night, I noticed Kimberley's kitchen faucet was leaking. I told her I would come over tonight and fix it for her. She introduced me to linguine and clam sauce, wedding soup, and tiramisu. Ima would love her mushroom, barley, and ginger carrot soups.

Her nightly feasts are moderately priced. The coffee-infused dessert is unlike anything I have ever had.

I am upset when I don't receive my regular letters from Walker. The gloom of war rages on. There are food shortages and nightly broadcasts that do not sound promising.

I miss you both. I pray for Walker.

Love Aron

Chapter 28
January 1918 Berlin, Germany
Amalia Eisner

Majestic linden trees run along the borders of the Unter den Linden. For kilometres their lime-scented flowers attract bees, as their dark-green heart-shaped leaves hang from broad burnt-amber limbs. Young seedlings have smooth branches, which are fragrant and pocked. A cover of foliage they provide affords a natural reprieve from the sunlight. Being physically active is a joy here in Berlin. There are plenty of parks, open green spaces, soccer fields and tennis courts for every citizen to enjoy. Mozes plays soccer with the children in the park, weather permitting. Covered in perspiration, he became the envy of other young fathers. He plays with wild, childish abandonment. His affable nature preserves his youthfulness. At the invitation of a few guys from our synagogue, Mozes joined a tennis association. He's never played before. We moved here to achieve. Business expansion and new contacts can crop up anywhere. By embracing change, we're developing something of our own.

Maurice loves music, and Mozes bought him and Francois' wooden recorders. Gideon would have preferred drums. We attended regular outdoor evening concerts. Some events were for the boys alone, others involved the entire family. Berlin is luxurious. Our family is our greatest jewel. Nurturing them, reminding oneself to exist in the moments makes our life special. My simple love for Mozes allows this world. His pull on me is magnetic, but he doesn't eclipse me. Life knocks me around, but I always fall in his direction. His devotion elevates me to a new stratosphere.

The children drop off to sleep without incident after a full day in the sunshine and a belly full of chicken and potatoes. The night is ours. Mother pointed out the key to stable marriage is to make your husband your king. Your home is the castle. He'll slay dragons to protect what is his.

"A present arrived," I coo.

Mozes turns to me and in a low growl says, "I love a surprise."

His posture relaxes like a wave on the shore. Diving in, I ignite his unrelenting passion.

I move my bosom into his face.

"Mozes, can I put the new dress on for you? The hatbox took two hands to carry."

"Have you tried it on yet?" he asks urgently.

"Not without you." I kneel down and remove his loafers.

I glance upward, "let me show you."

He removes his day coat and vest. I unbutton his shirt. He reaches for me, and I race to our bedroom like a mouse running from the light, he slaps my derriere.

The dress is Lapis blue with cobalt velvet running the length of the sleeves. Additional detailing gathers and accentuates my bosom and my waistline. Scalloped cuffs with mother-of-pearl buttons adorn delicate sleeves. The dress has a zipper that runs along the back. I'll finish the buttons and leave the zipper for him. Like a panther tracking its prey, he pursues me. I giggle like a virgin on her wedding night.

"You are my reward, my prize."

His heated breath dances on the nape of my neck.

"Wear your hair up. The soft bend of your neck makes me crave you."

Chapter 29
April 1918 Berlin, Germany
Aron Rechtschaffen

Freshly baked bread drove me towards Herman Newman—an elderly man, with a gruff tone, and a cordial face. He carries a wicker basket brimming with dinner rolls. The buttery aroma reminds me of home. With a throbbing heart and a watering mouth, a lifeline stood before me. A grin stretches across my face as humanity and community enter my world. Herman offers me a roll and asks penetrating questions, bringing me out of myself. I ate roll after roll and enjoyed speaking to him. A simple fellow, his clean-shaven face is the only hairless part of him. His knuckles eclipse my palms. I lose track of how many rolls I've consumed.

He wipes his chin, and says, "children from the farm don't sleep well in the city. You'll tell me why one day."

His observations mask obvious concern.

"Your generous temperament is exactly what I needed."

The warm buttery rolls were outstanding.

"I haven't eaten food like that since I left home."

"Where is home?"

"Poland."

"How long have you been here?"

"Six months."

"How has it been?"

I consider my answer. Sweeping floors in a warehouse keeps me out of the elements. Food isn't scarce, but nothing tastes memorable. I've made friends but miss my family. How has it been? I search for the right words.

"It's been an adventure."

"You remind me of my son before he left. A good boy who followed the rules and listened to his elders. The Germans lost him, somewhere in France."

Herman and I spoke at length and started a friendship. He showed concern for my well being. He's invited me over for dinner more nights this week than last. He bakes bread, cooks stews, and devours his cucumbers with thinly sliced white onion and vinegar. We'd end our supper with a shared pot of tea and sliced lemon. Afterward, we walk around the neighborhood because the movement benefits his digestion. A month or two into our friendship, deep sloppy puddles of rainwater riddled our pathway throughout the park. Herman stopped abruptly, and the binding on his left shoe separated from the sole. After devoting a summer to fixing shoes, I could fix his shoes for him.

"You are unusual, Aron. You deserve more."

Herman's house buckled under the need for repair. I roamed, replacing stripped screws, caulking grout, tightening loose bannisters, and restoring damaged or rubbed down tiles. His friends visited, looked at my work, and the word spread. The aged, whose heirs had gone off to war and not returned, required me. They repay me with home-cooking and nice clothing. Occasionally, I find money concealed in a pocket. The charitable spirit of the German people never ceases to amaze me. Herman met me at the train station. Visibly agitated, we walked to his home in silence. When he was ready, he would tell me what was wrong. We walked right into his sitting room and there it was. His favorite wooden rocking chair broke.

He said, "I love that chair. My father, Bear, cut down the tree that made that chair. He made one for his father, his mother, himself, and my mother. When I left home and married my wife, my father gave me his chair."

His head was in his hands.

"He demanded I build a cherished home where the chair could be in the center of love and family."

"What a wonderful blessing," I say.

"I fed my son from the chair every night. One evening, he had a terrible fever and a rash over his hands and the inside of his mouth. I used a cloth soaked in cold milk to nourish him." He stopped, lost in his memories. I give him time.

"My last memory of my wife Clara is of her sitting in that chair and smiling at me, rubbing her pregnant belly, before she went into labor."

My mouth goes dry. His outpouring of emotion is raw and prickly. I don't have adequate words. I suck in my breath, hoping something comes to mind. He trusts me like family. I put the pieces together and realised his wife died in childbirth and he raised his son alone. The Germans never found his son's body. There is a small part of him that believes his son is still alive. He does not need my sympathy, but he needs my company.

"My father works in the timber trade," I offer.

"You speak little of your family," says Herman.

"I miss them," I admit.

"Good," he says smiling.

"That means you love them." The abandoned chair doesn't work the way it's meant to.

Objects have purpose and like our bodies resist change.

When their natural state of being is disrupted, it's hard to repair. I relish the challenge. Running my fingertips over the polished wood, worn soft, I sense the oak seat is weak on the left side. The exquisitely crafted joint is worn down. It will take some time. I'll need timber, a saw, and a sander. I wrote us a list of supplies needed and off we went to old man Verlin's hardware store.

Ryan Verlin, injured in the war, sits behind the register. He lost a lung saving five German lives from drowning in the Black Sea. He used to be an Olympian swimmer. With a serene face and a mouth of gleaming white teeth, his optimistic spirit is untouched by hardship. His wife, Herr Nicole Verlin, and their daughter Maya are present. Maya, an inquisitive curly-haired blonde, no bigger than a wisp, manages the inventory. She knows where every item in the store is located. Her smile and sweet laughter draw you in. Fiercely independent, she doesn't like it when her mother hovers. Yet Nicole maintains a watchful eye on her jewel. Nicole's customer care is beyond compare with a great mind for detail and a nose for gossip. She knows everyone. Today wasn't about tools at all. Herman was introducing me to Herr Verlin. Before we left, Herr Verlin pulled us aside.

"Herman, have him join the Neuve synagogue."

Herman and I thanked her. "Important men with beautiful daughters fill the congregation."

Her decree was decisive. Until our walk home, I hadn't recognized her pointed questions. While her daughter navigated the store, Herr Verlin pressed on and learned more about me in ten minutes, then people would know about me after ten years. That Friday night, she walked me over to the temple.

Edee Verness met me at the door. He gave his hand and said, "any friend of Herr Verlin is an ally of mine. Welcome to our community. Aron Rechtschaffen. There are plenty of young men and women your age."

Chapter 30
June 1918 Berlin, Germany
Mozes Meijer Eisner

Easily identifiable by their headgear and dress, a Hasidic Jew is considerably more than their outward presentation. The shape of their velvet hats denotes which Rabbi a religious man follows. Some hats are wide, tall, and thin, mirror a crushed fedora and others wear their hats backward, positioning the bow over the right ear.

While on a stroll through Monbijoupark, a Hasidic family crosses our path. Strolling single-file and reticent, passerbyers are conscious of their presence. The haggard father wears worn through black trousers with mud caked onto the cuffs. His wizened beard grows wild and untamed.

Under my breath, I mutter, "it's a dream out of Dobromyl."

Marjem demands, "where are they going?"

She points and withdraws within an instant.

Intrigued, I ask, "where do you think?"

"To synagogue?" Henie and Gittel giggle.

Cyla says, "Marjem, why do you say that?"

"I don't know," she says.

"The mommy is pretty," says Henie. Gittel nods in accord.

"She is. Her hair is blond and curl," add Amalia.

Their teenage son lags behind.

Marjem asks me honestly, "Why do they prefer to stand out?"
Her stare pierces me deeper than a flesh wound. She strives to read me. Fully aware her position is judgemental, she continues.

"Are they closer to God because they're more faithful?"

"Hasidic boys are obvious marks. As a child, their vulnerability shamed me. I didn't want to understand them. We pray to the same God, but they don't value what I do. My spirituality is private."

Marjem stands with her feet hip-width apart. She demands attention when she does this.

"Are you ashamed of being a Jew?"

Gittel audibly gasps. Henie and the boys are engrossed in the answer.

Amalia says, "You go too far."

Marjem's eyes widened. Marjem does not listen to me.

She is concerned about why most people hate Jews.

Marjem asks, "Did you want to be friends with the boys who hate Jews?"

I am astonished. To me, being Jewish never mattered, but it affected everyone else. Marjem thinks differently than me. She does not worry about pleasing others the way Cyla and Gittel do. I do not want to tame her spirit. I laugh out loud.

Marjem says, "You say being Jewish defines you."

Amalia and I both take a moment and consider her.

Her sentiment is clear. Her advanced vocabulary belies her youthful age. The older women in the synagogue stare when she speaks.

"Judaism is an honor. Growing up, boys worked side-by-side beside their fathers in the fields. Others worked in small village shops."

I take Marjem's hand in mine. Their ability to trust in their faith and purpose above all else makes them confident. They value humility. Studying, challenging, devouring the Talmud and Kabballah brings them closer to God, and the laws laid out to reach wisdom and bliss.

"Hasidic Jews value kindness. Their stories passed down through song recount lessons and adventures of their cultural traditions. Just like us, Marjem."

She analyzes what we've said. Her mind acts swiftly, and her snap judgements are generally correct. She interrupts everyone, even herself, and thus loses herself in her tumbling observations. Narrating her plans to all within earshot. Her thoughts are at the forefront of her mind. Compromise will be tough for her.

"Mama, your hair is pretty," says Henie.

Marjem rolls her eyes. Henie's smile is so bright it could light a dark room. Her black curls bounce as if syncopated to the lilt in her voice.

"Mozes, this is my moment. That Hasidic woman needs our sisterhood."

Amalia's commitment to her family and neighborhood is commendable. She runs over and introduce.

Chapter 31
September 1918 Berlin, Germany
Amalia Eisner

Jessica Jacobs is the president of the sisterhood at the Neuve synagogue. She's hosting our monthly meeting this evening. Originally from Holland, our mutual affection for home bonded us instantly. We both grew up near the water, swam before we walked, and hated the smell of the chicken coop in the mornings. Her warm brown eyes and envious corkscrew curls, remind me of my cousins back home. Tall and slender, she used to run along the canals until she moved here and married Steven. Her outrageous sense of humor makes her easy to like. As a mother of six, she accepts my limitations.

"Amalia, I raised two boys who never sat down," begins Jessie. There were plenty of mothers that judged me.

They had little daughters who would sit colour for hours at a time. My sons couldn't care less for colouring.

Creative nonetheless they wanted to explore the world around them. Her stories are messy and hilarious.

My cheeks ache when she gets on a roll. Her kind eyes reveal no judgment.

Her oldest friend, Renee, jumps in, "she's not lying. Our four children played together for years. I could draw a circle around my daughters. Her children, good boys, never ceased running." Her joy highlighting her well-earned laugh lines.

"Those boys kept my weight down," admits Jessie.

"My other girlfriends complained about how their shape changed forever. That wasn't my fate." The sacred inner circle of the sisterhood nod in agreement.

"Jessie never complained," said Renee.

She pulls a strand of grey hair behind her ear.

"Others were not as kind." After Jessie married off her children, her husband died of a heart attack. She adopted two more children in need. She revealed to me, Hashem infuses certain souls with the capacity to nurture. Her enriched toolsets obligated her to share these abilities with others. Their two souls would precariously drift without her intervention. She saved their lives. The entire community knows it.

Tonight, I brought Kira Sander with me to the sisterhood meeting. A buxom blonde who migrated with her partner and son from Krackow. I met her in the park and asked her to have tea the following day. She accepted, and I invited her to our sisterhood meeting. She is a twin whose mother takes care of the elderly. The women will like her. She's accessible to new friends, experiences, and advice. It takes her time to open up, but I suspect once she does, she'll keep me in stitches for the rest of my life. She's very smart and makes funny observations.

"I lived my whole life in Kraków," she begins.

She seems nervous. Her feet are crossed at the ankles.

"My parents and my grandparents are all from Kraków. My father owned a bookstore, and I read every book inside of it. My education prospered. Had I been a boy, my mother Judy said I'd be a great lawyer or judge."

Renee and Jessie look at one another.

"Kira Sander, these women are the shrewdest people in our community. We run the homes while our husbands toil and succeed. True power is all around you. We make the real things happen," says Jessie.

Renee and Emma nod in agreement. Kira Sander visibly relaxes. Like a deflated balloon, she's smaller but no less fantastic.

"I don't have a history in Berlin to base my decisions on. I don't know if I'm making my choices based on fact or my gut. Juxtapositions appear everywhere for me. Life keeps moving forward without enough time for me to ruminate."

"Welcome to our sisterhood, Kira Sander," says Jennifer Silverman.

A cute, upbeat brunette who volunteers at the three-year-old Hebrew nursery school. She also teaches classic dance classes at the synagogue. Fiercely loyal, she's a good woman to have in your corner.

Kira says, "Thank you for having me here. Berlin is a wild and thrilling new world for me." She leans forward eagerly. Her excitement invigorates me. Jessie's tone is as delightful as the result of a hilarious inside joke. She explains to Kira, "we celebrate the high holidays and don't attend Friday night services. I'm usually too busy cooking and enjoying a glorious Shabbat dinner with my family. After Shabbat services, we have lunch with friends and the children play. Judaism is joyous. Raising our families within our larger tribe instills a love for religion for generations. In Berlin, we aren't slaves to religious commitment. We celebrate Judaism on our own terms. Revel and love our lives and the beauty that Germany provides for industrious Jews."

Jennifer pours herself more tea and refills Renee's cup.

"The boys and girls attend Judaic academies, and our lives thrive without constant constraint and worry," adds Renee.

"Back in Roumania, my brother had to leave to get educated.

Thousands, if not more, immigrated here from all over Europe to learn. You're in the right place."

Jessie and I lean back, taking in the lively discussion.

She whispers to me, "we'll get to the agenda later. This is the real reason why we meet up together. To help and share. Maybe gossip a little."

"Your neighborhood is filled with professional Jewish business owners. There are plenty of opportunities here for your husband and family." informs Jennifer.

Her eyes beam. Karin Diperovich rushes into the parlor and joins the crowd, she's late for every single thing she does, but none of us mind, because she's a charitable individual. She takes care of three disabled adults. Her patience is virtuous. She sits down next to Jennifer, who immediately makes room for her, and squeezes Jennifer's thigh.

Jennifer brushes aside Karin's soft waves and kisses her on the cheek.

"What did I miss? And who is this beautiful blonde?"

Jessica leans in towards Karin, "Amalia brought a new friend tonight. This is Kira Sander."

"It's nice to meet you, Kira. Don't mind me, I'm always late. Don't take it personally." The ladies laugh.

Karin smiles all knowingly.

"We'll advise you on schools," says Renee. Kira opens her mouth as if devouring the information.

"We know how difficult it can be living in a new city. Children at your heels, depending on every decision you make, children need constant reassurance. It's exhausting. Allow our sisterhood to be your tribe and help you weather the storm."

"We hid our son several times from the Poles during the war," admits Kira Sander.

"We know your story all too well. Plenty of young Jewish men from all over Europe came to Berlin for the very same reason," I explain.

Karin says, "some boys weren't as lucky."

She needn't say another word. We understand the unspoken truth.

"I feel Hashem within the walls of the home I created in Berlin. Lighting the Shabbat candles and proudly displaying them in the window for all to see makes me giddy," says Kira. I remember when I first felt that sensation. Almost indescribable until you meet another kindred spirit. Once I felt the freedom from religious oppression, my personal and spiritual world exploded. My perspective changed. It used to be hard being Jewish. Sometimes in Holland but almost always in Dobromyl. Fear holds people back. Once fear stopped defining me, I found humor. The world changes fast and Berlin is a part of that. Making informed and smart decisions is what defines both Judaism and Germanic ideology. The sisterhood at the Neuve synagogue taught me that. They changed everything for me.

Jessie Jacobs will host the Chanukah Bizarre this year and asked me to be co-chair. The implication of her request is not lost on me. These generous women respectfully represent the community, and everyone is welcome.

When I return home from her sisterhood meetings, I cradle a new leftover delicacy. Mozes's favorite was Jessie's cherry and prune tartlets.

"You're happy here, Amalia?"

"Aron, Berlin is everything you promised," I say.

Chapter 32
September 1918 Berlin, Germany
Aron Rechtschaffen

I gathered every scrap and thrown-away button from my job at the fabric warehouse. I designed unique pillows and sold them. My friend Nathan bought a pillow for his Aunt Hinde. That sale led to another five. The following week, Herman stood beside a man in his fifties, waiting for me at my boarding house.

"Aron," says Herman, "meet Josef. He admired the cushion you made for his bride, Hinde."

Grinning, I extend my hand.

"It's nice to meet you." We sauntered over to a local cafe and ordered tea. He summarized his offer.

"I've known Herman for a long time. A man's name and good reputation are all a man has. You are industrious. I have a job for a young man like you. Someone unassuming, sympathetic, and sincere enough to handle high-level trade transactions."

Intrigued; I asked him to explain the job in greater detail.

"The luxury tax and import fees make business almost impossible. Although, if you can make it past negotiable borders, there's real money to be made. You would transport goods from Berlin to Prague. My best clients are Ukrainians. Herman says you speak many languages."

He softens his voice, "The Ukrainians can smell a Jew a kilometer away. The Poles need even less distance."

He eyes me.

"I don't care what you are. This is a dangerous job. But with great risk comes a substantial reward. Are you prepared to take the risk?"

"I've been traveling to foreign lands since I was nine years old. I know how to go unnoticed."

My parents would never agree to me accepting his proposal.

"You need someone brave and stupid."

"Probably more stupid than brave. I need someone likable. Someone who blends. Those poor bastards are starving to death under the Russians."

"The Russians aren't God-fearing people," I mutter under my breath.

"Is the work in Prague or Ukraine?"

"For now, Prague."

Smiling, I say, "The trade routes through there are striking. I will need a horse and a wagon."

"Agreed. Prague is the heart of Europe. I am getting older, and my new bride wants me closer to home with the baby coming. I need someone who can work for me, move merchandise from rugs to pots and pans, leather goods to wine. Are you interested?"

"I want a percentage of the profits. You cover transportation costs, food, and lodging when necessary."

"You know what you're doing, Aron Rechtschaffen. I am happy to have made your acquaintance."

He sticks out his hand and shakes mine. When the opportunity presents itself, leap.

Chapter 33
September 1918 Berlin, Germany
Amalia Eisner

Mozes explained to Marjem, "My father was brilliant, devout, and poor. He worked each day in the dirt. No matter how much he toiled, he couldn't get his fingernails clean. He milked cows, gathered eggs, and cleaned the chicken coop. The moment he picked up a shovel, he dug holes and planted seeds. While the seeds grew, he weeded and watered the plants. When the harvest came in, he collected and sold vegetables in the open market."

Mozes and I sit upon a red and black plaid picnic blanket. The sun is bright in the blue sky. Fluffy clouds sail across the sky as if they were in a race. Maurice, Francois, and Gittel run around. Marjem is indifferent in their games.

She sits beside her Papa, listening to stories of his childhood. Lost in his memories, I notice how Mozes's lips soften, his shoulders drop, and his speech slows. He does not speak often of his parents. Sometimes I think he forgets he was a child.

"Tell me more," says Marjem. She cannot consume enough of his affection.

"My father loved reading and devoured every book he could. In the small villages access to books did not come easily."

"Is that true?" Marjem asks Mozes.

We laugh at her innocence. She appears wounded, being excluded from her father's joy. To her, the sun and the moon rise and set with her Papa.

"When I first left home, there was so much I did not understand. I devised ways to figure out what I needed. I befriended people who could teach me and who were interested in helping me out. That is how I survived. Using the skills, I had inside of me to reach out to others who were willing to lend a helping hand. Once I returned home, I taught my father everything I had learned. His thirst for languages and cultural exploration were insatiable."

Marjem and Aron talk some more about his father and the austere lifestyle they led.

"My father," Aron began, "was a fractious and devoutly religious man. For centuries, the Jewish people believed in assigned marriages. My grandparents assigned him a bride. They considered it a brilliant match. His family's position for generations would improve with this union. Working in the town's flour mill meant steady work. But he loved another woman, a local orphaned girl with no dowry."

I add, "an orphan born into poverty has next to no opportunities. If she's lucky, she would marry a much older man. God willing, she would bear the man a son."

Mozes continued, "Four years later, the Cossacks invaded. There was a pogrom and the mill burned to the ground. Every family lost a loved one. They murdered my mother. They murdered the orphan girl. Kidnapped Jews were ransomed back to their families, but their loyalty was forever questioned." Marjem grows quiet.

"It's good that we live here and not there," says Marjem.

"Papa is right, Marjem, we are lucky to live here," I declare.

Marjem looks through me. Her Papa is the hero of her story.

"Marjem, your mother moved here with me and demanded

nothing. She knew Berlin meant a real future for us. Her bravery and faith opened a whole unexplored world to us."

Amalia, Henie, and David, 1925

Chapter 34
March 1919 Berlin, Germany
Aron Rechtschaffen

The terminal at the Berlin train station is a realm of blended emotions; lovers kiss in greeting and departure; husbands wave goodbye to their doting wives, and parents stand immovable as their children come back from war broken. The vaulted ceilings, iron encased windows, and stately staircases warm the otherwise industrial settings.

Walker hollered my name before I recognized him. Excitement rolled over me as he pulled me into a hearty embrace. I wanted to take the moment in and try to remember it forever. He made me feel like a little boy on the farm racing double step to keep up with his long strides. Walker and I had previously discussed the dimensions and weight of the machine he was bringing from London. It's called a feather cleaner. It might not look too pretty but it works. During the war, Walker learned to manufacture a plane. As a machinist, he maintains motorized components.

He applied his vision and education to create a compact feather cleaning machine.

It's hard enough to load the machine onto the train but it would be nearly impossible to move it through the streets of

Berlin without some sort of truck. Walker suggested I bring a dolly to wheel the unwieldy machine from the train to a truck. Herman used his truck to move Walker's machine. Walker and his friend Max worked well together. They used Herman's dolly and loaded the machine with little effort.

We drove home together and unpacked the machine. Herman prepared spicy sausages with ground mustard seeds, sauerkraut, and a basket of rye bread with caraway seeds for dinner. He suggested we eat before we do anything else. Max and Walker applauded the feast before them.

In Herman's kitchen, I prepared four larger-than-life carafes of quality beer. When I came back carrying them, Herman was happier than I have ever seen him; even his eyes were smiling. We dined the entire night. Walker and Max regaled us with tales of their travels. Herman told dirty jokes. We got sloppy drunk.

Max said to Herman, "I've never met a German I liked before. You remind me of my father. He is from Argentina. I am from Argentina too. I do not think Germans like Argentinians. Usually, Germans only like other Germans."

Walker slapped Max on the back of the head, the way your mother smacks you when you are stupid, then he laughed nervously. Herman grew quiet, then flashed me a wicked grin. He put his hand on Max's knee and gave it a good squeeze. Herman said, "trust me, you still haven't."

We laughed again and carried on. We unpacked the crate in the middle of Herman's dining room. We approached the machine and discussed how to put it together. We grunted, cursed, and laughed. Eventually, the machine started. The roar of the motor brought tears to our eyes. It was a group effort. We celebrated our success with another round of beers. Herman stayed awake with us as long as he could. He fell asleep with a piece of strudel on his chest. I placed a soft blanket on top of him. The next morning over eggs, bratwurst, and rye toast, Walker, Max, and I explained the business to Herman. The quality of our customer is as important as the product sold. Selling from a stall on the street attracts a customer who buys on the street. We need to create a realm of decadence because high-end clientele wants a unique shopping experience. Timeless elegance is noticed by those with disposable income.

Herman's wife took great pride in decorating their home and since her death, he's maintained her efforts. We'll transform the house into our store. We'll receive customers in the parlor with tea and small cookies. While women examine delicate berets and high fashion accessories adorned with long exotic plumes, their friends can survey the new double stitched accent pillows created from exotic textiles. We installed the machine in Herman's cellar, which remains cool in the summer and tolerable in the winter. There is a separate room that is perfect to sort, store, and dry feathers. We did a test run, and the machine eliminated the fetid odor from the feathers. With hard work, we will be successful. You are right. Germany is everything we ever dreamed of.

Love, Aron

Chapter 35
May 12, 1919, Perehisnke, Galicia
Naftali Herzl

The end of the war has caused mass confusion on a global scale. Broken and battered men roam great distances to return to a home and a family that may no longer exist. Widowed mothers and orphan children scramble in the streets rummaging through debris looking for sustenance or a warm dry place to sit and rest.

As a reward for his service the British military is providing train tickets for the entire family to meet up for a reunion in Berlin. Herman generously extended his home to our entire family. Aron is beyond excited and can't wait for us to meet Herman and see what his life is like in the bustling city. Walker explains that Berlin is the easiest place for us all to get together considering how spread apart we all live. He also knows that I've always wanted to go.

Convincing Tzizel isn't a problem. There is nothing in the world that she would wanna do more than put her hands on both of her babies again. Her concern is traveling.

The night before our journey, Tzizel whimpers and she falls asleep. She doesn't want me to comfort her in fact she would rather that I ignore what is happening. I know that she's embarrassed by her fear of the unknown. I need to give her time and space to push herself beyond her comfort zone. The boys are excited about the new business. It's all Aron can talk about lately. Herman provided his home as the base for the business. They'll showcase new duvets and pillows in the dining room, and Additional chairs, couches to the day room for customer overflow.

"Naftali, when we sent our eldest son away to England a little piece of my heart died. Having a loved one so far away from me where I couldn't protect and cherish him was an ask made of me that was too much to bear. When England drafted him into the war, I blamed myself because we gave him away. Even with the best of intentions, we abdicated and allowed the world to separate us. I've spent many sleepless nights asking myself why we made the decisions that we did? I always come back to the fact that there was no better decision to be made. When he returned home from war unscathed, I thanked him and said I will never ask for anything again."

The anguish etched in her face is from years of bottling up indecision and anguish. I owe her my world. She is the breath in my body and the blood in my veins.

"I hated you for a long time. It wasn't your fault we sent the boys away. It was a mutual decision, but I needed to focus my pain. I had to name my loss and I blamed you."

"Tzizel, you never told me."

"How could I tell you? I could not even look at you. The more I hated you, the more I hated myself. The pain of his departure never stopped. The magnitude of my despair was greater than my faith. The hole in my heart created by Walker leaving never sealed over. When Aron left, I went numb."

"We can now set you free of all the loss and all the pain. They are both happy and thriving in different countries. We can close our eyes at night and not have to worry any longer."

Tzizel says, "Children are little pieces of your heart on the outside of your body. When you send enough pieces of your heart away, it can't beat properly."

"I hate for you to suffer."

"No matter the surrounding maelstrom, you are my safe harbor," she says through tears of relief.

Chapter 36
June 19, 1919, Rozniatów, Galicia
Tzizel Rechtschaffen

The man before me has the essence of Aron but isn't recognisable. Well over six feet tall in height with biceps straining against his short-sleeved shirt. He could carry a tree trunk on his shoulders. His chest is twice the thickness of any man I've seen before. My eyes drink him in. When I surrender Naftali's hand, he takes off like a shotgun. Aron scoops his Papa up like a rag doll. Exultation escapes Naftali's lips and I cry out. Aron sets him down and kisses both his cheeks. Aron euphoria vibrates. His embrace knocks me off my feet. He twirls me around like a princess. I squeal. Naftali laughs merrily and claps his hands. I hug Aron again and bury my face right into his thick neck. I smell sunshine. He's mine. I made him. Hot salty tears stream down my cheeks. I have never known joy like this.

Through laughter, I say, "I promise you both that these are tears of joy." Naftali and Aron laugh.

Years of pent-up stress, sadness, and worry evaporate. Aron reaches for our three bags and carries them in one hand. We leave the train station and I'm displaced into a foreign world. The scale of buildings, boulevards, and wealth is a revelation.

The magnificent Unter den Linden is made for kings and queens to parade, though.

Herman treats us to delicious cakes almost too attractive to eat. Artificial colors, never seen in nature, make my mouth water. Outdoor concerts enchant our nights. Museums capture untold history for me and every room explains a different era in history. Oil paintings are my favorite. The hues, strokes, and texture create a realness for me. Mozes catches me trying to touch one painting. It was the size of the room. I blush, and he giggles.

He makes me remember my youth and vitality. Aron loves Monbijoupark. I soak up his stories like warm Challah dipped in honey on Rosh Hashana. Sophistication doesn't jade my Aron. Innocence lives behind his eyes. Seeped in education, his daily interactions are part of a world beyond my scope. Aron brings me in and shares his life.

"It's my little taste of Rozniatow. Inside the park, life grows smaller and slower," comments Aron.

His heart is wide open. He's not a suspicious person. The new world order suits him. He will thrive in a changing world. Understanding German policy, laws, and language allow him an advantage. Naftali holds on tightly to Walker. Walker grabs him like a lifeline. We bore witness to my chubby grandchildren. Their carefree nature softens me. A parent creates vulnerable little beings. You rejoice in them. Your offspring are your second chance to get it right. Ensuring their prosperity is everything. Walker turned into a generous and sympathetic father. Rosie makes him smile quickly. He worships God and is spiritual beyond any Rebbe I know. His time in the sky changed him. His devoted wife fulfills him. She compliments his vulnerabilities. Hugging, knowing, kissing my grandchildren is a privilege.

Chapter 37
August 1919 NYC, New York
Karl Eisner

Dear Mozes,

The decadence in New York astounds me. Every day I take in clean suits and steam them. The hardest stain to clean is lipstick on the collar of a dress shirt. Guilty cheating husbands sneak their clothes to me after work. Otherwise, their wives drop and pick up the dry cleaning. Unknowing wives pick the shirts up the following morning. The textile industry shows potential. I will discover my niche. Excessive drinking is a complication here in America.

Fridays are payday. Irresponsible drinkers spend their wages on strangers and let their children and wives starve and waste away from negligence. The temperance union believes men spend too much money on alcohol and spirits. For the first time in American history, consuming liquor is a criminal act. Americans like their spirits. The underground found a way to fulfill a giant market. A new industry sprouted overnight spearheaded by fugitives and mobsters.

Your letters keep me close to the family. You tell stories and I roar in laughter. Parenthood sounds difficult and heart-

warming. *Gideon is happy in Belgium. His business partners are old friends of mine. They are political and free thinkers. Good men, who run into battle for any bleeding heart. Gideon is in good company. François and Maurice love Paris. Work hard and you can make a life for yourself here in America. I am in control of my future. Love to you and the family.*

Karl

Chapter 38
November 1919, Berlin, Germany
Herman

There is one beer garden in Berlin for every hundred households. The competition is fierce and once you find the right group of people to drink with, you remain loyal to one beirgarten.

My allegiance is to Prater Garden. An old staple with simple rules and good food. Long wooden benches run the length of the establishment. I went there alone for a quiet meal and left with a new group of friends. Every meal for me begins with a stein of Weissbier. When I returned home from the Boer wars in South Africa the world around me didn't make much sense. It all comes down to luck, because dead is dead and there's no more tomorrow when you're dead.

War is senseless. The value placed on your life once you survive a great battle is steeped in guilt. Survivors question themselves, and what their purpose is in life as if there is some grand scheme laid out because they survived. You're either able to let go of the uncertainties and the endless questions or you'll go mad. The only sense you can make of it all, is to keep the company of those that experienced it with you. I served in battle with tremendous men who are still my friends today. These men have seen me in my ugliest times. During December 1899 I witnessed more death than I thought imaginable. A proud Prussian and inspired by Bizmark, I participated in the Boer War in South Africa. Barely seventeen, I fought valiantly during the Black Week. Armed with only a 7mm 1893 Mauser rifle, I ran out of bullets during the battle of Colenso. Burr Getthaub, a fellow Prussian, emptied his pockets and split his remaining bullets between the two of us. With a cocky sneer he says, "looks like we're in this together."

I laughed despite my chagrin. I owe my life to this man. He served alongside our friend Alexander Strauss who operated a 9 cm Kanone C/73 field gun. His arms and neck were thick enough to carry the gun by himself. Nowadays, Alexander drinks like a fish, sleeps standing up, and wakes up the next day at church sober.

He loves the ladies and manages to find himself a girlfriend whenever and wherever the opportunity lends itself. Alexander introduced us to Gregory Barron, a friend from his hometown who was injured and sent home after the battle of Magersfontein. Alexander and Gregory initially met at a battle over the Modder River.

My mouth waters smelling the pork seasoned in fennel and pepper sausage. The crackling sound of the sausage casing makes my stomach growl. Burr, Alex, and Gregory arrived before us. They're on their third round. Burr, the most social of the bunch, extends his hand first to Aron. He befriended every recruit in our unit before anyone else did. When death is all around you, you don't want to grow attached. Rookies make mistakes and mistakes in war are lethal. Burr didn't concern himself with that. Maintaining his humanity was paramount.

"Aron, Herman speaks highly of you. He says you're smart with an indefatigable work ethic."

"I consider Herman my guardian angel. When I first moved to Berlin, I didn't have anyone in my corner. Herman approached me with a basket full of bread and shared his bounty."

Burr, Alexander, and Gregory, laugh knowingly.

Alexander, a devoted father, says to Aron, "Herman said you are a good boy."

He too has seen plenty of men die in war and leave their sons fatherless and without guidance for the rest of their lives.

He understands what drew Herman to me.

"Herman spent many dark nights with me after my son disappeared somewhere in France."

Gregory sets his beer down, spilling a little on the tabletop, and wipes the white foam from his upper lip.

He grunts when he stands up, a wound incurred from a bullet that couldn't be removed from the war. Bowlegged he walks over to the food counter and picks up a tray of bratwursts and sausages. Burr stands up and takes the tray from Gregory. Burr pats him on the back. The two of them are like two peas in a pod. Their thick arms remain robust even without the daily exercise regimen of the military.

Gregory is a union man, and this beer garden had a strong union history. After the war, he found solidarity amongst ironworkers. The union felt like a unit in the military.

The organizational structure, a clear-cut purpose, the camaraderie appealed to Gregory.

Gregory says, "Germany lost the war because inferior breeding and communists are destroying us from the inside out."

"Don't forget the Bolsheviks, Gregory, and the Jews. They infest like cockroaches," says Alexander.

He's talented but he's small minded. Raised by an authoritarian German, he was parented by might and fear. His mean father was a snake. Men like Alexander, Burr, and Gregory were raised to defend their privilege. They live in a vacuum. It's important Aron understands there are good men who are antisemetic.

These men kept me alive on the battlefield and off.

Burr says, "The purest Germanic spirit should inherit the earth."

Aron listens intently and doesn't relay his feelings. I knew he was capable of holding it together because of the way he grew up, how well travelled he was, and how he continues to impress and surprise me on a daily basis. I knew tonight was going to be hard but important. Because these anti-Semites are going to be won over by a poor Jew from

Poland. Gregory replies, "I'll drink to that!"

"Extremist laborers are ruining society. It seems losing the war was not sufficient punishment for Germany. With each new degradation we suffer, society becomes further polarized." I add.

Alexander beams. One down and two more to go. Alexander won't find out that Aron is Jewish, he'll just do good things for him because my Aron is a good boy.

Burr interrupts, "The land grab written into the Versailles treaty was brutal. German citizenship stripped from innocent farmers and peasants? They gave their land over to another country, but those men and women don't know what it means to live in Poland or Czechoslovakia."

"The Germans are angry. The true German doesn't want to be comforted. We're sick of being weak. We want to strike back. Germans don't fight and lose. Germans are not victims. We will take what's ours. Not because we're owed it, but because it's our right," says Aron as he finishes another stein of beer.

Burr's inspired by Aron's declaration he gives him his fresh new beer.

"To Aron. To Germany taking what's ours."

Alexander and Gregory look at each other. They take long sips of their beer and polish off another plate of bratwurst and pickled red onions.

Alexander says, "My sister lives in Munich. The radical right wants more people to hear their message, but their fanaticism unsettles her."

"Do you think they're fanatics?" I ask openly.

Gregory says, "that remains to be seen."

He looks to me for support because the conversation grows awkwardly quiet. Sensing Gregory's increased discomfort, I redirect the attention upon myself.

"Didn't you show me a copy of that newspaper? What was it called, *The Good German*?"

Alexander says, "the paper is written by Dietrich Eckart. My son showed me a copy."

Alexander says, "he's a German volkisch poet and play-wright."

I see Aron has relaxed and the conversation moved on.

Aron raises his stein and says, "To Germany returning to its greatness."

My friends and I joined Aron's toast. The conversations between the five of us splinter off for a while as we continue to eat and drink.

"My son got a job at the new fire station on Oderberger Straße," boasts Burr.

His friends congratulate him and it's' another good reason to drink.

"That is wonderful news, Burr." An indefatigable spirit who cherishes his family.

His son's success means he raised him right.

"They'll pay him to put out fires! He can be a child for the rest of his life." Burr grows quiet for a moment.

"The fire department has brave men who are leaders in their neighborhood."

Alexander turns to Aron and says, "Herman said you're handy. The St. Elisabeth nursing home needs people like you. It is behind this beer garden. This could be a great opportunity for you."

"Alexander, what a great idea," I add.

Gregory says, "tomorrow Will go over and introduce you to the business manager. I know his father. After you get the introduction, you'll get the job and make yourself a nice bit of money."

Chapter 39
May 1921 Paris, France
Maurice Eisner

Heather Martine's family attends the Synagogue de la Victoire. Built in 1874, the grand sanctuary has over eighty-foot-high ceilings and stained-glass windows. I've never seen anything like it before. She is a French Jew, whose family is originally from Alsace-Lorraine. When France took back their homeland after the end of the war, the city cheered. Heather, a sensational redhead with an hourglass figure has creamy alabaster skin untouched by freckles. She introduced me to Paris through cafe lattes, churches and dancehalls. Yesterday she ordered us a hazelnut chocolate croissant. It's a dessert disguised as a breakfast pastry. She's heartbreakingly patient and outrageously funny. Ruled by mystery, she said she grew up in a bar and all she knows is beer and music. She laughs uproariously at jokes only she understands.

The grandeur of French architecture affects every aspect of your life. In Paris, if you're not a king you're a peasant.

The city thrives on romance, religion and industry.

I reach across the table and grab her soft hands in mine.

I stroke her long fingers.

She knew I was in love with her before I did.

"I'd like to take you out to dinner and treat you like a queen." Heather teases, "How about you take me somewhere good, not nice?"

We pass a man on the street playing a violin for money. He leaves a felt bowler hat on the ground in front of him and plays with his eyes closed. The clip-clop of a horse drawn carriages enchants the moment as we wind ourselves over ancient bridges on impossibly narrow streets.

She takes her hand from mine and wraps it around her cup of coffee. She talks about her past like it happened to someone else. An unremarkable childhood and a lot about wanting to see the world.

"I planned a life with a man who promised to grow old with me. Happy and oblivious to the cruelty of the world, I believed our dream would come true."

Her longing for another man tore my gut apart. But I couldn't help myself, like eating another piece of chocolate cake even though I'm full. I knew loving her would be my downfall. She confessed he died young and beautiful. Our world couldn't take all the love he had to give. I understood, then, that she was in love with a ghost.

A couple enters and they sit down by the window laughing with each other as if no one else is there. Young love is a gift all wrapped together in a ribbon of luck.

"Once I gave birth to Keira, I received notice that he's been killed."

A widow with a daughter to feed didn't have a lot of options. She found work with a wealthy family who needed a wet nurse. Their son and her daughter were raised as brother and sister. The lady of the house instructed her to learn German. When the children were toddlers, they kept Heather on and she taught them German and French, like a proper tutor. The Spanish flu took the life of the lady's husband. Her daughter was spared but was sick for a very long time. Influenza spread, there were piles of dead bodies left in the most obvious places, stagnant water, garbage everywhere.

People were afraid to go outside because they didn't know if they would catch the killing disease.

The lady of the house asked her to stay on and take care of the children. She stayed until the fever took the lady of the houses' son and her daughter.

We spoke for hours.

She said, "I'm no longer whole. You want wisdom, you want the truth, I have none of that for you."

She lit a cigarette and walked out of the cafe.

A woman named Raquel with ink black hair and olive skin enters. She runs the Outreach Center at the Synagogue and helps impoverished children and orphans. The ladies of the sisterhood ran fundraisers in their honor. A typical synagogue with arched doorways; they almost sold their chandeliers to fund the needs for many needy children.

Raquel sat down at another table and took out her book. I can hear Heather now, "our lives are dedicated to saving children. I want to make a difference or die trying." I realise I never see Raquel in the same room as Heather.

Chapter 40
September 1923 London, UK
Walker Rechtschaffen

Dear Dad,

At the latest picture show, we watched Mussolini march his army across Italy. He's corrupted. The execution of his bravado should strike fear in every man and woman in the world. Tyrants start wars. He won't bleed for Italy, but he'll bathe in the blood of its citizens.

Göring is another man to fear on the global stage. After the great Red Baron was killed, Göring galvanized Germany behind him and his piloting ability. Fighter pilot to fighter pilot, his capabilities demand respect. His own party betrayed him during the ROM push. Men are injured in battle and their survival is plagued in unimaginable pain. Many veterans become addicted to morphine and alcohol to allay the pain. Neither is an option but there are no better substitutes out there.

Being drafted smartened me up. I served with good men and their opinions on everything from winches to politics shaped me. Men who haven't served don't understand. Aron, I was lucky. I flew planes in the sky amongst the clouds. Blood and death weren't right in front of me. The guilt comes from knowing blood and death was the last moment for many. I dropped bombs and never looked back. Flying permitted me distance. Governments make careless decisions and don't consider their citizens. Without language, the inability to communicate stifles the passage to success.

After the war, the French government wanted to punish Germany. Carelessly redistributing borders between countries and stripping people of their citizenship and their language disallows healing. Until Germany is given the chance to heal, the unrest will continue. From what I read you are safer in Berlin then you would be in Munich. Let's pray for healing and no more war.

Let me tell you all about the children. The twins' personalities are really developing. Julie loves animals. She had me build her a birdhouse the other day and I put it outside her window. Julie painted the birdhouse, and carefully prepared a dish for seeds. Michael was more interested in climbing the ladder and hammering a nail above her bedroom window. Julie is soft and Michael is rough. Julie is elegant and poised and Michael is athletic and strong. Between the two of them, you'll always hear tears, screams and a crash. I never find out what the true story is because they protect one another.

Rosie's a little nervous by all the commotion they create.

I remind her to relax which never helps. To me, the commotion, tears, laughter, and love mean we are living a good life. It's important to be strong, healthy, and happy. I would never have been happy on a farm in Poland, but in the middle of London, I'm the happiest man in the world. I wish that love for you.

I'm proud of you for creating a life for yourself in Berlin. Do not forget to write and send another letter off to Ima and Abba. Your success is a testament to their parenting. I will continue to keep you in my prayers.

Love, Walker

Chapter 41
January 1924 Berlin, Germany
Mozes Meijer Eisner

"Amalia, Marjem's gift for math is undeniable. She scored the highest in her class for the entrance exam to university." I'm practically screaming.

"I love that she's smarter than me."

My daughter can be a university professor, a concert pianist, maybe a lawyer or judge?

"Boys and girls included?"

She asks without listening for the answer. Another question will come, but she won't listen to that answer either. Her mind is elsewhere. I see it in her faraway expression. We know how smart she is, the potential was there, but now she has real choices to make.

"Yes, boys and girls included." I look at her earnestly. Amalia is beaming with pride.

She says, "You either have what it takes, or you don't. Her mind will open so many doors..."

Pride bursts from my chest.

"She can be a banker, like me."

Amalia laughs. My unbridled joy surprises me. None of my other children have this level of promise. Maurice and François sought adventure and moved to Paris. My sons are the two sides of the same coin. François is funny and thrill-seeking where Maurice is reserved. His neurotic mindset anchors François. They are doers, and the limitations of Dobromyl couldn't contain them. Cyla married a Rabbi's son and moved to Holland. Gideon married a pleasant girl from Antwerp and runs her father's stores. He can fix anything. But Marjem is academic and strategic.

"You speak to her," urges Amalia.

"She'll listen to you." Amalia's hurt because she adores Marjem and Marjem pushes her away more than she pulls her close. Teenage girls are unpleasant.

"Amalia, you're overreacting. She is judgmental and assumes she knows better. Young people act this way."

"The words I choose with her are never right. At any moment I know I will annoy her."

Amalia straightens her shoulders and looks me straight in the eye.

"One day, she will admit something to me that terrifies her. She will recognize that I can handle it. Whatever comes her way, comes my way too."

I stroke the side of her beloved face.

"She knows how much you love her, Amalia."

"Thank you for saying it. I don't accept it, but I appreciate you see me."

"What do you want me to do, Amalia? I'm listening."

"Tell Marjem she can pursue whatever she wants until she gets married." What? What does it matter?

"What happens after she gets married, Amalia? She's brilliant."

"She can use her mind in any way she wants. Her getting married is important to me. Her day should begin and end knowing she is loved."

I study my bride. Strong and independent, she gave me a family and created a castle. I wanted somebody who was not happy to stand still. Amalia is a magnificent person. She never runs away in fear. She is my equal.

"We only get one life. Let us make it as exciting as possible. I will talk to her about university."

"Good. Make her think it's her idea." She grins.

"No one questions a mother's love and devotion. It's her job to test boundaries and figure out who she wants to be."

I kiss my bride on the lips, then grin back at her.

"Do you realize how lucky I am?"

Amalia smiles. I pull her up and into an embrace. I take my hand and slide it down her back until I cup her backside. She lifts her chin and exposes her collarbone.

"Smell my neck," she growls playfully. She runs her fingers through my hair and gives it a little tug.

"You know I can't resist your neck."

She smiles wickedly and pushes my face into her bosoms.

Chapter 42
May 1924 Berlin, Germany
Marjem Eisner

Coldcream has a way of erasing the day's effect on your face. The harsher days call for scrubbing but mere wash with warm water and soap is sufficient for today.

My Victorian vanity is my quiet place. The lights are bright, and the mirror doesn't deceive. Wiping my eyelid clean of eyeshadow with a cotton ball, I reveal, "I don't care about falling in love, Henie. I just finished school and I have a chance to work in the bank with Papa."

After I finish one eye I begin on the other. Henie is bursting. She's my biggest fan in the world. Telling her about my life makes everything more exciting.

"He's so dreamy, Marja, his dark blue eyes smolder."

His ebony eyelashes are so shiny they look wet. His lips are luscious. Henie is a hopeless romantic whose experience is entirely not practical. Her knowledge is gleaned from books, music lyrics, and silent movies. She twirls in a circle with a sweater clutched to her bosom. Her brown curls bounce flashing her red velvet ribbons.

"Just because a boy likes me doesn't mean I have to like him back. I don't even have to acknowledge his devotion. Lots of boys like me, but that doesn't mean they have to matter to me, and especially not to you. Just because someone chooses to love you doesn't mean you have to choose to love them."

Henie looks at me like I am from a different planet.

"Marja, go on the date. Stop getting in your open way. You're not even giving him a chance. You might be surprised."

Brushing my hair, I consider how boy-crazy my sister is. I'm supposed to care more about meeting a boy, falling in love and getting married but I'm not.

I want to see what I can achieve. Working and interacting with smart people all day thrills me. My mind races with ideas. Nothing has ever intrigued me more.

Henie can't relate, not because she isn't brilliant. She simply lacks my perspective.

I laugh. "He's cute."

"He's so cute, Marja. Do you hear yourself?" adds Gittel.

Gittel has joined Henie's team. They are a fearsome duo.

"He is cute," Henie says to Gittel.

Gittel stands on Henie's bed and falls back dramatically with the back of her hand pressed against her forehead.

"I will find love someday, the kind of love that takes my breath away; where the rest of the world disappears."

"Marjam, life isn't like the movies. Ever since Papa took us to see that movie about Nosferatu, you're dark. Love doesn't need conflict," reminds Henie.

Giggling, I ask, "How do you know, Henie?"

"Snarky isn't an attractive look on you, Marja," chides Gittel.

Henie jumps onto Gittel's bed. Gittel complains and pushes her off.

Ignoring them both, I conclude, "Love will come whether I'm ready or not."

Chapter 43
August 1924 Berlin, Germany
Aron Rechtschaffen

Dear Abba,

As the economy changes people must reinvent themselves to provide for their families. Their responsibilities never wane. There is strife but there's opportunity. Being single liberates me. Herman contends my traveling abroad makes our offerings unique. Our business continues to expand. We fulfil the needs of our regular customers, and our luxury offerings attract new recurring clientele. Traveling rejuvenates my spirit. Herman recognizes how the tumultuous city overwhelms me. Without quiet time, I retreat within myself. On my travels, I work the local markets, meet new people, and hear different languages and dialects. When it's safe to be Jewish, I attend a local synagogue and meet a multitude of eligible Jewish girls. To differentiate our offerings, I collect scraps of exotic fabrics. Some fabrics have small beads sewn into them while others sparkle like gemstones. These commodities, fashioned into accent pillows, unseen by the elite in Berlin drive our success further. Running our boutique out of Hermans' house is the right decision. Herman was born to play the host to wealthy older German women. They adore him, especially the single ones. When he frets over making a proper cup of tea, they swoon in admiration. Our business is clever on multiple axes. We cater to our recurring clientele and satisfy a vacancy in the marketplace. We're part of a new movement. Our family-owned shop inhabits a beautiful residential neighborhood. We're not alone in setting up shop inside a house.

From the street view, you wouldn't know anything was different, but if you operate within the right circles, you're privy to the secret gems of the city. While we use Herman's basement to sort, dry, and store feathers; others use theirs as artisan studios. Musicians, painters, and sculptors are willing to work in whatever space they can find.

Creative people are exciting to hang around them. They see things unconventionally. My latest discovery is another home-based restaurant. People sit on sofas, around a coffee table, a kitchen table, and a dining room table. No one is put out, and no one is bothered by how things are done - if they are done with kindness. The Jewish community is growing. Hassids leave Poland and immerse themselves quickly in German cities. They shave their beards, and frequent synagogues without fear or reproach.

The latest business concept to come to Berlin is called a department store. Imagine the Rozniatow Ringplatz indoors and on multiple levels. The walls of the department store are bigger than the Rechtschaffen's synagogue in Rozniatow. Zadeh would love the grandeur of the building and displays. The air smells fresh and clean. The premade clothing is soft to the touch.

Women frequent perfume counters. Silk scarves, men's suits, fine men's watches and housewares are sold and warehoused in one facility. Abba, you can spend money on clothing, tools, furniture, jewelry, and books, all in one place!

Our friend, Ryan Verlin who owns a hardware store is considering selling his shop and being part of the department store. He thinks the foot traffic alone would triple his business. I'm not sure. His wife, Nicole, isn't too keen on the idea. However, his daughter Maya, a teenager, loves the idea. Nicole Verlin never stops fixing me up with eligible women. She introduces me to plenty of women, but she knows love is not something that can be forced.

Love comes upon you and re-events the entire world around you.

I will write again soon. I love you and Ima.

Love, Aron

Chapter 44
February 1925 London, UK
Walker Rechtschaffen

Aron, my sweet little brother,

As Adolf Hitler defends himself in court, the international stage promulgates his fetid hatred. He's charismatic and his ideal world is relatable to many. Britain wants the violence in the streets of Germany to stop. There are reports of bad actors called The Storm Police victimizing the disenfranchised. Within two or three years, the police force has increased in size by nearly one hundred times. Hitler's passion is deadly. How dangerous are these pseudo-police? The London papers report there were nearly thirty thousand people in attendance to hear Adolf Hitler speak publicly.
I am your brother, and you need to listen to me. I've seen good men kill good men because only one person was allowed to survive. Crazy breeds crazy. Tell me you're safe.

Love, Walker

Chapter 45
April 1925 Berlin, Germany
Marjem Eisner

Tripping over her words, Rosa says, "We should see it, Marjem. Dottie's older sister told me. They went there last month. Peanut shells and sawdust cover the floor like a cheap bearskin rug. The lights are dim and smoke curlicues through the air. Ladies here wear long satin gloves, use elegant cigarette holders, and drink cocktails."

"Rosa, what's in a cocktail?"

Rosa laughs, "Marjem, I have no idea."

She wipes her nose with her gloved finger.

"What else did Dottie's sister say?"

"The music is hard to dance to. There aren't any words to sing to either."

"You really want to go?"

I try not to whine. She thinks I am being theatrical. I care about her, and I know she cannot go without me.

"We'll go with Dottie and her sister."

She's whining now. I see disappointment seeping across her eyes.

"Are you sure?"

Rosa says I overthink things. She's not wrong. We both want to hear strange new music and experience something exotic. Rosa and I talk ourselves into this.

******

My body buzzes. I wear my new leather boots and a smart coat with gold buttons.

Rosa wears a red coat and carries a matching handbag. Our hair is curled into the latest chignon hairstyle. We step off the trolley and walk down the stairs. I am not a carefree person and I prefer to avoid conditions that make me uncomfortable. The neighborhood is unfamiliar and grimy. Rosa's eyes wide in anticipation survey the poorly lit neighborhood for something familiar. Rosa takes her purse and pulls it closer.

I nearly scream when a hovering figure of a man in a trench coat stands before me. His face is shadowed.

Rosa calls out, "Dottie, Lizzie, wait up."

Her voice is pinched. Dottie and Lizzie turn and acknowledge how far from us they have walked. Rosa and I pick up our pace.

"Marjem, do you see the puddles?" asks Rosa.

It hasn't rained in days. I reflect.

A strange aroma tickles the inside of my nose. Sneezing makes it worse. Rosa smells it too.

"Stay away from the urine."

My stomach does a flip. I am not sure why I put myself in this situation.

Rosa turns to me and says, "I'm not sure about this, Marjem; I have a strange feeling in my belly and it's growing."

I appreciate Rosa's vulnerability. A trolley runs behind us and shakes the street. Lizzie laughs at Rosa, who is now shaking in fright.

"You're too jumpy."

"Don't be mean," says Dottie to her sister Lizzie.

"They're sheltered. It's not their fault."

Lizzie takes the address out of her purse.

"Where is it?" she says to herself as she scans the street.

"I don't remember," says Dottie.

"It should be here." Lizzie's voice is edged with uncertainty now.

"Is it gone?" asks Dottie.

"It is," says Lizzie. She sounds deflated.

"I can't believe how fast that place disappeared."

A woman walks past us and stops beneath a streetlight. I cannot help but stare at her. Her clothing hangs oddly on her curvy frame. Her cheeks are drawn. She's frayed around the edges, but if she cleaned up, she could be Gittel's twin with her blonde hair and light brown eyes.

Rolling through the details of the evening later while lying in the comfort of my bed highlights certain moments.

By candlelight, I write my impressions of the evening in my journal. Cyla greets me and asks how my evening was. I tell her enough to satisfy her. In my mind, I can't unsee the forgotten lady from under the streetlight. It is like popcorn. When you have a rotten piece of popcorn after handfuls of delicious popcorn, that one lousy piece ruins all that came before.

Chapter 46
March 1925 Berlin, Germany
Naftali Herzl

Dear Aron,

Your letters uplift me. Your life in Berlin is beginning to come together. Mother says as soon as you feel the ground securely beneath your feet, everything else will fall into place. When Rebbe Rechtschaffen first came to Przemyśl, I would not have accepted the invitation if I couldn't secure my transport to Rozniatow. When the great war ended, Germany was understandably demoralized.

The economy has yet to recover. Fascism, a dangerous movement fueled by pervasive hardship, wraps its tendrils around the willing and the weakened. Similar to planting the three sisters: corn, peas, and squash. The corn provides a strong stalk, a solid foundation, for the delicate peas' tendrils to wrap itself around. The squash provides nutrients needed for both the corn and the peas to flourish. Anti-semitism has a long history across continents and oceans. Jewish people are easy targets: we speak a different language, eat specialized foods, and dress stringently.

Antisemitism is the squash which replenishes the earth with nutrients. The corn is the passionate nationalism felt by the German Volk. Political uncertainty or the peas, who cannot sustain without the foundation of fervent nationalism to sink their tendrils into. The entire ecosystem is continually replenished by the nature of constant antisemitism.

When you face a lion or a bear which are you more afraid of? We covered the lion, now let's talk about the bear. Communist Russia wishes to rule the world. Their culture is desolate and unforgiving, like their humor.

They don't like themselves, but they are particularly loathsome of Jews. Your Uncle Shalom is a Zionist which is particularly hard for your grandfather to digest. He is a traditionalist and a devout Chassid.

We Rechtschaffens live this way, like the Rechtschaffens before us, and the ones before them. For hundreds of years, long coats and fur hats have made sense. The Zionist movement has spread. Trading their traditional coats for short jackets, and their fur hats for stylish caps. Shalom formed a Zionist club with the Wasserman boy. They brought a modern haslaka, a set of beliefs, to Rozniatow. Uncle Shalom rides the line between both worlds.

He stays traditional out of respect for Grandfather Hersch, but make no mistake, he wants to wear the shorter jackets and the stylish caps.

He started an acting troupe in town, and they performed The Jewish King Lear. Barnik and Issachar Stern dressed up as women to play the female roles. Remember Jeckel Spiegel? They used his house to meet before he emigrated to Palestine.

Walking through life as if you have no control is crazy. Allowing others to determine your destiny is crazy.

Standing still and not choosing to take everything you can it's not the way. You don't have to step on others to have a *wonderful life that you are in control of. Germany has endless opportunities.*

Love, Abba

Chapter 47
June 1925 Berlin, Germany
Marjem Eisner

My sister pirouettes across the room, not listening to a word I say. In her left hand, she carries a new red hat and perilously high heels.

I say, "Henie, slow down, I can't figure out what you're saying."

Her syncopated breaths mirror her bouncing brown curls that never lose their freshness. She is the envy of any lady with smooth hair.

"He brought me flowers," sings Henie.

"Long stemmed roses!" Roses like Henie smell beautiful and look delicate but they're resilient and strong with their thick stems and thorns. If you hold the roses too tightly, alike Henie, you'll walk away scratched and bleeding.

"Tell me," I invite.

Henie spins around, full of joy. Excited and moody, she lives without hesitation, going full speed in whatever direction feels right at that moment. Not one to plan, she can throw together people, a party, or an inspired fashion statement in a heartbeat. Her spirit is singular. Henie will not listen to others. You cannot tell her what to do. She does what she wants. She rambles through her story. At a party, Henie met a man with blonde hair and Clark Gable eyes. Her friend Shifra who lives with her older sister works in a movie theater. They throw a lot of parties. Shifra's Parisian beau is older than her sister. Shifra is not on a path destined for Henie. One can't bully Henie into anything. Henie is going to screw up, and maybe lose her way, but her heart is in the right place.

Henie says, "He's from Paris. A violin player - a virtuoso. His spirit is poetic and when he plays, I want to cry. He's such a passionate man."

She pauses and looks uncertain. The sparkle in her eye dims.

"He isn't a brilliant talker, Marja."

She opens her mouth to speak but reconsiders.

"Not everyone is good at everything," I say to comfort her. Sharing in her excitement is way better than dampening in. Unfortunately, this love will not last. For as headstrong as she is, Papa's approval is paramount to her.

"I wish I could play the violin. I always wanted to be musical. Remember when Mother got us both piano lessons?"

I laugh as the memory floods my mind. Henie had no intention of learning how to play anything. The two of us devised a plan. I would play the piano and she would dance. Our recitals captivated the family.

"Henie, what is your next step?"

"Marja, he wants me to meet his parents in Paris."

She takes me by the shoulders.

"Will Mama and Papa let me go?"

She spins away and says, "Can you escort me?"

Wait? What? Paris? He wants Henie to meet his parents?

"Henie. When you start a job, you must build up time before you can take a vacation."

Stalling for time, my mind is not moving fast enough to slow Henie down. She can't go to Paris. Mama and Papa will forbid her. The fight will shake the walls. Papa will get red in the face and beat the table with his fists.

David will not be able to eat for the rest of the evening. Henie is an entertainer, an inspiration and an impresario. People want to be around her even though they don't know why. She is non-threatening but isn't to be ignored. She is the carrot. Her company is a reward. Her light and wonder are wild and unruly. A silly man from Paris isn't enough for her. If he knew her, he'd never ask this of her.

"Marja, the heart wants what it wants."

Her breathing slows as I hold her in my arms. Papa will not stand for any of this. Mother will rest her chin in her hands and pull her knees together. She will smooth over the non-existent wrinkles on her skirt and cross her legs at her ankles. She wraps herself up in the most feminine way.

Papa can't resist her. He will always choose her, and her loyalty to him is uncompromised. I want that. My parents are in love. What Henie has with the Parisian violinist is not love, and Henie's dreams will not survive their judgment.

"Marja, I love him."

"I see that." I stroke her hair.

She smiles brighter than I ever dreamed imaginable.

"It's happening fast," Henie says more to herself than to me.

"Does that bother you?"

"Impulsivity excites me, but marriage," she sighs, "is for life."

I ask, "When will Mama and Papa meet him?"

Her eyes grow wide in response.

"You should invite him to dinner. Give Mama and Papa a chance to see how much he loves you. Invite him over a few times. Allow our parents to get used to him. Then you can bring up Paris."

She considers this. It is better to make a gentle suggestion and let her ruminate.

Chapter 48
April 1925 Perehinske, Galicia
Naftali Herzl

Dear Aron,

The military made your brother, Walker, the man he is today. I recognized his intelligence from a very young age. We had a leaky faucet and Walker took the whole contraption apart and put it all back together without any guidance. The lessons he learned during the war will benefit him for the rest of his life. Flying planes gave Walker purpose. The cockpits' controls captured his attention. Dials to interprets and fast mathematical calculations keep him sharp. While in the war, he felt tremendous purpose. Once he returned, like many others, transitioning back into civilian life proved difficult. Rosie saved Walker. He had trouble sleeping and he would write letters filled with ghoulish activities like people stripping the dead to steal their supplies. The rules of humanity change when you're fighting to survive.

Once home, the children grounded him. He likes working with you and Max. He sees the value in building your business, but he needs more. Here in Poland, unemployment is rampant, and the housing market has changed. Existing homes cost too much for anyone starting out without equity. New immigrants can't afford to rent an apartment. Immoral landlords take advantage of a bad housing market and allow apartments to remain empty. These abandoned apartments attract bad people. There is no new construction. There's a lack of opportunity for growth.

In better news, apothecary Benjamin started a bus service back-and-forth from Rozniatow to Perehinske. He enjoys making his lotions and medicines. His friend Newman recently lost his eyesight. People say it happened from the sugar disease. Either way blindness wasn't going to limit Newman. Benjamin made Newman a solid walking stick. Everyday Newman stands across the school and shuffles the children back and forth. The parents appreciate the help and Newman has a purpose.

Follow your dreams, Aron.

Love, Abba

Chapter 49
September 1926 Berlin, Germany
Herman

When Burr's son Hans joined the local fire department, we relished in his acceptance for days. A star athlete in high school, Hans is happiest when moving, running, or climbing. He makes an ideal fireman.

One fateful night a fire raged in a small local bakery. The stout structure couldn't withstand a fire of that magnitude. When Hans ran back into the burning building, he saved the owner, a baker, his daughter. Covered in soot and tears, she pledged her life to Hans. After she openly wept in Hans' arms, Burr knew how his son would react to her.

The deal was sealed. Within a month the two lovebirds married and nine months later welcomed a baby boy named Henrick. Hans said to his Vader (father,) he's as much mine as he's yours. Burr takes care of his grandson during the day. He feeds him breakfast, takes him on a walk through the park, and places him down for a nap while his daughter-in-law prepares dinner for the family.

When the baby was born, they moved in with Burr. Early in the morning between two thirty and five, Hans works for a political paper called *The Attack*. He runs the printing press and distributes flyers. Hans is an ideal recruit.

As a firefighter his unrestricted access to the municipal buildings makes him valuable. Physically, he embodies the Aryan ideal: blonde, lean, and muscular. Burr and his son share their slant to the radical right. Gregory and Alexander aren't far behind. No one really knows where I stand. I agree with everybody in every conversation every time I get the chance.

Hans explains over a carafe, "the divided Volk yearn for security and government accountability."

The uncertainty leads to protests, most of them peaceful. Firemen and their trucks arrive to protect innocent bystanders and maintain civility. Last week, a protest ended with a fire at the Halle. The fire consumed the building and Hans. Hans' burial is a reminder of what Burr and the world have lost. Burr wants to grieve in private. Alexander and Burr walk to the cemetery together in silence.

Gregory and I meet them at the front gate. Before the funeral can proceed, the coroner needs a witness to identify Hans' body. A standard gruesome procedure that must happen before a burial may continue. The coroner turns to Burr, and Alexander steps forward and assigns himself the task.

"Are you sure about this?" asks Gregory.

"I'm sure," says Alexander. It's horrible.

We walk to the graveside and wait for them to bring out the coffin. Hans' entire firehouse arrives with an additional fifty people in dress uniform. It's incongruous to bury your child. Burr prefers to grieve in private. However, the Nazi party has an alternative agenda. We've seen them turn a burial into a recruitment event.

Burr looks down at his hands and wipes away invisible dirt.

Alexander says, "Hans was respected and loved."

Drums beat in syncopation strong enough to shake my body.

Marching Hitler youth regale the crowd in crisp white shirts and pressed black pants carrying green wreaths.

Dismayed, Burr turns to me and says, "I don't understand what's happening. This is not what I expected."

His voice barely above a whisper, holds back cracking in despair. Two young men approach Hans' widow with a folded Nazi flag.

"Who are these people?" I ask Burr.

Burr's face is blank.

He admits, "I don't recognize anyone."

The elderly men wear elegant cross body sashes decorated in Nazi regalia. Their wives don fine silks and fox stoles. None of these people belong. They're not here to mourn the loss of a young life taken too soon. The Nazis don't respect what happened to Burr. Beautiful blonde girls with rosy cheeks carry baskets of edelweiss and sprinkle the earth before Burr's feet. Following the young girls is an officer. He leads a group of five soldiers carrying rifles. They march before the crowd and stand in front of Burr. The officer stops and commands his soldiers to fire. They fire five shots into the air. Each shot pierces me and I recoil. Burr grabs my hand. Afterward, the officer hands Burr a folded Nazi flag. The funeral ends and a lorry rolls down the street scattering Nazi propaganda into the streets. The stark red, black and white pamphlets promise people a better future with the Nazi party at the helm.

Gregory says, "the Nazis are proud of Hans. That is clear." He glances at the folded flag in Burr's hands. Burr eyes are red and sore. He places his hands on Burr's shoulders. Alexander says, "Munich is the heart of the Nazi party. To become a powerful party, they need Berlin. Hans was an active member. He took great pride in his responsibilities. This is how the party chose to honor him."

I used to think the definition of honor was straightforward. What the Nazis did was advantageous, it was the farthest thing from honourable that there could be.

Chapter 50
November 1927 Berlin, Germany
Aron Rechtschaffen

Dear Abba,

Belovezhskaya Pushcha is the singular reason to visit Gdynia. The smell of the oak permeates your clothes and fills up your nose. The placating scent relieves any congestion in your throat and chest; the quality of the air is better. Bison, deer, and elk run wild across our vast terrains. Squirrels and chipmunks play in the trees. Spring commences when robins with rust-coloured tinted chests soar from tree to tree in pairs. Inland you can smell the sea and taste the salt on your tongue. Sleeping beneath the stars is preferable because the evenings are warm but not humid. A soft breeze lulls you to sleep like a childhood bedtime story. The night sounds of tree frog calls and gophers scurrying across wilted leaves reminds me of home.

Sopot, the port, was built in 1827, and it has the longest wooden pier in Europe. People sit on the beach and watch the waves crash for hours. One day at the market is never like the next. Vendors with large personalities, bronzed skin, jewelry in their ears and hair peddle their wares to willing consumers. Men and women from all walks of life converge for the same purpose: consumerism. Merchants raise their voices above one another to entice the next shopper. Fish seared with spices and citrus makes your mouth explode with flavor. Food never tasted better than when it's fresh from the ocean and practically squirming on your plate.

After the war ended, Poland relied on this jewel in the Baltic Sea. When I return and tell Herman about this slice of Eden, he'll be afraid he'll lose me to Sopol. The simple life by the water is not to be overlooked. Counting time by the crashing of waves is uncomplicated. Appreciating what's given comes naturally here. Life here is closer to Rozniatow than anywhere else. I wake up early to make the first footprints in the sand before anyone else. Dredging my toes in the warmth by the seashore connects me to the world.

For a long time, the routes through Gdynia proved profitable. As of late, the relationship between Germany and Poland has strained. Germany decided to impose import taxes on all foreign goods. More obstacles to navigate. Better men have solved harder problems. Reams of exotic textiles prove difficult to transport across the border unless I can bring cases of wine as gifts for my border guards friends.

Stay safe, Aron

Chapter 51
December 1928 Berlin, Germany
Marjem Eisner

Most of my Jewish friends go straight from high school into marriage; the other ones merely count down the days till their ceremonies. Marriage isn't my ultimate goal in life. To the chagrin of my mother, establishing my place in the world fills me with hope and excitement about the future. Working at the bank is important and a privilege. I interact with clients, help them resolve their issues, and feel necessary. It's satisfying work. Reconciling numbers brings me great peace. Mathematics doesn't fluctuate; there's no room for interpretation. The absoluteness of it makes sense to my foundation. Many brilliant young unmarried girls become bank tellers. They shop for husbands batting their lashes, wearing inappropriate lipstick, and dressing in sweaters that are too tight. Sociable and friendly, they gossip freely at lunchtime and after work in cafes.

A tall thin man walks into the bank and stands in my queue. I can't take my eyes off of him. His hair is brown with reddish undertones and his skin is the color of fresh cream. When he approaches, he removes his hat and smiles boldly. After he clears his throat, he introduces himself. Soft-spoken with sweet penetrating eyes, he disarms me. He comes in every week and makes another savings deposit. He's a man of habit. Arriving at the same time every week, choosing my queue to stand in and when it's his turn, he clears his throat and reintroduces himself. I told him how I remember his name. His response is to smile broadly. For three months, this is how we interacted. Last time I saw him he had more to say to me than ever before. He inquired about my day and listened intently to my answers. He picked up on the nuances and continued our conversation easily. When he left, he presented me with a tall yellow and white daisy.

The center of the flower smells of sweet pollen.

The white petals are diaphanous yet durable.

They grow in meadows, by the roadside, and in both wetlands and direct sunlight.

Aron Rechtschaffen missed his deposit last week.

The thought of him lingers in my mind. When he doesn't appear the following week the nagging concern grows inside of me. My emotions swing like a metronome.

He occupies my thoughts more than he should. I think of him at the strangest of times. Monday, I thought of him while I was drinking my morning coffee.

Last night, I imagined how it would feel if his hands touched my hair.

Chapter 52
February 1929 Berlin, Germany
Aron Rechtschaffen

Dear Abba,

Establishing oneself is not easy. Young men wear themselves down to small nubs proving themselves. Working with feathers is messy work. Tedious and meticulous work, feather dust is as insidious as hay dust. The dust lodges between my fingernails and cuticles, collects inside my ears, and dries out my scalp. Can you imagine waking up in the morning and your tongue is dry? For months, my throat has been sore. My Dutch friend, Paul, invites me to his ancestral home to take a much-needed vacation. I've never regretted leaving home and moving to Berlin, but I crave the quieter moments more than I used to.

A series of handcrafted guitars line the dining room walls of Paul's childhood home in Holland. Paul's father Thom explains, playing the guitar is part of their family's shared identity. Three generations ago his great grandfather Dan Daniel built the very home we're standing in with his own two hands. He made the money to buy the nails by singing and playing his guitar in the town square. He chopped the trees down and prepared the wood himself.

"We have a lot in common," I explain to Thom.

"My grandfather built his home with his own two hands in Rozniatow, Poland." Thom's traditions are close to ours and even occur during the same times of the year. Our lives orbit around the changing of the seasons.

After dinner we convene outside around the fire pit, and the men play, sing folk songs from their childhood, and allow the fresh air to heal. After dinner, we discuss the day and recount the high points, the low points, and the moments we wish we could do again. It's a wonderful way to reimagine the time we spent and cherish the more important moments. Holland produces red and orange peppers, purple beets that stain your fingers, canary yellow squash, and bright orange carrots. Fields of tulips and yellow, pink, and purple wildflowers scatter the countryside.

The Dutch are fun-loving people, but make no mistake, they aren't pushovers. They are passionate about a healthy family existence; they love water, and the lucky ones live on houseboats. Living by the water and breathing in the freshest air I've ever enjoyed, helps me rest. Paul and I made a table. Thom and I built a bed and a bookcase. His hands are gifted like a surgeon's and the quiet focus intensive work suits me. Seeking shelter in a new land is the change I needed to recharge.

I'm heading back to Berlin to capture Marjem's heart. She works in a bank. Her purpose is bigger than just herself and she's proud of her accomplishments and intellect. She's a modern woman, built in the image of God, but exists in the secular world. Raised in Berlin she attends synagogue every Shabbat. Herman consulted Herr Verlin. You remember, she's the one who introduced me to the synagogue a few years ago on the bequest of Herman. She cares for me the way a good aunt should. Think of her as my local Aunt Bluma. She implied a woman like Marjem will notice a solid work ethic, kindness, and loyalty. She's actively moving me three steps ahead towards Marjem. Herr Verlin is kind and calm. Upon her recommendation, I deposit my wages once a week during her shift at the bank. I'm making myself a habit in Marjem's life. Standing before her at the teller counter makes my mouth run dry. All I'm able to manage is my name and a goofy grin. The second week I politely re-introduce myself. I wrote my name down on a piece of paper, so she could reference my account. I didn't want to spend less time with her, but I wanted her to spend more time on my name. She remarked on the gesture, tilted her head to the right, reread my name again and smiled. The unconscious movement meant she was registering my name in her long-time memory. The third week, I politely re-introduced myself. The fourth, I made a feeble attempt at a self-deprecating joke regarding weekly deposits. She bristles and tells me she finds my regular deposits reliable. "It's refreshing to see members of my own generation caring about the future." She smiles shyly at her impassioned response. Herr Verlin is right again. She likes my routine. Before I left for Holland to take a short vacation and regroup, I bought her a single sunflower. Something simple, sweet, and memorable.

Love, Aron

Chapter 53
April 1929 Berlin, Germany
Marjem Eisner

I felt him before I saw him. My insides buzz like fireflies trapped in a glass mason jar.

He approaches and I've forgotten everything I've rehearsed anticipating this moment. Negligent to remain disinterested as Henie instructed, I blurt out, "Good morning, Aron."

There isn't any casualness in my tone. I'm too familiar with him and unprofessional. My heart pounds in my ears and I lose my train of thought. I'm focused on the anxious dialog in my head. He reaches out with his hand and places it on mine. My pulse quickens but I quiet down.

"It's good to see you again." He says calmly.

"I missed two deposits."

His touch expressed more to me than any words could.

"I noticed." I say before I can stop myself.

I don't want to ruin this real life fantasy playing out before me. He is so good looking and kind. I want him to like me and ask me out. I've never felt this passionate before. This is how Henie acted when she was a teenager and fell in love for the first time.

The hair on the back of my neck stands up when he catches my gaze. His lips are pink, and I want to kiss them. The idea of his breath on my neck makes my knee tremble.

"A friend took me to his home in Holland. The time away was great for my health and spirit. But I missed my new routine." He trained his eyes on me.

"I wanted to pick up where I left off."

He's a grown man with adult intentions. I'm on fire. As the heat rises from my neck, I wonder if he can feel it too?

"How nice." I remark. "You have good friends."

"Yes, thank you." He removes an envelope from the inside of his trench coat.

"Please see my deposit."

His fingertips brush my hand as I take it from him.

"Giving you a sunflower made my intentions known. I apologize if I caused you any trouble. Your privacy is important to me."

He pushes a letter towards me.

"Read this when you're alone. Next week, I will ask you on a walk through Monbijoupark at lunch."

"That... That sounds wonderful, Aron."

Bad Buckow 31.7.1927.

Chapter 54
September 1929 Berlin, Germany
Aron Rechtschaffen

Dear Abba,

Political unrest rules the streets of Berlin. The Nazis hold rallies and propagate hate for anything non-German.
The extreme leftists weaken the entire country.
The Bully Boys, an organized group of militants, conduct regular acts of minor violence. I'm unsure of who sanctions them, but their power is real. We see them attacking the disenfranchised without repercussion. Tensions have eased a little in certain circles. Unemployment is down. If the unsubstantiated attacks on socialists, intellectuals and communists who are out of step with society stop, extremist views can't take shape.
Herman's friend, Burr, a fellow veteran, wanted a quiet small burial for his son, Hendrik. Herr Verlin attended out of respect. His fire station attended.
A sycophantic crowd of Nazis overtook the service. After the funeral, Burr was disenchanted with the Nazis. He put his faith into a movement that used him. It's edifying to see how

his mind was changed. I'm hopeful, if he can change by witnessing the true action of the movement then others can too.

Love, Aron

Chapter 55
November 1929 Berlin, Germany
Marjem Rechtschaffen

I cannot remember a moment of my childhood without Henie by my side, nipping at my heels. My precocious little sister charms everyone she meets with her outrageous laugh and easy-going nature. Her personality fills the room. Henie loves the sound of her own voice; she sings in her sleep, while she dresses, and when she prances around the house. She eclipses me but there's no one else's opinion I hold in higher esteem. Rushing into our bedroom, I tell Henie, "He came to the bank again today."

Tossing my bag on the bed, my body hums with intoxication. My mind is foggy. The edges are softer, and I've never felt so alive from a man's attention.

"What did he say?" asks Henie, leaning upon her elbows. Her eyes sparkle, waiting for a tasty morsel to sink her teeth into. A romantic at heart, Henie loves love: falling in love, being in love, and the quest for love.

I walk over to my vanity mirror, sit, and turn on the Tiffany glass desk lamp. I remove the bobby pins from my hat while I choose my words. I brush through my hair and remove my pearl earrings, then take my index finger and touch the plump, soft flesh beneath my right eye.

"He wanted to make a deposit."

"Who cares what he wanted to do. What did he say?" she demands.

Twirling towards her, I say, "He asked me about my day." His smile makes me shiver inside. He's the man for me. A good man whose sweetness comes easily and generously.

"That sounds nice," says Henie in a dismissive tone.

I lost her interest once I started talking about his sweetness. Gentleness isn't sexy. I want someone who excites me for the long term because he cares about the right thing.

"He asked me if I was outside today. I told him not since early this morning. He reflected on the cerulean blue sky. No one should miss out on the chance to walk in the sunshine, he said."

Retelling the story makes me flutter. His words came fast. Penetrating. Decisive. He held my attention for every moment he was near me.

Rolling back over, Henie looks right at me.

"He sounds romantic. I love a good romance."

She jumps from her bed, plants her feet on the floor, and says, "This could be your great romance, Marjem. A man from a distant land, tall, dark, brooding..."

"He isn't dark, Henie. He is fair, with auburn hair and hazel eyes. But he is tall. Sexy tall. When I twirl, I will be a delicate whisper of a woman in his arms."

"When were you in his arms?" She sounds panicked.

She's going to fall on the floor bouncing around like that. "When were you in his arms? What are the details? Speak! Each word is important."

"Who do you take me for? I haven't been in his embrace yet. I'm imagining it."

"You've found your love. For you to imagine a man's embrace means he occupies your mind, your heart."

"Henie, you see right through me. The same way you see through everyone. You're perceptive. People can spend their whole lives not understanding why they do, what they do. That'll never be your problem. You understand exactly why you do what you do, what you want, and when you want to do it. There's an emotional genius to it. If everyone else had you in their lives, they would understand what truly inspires them."

She raises one eyebrow and responds to my impassioned reply.

"You're noticing the right things. He's more than a passing interest."

"He's different from the other men I have met and dated. He's not cultured, but he isn't unsophisticated either."

"Marja, you like him. You're not even toying with me."

She is sullen. She enjoys how we tease each other.

"Common does not suit you. Plain will not hold your interest. You're too smart."

Henie's version of me is exquisite. She takes the hairbrush from my hands and brushes through her hair. She needs something to occupy her hands.

I'm surprised she sat this long.

"He's traveled and independent."

"Well don't you sound proud?"

Her accusation throws me.

"I'm kidding, look at your face. I am teasing. It is good you are already a little possessive. It means you're invested."

I'm exasperated.

"I don't remember that happening..."

Henie's Cheshire cat grin says it all.

"What did you say about the offer for a walk?"

"I said, I noticed the weather was especially warm today."
She's right, I've been caught up in my thoughts all day. I remember every word of our conversation together and replaying it in my mind brings me great joy. I don't remember the rest of the day after Aron brought me back to work. I've never felt this way before.

"I told him; I can't very well take a walk with a man I don't know."

Pounding her fists on the bed, she says, "you know his name. His name is Aron, and you've been talking about him for months."

Maybe I'm playing a little hard to get.

"What did he say?"

"He excused himself, tipped his hat, and cleared his throat. 'I am Aron Rechtschaffen. Would you escort me on a walk at lunchtime around the lake?' He stepped back and smiled ear to ear. There's a mystery behind those eyes. I nodded yes, and he asked me when he should return. I told him I was taking my break at twelve-thirty. He said he would return then."

Opening my bag, I remove a box of chocolates.

"I forgot, he brought me these."

"Ooh let me see," says Henie, taking the box out of my hands before I react.

"Save some for Gittel."

Ignoring my request, she continues, "I love the chocolate covered orange nugget squares. Those are the best."

She handles each piece of chocolate. She takes a bite, pulls a face, and puts the second half back in the box. She tries another piece, again replacing the second half in the box. If I don't stop her, she'll make her way through the entire box of chocolates.

"Henie, stop! That's gross."

Laughing, she says, "I did you a favor. Now you know what's inside of each chocolate."

"He's funny. Like, hilarious. He packed a picnic lunch for us."

"What did he bring to eat?"

"He packed a salami and breadboard, a bunch of red grapes, two red delicious apples, two cherry Danishes, and grape juice."

"Sounds like a child packed the lunch," says Henie derisively.

"No, no, it was perfect. He packed his favorite things. He told me how apples are his favorite fruit. salami can be spicy and salty at the same time and red grapes are the perfect self for a refreshing burst of watery sweetness. Open and honest, his nature made it easy to get lost in his conversation. His gaze penetrated me when he spoke. Spending an hour with him was the most fun I've ever had. There's so much to learn about him. He's taking me out to lunch again tomorrow. I'm going to wear my green sweater which really brings out my eyes. He said he picked cherry danishes because the cherries make him think of my lips."

Chapter 56
January 1930 Berlin, Germany
Aron Rechtschaffen

My father loves books. Every celebration and holiday are valid opportunities and acceptable reasons to buy more books. Reading makes you smart, and education is a central tenet of Judaism. Inside the front cover of every book my father purchases he writes down either my name or Walker's.

He explains, "When I die, no one will fight over my treasures." Walker laughs, letting uncomfortableness slide off his back. I don't take his words to heart. Today I'm at the largest collection of Jewish texts in southern Berlin. The bookstore is called J. Noble. Books, historic texts, religious and ceremonial tomes line the bookstore from floor to ceiling.

Dust particles dance in the rays of light streaming through the dirty windows. The sparsely lit store can tell more stories than the books it contains. Stories of men, women and children visiting, deciding which cherished text to choose today, feels mysterious. Two overstuffed burgundy leather chairs are wedged against the southern wall next to a small glass table covered in discarded books.

Walking through the aisles, I run my fingertips along the countless weathered leather spines landing on one hardbound book. My nostrils fill with the smell of ink-soaked parchment. I bought a German-Hebrew Hagadah published by Gonzer & Lewin. When I build my family, I will lead my Pesach Seders with this Hagadah.

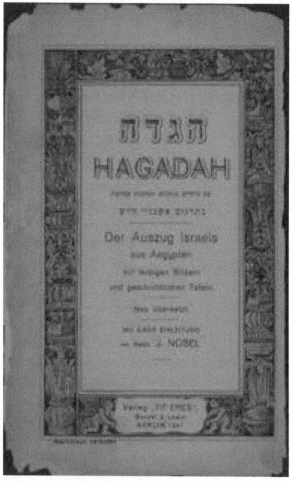

As a child, we prepared for Pesach the same way every year. My mother unpacked the Seder plate, Abba gathered the

Pesach dishes, and I unpacked the Hagadah. I handle my father's Hagadah with great care.

Exquisite calligraphy adorns the Yiddish on each page.

The stained pages tell the stories of Seder's past. Another Hagadah belonged to my great-grandfather Naftali.

His beliefs weren't shared by many.

His robust mellifluous voice would shake the windows in their frames on the high holidays.

I pass the butcher and see men and boys line the block gathering last-minute ingredients for Pesach. The extensive preparations alone for the Seder bring me back into my mother's kitchen.

She cooks for weeks to prepare for Pesach. She's one of the first to place her order at the local butcher. She wants the first pick of chickens, a shank bone, brisket and schmaltz needed for the week of Passover. She uses forty eggs throughout the week. My mother's Pesach menu includes: fresh fish, chicken, brisket, mashed potatoes, kugel, tzimmes, and matzo ball soup. The pickled carrots and beets she serves with her gefilte fish make my mouth water year round. My father told me how he went over my mother's heart with a bouquet of wildflowers. They're personal, untamed, and delicate. Resilient and fragrant, they grow in forests, fields, meadows, and by rivers and lakes. You can't buy wildflowers in the flower market. Gathered by hand, they come in hundreds of varieties. One of them is a sunflower. Sunflowers are majestic. They can grow taller than a human being. Marjem is my sunflower. Her luscious golden blonde hair and her exquisite ruby red lips confound me. She has an inquisitive nature. We've gone on six dates, and each one ends laughter with a promise of more time with her.

Chapter 57
February 1930 Berlin, Germany
Marjem Rechtschaffen

Henie notices my changed behavior and offers me daily in-spiration. This morning she left a new lipstick on the vanity for me to try. Sometimes she'll leave one of her favorite blouses on my bed knowing that I'm going to see him. I show him my Berlin from museums to cafés and I even chose a couple of nightclubs, upon Henie's suggestion to appear more sophisticated and worldly than I am. At night I pick cer-tain streets for us to walk through after a dinner date where jazz music fills the streets without exposing us to smoke-filled rooms and excessive drinking. My childhood was the antithesis of Aron's. Children should laugh and play, allow themselves to be reckless and sometimes stupid, to cry over skinned knees and stay up past their bedtime. I was allowed to learn and fail under their protection. None of those allow-ances were given to Aron. Yet, he doesn't express anger or regret. He's hopeful for a generous future he will craft for himself. His world changed when he was thirteen years old. In the springtime, he travels to the unknown without fear; in fact, he thrives. I love that he can survive on his own. I don't know the first thing about survival. He can build a tent, make a fire, fish, and cook food. He tells me about his childhood when his entire extended family gathered to welcome Shabbat together. Scores of Jews singing into a starry night sky in the shadows of the Carpathian Mountains. Sometimes their voices were powerful enough to part the clouds in the sky. He said he felt God on those nights. I have never come across someone like him before. I keep his vulnerabilities private. His openness is beautiful. Wanting the nicest things in life isn't everything in life; your humanity is.

Chapter 58
February 1930 Berlin, Germany
Aron Rechtschaffen

Dear Abba,

Berlin is beautiful and full of promise. The parks, museums and theaters enchant tourists and enlighten the locals. Marjem and I basked beneath the twinkling stars while attending bewitching evening concerts of Bach, Beethoven, and Mendelsohn. Live music on this scale evokes euphoric joy or melancholy depending on what we're listening to. Marjem pushes me to express myself, which I agonize over. Her pledge is: there's no wrong answer.

Marjem glows like the warm soft yellow sunshine.

She reminds me of sunflowers and baby chicks at Easter time. She's the finest piece of art I've ever seen and evokes wild emotions in me. My heart races whenever I see her. She's not a frivolous person and she doesn't want to waste money on restaurants, but she wants to see every movie that comes to our local movie house.

Marjem has great ideas about the business. She found two ways for us to save money. In case you wondered, the business is strong. No matter the economy, people need a good night's sleep and will pay for a quality quilt.

Herman developed a persistent cough. He's slowed down and walks as if in water. I want him to keep eating and sleeping well. Marjem and her mother Amalia prepare meals for Herman. Amalia's specialty is soups.

She and Herman have a game. She prepares a new soup, and he must identify the ingredients.

I am happy and healthy.

Love, Aron

Chapter 59
March 1930 Berlin, Germany
Marjem Rechtschaffen

Aron carries a small book in his inner coat pocket. Never without it, he fills the pages with his precise penmanship. He uses a small pocket-knife to sharpen his pencil tip when it grows dull. He takes notes on whatever crosses his mind: there is a diagram of a wooden rocking chair, a barn with majestic mountains in the background, diagrams of shoes, wheels and wagons, fabric designs, maps of Poland, Belarus, Ukraine, Holland, and Belgium. Certain maps show rivers and lakes, others show train tracks and backwoods paths; kilometers logged, and train timetables noted with circles. Lists of ideas, lists of words and their definitions, endless names and addresses of connections and friends all over the world.

He reaches across the table and takes my hand.

"Tell me Aron, what do you enjoy about the work you do?"

"Meeting new people. Finding connections between the product and the need is fulfilling."

He gazes into my eyes.

"Because of you, Marjem. I don't want to miss out on my time with you. A life with you is my dream. You're as delicious as an almond Danish soaked in rum and tossed in powdered sugar."

"You see me."

I stop.

Henie says mystery is important. If I say too much, he might lose interest.

"You notice my needs, Aron."

He strokes my index finger with the side of his. It's sweet and sexy.

"Marjem, I want you to share your world with me. Tonight, let us go hear the new concert in the park. Let's walk through the gardens and watch the leaves change."

I stare at his lips, willing him to see my desire.

"I want to kiss you, Marjem."

I whisper, "Your words take my breath away. Kiss me and never stop."

He takes the back of my head in his hand and pulls me close. Our lips touch. I press in and kiss him harder. I pour myself into our kiss. His lips are firm and when he takes hold of me, I am home.

Chapter 60
April 1930 Berlin, Germany
Aron Rechtschaffen

Dear Abba,

Marjem is impeccable. I asked her father, Herr Eisner, for her hand in marriage. I have the means to support her in a very comfortable lifestyle.

I explained my business, my prospects for the future, and I opened up my finances for him to inspect. He was very impressed with how I had accomplished so much. I insisted he meet Herman.

A few days later, Herr Eisner came over to Herman's house. Herman prepared a delicious brunch of egg and tuna salad sandwiches made on the most delicious rye bread with caraway seeds. There was a platter of sour pickles, pickled peppers, white fish, white onions and herring. Herman did not miss a single detail. Herr Eisner bought lemon and cherry danishes for dessert.

They discuss the business between them as if I wasn't in the room. Herr Eisner understands our machine from England is the key to our success. By not outsourcing the cleaning of the feathers, we save money. He suggested we move the machine into a new building, more centrally located. His ideas are good, but I do not have the capital. The more they talk, the deeper the strategy goes.

Herr Eisner and Herman are mutually impressed by two young brothers in different countries coming together and creating a substantial business.

Herman offered to pay a dowry to Herr Eisner. Herr Eisner said, "I appreciate your respectable nature, Herman, but that's archaic. It is up to Marjem to choose Aron. I hope she does - she is happier than I have ever seen her. She is a serious girl, but there is a new lightness in her, which I realize has everything to do with Aron."

Marjem's family is moving back to Holland next year.

By the time you read my next letter I will have proposed.

I'm ready for the rest of my life to start right now!

Love, Aron

Chapter 61
April 1930 Berlin, Germany
Mozes Meijer Eisner

Aron doesn't recognize he's won. The golden ring is in his grasp. Herman graciously invited me over for beers to discuss the children's future.

Herman insists, "Aron gave me a second chance at life. Without him, I had no reason to go forward. I saw a tall young skinny boy without a family. The sight of him made me sad. In any other time, and any other place, a boy wouldn't need to raise himself. An unspoken atrocity sent him away from his family. He resembles my son. If my son were without me to protect him, who would step up and help him?"

"He was lucky to have met you," I say.

"Mr. Eisner ..."

"Call me Mozes, please, we will be family."

Herman laughs, and the sound warms me. He's genuine. I see why Aron likes him. We exchange stories of our childhood. We both knew loving parents. Our fathers worked hard. Neither one of us raised ourselves. Herman made a cup of tea, and I brought a box of danishes for him. We shared the dreams we had as young men.

"I would've visited Paris. I was going to take my son before the war. We didn't go, and I can't even remember why. Mozes, I want Aron to live without regret."

I say, "the real estate market is volatile. But if you have enough money..."

Herman interrupts, "isn't that true of everything in life?"

I nod in agreement.

"I lived my entire life in Berlin. When I was a young man, I took my savings and purchased this house. My wife and I built a beautiful life with each other, and she gave me a son. God took her away. In retaliation, I stopped speaking to God."

I put my hand on his shoulder, "I'm deeply sorry to hear that. Atheists are some of the most honest people I know."

"Thank you. My tragedy happened a lifetime ago. Aron healed me. I met his brother Walker, and his parents, Naftali, and Tzizel Rechtschaffen. They are quiet, hard-working folk. Deeply religious and faithful to their Jewish God."

Aron's ability to share his entire family with Herman, makes me prouder than I realize. Aron says his books are well maintained. They are, I check them. But Marjem cleaned them up. The business is profitable. Herman adds, "running the business out of my home has led to great success. We have a receiving room for the elderly ladies of Berlin. There's adequate space in the basement for the feather cleaner. But there are always ways to expand the business." Herman and I met three more times and laid out an immediate and a long-term plan. The next time I see Herman, I arrive unannounced.

Others consider it disrespectful, but Herman understands we're devising a plan and the ones who move fast win. Before I remove my coat and hat, I tell him my good news.

"Grobe Hamburger Straube is the perfect street. The Jewish Cemetery is there. Their children will attend Jüdisches Gymnasium Moses Mendelssohn. We can buy it for a song. The bottom floor is a boutique. We can refinish the floors. The top floor needs new doors, new windows, and a paint job."

"Aron can manage the repairs," says Herman.

"Exactly." We shake on it.

"Marjem and Aron will occupy the second floor. We move the business into the retail space on the bottom floor. They can rent out the top two floors to whoever they want."

Herman says, "I have a great idea."

"What is it, Herman?"

"I will put my house up for sale. The money will cover the upper two floors."

"Herman, how generous!"

"Not really. I will occupy the top floor. Thank God for Aron. He won't let me die alone. When you get to be my age, those thoughts occupy your mind."

"Your devotion is admirable, Herman."

Unemployment is raging. Herman and I can provide security in the middle of the maelstrom. We made an offer on the property, and they accepted it.

Herman says, "Aron can keep his savings for a rainy day. Amalia and Marjem can decorate the retail store on the bottom floor. The closing is set for Thursday."

The best way to celebrate our surprise is to cook an elaborate dinner.

******

The adults sit on a couch in my living room. The children stand before us. Excitedly I jump up and announce, "Aron and Marjem, your wedding is right around the corner. We found an elegant home for you to live in. On Thursday, we'll go to the lawyer's office, and you'll sign the paperwork."

"Papa!" Marjem screams.

Aron looks at me.

"How can I accept this? We are just starting. I want you to respect me because I will take care of your Marjem."

Herman says, "We know what a wonderful job you'll do taking care of Marjem. Save your earnings for a later day. Now graciously accept and compliment Amalia on her extraordinary dinner."

He turns to Amalia and bows, "you show no greater honor than cooking with such love and talent. Unfortunately, I am full, and I've grown tired."

"Herman, you embarrass me," says Amalia, blushing.

I'm distracted, watching the flush climb up his neck.

Aron turns to Herman and asks him, "Are you alright?"

Herman says, "Aron, your life is about to begin."

Aron begins to speak, and Herman holds up his hand. The room grows silent.

"I sold my house. I bought the building with Amalia and Mozes. We're going to set up the store on the bottom floor. You're going to live on the second floor. I'm going to live in one apartment on the third floor."

"Herman ...." begins Aron.

"On Thursday, we will all go to the lawyer's office, and you will sign the paperwork. I sold our home, so you're moving with me."

He laughs.

"It's late, I'm old."

He spread his hands in a gesture of peace.

"Aron, you know it's not good for my heart to fight."

Aron says, "Yes, sir. I know. Thank you for the most gracious gift."

Marjem walks over to Herman and hugs him. She kisses him on the cheek. Happy tears stream down her face, then she turns to hug her mother and me.

Marjem says, "We're going to walk Herman home."

Her smile is ecstatic.

Herman stands up and says, "Mozes, it's been a pleasure conspiring with you for the past few months. Nothing makes my soul happier knowing we're taking care of my boy and your precious girl."

Chapter 62
May 30, 1930, Berlin, Germany
Aron Rechtschaffen

Once the snow melts and the cold snap in the evening air dissipates the sparrows and robins return. Within an hour of their first call the sun rises and filters the sky in shades of yellow, rust, fuchsia, and orange. As a new day begins, the morning dew coats the grass and soaks my shoes. Spring means Pesach is upon us. My favorite memories of my family are during Pesach. The Seder, songs, prayers and the rituals all contribute to its sanctity. Mama uses the outdoor kitchen during Pesach and Papa built a special table to enjoy our meals under the stars. Our Pesach commences when Papa asks for his tools. He's a serious man with an unruly beard which frames his face and highlights his cloudy gullgray eyes. My older brother, Walker, is ready. He hands me a feather, a handkerchief, a candle, and a wooden spoon. Walker shadows Papa and repeats each gesture. Walker instructs me to hand the candle to my father. A match is struck, and the candle is lit. Papa hands the candle to Walker and I hand the feather, the handkerchief, and the wooden spoon to Papa.

Walker hands the candle back to me, and then leads me from room to room as Papa locates and removes each piece of chametz (bread) we had hidden. We start in the kitchen, then head to the family room, and end in their bedroom. I held the candle close, and it illuminated Papa's face. Papa swept the chametz with the feather onto the wooden spoon. He secured the chametz by wrapping the handkerchief over it as we moved from room to room. To our amazement and delight, he found every piece. Tonight, the Seder is at my house. After the Motze, my father-in-law Mozes stands up and walks towards my mother-in-law Amalia, relieving her of the plate of macaroons.

She turns to me and says, "Aron, we prepared a gift for you. We want you to hide it in a safe place for an emergency."

Herman turns to me and says, "your family loves you very much. I feel tremendous honor being part of your ceremony tonight."

He turns to my father-in-law, and says, "Let me remove myself and say good night. Your family can continue your celebrations in private."

My father-in-law says, "Herman, you are family."

A smile more genuine than I've ever witnessed in my life spreads across Herman's face. I wish it was you by my side tonight, but the second-best is Herman.

Amalia hands Marjem a large green, silk bag. handkerchief.

"Oh goodness," gasps Marjem as she opens the bag.

Her eyes widen and she says, "jewelry...gold bracelets, necklaces, diamond earrings, and rings with every gemstone you can imagine..."

She fingers a particularly lovely diamond ring.

"Governments come and go. Paper money can be more valuable to feed a fire in your stove than to the butcher when you want to buy a chicken for Shabbat," says Mozes.

"Sir, we're doing well. I appreciate your gesture," says Aron, handing back the jewels.

"Don't insult me, Aron. I need to know my children are safe. Having wealth, transferable wealth means power over your destiny. Spending my life with Amalia makes me happy. I have peace because I have everything I need. When I place my head on the pillow at night, I'm asleep before Amalia has turned off the light."

"It's true. He never covers himself. I always tuck him in," teases Amalia.

She pushes Aron's hand with the bag of jewels back towards him. She smiles and says, "Take these and save them for a rainy day."

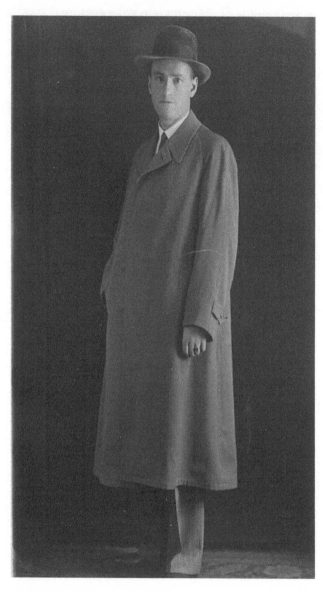

Aron, 1930

Chapter 63
October 1930 NYC, New York
Karl Eisner

Dear Marjem and Aron,

I received the most heartfelt letter from my cousin Gerta. She was greatly impressed with Marjem and most of her letter was dedicated to your newfound friendship and your life in Berlin. My heart filled with pride knowing that your family is a true representation of the greatness we have inside of us all. Gerta was scared to leave home and I promised it would be worth it. There wasn't any future for her in Dobromysl and she needed to understand how much bigger the world is and that there's a place for her in it.

We mutually agreed the timing of her arrival wasn't optimal. You're both newlyweds and you deserve the joy and freedom two young adults deserve once they're married. You never made her feel uncomfortable. Again, a testament to your class. She told me about Herman and the friendship between him and Aron as it relates to your business. Again, it comes back to the business you've created in Berlin. I'm inspired and I'd like to believe some of the ideas that I've been talking to Aron about for years have helped.

I've arranged for an affidavit for Gerta to come to America. I found her work as a schoolteacher in Long Island, New York. She's changed her mind and sees greater potential working in a department store. However, she understands a job in hand equals success. New passenger ships from Europe arrive daily filled with impoverished souls hoping to use their skills and find their own version of the American dream. I came here as a tailor. My beautiful wife, Bertha, is a schoolteacher and turned into a wonderful mother to our three children. This is the life that you deserve.

The rules just changed, unfortunately. The great depression and the stock market crash has turned the entire country up-side down. Especially New York, the financial heartbeat of the country. When New York suffers the whole country feels it. Overnight people who invested in the market lost every-thing, all their savings. Period. Friends lost jobs and others can't find the money to pay their own rent. People are being evicted from their homes and they have nowhere to live. Friends are taking in people. My family will remain fine. I've moved my business back into repairs and alterations. I've be-come a busy tailor once again. I've maintained access to a large variety of inexpensive textiles I can repurpose into whatever people need. Creating demand when people are starving is bone breaking.

The collapse is coming to European shores. Germany's been living very high off, of loans from America for far too long. When those loans are recalled, the global repercussions will be epic. Overnight the economy will be moved into freefall. With global discontent, fresh voices come into power. There are many Americans who find Adolf Hitler to be a mesmer-izing orator. He's the man who can galvanize the masses when there's pervasive strife. His ability to appeal to the

educated makes him threatening. He has an army—a paramil-
itary force called the SS. In America, we see them marching
in the local news reels; they're sharply dressed and command
fear. I wouldn't want to be on the wrong side of a fight with
these bullies. Stay safe, I love you.

Karl

Chapter 64
December 1930 Berlin, Germany
Marjem Rechtschaffen

Aron sits at the dining room table reading the newspaper lazily stirring a steaming cup of tea beside him.

"Aron, guess what came today?"

I rush over and kiss his sweet face.

"The new Berlin directory!"

Aron smiles, but I can tell he doesn't understand how exciting this is. This is the first time our names are listed in the address book as married husband and wife. We're officially bound and documented.

"Your delight in seeing our union made public in the most boring and bureaucratic way means everything to me. You honor me with your adoration, Marjem," says Aron.

I don't tell him how much I enjoy writing my new name on any piece of paper I can find. The novelty will wear off, I'm sure of it, but for now it is an extra special secret treat that belongs solely to me.

"When a new piece of mail comes to the house with the married name, it tickles me."

"Until you realize it's a bill," says Aron.

Laughing, I agree, "Absolutely true."

We laugh together and Aron surveys the other mail.

"Do you have it?" Aron asks.

I run into the bedroom and grab the new address books.

"Why are there two copies, Marjem, are there always two?" asks Aron.

"Yes. One for residential listings and one for business." I don't understand his consternation.

Aron says, "Marjem," then stops himself.

He regards both covers and turns them over in his hands. Opening them both, he locates our name. He closes them again. Unease fills the air. Something is wrong.

"Why would the German government print a directory with only Jewish residences and businesses?"

We've never had a business together before. I can't say I've ever noticed. Aron understands something I'm not catching. By nature, he's more cynical, constantly asking questions to understand other people's motives.

"The Nazis devised a way to quickly locate the Jews who live in Berlin and run businesses. Were similar directories created in Nuremberg? How will this impact us?"

My excitement fades, the sweet taste in my mouth grows sour.

"I want you to talk to Herman and get his opinion. I'm sure his friends have a lot to say about it. This would be a good time to be on the fly on the wall and hear the disgusting truths coming out of the monster's mouths."

I had thought, how convenient. We usually wait until after the high holidays are over to get the synagogue congregation list for the new year.

"I feel stupid. My mind took me to convenience, and I thought about the sisterhood at the synagogue and how practical an address book like this would be. I hadn't considered any other outcome."

Aron says, "This list shows where every Jew in the city lives."

Chapter 65
January 1931 Perehinske, Galicia
Naftali Herzl

Dear Aron,

Distinguishing between what's important and what's simply noise is a skill you can take an entire lifetime to master. When I'm calm, I'm happier, and the flowing sound of water eases me. The big decisions I have to make in life I choose to make when I'm in a state of calm.

Unfortunately, fear drives more decisions in your life than everything else. Most people succumb to fear. It wears down most good people. Each one of us can only tolerate so much before we reach our threshold. It does not make us weak or wrong. It makes us human. There are two choices in life: grow or die. You chose growth. Walker chose growth. You both make me so proud.

The Jews of Galicia survived another pogrom. It is unclear who drove the violence. Russians, Polish, and Ukrainians soldiers relish spilled Jewish blood. This year, on the last day of Passover, the Cossack beasts set ablaze an entire village. Smoking embers of the Torah are the only remains of their

synagogue. The Rebbe and his family escaped with their clothes on their backs. The terror of future invasions has galvanized Russian and Polish Jews to immigrate to Palestine. Zionists call Palestine heaven on earth. Each person who has immigrated there and written home says the same thing, "Stepping upon Palestinian soil brings a heavenly peace."
Everyone here is talking about the recent election in Germany. The president of Germany cannot inspire unity.

A Prussian and an aristocrat, he is used to his orders being met without rebuke. A splintering society does not reflect well upon its leadership. The government collapsed because of the depression in America, and German citizens seek answers. In September, six and a half million people voted the Nazis into the Reichstag. A new national force seized control. The government has its hooks into society but the rabblerousing brownshirts delegitimize them. The uneducated thugs hurt the legitimacy of Adolf Hitler and the Nazi party. As the great depression continues, more men volunteer to become part of the SA or the SS, the Nazi elite force. The world outside of Germany noticed a shift in the party between the ruling factions. The mounting levels of power within the party are the very thing they can tear it apart. Rolm, who organized the disastrous Rohm Push has returned from self-exile in Bolivia to run the SA. They continue to target intellectuals and communists. The world outside my doors is in turmoil. The love and warmth inside my home between my beautiful wife and myself keeps us safe. We make a good living and eat chicken every night. Know in your heart that we are safe and if there comes a time when we're not, I will not hesitate to take my beautiful bride to somewhere safe.

Until I hear from you again,

Abba

Chapter 66
January 2, 1931, Berlin, Germany
Mozes Meijer Eisner

My dear Marjem and her wonderful husband Aron,

The nights have grown short and winter is upon us once more. The canals in Holland are the most fun during the winter season. I walk a little slower, but my ice skating is as fast as it ever was. When your mother puts on her skates, she looks sixteen. Her ebullience on the ice is unmatched. I can sit for hours and watch her skate circles around others. She takes small jumps and spins. I fell in love with her the moment I saw her. If it meant I would miss an appointment for the chance to watch her skate, I would do it. Her ethereal beauty could capture the heart of a king. We never found a good place to enjoy ice-skating in Berlin. I'm glad I've come back in my retirement years to enjoy your mother this way.

Herman sends me letters and keeps me up to date on the business. He tells me how happy you both are. Your mother thinks I'm ridiculous to have a spy in my own children's home. She's just annoyed she didn't think of it first.

Your mother and I received a letter from cousin Karl in New York. He says the financial collapse nearly destroyed his business. He laid off his delivery boy, and his wife is at the register. The wave of unemployment is worrisome. He sees good people starving on the street. When he can provide work, he chooses a family man. With financial instability comes extremist political solutions.

Uncle Karl says communism and socialism are upsetting the democratic sensibilities of the United States. He told me about our cousin Gerda. I understand she wasn't in your home long before her affidavit cleared for passage to America. I'm very proud of how you treat all members of our extended family. Your mother couldn't be happier. She spends a lot of time with your sisters and their children.

In a few months, Francois is going to come to visit. He will then escort your mother and David to Belgium to visit Gideon. David is interested in establishing his own life in Belgium along with Gideon and Gideon's family.

Gideon could use the help and it is time for David to venture out and become the man he is destined to be. I'm afraid I might've held him back; perhaps I kept him at home for too long. Your mother has given me seven beautiful children in a decade. An empty nest is difficult for her and for myself. You're all growing up too quickly. Each one of my children brings me pride. Marjem, from the moment you could speak, I knew I had to work harder than I ever have before.

I had to stay a step ahead of you for as long as I could manage because you respected intelligence and deserved every opportunity. Moving to Berlin meant you could have whatever your heart desired in life. You attended the best schools, frequented museums, enjoyed live concerts and theater. You made all the right choices. You and Aron should only have love and light in your life, and I should only be around long enough to watch you create a beautiful family.

*Every night before I go to bed, I say a prayer. I want to remind
Hashem to look out for every one of my children.
I hope to see you before we celebrate Pesach again.*

Love, Papa

Chapter 67
February 1931 Berlin, Germany
Marjem Rechtschaffen

Rosh Hashana celebrates Hashem opening the book of life for the New Year. If your name is written in the book of life, then you live for another year. It sounds simple. It's understood that if a person dies during the high holidays, that person is deemed righteous in the eyes of Hashem. Papa can't tell me what I need to do to have my name written in the book of life, but he says it's something I should worry about. He says the people who should be concerned are old people because they are closer to death.

Rosh Hashanah was my Papa's favorite time of year. The air is crisp, smells of pine, and sleeping beneath a down feather blanket is heaven on earth. Rosh Hashanah is dipping apples into honey and Mama making a delicious brisket with corn, mashed potatoes, cabbage rolls, stewed carrots, and challah. Rosh Hashana is when Papa uses his Tallis as an aegis to protect him and I from the rest of the world's judgement. That's where he would spend extra time teaching me how to read Hebrew because it didn't come easily. The Jewish alphabet would dance around the page, and I couldn't make sense of it. Rosh Hashanah was our time together, where my weakness bonded us together. Every holiday he would try again and to this day no one knows I can't read a word of Hebrew. But I don't have to when I stand beside my Papa. I don't have to know the words because my intention is as pure as his blessings. Papa said we are alike. When we prayed, I snuggled into his chest. He wrapped his arm around my shoulder. The world fell away, and it was only us in the synagogue. When he sang, his prayers made sense. Papa's vibrant tone was meant for Hashem. My love for Judaism is wrapped up in my love for Papa; he's as sacred as the high holidays.

On January 10, 1931, I stood over Papa's casket.

He was inside, but I couldn't touch or see him. He wasn't part of my world anymore. I put my hands on the casket and wept angrily. There were so many things that were left unsaid. How do I tell him I wasn't finished needing him?

I want him to be proud. I love myself and that has a large part to do with him loving me. Did he know how much I cherished him? My tether to the world is gone.

I drift in a churning sea where the sky is stormy and there is no horizon in sight.

Will he see what I have become? I never doubted the existence of heaven before Papa died. I had absolute faith and trust that heaven existed. His death capsizes my belief. The foundation which was never supposed to crumble feels like sand running through my fingers. I chase Papa in my dreams through a field of wildflowers. We are back in Dobromyl on Rosh Hashana. We can't begin our supper before we say the evening prayers and light the candles. I'm sent to get Papa while Mama cooks. The faster I run through the wildflowers; the farther Papa moves away from me. When I shout out his name, he turns his head and smiles. His lips have always formed the most beautiful smile. When he used to kiss me on the cheek as a little girl his mouth was the entire size of my

259

cheek. I call him and say it's time to come in and we want to begin the holiday. He waves to me and walks in the opposite direction. I want him to stop. When I open my mouth to call his name, I'm rendered mute. I awake to Aron holding me as I continue to cry and scream out for my Papa.

I do not know how to exist in the world without him.

Chapter 68
April 1931 Berlin, Germany
Marjem Rechtschaffen

On Monday and Thursday nights, my heart quickens at the sound of Aron's key unlocking our front door. He saves all the backbreaking deliveries for these two days.

This prevents him from coming home for lunch.

"Have a good day," I say as my voice breaks, handing him his lunch on those mornings.

Our hands touch and he inadvertently shocks me. I squeal and his cheeks grow red. He is still the shy man who courted me at the bank. His stillness, a once-endearing trait, now frustrates me. Aron stands in front of the closed door, his eyes askance. He loves and desires me but is embarrassed by his loss of control when we are intimate.

Heading towards me he says, "I see you made a snack for yourself. I wouldn't want you to forget it."

He slips the snack into my jacket pocket. The aroma of his freshly shaven face excites me as I lean into him.

Touch me, I want to scream. My neediness consumes me.

I walk to the door and snatch my scarf from the hook and wind it around my neck, the way he winds me up. Walking briskly in the fresh air helps clear my mind. Monbijou park is my sanctuary. A walk along the river will be a great distraction from not seeing Aron today.

He whispers, "Does our growing son make you hungry?"

I fight back sudden tears.

"And faint, forgetful, and amorous. Do you think I am crazy?"

"Never," he rasps.

"There is nothing crazy about you." Our eyes meet.

His hazel eyes change to steel gray as his mood shifts towards passion. His intent soothes me.

I sense myself giving into his mood.

Aron's inherent patience contrasts with my prickliness. This morning, I closed a cabinet door on my finger. He asked if I was all right before I even reacted. He is observant and notices things I do not expect him to see. Pregnancy is hard. A continuous cycle of despair, annoyance, and elation exhaust the strongest women. I wear his compassion like a warm blanket on a rainy, damp day. His eyes darken further, and we reach for each other and kiss.

Breathlessly I say, "I love you."

He straightens himself and clears his throat. Aron collects the empty milk bottles and opens the door. He places them carefully on the step.

"Come along, let's walk to the park."

As I pass him, I lean in and whisper, "Thank you," lingering by his ear. He stiffens.

Outside the cerulean sky changes Aron's eyes from gray to steel blue, which matches my dress. I squint against the brightness and inhale the crisp air. The aroma of baked bread from Himmel's bakery wafts over me, and my mood brightens.

With Aron beside me, I am safe and happy.

"Marjem, most women stay home and don't exercise this far into the pregnancy."

"I don't know how other women are raised, Aron. Papa raised me to be me. I love salty foods, pickles, fried potatoes, and whitefish salad. But Mother said I must stay away from those foods. I am retaining water and being bloated and pregnant does not mix. I want to… need to clean the house and prepare for the baby. Walking clears my mind. My back is relieved because of the motion. My ankles remain slim, and my knees are less stiff, even with the additional weight."

Aron does not object. He listens and nods, "I want to take care of you."

My tone softens and I lower my voice, "I know you do."

He clutches my hand and says, "We chose each other. I knew what I was getting myself into."

He laughs at his joke, and I feign devastation.

"Don't forget, you pursued me for months," I charge.

He raises his left eyebrow, something I find particularly charming, and keeps the rest of his thoughts to himself.

Along Krausnickstabe street, a tall, thin man exits Mr. Greenbaum's shop. He is our local cobbler.

Aron calls out, "Boris, Boris, over here" and waves his arms over his head. Boris turns and sees Aron. They meet in the middle of the street. A store bell chimes, and Mr. Grossman's trademark jovial greeting, "Guten Morgen, Shalom," echoes into the street. I imagine he will greet us the same way after our child is born. We will be walking together down the street, the baby in my arms and Aron's arm protecting me. I will look up into Aron's smiling face and see his pride in us, his wonder in his child.

"Marjem, are you listening?" Aron asks me and I realize I have not heard a thing he said.

I am not sure when I stopped listening. This is not the first time I have become engrossed in something other than the conversation I was a part of. It happens to me more when I read. I read the first line of a story, and then I read it again and again. I might read the sentence five or six times. Then suddenly, I am in the middle of the page, and I have no idea how I got there. It is disconcerting. I am not sure if this happens to other people. I never told anyone. When it happens around Aron, he gets annoyed. I can explain to him a million times that it is not out of disrespect, but his feelings get hurt and that is why he gets mad.

"No, I was distracted. What can I do?" I say quickly.

"Speak to Shira and invite them for Shabbat dinner," says Aron. They are good people.

"Shira will have lots of advice about the baby."

"Aron, she'll ask me what she can bring for dinner."

"Ask her to make her tzimmes. Boris loves it and she makes it weekly, it'll be easy for her."

We continued to discuss our upcoming Shabbat dinner and Aron intertwined his fingers with mine. Our pace quickens as the sun finally rises over a residential four-story apartment building on our horizon. Rays of light filter through and illuminate the entrance of the *Moses Mendelssohn School*. Living down the street from the school makes the location of our building desirable. My child will have the best education available. He will learn about religion and science. He will understand ancient civilizations, math, history, art, and music. He will learn languages including German, Hebrew, and French. Our son will be worldly. He will not have to work with his hands if he does not want to. He will not slave away in the sun and leave the house seasonally to find work. His life will start differently than Aron's. I look at my Aron and smile. I know he worries. As he leads us through a score of boys, they jostle for attention, lanky frames blocking the sidewalk as their incongruent voices bounce off the brick facade of the school. The smells overwhelm me, pungent, musty, and sour.

Aron says, "Those children are the size of men."

"I had no idea boys this young would be so big."

I feel small and fragile, despite my big belly.

Aron explains, "Boys start puberty between thirteen and sixteen. The ones who start earlier look like puppies. They are all noses, feet, and hands at first. Their bodies need a chance to grow into themselves."

"Do you think our boy would look like that?"

I see a boy with thick blonde hair and a wide, pugilistic nose. I touch my own nose self-consciously.

"Marjem, he will grow into his nose," he laughs.

"You are so clever. I want you to teach him everything you know."

I think to myself - you will teach him to be a man.

"You'll teach him how to survive. How to be a man like you. You are gentle and confident. Where Papa was loud, you are quiet. A crowd of people constantly surrounded Papa. Part of him enjoyed the attention, but he did not seek it out. You prefer to not even be in the room."

Aron admits, "I'm in the room when I have to be."

He looks at me and says no more. He is kind and generous to everyone.

People respond well to him; he has a nice face, and he keeps the mood light.

"You could be around more. In the room from time-to-time. You are well-liked," I say to him, meaning every word.

The wives from the synagogue tell me how much their husbands enjoy their conversations with you. He is noticeably quiet and sometimes that is off-putting to more insecure people.

"I don't need a lot of attention. I don't like it, but I like going places with you," he says, squeezing my hand.

The clicking of our heels against the cobblestone street eases me. Papa said our distinguished address would open doors for future business. This pleases me immensely.

My stomach flips as we pass the butcher and I see raw meat.

"We need to talk about the business," says Aron.

I appreciate the distraction. When he is wrestling with a decision; talking it through, step-by-step, helps him get to the heart of the issue faster.

"What is the problem?" I ask.

"Your Papa wants to push more feathers through Berlin. The logistics aren't the issue," explains Aron.

He outlines why we need additional staff with specific skill sets that will eat into our profits for a while.

"Do you need to hire a new transportation manager?" I add, "If the routes are smooth, we can train someone else for the road."

The issues involved are complex and Aron breaks it down for me. When I was little, Papa would wake up in the morning before everybody else. He would sit on the couch outside my room reviewing what was on his agenda for the day. After I saw the light was turned on, I would climb out of my bed, put on my robe, and sit down next to him. I would look at the jumble of words and numbers before me and have no idea what any of it meant. Papa took the time to explain to me what was on the piece of paper. He would go through his day and let me know what parts he found exciting and what parts would be dull. This was our quiet, special time. No one else was awake. I did not have to compete for his attention, and I liked him telling me about what he did during his day. Aron respects my opinion. He brings me into integral decisions. When there is a problem to solve, we solve it together. We are stronger for the partnership.

"Maurice will train the manager; someone who speaks German and French. He can handle staffing, Aron. He has a good eye for talent."

I stop. Each kick from the baby takes the wind from me. The time is coming. My stomach is so large. I never imagined my body would expand like this. I am vulnerable. The security of my baby is my only concern.

"Are you alright?" Aron asks.

I cannot catch my breath, but I am alright. I am amazed by how quickly my body can fail me.

"I am fine." I do not want Aron upset.

"Distract me. Tell me more about the business."

The baby moves once he hears Aron's voice.

To straighten out my spine and give my ribs a little bit more room for the baby, I stretch my hands up into the air. Not being able to take a deep breath is terrifying. Aron takes his handkerchief and wipes my brow.

"You are panting. I want to walk you home," insists Aron.

"I need some sugar."

"Of course, you do. Let me get you a cherry and cheese danish." We start towards the bakery.

The florists' door opens, and fragrant roses divert us. Anita Strauss, a squat woman with round hips and a plump face, runs a beautiful store. She wears two pairs of eyeglasses, one for distance and one for reading, and changes one for the other regularly.

She saunters over, "Mrs. Rechtschaffen, you are a vision of health. I trudged through the valleys of the Carpathian Mountains for all five pregnancies, and my body still thanks me," she says and pats her hips.

I blush at her immodesty. My hips have spread as well.

"Thank you. Mrs. Strauss."

I will have to work hard after the baby to pull my body back into shape. Every day, I joke that my circumference has changed. I drop everything, I bump into walls, I constantly knock my left elbow on the bathroom sink.

"I walk along the river for moderate exercise."

"Good for you. Give my best to your mother," she says.

"I will."

My mood sours. I miss Mother more than words can express. Aron moves closer and places his arm around me. He angles us back towards Mr. Himmel's bakery, where the cakes and bread make his mouth water. I never eat sweets first thing in the morning, and he hopes I will lose my resolve. He loves sugar but it is not good for him. I feel myself waffle when Mrs. Doris walks out with a lemon Danish in her hand. The pastry shines with sweet butter and honey. The lemon center looks oversized, which I love. The freshness tastes luscious when it coats your tongue. Now I must have a Danish.

"Good morning, Mr. and Mrs. Rechtschaffen," says Mrs. Doris. She is a language and manners instructor whose greetings sound unduly formal. I stand up straighter in her presence. Her dress coat is vibrant green, which highlights the red in her long brown wavy hair.

"So nice to see you, Mrs. Doris," replies Aron.

He exaggeratedly tips his hat and I giggle. He cannot help himself. He does this for my enjoyment as much as his own. He is not a fan of people who take themselves too seriously and live stringently.

"Oh, no need for such extravagances, Mr. Rechtschaffen. Have a nice day," says Mrs. Doris as she walks away from us.

Turning to Aron, I say, "You be nice. She might be our son's teacher one day."

My smile betrays me. I am far too amused for my reprimand to be taken seriously.

Aron looks from the bakery back to me.

"Aren't we going in?" asks Aron.

"I'll get two lemon danishes when I return from my walk."

Aron smiles and licks his lips, "I prefer cherry."

With a wink, I reply, "who said you were getting any Danishes?" He feigns shock.

I walk in and buy two cherry danishes, one for Aron and one for me. On the way back, I will grab two lemons. Aron waits for me outside the door. I hand him a Danish and we kiss, then I cross the busy thoroughfare.

Aron, 1933

Chapter 69
May 1931 London, UK
Walker Rechtschaffen

Dear Aron,

I hear congratulations are in order! I understand Marjem is pregnant, and we are all extremely excited here in London. Becoming a father changes your perspective. The bond you have with Marjem will grow even stronger after she gives you a child. The child is not only a product of your love, but a representation of what the future of your family will be. Children are magnificent. They will push you to the edge in a second and then pull you right back with a simple smile or an overly aggressive hug. My life has meaning beyond my wildest expectations. My family is what grounds me when the world around us is collapsing. I take my strength from them. You must always respect the sanctity of your home. That will be your refuge.

The world is a mess. Every country has its version of financial depression. Unemployment is through the roof, people cannot afford to rent apartments, and good honest hard work is not easy to find. Most European cities are still in ruins. There is no money to rebuild. There aren't as many able-bodied people to do the work as there used to be. We lost an entire generation of men. Some people went back to their old lives without realizing you can't go back. Other people saw it as an opportunity to re-create themselves. The smartest ones, in my opinion, left everything and chose a new land to live in, where mistakes are not behind every corner like ghosts haunting you. I do not think anyone thought a world war could erupt over a murder.

The citizens of Germany have outgrown what President von Hindenburg can offer. He is out of touch. After the war, citizens of all countries began to reassess their role in society. Those who served felt great hardship for their sacrifice. Those who did not serve most certainly lost somebody who did. After Herman lost his son in the war, he became more active in the local veterans' club. He needed to find meaning from the greatest loss he ever felt.

The friendship he built with these veterans is substantial. The Republic values their sacrifice. They're provided special benefits and community programs. Herman's loss is no less painful but having others to commiserate with helps. We all share the pain of the past, but we don't talk about it publicly. It's the extra seat at the dinner table that will always remain empty. If the chair isn't there, there's no balance or harmony to the table. Yet the chair remaining empty is just as unseemly because you can't help but imagine the person who is missing.

The recent news reels show the rest of the world the new exciting German innovation. The Schienenzeppelin is fantastic? A propeller-driven rail car? It set a world speed record of 230 km/h on its way from Hamburg to Berlin! I would love to get my hands on that propeller and take it apart and then put it back together. I want to understand more about German machinery. Even here in Britain, German engineering is highly *regarded. Many British engineers would love to collaborate, but nobody trusts Germany anymore.*

We heard that Marjem's father passed away and we feel terrible for your loss. He was a magnanimous man who cherished family; the kind of man one should admire. The relationship you shared will only make you a better man in years to come. Your letters are always exciting to receive, and they feel like morsels of home. Stay healthy and be strong. Until I see your face again,

Love, Walker

Chapter 70
July 1931 Berlin, Germany
Marjem Rechtschaffen

Renee and her mother Erika arrive walking arm-in-arm. They look more like sisters than mother and daughter. Renee's chestnut hair is braided and woven at the base of her long, slim neck. Their relationship is enviable. I doubt Renee could last one day without speaking to her mother.

Erika says, "You are beautiful, Marjem. Steel-blue is your color."

We embrace; I close my eyes and drink up her tenderness. I hold on a little longer and she strokes my back. Her affection comforts me.

"Thank you," I say.

Erika kisses my cheek and regards my pregnant belly.

"Raising a family in Berlin is thrilling. We have the best of everything - art, literature, and music."

With a wink, she says, "Before you know it, you'll be hosting a Bar Mitzvah in the Neue Synagogue."

She squeezes my arm in endearment and notices the mother-of-pearl buttons at my wrists. She smiles knowingly.

"Your mother has the most exquisite taste. A mother notices the wrists and how the finer workmanship can take a simple garment to the next level."

Erika's eyes sparkle in delight, and she kisses me once more.

"Renee's eager for me to stop talking."

She waves goodbye and saunters over to her friends. Jealousy overwhelms me. I want my mother. We never ran out of things to say. Does Renee realize how lucky she is to have her mother here? I have difficulty swallowing.

A lump builds in the back of my throat. A mother's love is felt through her tea and toast. She would massage my swollen ankles, soothe my upset stomach, and take away my fear of the unknown.

Defensively, I cover my growing belly with my hand.

The mothers congregate in a shaded nook on the eastern side of the park near a duck pond. The greeting between bala-bustas is an art form, a methodical dance where they embrace, then hold each other out at arms' length to admire their refin-eries, and then embrace again. Each woman is as well-dressed as the next. The velvet hats are breath-taking. Some women wear silk scarves around the brim of their hats to make them look casual. Others wear pearl brooches or long ostrich feathers. These women are dressed for a night at the theater. My mother, if she were here, would be kibitzing with them. My heart contracts again.

Renee is feeling snappish.

"Let us walk and get a little distance between me and Ma. She kept me up late last night picking out her outfit for today. She declared at nine o'clock that the internal drama in the syna-gogue's sisterhood must be resolved. With Erika at the helm, she expects her volunteers to conduct themselves with the ut-most propriety. She'll need at least two hours to untangle eve-ryone's feelings."

Renee is visibly annoyed.

"She is getting on your nerves, but she's sweet. If the worst thing in the world is that she cares too much, it's not so bad, is it?"

"Since I became pregnant, I'm high strung," declares Renee. Did she say pregnant? I scream at the top of my lungs. She joins me in a shriek of delight. All our composure is lost. We hug, kiss, and revel in her unexpected news. I am sweating and my heart is beating fast. We hold each other's hands as we walk along the river which runs through the center of Monbijoupark. We absorb the warmth from the sun above. Friends and congregants mill within their own smaller circles of intimate friends throughout the park. Young mothers hold court with their infants and prams, and older retired men play chess on benches. Berlin is home to many affluent Jews who do not hide their Judaism, unlike Galicia where rampant intolerance made mindful Jews worship privately. Here, little boys wear *yamakas* and their *tallit* hangs out from underneath their shirts when they sprint across the expansive rolling greens.

The park is designed as a refuge from the bustling city. The Riverwalk, lined with white-washed wooden planks, offers a unique vantage point of the park. The city lies beyond the rolling green, but you can't hear it over the rustling water along the riverbed. The earthy smell of moss reminds me of childhood. Birds are tending to their nests in the tall oak trees. Nature's reverie helps me release the pent-up energy I am plagued with lately.

"I am thinking of Dobromysl. Life was simpler there. I am running with Gittel and Henie through the fields of pink and yellow wildflowers as tall as I am."

Renee says, "I love the idea of wildflowers being as tall as I am," grabbing my hand.

I have never known her to lack friends or attention. Renee's confidence guides her life. A crying child captures my attention, and a mother responds to her son's whimpers. A group of toddlers run down a small hill and squeal in delight. Young mothers watch, enraptured by their napping infants who lay undisturbed in the open air.

Renee raises her chin in their direction and says, "I'm terrified of that. What secrets can you tell me?" whispers Renee.

"Seltzer aids in digestion, as does hot water with lemon in the morning and after dinner."

My shoulders hang loose and my hips sway spaciously. Before pregnancy, kind glances and greetings from men were a daily occurrence.

It is refreshing how I am invisible now.

"I can't see my feet. If I drop a brush or a fork in the house, I do not pick it up. Bending has become complicated."

Laughing, she says, "Really? I should not laugh. That is not nice. In a few months, you'll be laughing at me because I won't be able to bend over."

"In the beginning, I was nauseous. In the second trimester, I ate everything in sight. I let my body tell me what it needed and didn't bother with anybody else's advice or suggestions. My hips have spread, I'm not happy about that, but I walk a lot. I let my body tell me what it needs. My breasts are sensitive. With six weeks left to go, I find it impossible to stop my ankles from swelling. You can't eat pickles or soft cheese. Whitefish salad, although delicious, makes me retain a lot of water."

Renee hesitates and looks like she is choosing her words carefully, "Herbert isn't interested in how I feel, but he is thrilled with the pregnancy."

"I'm sorry. Herbert's missing out - he loves you. Not all men can be everything we need."

I want to comfort Renee, but I can't relate. Aron's support has never wavered, and I wouldn't know how to go through all these changes alone. I am thankful for the relationship Aron and I have built.

"I allow myself to walk like a duck when Aron isn't around."

Laughing, Renee says, "Like right now?"

I give her a little shove. Museum Island is right in front of us. Bicycles litter the small footbridge that connects the island to the park. Renee and I hold hands and cross the bridge. We approach my favorite part of the park, the Palace, once the home of emperor Wilhelm I.

Walking through the ornate architecture of the palace, I feel like a commoner trespassing.

"Shall we take a quick walk to the Palace?"

"Not today. I don't want to leave my mother for too long," says Renee.

"Marjem, whatever happened with the piano debate?"

"I told Aron I don't play well, that I would rather send our child out to Mrs. Bauermann for piano lessons."

"Your mother would love a little artist," Renee says.

"We live in Berlin. He can be whatever he wants."

Renee inquires, "Are you going to get the piano?"

"What do you think?"

"It's nice that Aron wants to fill his home with music."

Aron did not have an easy childhood. He worked from a young age, like Papa, and created himself from nothing.

"You're right," I say.

"I should support his dreams for our son."

The ducks clamor out of the water, chasing after stale bits of challah. Their quacking and the downy softness of their feathers satisfies me. My earliest memories in Berlin are of Henie crying, Mama pleasing her, and Maurice and Francois chasing Gideon across the bridge.

"Our children will grow up together. They will run along these paths and feed the ducks. They will visit the museum to research school projects, and one day have their own families," I say.

Renee stops and her face is pale.

"Let's sit down," I say, and I take her arm in mine.

I reach into my pocket and open a linen napkin with cheese and slices of apple. I place one in my mouth and hand one to her.

"Eat," I instruct. She eats and closes her eyes.

"Pregnancy changes everything. You never know when you will feel winded. I keep small snacks on me at all times." She smiles and takes the second piece of apple. I thank Aron for thinking of me and my needs. I am incredibly lucky. "Francine bought a bigger apartment after she gave birth to her third child," says Renee.

"I see that look in your eye, and now you're biting your lip. You have something to say which is not kind. You're trying to figure out if you should put your breath behind those words."

"It's amazing to have a friend like you who understands what I'm thinking, knowing I don't want to say the words out loud. I should not judge. She's a lovely woman with beautiful children and a happy marriage."

"Marjem, I don't spend the way she does. It makes me uncomfortable how much she spends. It's none of my business, but it bothers me."

"How did my mother manage in Dobromysl on a farm in the wilderness with six small children? Before moving to Berlin, she never walked inside a library, a museum, or a theater."

"Savages."

She laughs to take away the sting of the word.

Chapter 71
July 1932 Berlin, Germany
Marjem Rechtschaffen

As Helena Auster enters my store, the SS hens straighten their backs, and their mouths reshape into obsequious smiles. Their façade is a feeble attempt to mask their acerbic whispers. Helena is not fooled. She carries herself with the quietude of one born into immeasurable wealth. I doubt she has ever hung up her own coat. A fierce and competent woman, it is rumored she made royalty wait on her once. Her chestnut waves bounce beneath a wide-brimmed blue velvet hat. She strides towards me, ignoring the hens who want to meet her gaze. Her smile reveals a small chip on her bottom front tooth. Her fashion sense is pure Parisian; the evidence is in the tailored lines of her rust-colored dress. Her captivating sea-green eyes, outlined in celery-and-cream eye shadow, look luminous. I notice the hens leaving the store. Perhaps they sense a threat and know a quiet exit is the best kind.

"I'm interested in the small pillows stuffed with fine ostrich feathers for my couch," states Helena.

Her request is simple, but she puts me on edge.

Working through my jitters, I say, "We have different kinds of feathers for various applications. Our feathers are the finest products in Europe from vetted and reliable sources. If paperwork is necessary for authenticity, that can be provided."

She places her white-leather gloved hands up, "I like the sound of your professionalism."

Taking a breath, I realize I am holding mine.

"We received a new shipment -- small and large feathers for duvets and pillows."

Regarding a list she's removed from her clutch purse, she squints her eyes.

"Where are my glasses?" she says, opening her bag again and removing a small pair of glasses in golden frames.

"I want a set of wedding sheets, a winter duvet, and four pillows."

She looks up at me, folds her list, and places it back in her clutch.

"That shouldn't be an issue."

I collect a few samples in my arms and ask, "Do you have a color in mind for the duvet? Are we reupholstering old pillows or creating new ones?"

She clenches her hands momentarily and then removes her gloves. While she considers my questions, I pour her some black tea. I add a slice of lemon on the side and there's honey in a small jar next to the steeping water. Her posture changes when she cocks her head to the left.

She regards the tea and says, "Your store is quite lovely."

As she clarifies her order, my agitation fades. We talk about her likes and dislikes in colors and fabrics, which reveal a lot about a person. Not only what her tastes are, but how those tastes were first created. A personal history unfolds when discussing décor. I like her. Her manner is serious and organized. Her beauty is intimidating. She is confident and considerate. After the second cup of tea, I feel a connection.

From then on, she visits often and comments on my regular flow of customers. She is impressed with the business and brings every out-of-town guest she knows to the store. Each one seems to outdo the one before. They buy a new duvet, a set of sheets, and matching pillowcases to ship home – Paris, London, Hamburg, Brussels. Each friend waits for Helena to give them a nod of approval before they make the purchase. Until she gives the nod, they keep ordering more merchandise. Every transaction that is due to Helena, is noted in the ledgers. I would be naïve to be unaware of her importance.

The front door bursts open and Helena says excitedly, "Marjem, a telegram demands my attention. I'm hosting an early Christmas Soiree; I'll need linens for a formal dinner of thirty people."

She is visibly agitated.

"I need paper," she says, and I hand her an empty order form. She looks at me and her face changes, "A high-ranking government official will be in attendance."

I take a step backward. My mind clears as the room spins. I sit down to collect myself. Squeezing my inner thigh with my nails causes enough pain for me to focus.

Taking in a deep breath, I say, "Helena, come and have a seat. Let me get us some tea."

But she is the one to walk to the door and flip the sign to CLOSED.

"You look like you saw a ghost, Marjem. I'll get the tea," she says with a laugh. Helena walks into the back of my store and gathers my teapot, tea, lemon, and honey.

"And strudel," I say.

She once confided in me how she craves privacy. These days, I close the store to give her that privacy when she needs it, and now she is comfortable enough to close the store herself. A placid atmosphere is better for everyone.

"Marjem, you are a class act," declares Helena.

Walking towards me with my tea and strudel, making herself at home, like family, I can see she is a true friend. She does not need to do what she is doing. She has all the friends and family she needs or wants. She reaches for a bar stool I keep by the window and carries it over to the counter.

After removing her jacket, she confides, "I would never object to a slice of your strudel."

With a sideways smile I say, "No one can resist."

Helena and I are about to create an order which will bring in a month worth of revenue in one day. She is bringing the Nazis literally to my front door with an event like this. The situation is so dangerous, yet I know we will be alright. I pinch my cheeks when she is out of sight to give them color.

"Your strudel tastes like apple compote baked into rings of cinnamon and brown sugar pastry swirls. Oh, if you added chocolate, I could open up a bakery and sell it!" laughs Helena. She stares at me in great surprise.

"Thank you."

She places two plates and two cups before us. She slices the strudel and I pour the tea. We have developed a shorthand relationship with one another.

"Let us work through the order. Aron can handle the delivery. Just tell me what you need. I always order extra in case."

We break down the order and drink our tea. A bite of strudel here and there helps me push down my nerves. I am planning the order for the party, but I am not going. What an ego I have. To think I would be at the party. I am a vendor. A friend of the hostess but a vendor, nonetheless.

Helena starts with the linens.

"The linens are the canvas, you know, for the entire table. Envision old-money charm, Marjem - we will go with a bone color. It will make any choice of dishes pop with splendor. Let me paint you a picture. Better yet," she grabs the order form and draws a large oval.

"Here is the basic plan for the table."

She begins to craft a story that will be told through the right set of platters, centerpieces, and small side dishes. Her vision is like nothing I have seen or imagined before. Never having attended parties at castles, I could not grasp the grandeur. It is exciting to be a part of the planning for such an event. Helena is an intoxicating fountain of information.

"The Reich requested this party," she explains, and my mouth grows dry.

Helena continues talking, but I stop listening. This happens when I am anxious. Mama called it daydreaming, but daydreaming sounds pleasant. This is a loss of time. I do not know what I have missed out on until it is too late, and then I have no idea if it was important. It is unsettling.

My heart hammers in my chest. I think I need to go to the bathroom. Shifting uncomfortably, I ask Helena to describe the place setting.

"Formal. Thirty people and ten waitstaff. I will purchase two Christmas trees, which I will fill with hundreds of white candles wrapped in brown paper. The trees will bookend the dining room table. Bright red delicious apples and fresh gingerbread men will add pops of color amongst the candles. I have hired a four-piece orchestra to greet my guests in the foyer. There will be champagne and two types of red wines: one light, bright, and aromatic, the other dry with hints of melon and grapefruit."

"I'm writing as fast as I can." I remark.

"I'm inviting the Kaiser sisters, the Staubers, a few high-level SS and their wives, a Prussian vet, and an American actor."

She winks and grabs my arms, "and you and Aron. I promise you'll have a wonderful time," says Helena.

How can we go to a party where SS officers are in attendance? Could we be arrested? Doesn't Helena know I am

Jewish? I am not sure what to do; if I tell her and she already knows, I might risk insulting her. Helena strikes me as a person in the know. She would not walk into a situation and not know who the players in the room are.

"Thank you for the invitation."

"I will also send over a lovely girl who can take care of Manfred for the night. You can stay out late and indulge. The next day you can sleep in, and the girl will prepare breakfast," instructs Helena.

"You're too kind, which isn't necessary. I don't have anywhere for her to sleep," I admit.

"She can sleep in the baby's room if there is one, or the kitchen, no matter. It's resolved."

She speaks with finality. After a few cups of tea and an entire strudel eaten, the order for an elegant Christmas dinner at Helena's is now complete.

Chapter 72
July 1932 Berlin, Germany
Aron Rechtschaffen

Dear Abba,

The loss of Marjem's father has been a tremendous blow to the entire family. Although Marjem and I live in Berlin while the rest of her family is in Holland, we still feel their pain over here. Marjem's youngest brother David was about to embark on a new venture and move to Belgium to live with his older brother Gideon. But David changed his plans and remained at home with his mother. The entire family is grateful for this, but we also understand David deserves a chance to find his own path in life.

Our baby Manfred's makes me happy. He is the best of me and the best of my beautiful Marjem. When I take him on a walk with me, I explain the entire world to him.

He is learning all the time. Having a child like him makes me a better person.

I love my life here in bustling Berlin, but I crave the solitude of life on a farm, where your time awake and asleep is scheduled by the sun. I know I made the right decision moving to

Berlin, finding a beautiful woman, getting married, and start-ing a family. All those were wonderful choices.

I would prefer not to spend time worrying about how I can maintain what I have. I want to simply enjoy what is around me, work hard, provide, and grow ancient with my Marjem by my side. The baby just spilt milk on the business ledger. I'll write more soon.

Love, Aron

Chapter 73
May 1932 The Hague, Holland
Amalia Eisner

Dearest Marjem,

Each morning, I wake and think of you. I count down the days until my grandchild is born. In the countryside of Dobromyl, through tall grass and dirt roads beaten down by centuries of use, I carried you inside of me in search of a river cool enough to relieve my swollen ankles and toes. Summertime was spent in the water until my feet and hands would shrivel up. Once we arrived in Berlin, while pregnant with David Joseph, I walked along the river every day at Monbijoupark. Mozes bought me Epsom salts to relieve my bloated feet. Your father found a way every day to make me more comfortable. On the weekends he'll make me a cup of tea around three o'clock in the afternoon because he knows I'm tired. Every morning when I saw his face I smiled. He belonged to me, and my life made sense with him in it. To me, it comes down to the partner you choose in life. Your father came from a place where being Jewish defined him. He could not own land and he watched his father slave away for an unintelligent goy.

Galicia did not allow him the chance to feel dignified. Lack of opportunity filled him with frustration. He didn't want to raise his family in a place where neighbours and countrymen hurt one another in the name of religion. He worked hard and saved money, built a good reputation, and made connections. We were a great team. While he travelled for work, I took care of the rest. Our partnership worked. When he heard rumblings, he found the opportunities, then acted. When we heard the Russians were coming, we left Dobromyl. Their pogroms wiped out entire villages and townships. Some lucky townspeople disappeared to Siberia or Kazakhstan. Others never made it out alive. When we left Galicia, we told no one. He bought train tickets and bribed a landlord in Berlin to get our first apartment.

Once he was in, he worked fast to fit in. It was not easy when we immigrated. Mozes wore the same suit, shirt, underclothes, and shoes every day. I soaked and mended his socks well beyond what I ever could have imagined. You children do not remember that time, and I am proud of that. You all thrived. Now you own your building and have a growing ostrich feather business. I want to make sure you and Aron stay safe.

Take care of each other. Your younger brother David is doing a wonderful job taking care of me. My days are spent either with Henie or Gittel. I miss your father every day. No matter what happens, I turn to tell him and forget he is not there. Sleeping through the night is difficult. I slept beside your father for the better part of forty years.

When I awake before sunrise, I lay in bed, and I talk to him. I tell him what is wonderful in the world. I believe he can see me in heaven. Life must have humor, dignity, and kindness. If these basic tenants are missing, then living lacks pleasure. The love your husband has for you is better than a best friend

and better than a lover. You choose a great partner because one day your life might depend on him.
His life is you and there is nothing that makes me feel safer than knowing that.

Love, Mother

Chapter 74
February 1933 NYC, New Yok
Karl Eisner

Dearest Marjem,

I write to you because life here in the United States is exciting. In a mere three years, the economy turned around. The President of the United States, Mr. Roosevelt, aka FDR, is an inspiring man who believes in the greatness of Americans.

When Americans were running to the bank and pulling out their money, FDR declared a four-day bank holiday. A few days later, FDR appeared on television and hosted a series of conversations with the American people. He called them fireside chats. This program created confidence in the government. He spoke directly to the American people like they were his own family.

He appealed to their sense of security and asked everyone to stop taking their money out of the banks. He said our nation cannot heal if we live in fear. Would you believe that millions of people redeposited their money to the banks? He shared the State of the Union with its citizens. He established trust and the American citizens respected him for it. I think New York City is the best city in the entire country. If you listen to the people around me, they all seem to believe the same thing. I wonder if that is an American sensibility?

New York City is filled with different nationalities and religions. When you move to New York, you become part of the melting pot. You keep your faith and your customs, even in public, but certain standards must be maintained, and overall society must work together. FDR could be an elder back in Perehinske. He is a community man. He thinks like an engineer and when faced with a problem, he climbs inside and works his way out. He is also capable of looking at a situation from the top down.

FDR established at least a dozen new public works programs. Tens of thousands of good people are returning to work. The country is bouncing back, and productivity is on the rise. This is the time for you to consider coming to America. I have made a life for myself here. I have never gone out of business even within the chaotic years of the financial crisis.

In the fog of financial instability and unemployment, a single voice is emerging, and Adolf Hitler is winning the hearts and minds of the German republic. He is not a general nor is he a Bavarian aristocrat. He has cast himself as an everyman who through education, military service, and aspiration has risen to the rank of chancellor. He represents the future of Germany. The old guard failed the people before, during, and after the war.

The nation will stand behind him, and the democratic process will lead Germany back to greatness with him at the helm. His charisma is unparalleled. If his goals align with yours, there should be no problem, but there is a touch of fanaticism about Adolf Hitler.

He tries to keep it at bay, but it could consume him and those around him. A man who craves power as much as he does is dangerous.

America should be your future. When you come here, I'll move your family into my house. Aron and I will work in the store, and you can help raise the children. If there is any additional free time, you can do extra work at the store. You will save money quickly. Then you can launch your own business and get your apartment.

You and Aron should consider it. I will open an application on this side of the ocean. I will sponsor your family and we could all live in beautiful New York City together.

Stay safe and continue to write to me.

We all love your letters

Chapter 76
March 1933 Berlin, Germany
Herman

I walk down the stairs and knock on Aron's front door. "Aron, open up. Grab your hat. We're headed to the beirgarden."

Marjem opens the door and smiles. She hands me the baby, freshly washed and swaddled. A halo of golden waves frames her heart shaped face.

"Would you like something to eat before you take my husband out?"

"No thank you, Marjem."

I kiss Manfred on the forehead. Aron passes Marjem, kisses her on the cheek, and takes the baby from me.

I turned to Marjem, "I won't have him out late."

Marjem heads back inside and Aron locks the apartment from the outside. The night is warm and the stillness in the air feels like a light spring jacket.

As we approach the beirgarten, I say, "Herman, I enjoy your friends even though our political differences are vast."

"Aron, they love their children. Just like you love Manfred. They take great pride in being Germans. They shop in your store."

"They know my beautiful wife."

Aron's face flashes in fear. I stop abruptly. He has nothing to worry about. My friends would do nothing to harm him and his family. I've made it clear to them that Aron, Marjem, and Manfred are family.

"They do not know that you are Jewish. I disagree with most of the things they say, Aron. But we all try for each other. We show up and are loyal friends. There will come a time when they'll figure it out."

"You think so?"

"Yes, I do, Aron. By then, they'll question the validity of their own beliefs."

My friends Allen and James are waiting for us at the Biergarten. As soon as we enter, brotherly hugs and handshakes are exchanged, and we all sit down together and order a round of beers.

I say, "I'm starving. I want some of that weird brown Russian soup they have here. The one that has little bits of unidentifiable meat and the scraps of every vegetable leftover from the rest of the week."

Burr jabs me. "You've never met a soup you didn't like."

Aron laughs with Alexander and Gregory. Their familiarity warms me. I want Aron and Manfred to have friends when they're old who they've known forever. People who know all the in-between and don't need an explanation as to why you feel the way you do.

"You don't make the soup sound appealing," says Aron.

Herman says, "You're missing out! I know it sounds disgusting, but it is hearty and delicious. Let's have some pretzels with hot mustard."

The beautiful barmaids weave through the tables and deliver beer. Four beer steins are placed on the table. James takes a bite of a pretzel and finishes his beer in one gulp. It is an impressive display of gluttony.

Allen says, "Herman, it's great to see you. Let me introduce you to my friends Samuel and Joseph."

The men exchange handshakes and join us at the table. Samuel stands up and waves his arm in the air. He gets the attention of the waitress and holds up six fingers.

Joseph says, "did you order some food for the table or just beer?"

James says, "Yes, we've ordered soup, bratwurst, pretzels and hot mustard."

Aron says, "Sounds like a feast to me."

Joseph walks over to the kitchen.

James says, "Did you hear about the Reichstag fire?"

Burr looks at him and says, "You would have to live under a rock to not have heard about the fire. The question remains, who started it?"

Gregory walks over and sits down, dipping a big piece of pretzel into the hot mustard, and says, "We need a doer. A thinker is great when you are building the ideals of a society. We need an organizer."

I am distracted by the amount of hot mustard on his pretzel. I am convinced it will be too hot and he will burn the skin off the top of his tongue.

The waitress walks by, and I reach out gently.

"Would you be so kind as to bring to the table a plate of carrots and celery?"

She says she will be right back.

Allen says, "The communists set the fire."

Joseph returns with a platter of treats directly from the kitchen. Every appetizer they offer is on the platter before me.

The waitress arrives and places another eight pints down on the table.

Joseph smiles and turns to Samuel and says, "What did I miss?"

I ask, "How can you be so sure, Allen? What would the communists gain from setting the fire? They already had the largest share of control in the parliament. They've been hounded by the Nazis for quite some time, and they never engage."

Burr says, "The communists have the power. They have nothing to prove and more importantly, nothing to gain."

I am shocked. "Burr, are you working for the ..."

James interrupts, "The fire gave Nazis power. In order to control Germany, one must have control over Berlin. Munich is not enough. To burn the parliament down to the ground is an act of treason. You can deconstruct it anyway you like, what remains is who has the most to gain?"

Allen says, "I did not fight in the war to have my civil liberties taken away." James and Burr agree.

"There's a lot of beliefs they have in common. The primary difference is that James did not lose his son during the war."

"The Nazis are trying to protect the Germans. They believe the Communists are going to stage a coup."

Burt takes a large swallow of beer. Aron opens his mouth and then closes it again. Good boy. Better to be quiet and listen. There is no reason to find holes in people's arguments. The point is to understand where everybody's allegiances lie. It is not a crime to listen. I would like to ask Aron who he thinks set the fire.

Allen says, "My son Jeremy is a proud member of the Nazi party. He says the organization is very well run. The trifecta of power will enable the Nazis to have their message made clear. Rohm runs the SA, Himmler controls the SS, and Göring oversees the Gestapo."

Gregory says, "I think the country would be much happier without Marxism."

"Gregory, I think you are right. Haven't you noticed the popularity of the Nazi party has exploded over the past couple of months? It appears many citizens felt threatened by communism and the Nazis' ideals appear to be looked on favorably by the Volk," I say.

Aron continues to say nothing. But if he is not careful, they will start to take notice and then wonder where his allegiances fall. Gregory stands up to excuse himself. James says, "Greg, are those knees bothering you again?"

Gregory says, "Every goddamn day since the war. I sat in those trenches either a minute, a day, or a week too long. I have never been able to get rid of the stiffness. My wife rubs my knees every night with Vaseline. The doctor says to me, the more I walk, the less pain I will have. I told the doctor that when I walk, I'm in pain, so I should just sit down." Burr snickers.

James replies, "Doctors don't know anything. They make it up as they go along, and they practice on us poor fools."

Aron nods. Jim raises his beer to Aron, and they toast each other. Burr stands up, waves the waitress over, and says, "My men are becoming melancholy. We need more beer."

He proceeds to bang his beer stein on the tabletop. He is not doing this to be offensive, he is simply drunk. This is what the men do in the beer garden.

One man begins to sing an anthem. Men stomp their feet with their hands on their hearts. The beer garden is filled with patriots. This is magnificent. I do not agree with most of the men in this room, but I do love my country. When the patriotism dies down, we drink another round of beers and continue talking.

James turns to Aron and says, "What a bunch of fools you must think we are. Old men who do not have a place in the world anymore, but still cling to their youth. I was watching you listen to the rest of us boast about our knowledge of current events."

I look at Aron, but he does not appear to be uncomfortable at all; he is an impressive boy.

"James, if I were given a choice on who to back, between Göring or Himmler, I would have to back Göring for this one reason: my brother is a fighter pilot. He says that Göring's ability in the sky is God-given. The way he navigates a plane is the same way a conductor directs his orchestra."

Burr says, "That reasoning is sound."

Chapter 76
1933 Paris, France
Maurice Eisner

I haven't seen Heather for at least two weeks. She went to the countryside to find more recruits. Young girls around twenty-two who most people look right through. They should be pretty but not wildly attractive. Heather looks for girls who are smart. France depends on the information these girls can obtain. I sit by the window of our favorite café sipping coffee waiting for her to arrive.

My beauty rushes in, "Moe, I missed you so much."

She's all passion and no pause.

It would be easier if I could tame her, but I wouldn't want her any other way.

"Heather, lightning struck and seared your name on my soul."

Heather laughs and brazenly mocks my love. I feign horror and she laughs harder.

"Are you ready to come with me on a short trip?"

The two of us can wander along the countryside like newly-weds. Her mission is surveillance. Is there police intervention near the border? Are there spots to slip through? Are we traversing a forest? Hills? Open plains? What's the easiest way across the Germany border? Do they fear communism? Heather is detailing new protocols she must endure to protect herself. The new recruits must be physically fit. Can they handle subterfuge? Are they clever enough? Can they remain cool under pressure? Surveillance is subtle but sabotage takes a more delicate hand.

"The storm ravaging Germany has just begun."

I reflect for a moment, "Unemployment is over twenty-five percent. The economy couldn't be worse."

"Moe, your sister is in Germany with a baby. Losing my daughter convinced me time is no longer infinite."

Heather fumes, "these feral boys are bereft of role models. The Nazis foster these youth and turn them into a private police force. Drunk on power, these hoodlums roam the streets tormenting good citizens. Who is teaching these boys how to become men? How to appreciate and love a woman?"

"Heather, they prey on the weak. Their hatred emboldens the marginalized. These degenerates should remain hidden. Society should not tolerate fundamentally immoral beings."

I've seen disorganized brown shirt SA thugs that no one can seem to control. There is the SS, which functions as a paramilitary force, a private army if you will, and now there is a third group of detectives and intelligence officers called the Gestapo. Their directives are secret, the power is growing as are their numbers.

"I couldn't agree more."

Heather leaves abruptly without saying goodbye. It's very Irish of her. Heather is singular in her goal to make a better world for children. Something clearly came up. Raquel enters the café. An air of arrogance surrounds her. Brilliant and well-read, she can change a tire, run a telephone switchboard, and do it all in a cocktail dress and heels without breaking a sweat. Her physical beauty attracts many, but she doesn't care. That's the power the truly beautiful have. They know they're beautiful, they don't need to be told they are and they shun compliments which highlight their beauty.

For them, their beauty is a burden.

She motions to the waiter for a fresh cup of coffee. Remaining silent until the coffee comes, she liberally pours in cream and adds two spoons of sugar.

"They will be rationing us soon enough. You wait and see. We'll have to survive without coffee, chocolate and God forbid cigarettes." Raquel trained Heather.

She plots and schemes beneath traders' noses.

She turns to me and says, "we're going to Belgium. The borders are open. Military action in Germany is under-reported. We need to draw maps and follow border patrol movements. Identify porous locations to slip through the border undetected."

Women like Heather and Raquel are impossibly brave. There's no training for them to undergo. They're merely told to be brave. So much is expected of them without any guarantee of survival in return. Raquel is tough but fair and wouldn't ask anybody to do something that she wouldn't do herself.

She's intolerant and sometimes harsh to the weak and feckless, but that's because she believes in what people are capable of doing.

She doesn't care for excuses; she responds to solutions.

Raquel's sister Leah comes in. Two lovely Jewish women who give their lives over to charity every day. Well-connected through the synagogue they show up and make a difference. Leah has a gentler touch than Raquel.

They are like two sides of the same coin, both precious and important yet uniquely identifiable. Leah is good at numbers and fast calculations. Her perception of distance is unparalleled and she's an excellent cartographer, but she will take the uninspired by the hand and explain to them why it's essential they care and take action. She is one of the best recruitment devices they have. Everyone she meets wants to be her friend and in order to do that you must step up and work towards a better tomorrow.

Chapter 77
May 4, 1933, Berlin, Germany
Aron Rechtschaffen

Marjem rushes into the room, panting, "Samuel Eichtstein was arrested by the SS last week."

She takes a breath and allows me to absorb the news.

My blood pressure soars.

"Yesterday, Beatrice delivered a substantial bribe to the SS administration office as instructed. Her reward was her husband, Samuel, in the gutter next to the front door with both eardrums punctured."

I can't imagine what she went through when she heard about this? The depravity is too close to home and the story rolls over me like a cement truck. Marjems alarm is palpable. An explosion is right in front of me and I need to absorb the impact to help save my wife.

Samuel Eichtstein's family and I have a long history.

They own a large warehouse in the industrial plaza. His family business began in the 1890s. When I first arrived in Berlin, I saw a man tripping over gravel. I dropped my packages and ran to catch him before he hit the ground. His gait was pinched, and he reminded me of my father. There was a lot of wisdom behind his sharp and clear eyes. I walked him home. When Solomon's wife answered the door, she ushered me in before I could object. She served me a heaping bowl of hot stew with potatoes and carrots, and I dug in before my manners took over.

"Your generosity brings tears to my eyes and makes me miss my parents. You didn't need to feed me but you did. Thank you."

Herr Eichtstein laughed, looked at my plate, and smiled brightly, "Clearly your stomach knows more about what you need than your brain. I would've made you my roasted chicken and sweet honey cake for dessert if I knew you were coming."

I wanted to cry out of sheer joy.

After supper, Solomon walked me out and asked me if I wanted to see his warehouse.

"Our business has employed good, hard-working people since the beginning of the war. They're an extension of my own family."

That is what I am looking for. A place to plant my roots and belong to something greater than myself.

"No one should be alone in a big city like this."

His family became an extension of my own. When Solomon passed away in 1922 from wounds inflicted during the war, Samuel took over the business.

Marjem continues, "Beatrice said imposing men with chests the size of the door filled her vision. No light filtered past them. They pushed her aside and made themselves comfortable at her dining room table. The Gestapo demanded the entire family be present. They cataloged her possessions, showing great interest in their artwork and silver from dinnerware to candelabras. Their greedy paws left oily fingerprints on everything. The Brown Shirt took her mink fur coat from inside her closet."

"Thank goodness Beatrice and Samuel don't have a daughter. The Brown Shirt pigs ogle teenage girls. Marjem, I want you to sit down, take a breath, and start from the beginning."
She explained the entire story again but this time the words came out slower.
"Since Samuel's arrest, the entire neighborhood has been scrutinized. Her neighbors are afraid to talk to her.

******

The Nazis change the rules daily. Today Jews aren't acceptable teachers. They're driving intellectuals indoors and underground. When Jewish children returned to school, the school forced them to sit in the back of the classroom, behind an empty row of desks to separate the children. Hoping the Jewish family would be uncomfortable enough to no longer return. Jews are made to feel their religion is contagious like a virus. Two weeks later, twine rope was strung across the room separating the Jewish children from the rest of the classroom.
"Aron, is this going to stop? Everybody is going to wake up and realize they don't want to live around all this hatred. First Samuel's warehouse, tomorrow it's the rest of the block."
"They're acquiring industrial buildings for a reason. My reasoning says they want to stockpile goods they don't want anybody else to know about."
"I don't understand, explain it to me," she cries.
"It's illegal for Germany to remilitarize itself. If the Nazis are hoarding munitions or guns, it could become an international incident. Warehouses could be filled with silk for parachutes or blankets for soldiers."
"Or gasoline for tanks and trucks?"
"Exactly, Marjem. There could be barrels of oil or guns and rifles. If they're taking over warehouses, this is the kind of information you need to send to Maurice."

"But how can we possibly know what's going on? There is only so much I hear at the store. I understand how vital the information is. Helena keeps her ear to the ground, and we stay as informed as possible. Their deception is rampant, and it makes my head spin. Playing a calm person every day is exhausting."

I hug my wife, relishing her strength and bravery.

"How is Beatrice now?" I ask.

"She buried her wedding ring in her backyard in a tin can with her diamond earring studs. She gave her favorite winter coat and hat to her non-Jewish neighbor."

Beatrice put herself at great risk when confiding in Marjem. I know how trustworthy she is, but we live in a time and a place where morality is on a sliding scale. Loyalty and friendship don't mean anything if your life is being threatened or your loved ones are in peril. You will do anything to protect them.

"Beatrice has to be careful. She doesn't want to offend the wrong person thinking how dare a silly Jewish woman think she knows better than a good German."

"I don't want those dirty bastards touching any of my treasures."

"Marjem, they're just objects. They mean nothing." Marjem's face changes and she looks like she's a million miles away. That means she's hatching a plan. She walks into the kitchen and starts opening and closing cabinet after cabinet.

She wipes the same spot clean for nearly three minutes.

I say, "soldiers enjoy beer. I should start buying more beer and bring it along to all my deliveries. Especially the late-night ones, those men work the worst shifts; they might be friendly when it matters the most. If I make the relationships sweeter now, I'll be in the "pocket" when I need to be."

She turns slowly to look at me.

"Aron, were you surprised by what Beatrice said?"

"Surprised? Nothing the Nazis do surprises me anymore. You know better. You know not to talk. But you also know when you need to listen. Paranoia is a deadly bubble to live within. Feeling targeted by a powerful force, like the government, makes your world small."

"Aron, the Nazis came after her. She is in the thick of it."

"Marjem, Beatrice is a target. She has proof of their malfeasance. Do not shun her. If we do that, we are no better than them. Let us lead and not follow. One day, it will be our turn caught in their crosshairs."

I do not need to scare her any more than she already is.

"Taking the warehouse wasn't enough for them. They wanted to make Samuel's family suffer. They are sending a message. Resistance is futile."

Marjem whispers, "They want everything."

"Marjem, they'll come for the entire block."

The bloodthirsty thugs' stream through our neighborhood. Riding motorcycles, racing down streets, trucks peel by our home late into the night. Pounding jackboots shake everything that's within earshot. I wait for Marjan to fall asleep and then I suddenly climb out of bed, grab my baseball bat, and sit down in front of my son's door, waiting.

Chapter 78
July 1933 Berlin, Germany
Aron Rechtschaffen

As the sun streams through the sliver of curtain not pulled fully across the window frame, the day begins again. Marjem prepares breakfast with Manfred by her side. He holds onto her apron, cruising around, learning about the world with his Mama within his grasp. She is never burdened by his endless distraction. Manfred, our favorite henchman, charms our patrons during the busy afternoon hours before his nap. I can hear the two of them talking right now in the kitchen. Manfred happily babbles and Marjem talks to him as if she understands what he is trying to say.

"Good morning sweetheart. Yesterday, Herr Bavermen's wife came into the store. If she asks to see my samples one more time, without placing an order, I will lose my temper."

"You say you will, Marjem. But you and I both know you won't."

"She's sweet but she never stops talking. She raves about the new double seams on the duvets. She discusses craftsmanship like it is her field. She can never settle on a color. She even told me that last spring she gave her old duvets to the maid, which is exceedingly generous. The rich are frivolous. This winter, the forecast calls for lots of snow. A frigid and unforgiving winter would be hell without a marvellous new duvet to keep warm underneath."

I cannot help but laugh. Marjem told me this story countless times, but I cannot get over how well she impersonates Herr Braverman's wife.

"She sounds like a person who has plenty of means, but a real inability to pull the trigger and make a decision. Perhaps you should use your skills to influence her in the right direction. Today might be your lucky day."

I smile at her expression.

"Do I give special pricing on a bulk order of ten quilts? If she orders ten quilts, I will need to hire someone."

"Marjem, that is a good problem to have," I say.

"Her big mouth brings in a lot of business. She is a braggart, and her inner circle of women will not be outdone by one another. The more she broadcasts, the more orders will come in. The hens cluck and additional orders flood in. Aron, when they come to roost at our door, we'll make a record number of duvets this summer for fall delivery."

"You're exceptionally talented at this side of the business. You know how to read people and meet their needs."

"Let us hire two part-timers. We have friends who can use the work," suggests Marjem.

Everyone has mouths to feed.

"That isn't a bad idea, Marjem."

I propose we should hire one non-Jew, someone who specializes in zippers and buttons. Hiring someone outside of her circle is hard for Marjem to accept. She needs time to warm to this idea. But it makes good sense for our business.

"You should use your connections with the gatekeepers. Those are people we might need at some point. That reminds me, the new custom duvet you ordered for Herr Verlin is

ready. I will have a custom wrapped and then you can deliver it tomorrow."
"Did the matching set for her daughter Maya arrive?"
"Yes. Both arrived in plenty of time for the wedding."
"Marjem, our wedding gift is going to be the nicest."
She laughs delightfully.

"You were saying we Should hire a mother who needs some extra hours and is great with zippers and buttons."
"An elderly woman might be a good idea. Everyone appreciates when you help the elderly. She can work from home. You can handle that part. I will send examples and instructions." She looks away.

"I don't want any of them near my Manfred."

"Fair enough."

She looks back at me, her eyes hard and cold.

"I entertain the wives of the SS daily. They do not respect me because I work. I do not respect them because they do not. I command my own life and freedom when most women cannot. Most women have husbands who are afraid of their wives' power. They look down on me because I work but working allows me to command my life and freedom. I witnessed how they decorate their homes with open wallets. These women spend in ways I find embarrassing."

"They spend their husbands' money thoughtlessly," I say.

"They spend their own money thoughtlessly. If a husband does not allow his wife to work, then the money that he earns is for the entire family. That is how we live. One bank account. What's mine is mine and what's yours is mine."

She smiles at her little joke. I am glad she can find some humor in this.

"German men are vain. They want to be surrounded by beauty, but they are not interested in showing love. They are unfaithful to their wives as if it is part of their vows. All they want to do is outshine one another. Whoever's left standing at the end and is the most sparkly wins."

"Aron, use their weaknesses. I made you four new sets of pillows from the scraps of foreign fabric. No two sets look alike. Your men can give one set to their wives and the second set to their mistresses."

She walks over to me with her new pillows packed and ready for delivery. She touches my cheek.

Leaning in, she whispers, "Giving away these samples was a brilliant idea."

The recipients of the pillows find their way to our store. Then they buy duvets, sheets, and pillowcases.

"Just last week, Herr Bavermen's wife brought in two of her best friends. They walked around and around, touching everything - I had to refold things multiple times. They only spoke to each other, and I gave them their space. I brought out my teapot and some honey cake. One lady, the younger of the two, purchased three pillows. She said her beautiful new white couch was devoid of color. The way she said it made it sound like a modern tragedy." She grins.

"Marjem, I love it when you tell the story; your snarkiness is hilarious."

My hand strokes down her hair.

"I told her how envious I was of a brand-new white couch. The way she looked at me made me realize I had made her uncomfortable. I quickly followed up by saying, do you think exotic accent pillows would be suitable? She considered my question like an academic expert, and I knew I had her at that moment. She asked me to find her something that no one had ever bought before. To prove my authenticity, I showed her the fabrics. I told her I could have them custom-made and she could pick them up tomorrow. It would cost extra but the customization ensures that no one else will ever have those pillows."

"Tell me more."

"She asked if I could add a certificate with the purchase to validate the authenticity. I told her that was standard practice with original items, but at an additional charge. Not to be outdone by her friend, the other woman ordered three throw pillows for herself with the validation paperwork."

"These stories are golden nuggets, Marjem. We need to increase our imported fabric order this month," I add.

"Okay," she says.

She is not even looking at me.

******

Every night after dinner, she opens the books and runs through the numbers. Numbers relax her as they always have. She checks and then rechecks the figures to make sure each column is accurate. Her diligence is born from years of working at the bank.

Looking up, she says, "My older friends hesitate before coming into the store when they see the hens. I understand why they are nervous but that does not mean I do not miss them. Their jokes and presence provide me with a needed break during my busy day."

"I understand you miss your friends," I say, placing my arm around her shoulder.

"The streets are packed with foreigners, and these migrants fleeing Russia make the locals nervous. Lately, I see fewer faces that I recognize. The black hats and long beards belong in Perehinske or Rozniatow. They aren't even trying to assimilate."

Peasants from the farms of Poland and Czechoslovakia do not look or act like Berliners.

They reek of poverty and desperation. Emigration like this will tip everything in the wrong direction. The key is to not push your Jewishness onto anyone. Deeply religious Jews are not subtle. They create division.

They make people fearful.

"One lady in the store spoke of her sister who lives in Ansbach. She said mobs of unemployed veterans, communists, and orphans with nothing else to do fill the streets at night. The citizens stand by and watch the vulgarity and do nothing. These thuggish uneducated Nazi youth bully everyone. Are they going to bully us too?" asks Marjem.

She is not working on the books any longer. She is fully focused on me, her eyes wide and bright. Manfred is in bed and Marjem wants to talk.

"I've heard the same things from other men in the synagogue. Unemployment is rampant in cities such as Düsseldorf and Essen, yet the local chapters of the brown shirts leave their citizens at peace while only occasionally arresting a Jew to maintain order."

Chapter 79
August 1933 Paris, France
Maurice Eisner

Dear Marjem,

I miss you terribly. I'm afraid everything I have to say you already know. If I keep my fears inside of me, they will pollute all the good work I am doing here. Adolf Hitler is a venomous monster who must compromise to form a ruling coalition. The election proved how divided the people are. Are Germans happy? Is nationalism in the air inclusive? At some point unemployment will catch up with inflation and then no one will be able to buy bread.

I'm not coming up with this all by myself, like I said, I'm not the smartest person in the room. François brought the book to me. Adolf Hitler is not a genius, but he is thorough and relatively transparent about his disgust for Jews, gypsies, intellectuals, and religious institutions. He's charismatic and bombastic. Whilst he is young, thin, with soft features and very little facial hair, he becomes a non-threatening option to women and children.

The Volk are balancing on a precipice.

If dad were alive, he would come there himself and take you out of Berlin. Be the force he was and protect Manfred. Resist the opportunity to get in your own way. This is not the time to choose the hardest path.

The time to act is now.

Love, your big brother Maurice

Chapter 80
September 1933 Berlin, Germany
Marjem Rechtschaffen

The streetlamps cast a warm glow along the Unter de Linden. On the night of Helena's party, couples huddle beneath shared umbrellas and light fluffy snowflakes fall from the sky. This snow sticks to wool coats and holds its shape long enough to be admired. A horse-drawn carriage pulls away from Helena's curb as we arrive. Two motor cars are parked on the street. Aron rings the bell, and a butler opens the door. Two lady's maids approach and with German efficiency, remove our snow-laden coats and umbrella. Led into a smaller room, there is a plush velvet couch and smaller black leather benches for us to sit on to remove our galoshes, then through a narrow hallway overly decorated with old paintings lining the walls, another lady maid greets us. She presents a small bowl filled with scented water to refresh our hands. The second maid hands us plush hand towels. I want to smell my fingers but that would be tacky. Lavender and lemon notes fill the air, and a grand staircase leads us upstairs.

"Welcome," says a lovely maid dressed in a smart black shirt and skirt with a small white lace apron, offering a tray filled with tall crystal flutes of champagne.

The doorbell rings as we enter a larger parlor. Aron and I glance at one another and touch our glasses and are charmed by the ringing chime they create.

He whispers, "L'chaim," and winks at me while I take a long sip. Another maid greets us with a canape of smoked lox and capers on a toast square. Aron and I both take one.

I remind Aron, "Eat slowly, this might be the last food we see for a while."

Couples are engaged in conversation. A maid offers a tray of mini meatballs served on toasted rye in a pepper cream sauce to a man with a thick white mustache. Aron pops the smoked salmon into his mouth and waits for the meatballs to come closer. Mini quiches are being circulated and I can see Aron's eyes following the shiny silver tray.

"You don't know what else is to come," I say to Aron as he wipes pepper cream sauce from his lips.

I spot an evergreen branch decorated with cranberries balanced precariously on the top of the window frame.

"It feels like my own home, but so much nicer."

This from a woman in a lovely red satin dress. Her name is LisBeth Stark. She is married to a doctor and visited our store last month.

"I love that Christmas smell," replies a tall man in a tuxedo with a cane who walks over to another man leaning against the piano. LisBeth Stark kisses the man leaning against the piano, who must be her doctor husband.

A serving maid passes with Zwiebelkuchen – an onion cake made with ham, sour cream, and chives. The unctuousness of the cake is heavy, but it is a classic staple at formal dinners. Aron notices the cake, but I place my hand on his arm and mouth soundlessly, "Ham."

He turns away from the cake and takes another flute of champagne which is sweet and zippy.

"Helena promised a feast to impress," I confided in Aron.

"Marjem, the champagne is delicious. It's all about the bubbles, the smaller the bubbles the finer, the grapes."

"Where did you learn this new fact?"

"I heard a woman tell her friend over there. I should walk around and see what else I can learn."

"Go have fun," I jokingly suggest.

A brass-colored redhead with a flecked face says, "I hope we sing carols after dinner."

Her hair is set in finger waves and parted to the side. The clear beading along the cowl neck of her dress adds texture to an otherwise simple green silk dress. Unfortunately, silk is unforgiving in a fuller form.

"Her piano is too beautiful not to play."

"Just wait until drinks are served after dinner. We'll be singing wartime classics in no time," says a man in a military uniform.

Patrons from our store, like the Kaiser sisters, are here. They are Henrietta and Edith, Prussian nobles who are well-connected to the Reich. The Kaiser sisters are also active in the local art scene. Henrietta wears a long ivory gown with cutouts on the sleeves beneath her shoulder. The placement of a thin high-waisted seam under her bust creates a long line that leads the eye smoothly to the floor. Her matching silk gloves fitted on her hands and bunched just past her wrists add an unevenness against the softness of the gown.

"Marjem, you are a vision in cobalt blue," says Henrietta.

"Thank you, Frau Kaiser," I reply.

"You and Aron should call me Henrietta," she says, gesturing to her sister, "And call her Edith. Tonight, we celebrate together."

Edith grabs my arm and says, "Blue is your color. Your eyes are almost steel gray against your dress. I haven't seen that color anywhere."

"It's a gift from my mother in Holland," I admit.

"Her taste is splendid."

"Thank you, Edith," I say sheepishly.

I do not take compliments well from other women.

Aron says to Henrietta and Edith, "We are blessed to bring in the holidays with each other under such a lovely roof."

"Yes, we are lucky, indeed," Henrietta notes.

Aron takes my hand, and we walk down one side of the grand table. In the center of everyone's plate is a small card with their name handwritten in calligraphy. Helena's table plan matches friends with strangers to ensure a dynamic mixture of introverts and extroverts, political types, artists, industrialists, and actors. Helena told me all about the sitting arrangements last week.

"Marjem, you will sit across from Aron. I wouldn't want you to feel nervous," says Helena.

She leans in, "But you will be next to people you do not know. Which shouldn't be an issue for you since you run a thriving business and have to speak to people every day who you don't know."

"I appreciate the warning, Helena. I know your guests will be lovely."

Tonight, we will dine on royal Bavarian china dusted in gold leaf. The embroidered lace inlays in the tablecloths were well worth the time it took to locate. I called in a few favors to make that happen for Helena. She is worth it. She is such a good friend, and the table looks extravagant. As the light reflects off the chandelier's crystals, patterns dance across the walls. I feel transported into another beautiful world where champagne flutes overflow with fresh strawberries. Lifting a fork and sensing its heft, I confirm the silver is not plated.

Four forks for different courses lay to the left of the plate, and a spoon, three knives, and a bigger spoon on the right. The place setting is completed by a small finger bowl above the plate to the left.

"Marjem, the place settings are wonderful. Your mother would love to see this," notes Aron.

"This party is legendary. Everything she loves about the upper crust of Berlin is all here," I whisper.

A bell chimes and Helena emerges. Her gold metallic lame dress sparkles with shimmering glass beading. Her chestnut hair is fashioned into a sleek elegant upsweep. The keen application of cream-colored eyeshadow contrasts dramatically with the darkness of her magnified mascaraed lashes. When wearing a natural blush pink on her lips, Helena's elegant, contoured cheekbones are enhanced.

"Helena looks spectacular," I confide in Aron.

A high-ranking SS official sits to the right of Helena. The military presence in the room unsettles me. I am not unaccustomed to uniforms, but not at dinner. I do not socialize with people like this. Aron does not either, but he appears unfazed by it all. I know in my gut that he is on the alert. My stomach churns over and over. The SS official does not seem to notice anyone else, which suits me fine. On the other side of Helena is an American actor. He is gorgeous; six-foot-four, dark hair, light misty eyes. The arms on his suit tighten around his broad chest and biceps. It is undeniable how classically gorgeous he is. His hair is so black it is almost blue in the glow cast off the candles in the center of the table. Helena's eyes sparkle when he speaks to her. She laughs and throws her hair backward and exposes her neck. Any man would continue the conversation, if possible, to keep her attention. She plays with fire as she twirls her hair around her long slender fingers accented by a scandalous red nail lacquer. Why can't she entertain her movie star after the Nazi leaves?

Sitting to my right is a lovely woman of fifty wearing a fox stole around her shoulders and diamond drop earrings the size of almonds. She speaks to the Prussian veteran to her right. Her charcoal gray satin dress fits with a fluidity that compliments her fuller figure. Her grace shows me that she was born into wealth. The opulence around us is not special to her or the Prussian, but it is special to me and that is what separates me from them.

I want to touch Aron for reassurance; I feel insecure. I press my palms against the side of my dress. The dinner is about to begin. I find introductions can be awkward. Once I know someone, I am much more at ease. It is the initial conversation I find unappealing. Turning to her left, my neighbor introduces herself.

"My name is Emily Kruger. Helena is well known for her amazing parties, so I am sure we will get along famously. She is never wrong."

She extends her gloved hand.

"I understand that your family is in the ostrich feather trade."

Shaken by her brazen introduction, I breathe in through my nose and out my mouth. My heart beats in my chest.

"Nice to meet you, Frau Kruger."

"How exciting to meet a young woman running a business alongside her husband."

She regards the table and spots Aron.

"I find it all modern and very appealing. Helena maintains that you are old-school charming."

She says so much at once I am not sure what I should respond to.

"I am lucky to have someone who believes in me as much as Aron does," I say all of this before I can think my words through. My cheeks flush. I am a little embarrassed that I admitted so much to a stranger.

"Women nowadays have so much more freedom than our mothers did."

"My mother's life was full of adventure, but there are many others whose husbands chose for them," I say.

"That practice has defined women for centuries, unfortunately."

She looks down and clears her throat, "I think we have delved into a topic far too serious for this lovely occasion."

"I agree. I must say that your dress is lovely."

"I love fashion. Scarves, dresses, coats, and hats."

"We should talk more about hats," I say to keep the conversation moving. I like her.

She is intimidating but she seems smart. I bet there is a lot to learn from her.

"We'll talk later about accessories. Have you thought about other applications for your feathers and beads?"

"I love hats. My sister, Henie, attests that a hat, when accessorized properly, can change the entire mood of a dress."

Aron leans forward, "Hello, I am Aron Rechtschaffen. I see you have met Marjem, the brains behind our business."

"What a pleasure to meet you, Aron. Marjem and I are about to discuss accessories," divulges Herr Kruger.

"I will leave you to it," replies Aron.

"I would never dare interrupt a conversation between two beautiful women discussing accessories. That is well beyond my depth."

He smiles sweetly.

Frau Kruger reveals, "Strudel. Helena tells me your strudel is better than any bakery along the Unter de Linden. Every Jew I know has a special dish they can make."

She laughs at her confession.

Before I have a chance to recover, a short lady sitting askew to Aron discloses, "I detest oysters, but I love green turtle soup. The sherry sweetens the celery and onions. My friend, who is a chef, explained that the stewing process removes the brine aftertaste."

"The food has been exceptional so far," adds Aron.

The short lady is wearing a v-neckline red chiffon dress detailed in fine black beading. The diagonal seams create contours that allow for greater movement. Her custom-made matching hat is accented by flowers.

"She's wearing an original Bruyere," whispers Herr Kruger.

"She has to be, it's tailored impeccably," I respond.

"...for what it cost to have it made in her size," winks Frau Kruger. I am intrigued by Frau Kruger. Her tongue is sharp and witty. If I do not catch myself, I might laugh too loudly at her snarky retorts. Her understanding of people is keen. Thriving in inner circle status, it is unclear how far she will go to maintain that standing.

As wine and champagne glasses are refilled, the others join the discussion of turtle soup versus oysters. Leaning in towards Aron, I can see that he has not touched his soup. He smiles weakly and I know he will not eat a bite. Aron mutters, "I'm stuffed from the appetizers. I need a bubble." The guests settle into their meal and the room grows quiet with sounds of chewing. Helena's laugh captures my attention. She places her gloved hand on the American's forearm. Not to be outdone, the SS officer motions to the waitress to refill Helena's flute with champagne.

"How do you know Frau Auster?" asks a Prussian officer seated across from Emily Kruger.

My eyes meet his, which are bloodshot and hazy.

"Frau Auster is a top customer of our store."

Aron extends his hand to the Prussian officer.

"I see you have met the beauty behind my business. Allow me to introduce myself, I'm Aron Rechtschaffen and this is my bride Marjem."

Aron's presence fills the room around me, like a cloak around my shoulders. The oxygen feels lighter. Breathing is easier. "I'm Herr Karl Lenkeit. Please call me Karl. May I call you Aron?"

"Please do, Karl."

Karl wears an extensive array of medals pinned to his lapel.

"Helena is my sister. She tells me wonderful things about your store. I am pleased to meet you and your lovely bride, Marjem."

"Pleased to meet you, Karl. I see you are a military man."

Aron leans into Karl.

Karl's face brightens, "I was a pilot in the military. Now my eyes are no longer what they were."

"No one stays young forever. What matters is your experience."

I enjoy watching Aron navigate a room. He obtains information and allows people to talk about themselves. Typically, men like Karl, fit this profile.

"Hitler has me reorganizing the police force by integrating successful military tactics."

"That makes good sense. You must see some carelessness in the current system. Are you given the authority to make a swift change?" asks Aron.

"Lately, I receive complaints about the Brown Shirts; a rough and mostly drunken bunch of hoodlums who prey on the weak."

"They are a scourge on Berlin's beautiful streets,"

I say quietly. My palms sweat. I might have said too much. Taking a deep breath in through my nose and out through my mouth, I work at calming myself down. At night, when I try to fall asleep and feel unhinged, I place my hand on Aron's shoulder or chest. Feeling the slow steady rhythmic thumping of his heart through my fingertips reassures me.

"The Brown Shirts get in the way of good men being industrious," adds Aron.

"Yes, there are no easy answers. The SA will reign in the Brown Shirts. These measures should curtail the deviant and distracting behavior," enforces Karl.

"It's good to know that the problem is localized," adds Aron.

"Ah, but the Brown Shirts are well beyond Berlin. They are doing the initial hard work of cleaning the streets of the depraved, the mentally ill, and communists," confides Karl.

"There are Jews and communists all over Germany," proclaims one man to his wife near Aron's side of the table.

"Under the right hands-on leadership, the Brown Shirts can inspire the young and directionless," declares Erich.

I do not like Erich. He and Karl are dangerous and could create problems for Aron and me if they find out we are Jewish.

"The existing prisons are overwhelmed, and we need a greater institutional model for our prison network," declares Karl.

"The Brown Shirts are an ominous presence in front of my father's warehouse ..."

"That is Kirk Sommner, he and his family recently moved from Paris to Berlin," Emily informs me quietly.

"Perhaps the government will buy up some of these warehouse blocks and create industrial space for the military," reveals Karl.

Aron asks, "What would the Reich put in all the warehouses?"

Kirk replies, "Whatever the Reich wants to organize and rearrange in private, I suspect."

"Like uniforms, bedding, webbing, materials needed for supporting troops," adds Karl.

Aron presses on. "Hitler has a vision of a bigger role in the world for Germany."

"Any country worth their sovereignty needs a proper military," professes Karl.

Lena Klein, a new patron to our store who mixes with the SS hens, although her husband is non-military, confesses, "Erich, remember when they grabbed the old Jew and pulled his pants to the ground near the bakery we love?"

Flustered by the non-reaction to her statement, she drains her wine in one unseemly gulp. As her neck and cleavage flush, she relieves herself with a Parisian silk fan. The conversation continues to bounce madly around the table.

"I cannot visit that bakery anymore," says another woman.

"The police should leave the elderly to the ravages of time," avows Emily Kruger.

"Aron, we are opening a new prison called Dachau. Several well-paying positions in middle management need disciplined men. Good Germans can find honest and safe employment in Germany's new regime," adds Karl.

"But Karl, Marjem and Aron deal in linens and duvets. Perhaps you and Aron can discuss that?" instructs Emily.

"She is rarely wrong," admits Karl.

"I have several new work orders to fulfill. I can see why Helena brought us together."

Emily turns to me and says, "I must admit, I don't know how Helena knows the American actor. I wonder if he is intelligent. What movie did I see him in?"

We both turn and gawk at the American actor.

Snickering, I whisper, "Does it matter? We get to look at him now."

Emily smiles at me and nods. She appreciated the snark.

"Excuse me," says the lady, who announced earlier that she could no longer visit the bakery.

She leans towards me, "You know my sister, Joan. I am Irene Auster. You were generous to send that delicious chicken soup."

My mouth goes dry. A tingling sensation forms in the pit of my stomach. It does not hurt, but I want it to go away. The feeling intensifies and my palms grow sweaty. She knows I am Jewish. I do not want this crowd knowing anything about me. These people could be dangerous to us if they know.

"Hello, Irene," I say sweetly.

"Joan is a good and dear friend. We were sorry to hear about your mother's fall and your interrupted trip home."

She takes my hand in hers and winks, "it's comforting to put a beautiful face to a kind heart."

"Thank you, Irene." I turn to Aron to introduce him.

A hush covers the room like a blanket as the wait staff enters in two long lines and circles behind the guests. Each one holds a large silver platter and bowl. The butler clicks his heels, and each server places their platter down simultaneously. The synchronization of their movements enhances the overall elegance of the evening. Platters overflowing with potato dumplings, red cabbage, and caramelized chestnuts amaze my eyes. Two large bowls of creamy sauerkraut and chives pass in front of me. The servers return and each person receives a full plate of roasted duck in gravy with mashed potatoes and pickled carrots.

Additional plates of horseradish-roasted vegetables occupy the remaining space on the table.

"This meal looks delicious," murmurs Aron to his neighbor.

Karl stands and raises his glass, "To Helena, the most important person I know. Every day is better with you in it."

"To Helena!" chants the crowd.

Helena stands and raises both arms to quiet the chant.

"Tomorrow is never promised, but for tonight, we feast together in friendship."

She raises her glass to the crowd, and everyone toasts their neighbor. The room is festive and smells of cloves, pepper, fennel, and brown sugar. Someone clears his throat, and the room grows silent. Helena's priest asks everyone to bow their heads and hold hands. He blesses the food, gives thanks to God, and asks that we all live together with kindness.

"Lovely sentiments for the holidays," testifies Emily.

I dive into the delicious duck, and we discuss the spice profile in the gravy. The meat, topped with crispy skin, is cooked to a perfect medium with a hint of pink in the center.

"Marjem, did you try the creamy sauerkraut with chives? It's luscious and heavy like a hug," admits Aron.

He is happy and enjoying the food tremendously.

"The horseradish vegetables cut the silkiness of the sauerkraut," adds Emily.

"I add horseradish to all my meats," I admit.

"I have to be careful with richer foods."

"Horseradish aids with digestion. Same with cucumbers and white vinegar. Every meal should have a side dish of cucumbers."

"My mother ends every meal with hot water and lemon," states Karl.

Amused, I place my fork and knife down. We might have more in common than either of us knows. Helena's circle of friends is complex. Her brother is a highranking veteran of the Prussian military. Her favorite priest is from Vienna and her accent is Austrian. The more I try to see the tapestry of her illustrious history, the more the design unravels. How did she meet the handsome American actor? Why would she give a dinner for an SS officer and allow a brash American to openly court her attention? Unconsciously, I glance over to Helena, and she catches my stare. She raises her glass.

Mouthing the words is enough to communicate with her. "Wonderful evening!"

Hunter Miles, the gorgeous American actor, follows her glance and catches mine. His smile widens and his teeth gleam white. I sit up straighter and cock my head to the left. Do all the men in Hollywood look like him? Do all the men in America look like that as well? Emily continues to talk about the ingredients in the gravy. I agree that I would like to recreate these dishes at home. Helena was right, I feel like we have known each other for a long time.

"Helena is a woman of many gifts. She knows who should be in a room at any given moment. She is savvy, but she must be careful with that aptitude. Never underestimate someone like Helena," warns Emily.

"It is a talent to be able to work a situation to your benefit."

"Miles Hunter, you are not in America. You can't say such things," screeches Helena in delight from across the table.

"Live and let be," advises Karl to the man at the far end of the table.

"But be prepared to defend what is yours in case someone else wants to take it."

"Youth is a gift wasted on the young. When you are young, the world looks easy. When you get older, you know exactly how much effort must be invested to get what you want. The effort changes the intrinsic value. The weak are eaten alive when wealth, security, and power are not enough. Perhaps it is better to live simple and small? Save for a time when your life is flipped upside down and inside out," confesses Emily. She finishes her wine and a steward rushes over to refill her wine glass.

I am at a loss for words. Her honesty feels motherly.

"Aron and I used to take walks after dinner along the Spree in the Springtime. Now the atmosphere is unsafe."

"Smarter to stay in after dark nowadays," agrees Karl.

"Berliners don't cower and stay indoors well," says Emily. "We are proud and strong. Berlin is cosmopolitan and educated. The hoodlums are the problem."

"The war caused serious problems. Immigrants flooding into our country are polluting our society," adds Erich.

"Otto, you take me too seriously. I live in a different place. I don't have to be told what to think," explains Miles Hunter. Helena seems agitated. She pushes herself back from the table to create space between herself and the two men.

"A life lived in fear is not a life well-lived," summates Aron to Karl. Pulled back into Aron and Karl's conversation, I can see that Emily is upset.

"True, but a life without your Marjem is not a life you want. The ruthless brutes aren't contained for now, but that will change. The chancellor will not allow this situation to last for much longer; he is a serious man with plans to make Germany great again."

Otto Mueller's voice rises louder as Miles Hunter openly disagrees with him. Their argument now demands the entire table's attention.

"A leader like our Chancellor will give our people a country to be proud of again. The Great War hurt the psyche of German citizens. Battered men returned home and were thrust into poverty."

"That's what happens when you lose a war," challenges Miles Hunter.

His jet-black hair and smoldering dark eyes thrill me. Miles Hunter is provocative, like America itself. He speaks fast and loud and likes when all the attention in the room is on him. He smells like a ranch hand on a chicken farm. Maybe Americans like the smell of sweat and dirt but I would rather leave that smell on the farm in Poland.

"Are you saying we don't have the right to rebuild our nation?" seethes Otto Mueller.

"That is above my pay grade," softens Miles Hunter.

Helena exhales audibly.

"Young men raised without fathers need proper direction and purpose. There are men all over Germany who fit that description," alleges Otto.

"After the Great War, dozens of countries lost their fathers and husbands. War strips countries for generations in many unspoken ways," adds Emily.

Otto attests, "The Chancellor asserts that he can make Germany great again. I believe him. It is smart to trust him."

"He understands the German need for excellence," adds Helena.

"His expeditious response to the Reichstag got America's attention. Hitler weeded out the troublemakers," agrees Miles.

Otto finishes his beer and opens his mouth to speak but stops when Helena places her hand on his. He takes another sip. Otto does not like being challenged publicly. I enjoy watching him squirm. Innocent Jews squirm every day under the watchful eye of the Brown Shirts and their thuglike mentality.

"The Chancellor cleared the courts of Jews, thus ending needless litigation. The Jewish people lack discipline. The courts became congested under their leadership," explains Otto to Miles.

"There are a lot of Jews in Hollywood," mentions Miles.

"Even in America, the Jews invade and place themselves in everyone else's business. They make nothing. What is their talent? They profit from the industry of good men," asserts Otto.

"The Jews run the studios and negotiate contracts. I admire their taste in women; all their secretaries are young, gorgeous, blonde country girls. My favorite makeup artist is from California. She immigrated from Odessa with her mother and brother. All the stagehands are Irish or Polish, strong like oxen," certifies Miles.

Miles seems to like everyone but the Jews. I had not realized Americans hated the Jews as much as the Nazis. Uncle Karl paints a different picture in his letters from New York City. Aron glances at me strangely. He wants to ask me something but stops himself.

Edith interjects her opinion now.

"Several German manufacturers and producers are banding together under the guidance of the Reich. I was offered work on a new committee after the successful book burning."

"The upcoming Olympics?"

"I could have chosen the Olympics, but I was more interested in purging the Jews from the fashion industry," maintains Edith Kaiser. Emily and I both turn our heads in her direction.

"How do you get these families to sell and leave their businesses?" inquires Mia.

"That's simple," adds Karl, "Institute sanctions, forced buyouts, boycotts, pressure tactics."

He compiles a list in seconds.

My stomach tightens. Aron glares at me with thunderous eyes and my skin grows cold. Placing my fork down, I notice my wine. If I hold my glass with both hands, I can control the shaking. My heart races in my chest and I panic. I finish my wine and ball up my napkin in my hand until my fingers tingle.

Emily whispers, "Fashion isn't duvets and comforters. The Reich isn't interested in taking over your business."

Emily does not know that we are ready to leave Berlin as soon as the Nazis let us.

We are not naïve, but for now, we are still safe.

"...daughter was accepted to the Deutsches Mode-Institut," gabs Mia Strauber.

"How impressive. They have the full support of the Ministry of Propaganda. Establishing fashion independence from the

French is important for the German economy and psyche," reports Henrietta Kaiser. Edith nods in agreement.

Helena exclaims, "Count me out! Do you think a German could make this gown?"

She stands and twirls around in emphasis.

"Germany is elegant, not exotic. I love having the ability to choose from the best. Being a German allows me the access I desire. Isn't that exciting enough?"

She turns to Otto and pouts a little to emphasize her brazen opinion. He drinks her in and rubs her hand. She controls men the way Henie could. Whatever she serves up, they eat with delight.

"Leaving the League of Nations is the best move Hitler could make, in my opinion. We have the right to defend ourselves and re-establish our military. I don't believe other nations have the right to determine our fate," declares Karl.

"Let each nation stay out of each other's problems," adds Emily Kruger wiping her mouth and placing her fork and knife down.

The platters shuffle before us and desserts appear. Each person has a cherry quark and pumpernickel trifle served in a wine glass. Quark is a German specialty served with all kinds of fruits.

"Cherries and ducks enhance each other. Helena has chosen well again," I say to Emily.

The refreshing bite after the richness of dinner is a digestive relief. She also serves traditional dishes like Dresdner stollen, which is made from nuts, diced cranberries, apples, cherries, and pears soaked in sugar and baked into a cake.

"Your Dresdner stole is beautiful, Helena," praises the redhaired woman sitting next to Miles Hunter.

"The diced almonds are a lovely addition," notes Emily.

"…we spent months at the Nazi Propaganda Ministry organizing the book burnings. I had to find other women, mothers mostly, who could identify the true German message. People who were strong enough to filter through dark and transgressive material. We developed lists of offensive authors and topics. The mission became personal," admits the redhead to a woman seated directly across from her.

She touches her breasts with her hands, like a savage, to reinforce her point. I recall the chanting crowds undulating in the streets guided by torchlight. Thugs, teenagers, and desperate adults fueled by hatred who looted libraries and schools. Albert Einstein and Sigmund Freud's treasures were incinerated. It is now a crime to read or possess anything deemed not traditionally Nazi-centric. The culture and ingenuity I have embraced here in Berlin, gone. This Berlin has become frantic and cruel.

"...Joseph Goebbels speaking in the Berlin Opera Square was inspirational. Forty thousand true German citizens condemned books written by Jews, liberals, and foreigners. He called it "the cleansing of the German spirit," recalls Otto.

"How exciting to have been there in person!" enthused the redhead.

"You should never miss a chance to hear him speak," admonishes Otto Mueller.

"Goebbels has such a command of the German language," pines Sommer.

"After I heard Goebbels speak in 1932, I enrolled Wilhelm in the Hitler youth," remarks Mia.

"He's learned so much already. He can shoot like a sniper," affirms Henrik Strauber.

"My daughter joined the League of German Girls, and it changed her life. She talks about community and the importance of excellent health standards. Gretel runs sprints and she is so popular," boasts Henrietta Kaiser.

"She is blossoming before our eyes," agrees Edith.

"Did we care about such things when we were their age?" Helena asks Otto.

"Children are so political nowadays. They care about the state of the world and the future of Germany. Imagine how far ahead Germany will be past the rest of the world. After the Great War, Germany was expected to grovel forever. When Germany rises under the leadership of Adolf Hitler, won't the world be surprised?" voices Mia to her husband.

Chapter 81
October 1933 Berlin, Germany
Marjem Rechtschaffen

Aron spends the morning cleaning the apartment.

"Marjem, I am thrilled for the distraction," he explains as he fluffs a pillow and places it on the wrong couch. I chastise myself for noticing his poor placement.

"I don't even mind cleaning," he says and laughs to himself.

"Don't let me get in your way," I say coyly.

He passes by me and hands me my glass of water from the end table.

"You are never in my way."

"Thank you, Aron, I am a better version of myself with you by my side."

"It will be great to see our friends."

"I miss them too. Today will be excellent."

I hear the excitement in my own voice. His eyes are wide, and he looks almost childish.

"Aron, let us feel normal today. Unimportant. We can toast being unremarkable," I say.

Aron interrupts, "Yes, we will toast to love and family. You will show off the baby and the men can discuss the economy."

"I'm excited to see Missy, Rochelle, Kira and Jessica."

"Maurice is coming."

"What a fantastic surprise. I can't wait to see him; it's been too long."

"He does important work. We don't discuss it often, but the work is dangerous."

"I don't know what he does. I do not think any of us understand. He's established himself in a thriving Jewish community in Paris and his connections help our business."

Aron says, "He is a logistics connoisseur. His deep relationships in the railyard are invaluable. Lately, Maurice has been going back and forth visiting Gideon in Belgium. Gideon's business is successful, and he has expanded. He purchased a building and is rehabilitating it to its original glory."

"Gideon has tremendous abilities. No one in the family can do what he can. He was compelled to understand what was inside of everything."

I remember his first full sentence was, "How it goes?"

I smile at the memory.

Aron asks, "What do you think Maurice and François are trying to do with Gideon in Belgium?"

"I don't know. Gideon's wife, Laura, volunteers with the veterans. She is a blessed woman. Gideon loves the community. He credits Laura for everything good in his life. His life is so much bigger than I ever thought imaginable."

"Lately, Marjem, I see small businesses closing and vagrants congregating near warehouses. It is happening in Essen, Dusseldorf, and Hamburg. The boycott is rough. The government stays silent. What can we find out from Maurice?"

"We can't ask him anything directly."

"He'll let us know what we need to know. Our economy is on pause. I have never seen this before. I believe his perspective will validate my suspicions," says Aron.

"Sounds good to me. Why do you think he's here?"

"He's on a mission. Here. Holland. Belgium. That's all I know."

"He'll come, see the baby and cover him with kisses." Marjem starts laughing.

"I had a picture taken of the baby as you requested. Now I understand. You knew he was coming."

"I didn't want to get your hopes up in case his plans changed. Once he hears the juicy titbits you get from the hens, he will need at least an evening over a good solid roasted chicken dinner and wine to digest the necessary information. The gossip you hear is invaluable."

"That reminds me ...."

"Marjem, seriously, I need you to think about what you have heard at the store," says Aron.

"The Nazis arrested Mrs. Leila's husband. They dragged him from his house without his shoes on. He collapsed before he could even board the truck. The Nazis threw him on the truck like an oversized rag doll. Someone else pulled him in further before the truck door slammed down and severed his legs at the ankles. It made bile rise in my throat. Her store has closed, and she disappeared."

"Who told you all of this, Marjem?"

Aron looks ready to punch someone.

"No one tells me anything. I listen to their gossip. Two hens shared a story of a person they knew nothing about. Their husbands hurt people for a game, and they relish in the calloused details."

"They are pigs! Is there more you can tell him?"

"Helena came in with a new older woman. When the hens saw her, they rushed out of their seats to stand near her. Helena smiled at me, and I nodded. The hens wanted to find a way to ingratiate themselves but were not sure how."

"Why would Maurice be interested in this?"

"Because one of The Hens started to weep openly. It was tragically graceless. Helena was visibly shocked. The hen could have been standing naked on the Unter der Linden and it would have been better for her than crying in front of Helena's friend. The woman was crying because her husband was assigned to East Prussia."

"East Prussia? What else?"

"She's pregnant and his commander doesn't care."

Aron is quiet.

"I'll tell Maurice, and he can determine if the information is important or not," I say.

"Maurice won't care if the wife is pregnant."

"He will care when I tell him her husband is a logistics munitions coordinator. The husband figured he did his time being sent away to Africa, but now he's off to East Prussia."

"You are right. Your information is important."

He massages my shoulders. I tilt my head to the left, and he strokes my neck from my ear to my shoulder. He takes my head in his hands and repeats this deep massage on the other side.

"There are more people out there like Maurice and Francois. All the connections are links in the chain. Each link saves lives. Marjem, you know what matters. Your animosity for the hens must remain in check."

"I pity the hens in their pretty shoes, leather gloves, and silk nylons, stupid and vacant. Their lives are simple, and nothing is expected of them. I wouldn't be happy being that kind of girl."

"Marjem ..."

"I pitied them then, Aron. Now, their smiles, their easy laughter, make me jealous. Their lives are uncomplicated. All they have to do is be pretty and amenable."

"And non-Jewish." And it comes full circle again.

Struggle, hardship, and strife are the opportunities for a Jew.

Chapter 82
October 6, 1933, Berlin, Germany
Marjem Rechtschaffen

Jessica Jacobs always cheers me up. My home or hers she takes on all hosting duties whenever she's around. Over the past few years, she has grown even closer to my friend Kira. This fall, Kira became vice president of the sisterhood. Everyone enjoys her company. She's wonderful at managing a large group of women. She raises almost as much money as Jessica Jacobs for charity. Her bubbly personality is disarming. She also has a knack for home decoration. Missy Farber and Rochelle Haag are active in the sisterhood. They are both former elementary school teachers. Missy wears her hair in a short pixie bob cut. Her delicate features are accentuated by her close-cropped hair. She says, "There are plans we make inside our hearts that we don't share with anyone."

Missy's cheerful cadence matches her trim figure.

Pretty and sharp-witted, her brunette bob of hair is held together with a red ribbon headband.

"My dreams can be selfish and stupid, but they are important to me. I dreamt of having a baby boy to feed, love, and watch grow."

Rochelle adds, "I dreamt of my baby boy's bar mitzvah. Standing with pride amongst my friends while he impressed us. My waist would be impossibly small in my dress and my curled hair would cascade down my back."

Rochelle is an impressive woman with enviable olive skin and thick black Sephardi hair. She and Missy have been friends since diapers. When the two of them get on a roll, they leave me in stitches. I giggle at her vanity.

Missy says, "I dreamt my son would graduate medical school. I want to stand in the market one day and have someone walk up to me and say 'Your son saved my life. You must be so proud.'"

"I like your dream," I say to Missy.

Jessica and Kira agree. Kira mentions the new violin teacher she hired for her daughter, Sadie. Sadie is talented. Her father is looking into a school in Vienna for her.

Rochelle says, "Don't encourage Missy. She's carried that idea in her head since she was ten. One day in synagogue, we heard one old woman praise another during the Shabbat kiddush."

Missy reminisces, "It was such a touching moment." Rochelle places her hand on Missy's arm.

The familiar gesture between the two of them is gracious.

Kira says, "Motherhood is every emotion over and over, one on top of another, all at the same time."

Jessica says, "No matter what you do in the beginning you think you're doing everything wrong. You are not. But you don't have the clarity of mind to realize and trust yourself. Trust yourself. You're smart."

Every mother in the room nods.

"Missy, I'm sweating. Why am I sweating?" I ask.

The women look at each other knowingly. I wait.

What is the secret?

Missy says, "Your hormones swing wildly for months after giving birth. If doctors took the time to explain to women the changes their bodies will undergo after giving birth, women would be grateful. It is terrifying to not understand what is happening to you. Sometimes nurses in hospitals give you a little advice, but the best resource you have is us."

She squeezes Rochelle's knees.

"Nursing a human is exhausting. Are you impossibly hungry?"

"Yes! I could eat two baked potatoes every night," I admit without guile.

Jessica adds, "Nursing helps take off the weight from pregnancy. You didn't gain too much weight in the first place, which was wise. That makes it easier to bounce back."

"Make sure you keep eating because the baby eats first. You'll be left with nothing. You must maintain your strength to nurse the baby," advises Rochelle.

"She's right," says Missy.

"Babies are like fairies. They believe in magic and monsters. Scratches and bruises can be cured with a kiss. A warm bath and Epsom salts are a perfect salve for rashes, aches, and fevers."

Kira says, "The days can move impossibly fast."

"Every morning, Stanley kisses Charlie and me goodbye and heads out to the factory. He prides himself on arriving first and leaving last. Charlie and I walk together to school and he tells me about his friends and the teachers," says Rochelle.

Jessica smiles. She is in her element. "The school has great teachers."

Rochelle says, "His teacher at school says, 'Charlie's world is like a children's drawing that is yet to be filled in with color. When he focuses on one aspect of the drawing, he colors so intensely.'"

Aron and the men walk into the living room with a silver serving dish piled high with slices of honey cake. Missy's husband carries in a carafe of hot water and Rochelle's husband Stanley carries in a tray of teacups. Maurice follows with two bottles of peach Schnapps and a white paper box tied in French pastry ribbon. We all sit down and admire Maurice's gifts. He straightens and fetches another sack. He hands Aron two bottles of cognac and a box of cigars. The men hoot and holler in delight.

"Maurice, you are way too generous," says Aron.

Both Richard and Stanley stand in appreciation. Stanley extends his hand.

"Thank you, Maurice," says Stanley.

"I can't remember the last time I enjoyed a cigar."

"Richard loves cigars, don't you Richard?" adds Missy.

"Who doesn't?" says Maurice.

"A toast to us all, whatever we can do to extend happiness."

"Cheers to friends," sings Jessica.

"Cognac and cake are the only way to end an evening with friends," I say.

Missy and Rochelle scooch forward on the couch, pouring peach Schnapps into their tea. Kira offers up her empty glass and giggles.

Maurice says, "It's the simple things that get us through the stressful times."

Missy says, "Yes, I agree."

Maurice sets his glass down with a solid click.

"What happened at the school?"

Richard says, "Good teachers are essential. I had one teacher in fifth grade who changed my life. He explained math to me. I will love math forever because of him."

Stanley says, "A good teacher means everything."

"We all thought we made the right choice with that school," says Missy.

"How can anything go right with the Nazis chasing off the intellectuals?" adds Richard.

I look at Aron. He reads my expression and looks down to the floor. Kira looks uncomfortable. She stands up and walks around the room.

"First the fire, and then the Reichstag decrees…" says Maurice.

Aron explains, "No, first the communists disappeared. They loaded them onto trucks and shipped them off to labor camps. There were no arrests or trials."

"The Nazis are the government and their absolute power rains down on anyone associated with the judicial system. Jews are no longer allowed to be lawyers or judges. Jews can no longer pursue justice in the legal system. All non-Jewish lawyers were advised not to take on Jewish clients," says Daniel.

"There is talk at the store about the new work camp," adds Rochelle. Awkwardness fills the room like backed-up dirty dishwater in the kitchen sink that cannot make it past a clogged drain.

"Paris doesn't have the obvious unemployment I see happening here," adds Maurice.

"Week after week of double-digit unemployment leads to massive social problems," explains Stanley.

"Yes. We need good people in service positions to keep the city running properly," says Daniel.

Richard says, "Income is an emergency matter. The war ruined any kind of social safety net."

"The war ruined Germany," says Rochelle.

"I need more Schnapps," Aron declares, then laughs. Maurice stands up.

"Let's refill the ladies' glasses."

The men loosen their ties.

There is a buzzing around my eyes.

"Hitler is ruining the Berlin I grew up in," adds Missy. Richard walks over to her and places his hand in her lap.

"Berlin is where I fell in love with Missy," says Richard reassuringly. Missy takes both her hands and holds Richard's face. She closes her eyes and pulls his face in for a long loving kiss. Their affection is sweet to witness.

I say, "You are right. We have to prepare ourselves to live in a world that makes no sense."

Aron says, "it might get worse before it gets better. Poverty, malnutrition, and a lack of education compound the problems."

Aron turns to me, "There are good people who still want to live in a moral world."

"That is sweet, Aron," says Jessica.

Aron smiles.

"And important," says Kira.

"Are you enjoying fatherhood, Aron?"

"Parenthood. It's new and exciting and exhausting".

The ladies laugh.

"Each night as I fall asleep, I recount my day to Aron until I fall asleep."

"She talks until she starts to snore."

Appalled, I gasp, "Which is never!"

Daniel and Rochelle exchange a few quiet words.

"We're safe to say things here."

She turns to the rest of the group.

"Daniel is terribly upset. His brother Benji is a doctor. He set up a small pediatric practice and a month ago, the SA broke his glass windows and set fires inside his garbage baskets."

She looks at Daniel uncomfortably.

"We couldn't have done any more for him. We are powerless, and whenever we think about him, it hurts."

"We watched him build his dreams and have them crushed by a shiny leather jackboot," says Daniel flatly.

"Mr. Baker led the Berlin orchestra for two years. Then he stopped to take care of his sickly wife, Marie," says Missy.

"He enjoyed leading the chorus and orchestra at Charlie's school. He offered Charlie piano lessons on Thursday afternoons. He thinks Charlie has a real ear for music. We enjoy the time Mr. Baker and Charlie spend together," says Rochelle.

"You should tell the other mothers, Rochelle. Music and math are important. Life will resume, children will go back to school, and our children will not be left behind," advises Stanley.

"Stanley worries about the boys remaining competitive," says Rochelle.

"The world waits for no one," says Aron.

I look at him incredulously. He does not sound like himself. He looks at me searchingly. My heart races.

"Marjem, you look a little pale," says Aron as he lifts Manfred from my lap. Jessica moves closer and places a small piece of cake in my mouth. The cake is sweet and soft. The scent of nutmeg and cloves fills my mouth and nose.

"School's canceled," says Jessica.

"I wake up and plan our days together. Groceries, cleaning, laundry, teaching the children; thinking about it gives me a headache."

"It's hard to raise a family when you're scared all the time. You feel a tightness in your chest and wonder, why?" says Maurice.

"It's your family, it's my family, It's all of us. We're all affected," adds Rochelle.

Richard says, "I don't want to be a cautionary tale. We do not understand what is happening around here. No one can give us a real explanation."

"We have to dig deep and care for one another. We must show everyone around us we are good people who have the same values everyone else strives for. I must believe that this nightmare will end. At the same time, I can't stick my head in the sand."

"Stanley finds it difficult to have the children home all the time. School was a necessary break for all of us. Without guidance from proper instructors, children will be as capable as we are as parents. Rochelle is good at math, but she is not good at languages. The children need to be around their friends and learn from one another. There needs to be competition and achievement."

Rochelle says, "We read the classics together. Every night after supper, Stanley makes me tea with lemon, honey, and a splash of rum. He brings it to me while I am in the bath."

"Sounds luxurious," I say.

"A nightly bath is very relaxing."

"I'll take note," says Aron sweetly.

Missy says, "Mrs. Horowitz is gathering a bunch of the young girls on Monday mornings to teach them sewing. Stella enjoys being with Hannah."

"We should involve more of the girls in a sewing class. We can keep it inside our apartments and not draw unnecessary attention," says Rochelle.

"Today, I arrived at Charlie's school, and I saw the Nazi stormtroopers arrayed before the front gate." I knew our lives were about to change. It was another measure taken against the Jews in the name of Mother Germany. Evil slithered its way right into my doorstep today. My stomach ached and twisted upon itself like a rock. I crouched over. The pain prevented me from standing up straight.

"What did you do?" asks Kira.

"I marched Charlie back home. I didn't stop until we made it to the house."

My hands start to shake. I had no idea this was happening.

"Marjem, I didn't want to tell you while you were pregnant with the baby. There is no reason to upset an expectant mother. At the time, I thought I would blink, and it would all be over. I did not expect it. I still don't believe it."

"What did you do?"

"I could barely get my key in the lock. Unfazed and innocent, Charlie did not pick up on my terror. I dragged my favorite lounge chair from the sitting room, you know, the one we keep under the Klimt? I wedged it against the inside of the front door. Charlie and I spent the rest of the day upstairs in our bedroom. I let him jump up and down on our bed and felt his weight impact the bedsprings."

"Did you bring Charlie back to school the next day?" I ask.

"No," says Stanley.

"I wouldn't have returned either," said Missy.

"That's the same thing I experienced with Joseph," says Missy.

"Except I didn't turn around and go back home. I marched proudly into the school and the headmasters' office. Filled with righteous indignation, I demanded answers. He told me the school would continue with some changes and I should change my tone. Gobsmacked, I tucked my pride inside. He continued to berate me. 'Mrs. Farber, I know you have been part of our school for many years; these new rules will not suit you. Your kind should reconsider where to educate your children.'"

I see the anger behind her words. She is not a woman to be silenced. She is a shark, not a minnow.

"When Joseph returned from school, he went right to his room. He shares it with his younger brother. I always hear the two of them talking. Joseph told him great stories about what happened that day or a game he played at lunchtime. Today, Joseph was silent; he did not want to talk to his brother; he did not want to talk to me. After an hour, he came out of the room, and I made him his favorite dinner. He moved the food around the plate to make it look like he was eating, but he was not. I knew it and he knew it."

That must have been terrible. Not being able to help your children. I have never imagined being incapable of taking away all their fear and all their pain.

Missy continues, "I drew him a bath and I told him to have a good soak before bedtime. Getting him to take a bath on a regular day can sometimes be a battle but the way he walked into the bathroom, sad and defeated, he looked like he had aged ten years in one day."

"Did he talk to you about it? Did he tell you what happened?" I ask.

"The next morning, he woke up. He got ready for school completely silent. He barely touched his breakfast. He did not smile; he did not even want me to walk him to school. I said we do not have to go - you do not have to go today. He asked why today is different than yesterday. I did not have an answer for him. I did not have anything to say that made any sense. He said his friends did not want to talk to him. They do not want to look at him. In class, they moved his seat to the back of the room. All the Jewish kids sit behind a rope. They are two rows of empty seats that separate the Jewish kids from everybody else. It is barbaric. Why are they punishing the Jewish children?"

Stanley walks over and puts his hand in Rochelle's lap. We all know why they are being treated the way they are. We know the reason. No one knows when this is going to stop.

"It's very strange when you can't do for your children what your parents did for you. Our children are not even allowed to attend school and our lives are redefined by the day," says Maurice.

Kira says, "Being a mother is hard enough."

Aron smiles at me and the silence soothes my beating heart. The ladies collect the dishes and bring them into the kitchen for me. "I enjoy being treated like a princess."

Aron laughs and kisses me on the head.

"Manfred's sleepy."

Rosa and Missy jump up.

"We'll join you. I love rocking them to sleep after a warm bottle," says Missy.

I watch my friends fuss over him joyfully. After ten minutes, we hear a commotion in the living room. The men are in a heated debate.

As we rush into the parlor, the men silence themselves.

"What's going on? Aron, it sounds like you are yelling."

Aron says, "Nobody was yelling. I'm sorry if we were loud,"

"Did we wake the baby?" asks Stanley concerned.

"The baby fell asleep easily," I say.

"Rosa, honey, it was me. I was saying I cannot stand the Nazi flags. The way they flit in the air, carelessly. Silk caressed by the winds and kissed by the sun. It makes me crazy," says Stanley.

"Me too," says Aron.

"The Nazis squeeze all the oxygen out of the air. At night, Rochelle awakes to gasp."

"It's true," nods Rochelle.

"I dreamt of their shiny leather, over-polished boots crushing my neck."

"Germany doesn't feel like my country anymore," says Irene.

"We live under a weird, dark masquerade of terrors," says Missy.

"On my last trip to Prague, all the locals in the cafés were talking about how Germany has invaded Bavaria and the world has done nothing in response," says Maurice.

"Too many people are afraid to say anything. The question remains - when they finally find their voice, will there be anybody left to listen," says Aron.

Rosa says, "Hitler thrives on fracture."

Missy says, "How much damage will Hitler do before the world wakes up?"

Rochelle says, "Don't work yourself up, Missy."

Stanley says, "It's the same story, as old as time. The Jews create industry, products, and services. Our communities are luxurious and joyous. We live well. There are plenty of people who would trade their lives for ours. Plenty of Jews lost their businesses. Others have lost their jobs and their homes. Many good people are on the move trying to find a better life in a new land."

Richard adds, "Hitler targets Jews. There is rampant distrust and indignity in the world. Our society believes him. This dictator is charismatic and dangerous."

Maurice says, "People in Paris can't believe what's happening in Germany. The French understand the reparations from the Great War still cripple Germany. Those citizens who choose to follow a volatile extremist are absurd."

We are all in agreement. No argument here.

"I have lived in Berlin, but -" he stops himself.

He does not want to insult anyone or make anybody uncomfortable.

"Maurice, I want to understand what other countries think about Germany. Anti-Semitism, anti-intellectualism, and plain and simple crazy are ruling our country."

I put my hands on my skirt and take a moment before continuing.

"Papa moved my family to Berlin before the great war. Germany has slipped off the track and we need morality, justice, and intellectualism to help right ourselves."

I did not hold. I am personally offended when Germany is the butt of the jokes. No one wants to live in a home with drafty windows, a leaky roof, peeling paint, and a crack foundation. There is no honor in that.

"It behooves us to consider leaving."

Aron and I would never admit this much to anybody. Aron should talk to Maurice about going to Paris. Maybe we can head to Belgium? I should speak to Gideon.

"Before I was pregnant with Manfred, I spent an entire day at the German embassy. I stood in line waiting to place my name on a waiting list for immigration into England. I paid for this privilege. I was sent home to wait for two weeks until I received a letter in the mail with further instructions. A month later, I was notified that my application was denied, which didn't surprise me."

"I remember when you came home that day, Marjem, exhausted and frustrated," says Aron.

"Those useless lines."

Aron looks over to me and concern is written all over his face.

"I think our conversation has gone a little too dour. Perhaps the men will reconvene in the parlor and the ladies can enjoy themselves here."

Richard walks in with a fresh bottle of wine and four glasses. The men leave and the women talk amongst themselves.

I sit back.

"Marjem, you'll recognize other mothers around you because it's in the way we move. It's how we react to different situations, and how we carry ourselves," says Kira.

"There's a softness around the jawline a woman doesn't have before she becomes a mother," says Missy.

Jessica says, "You will spend the rest of your life fighting for your child. You will never surrender. You'll never grow tired of protecting your child because to protect them is to ensure your safety."

Rochelle adds, "A mother learns how to exist in the world with a vital piece of her soul on the outside of her body."

Marjam, David and Manfred, 1933

Chapter 83
November 1933 Berlin, Germany
Marjem Rechtschaffen

Lydia and Boris Schwiner lived in a cozy home. Lydia wanted children, and they had two. Lydia hosted elegant gatherings for famous musicians and philosophers. Her husband, Boris, provided the means. He taught all the neighborhood children. When the Jewish school closed, he tutored Jewish youth in their home. Neighbors and friends paid with food and other basic necessitates. Three months later, the same parents declined invitations to dinner at the Schwiners. Good news spreads fast, but bad news propagates like wildfire.

Several stories circulated and none of them were flattering for Lydia and Boris. The SS arrived with a truck and a Mercedes Benz. Stormtroopers entered their home carrying boxes and a folding table. A tall thin man with glasses exited the shiny black Mercedes. He carried an oversized brown leather ledger.

In painstaking detail, Lydia painted a grim picture. The troopers threw Boris around like a child. When I cried out openly, his face turned purple. He stared at me and spoke every word of love he could through his eyes, Marjem, I wanted him to protect me. Boris told me to run upstairs and lock the door. I ran so fast my feet barely touched the ground. When I looked back, Boris was on his knees and being kicked in the ribs." I held her hand and massaged her fingers. There were no words I could say to comfort her.

"They cataloged all our silver, every piece, from the cake platters and the silverware to the candelabras. The thin man selected which artwork they should pack away onto the truck. The burly soldiers with calloused knuckles spent hours handling everything we own. They took the piano. That devastated Boris. They were determined to strip all of the ornaments we had collected to adorn our lives."

The second time the SS visited, they took Lydia's furs. The third time, they took Boris.

******

Lydia's neighborhood is in a state of disaster. The first-floor windows are blown open from the inside out and the second and third-floor windows are blacked out. Newspapers litter the street. I see a discarded picture frame in the gutter. The glass is broken, and the picture is gnarled and twisted. Disgruntled men gather on the corner near Rosenthefer, their voices raised and punctuated with hostility. My fingers cramp as my knuckles whiten from clutching the handlebar of Manfred's carriage. The wheels buckle against a man I had not seen as I turn the carriage in haste.

"Mrs. Rechtschaffen, it's me Ernest Harktaine. Do you remember me? I did some work for your husband in the apartment. Last spring, I fixed the leaky toilet upstairs from your apartment."

Recovering from our impact, he says, "Let me walk you home."

Looking concerned, he inches closer.

"It isn't safe."

Rolling through my memory, I recall seeing Ernest with my Aron.

"I am fine. I don't want to take you out of your way."

I am frightened, but I do not want him to know. My weakness saddens me. I want this moment to pass as quickly as possible. I was happy this morning, filled with hope and excitement for the day. My fear drains me and is slowly being replaced by anger. I wonder if we'll ever be safe again.

"Aron would be upset if I let you walk home alone in distress with Manfred."

He is right. Aron knows him and he would want me to feel safe. I am overcome with gratitude. I wish I did not need a man. What would happen if Aron were not around? How would I handle it? It is not something I ever thought about and now I cannot stop. I did not grow up to be fearful. I was not limited in any way. I am unsure all the time lately and I have lost the ability to trust my instincts. I would be naïve to think I will ever be safe again living in Berlin. Being a Jew in Hitler's world is a death sentence.

"Yes, let's go," I implore as Ernest, and I walk swiftly away from the commotion.

Each step invigorates me. When we arrive at my doorstep, the air around us smells of buttered rolls from the bakery down the block. My mouth waters. There is no strife or danger here. How can a mere few blocks separate me from a war zone? I invite Ernest inside for tea. He comes in and says he will only stay for one cup.

"Marjem, my son Solomon was relocated. There are other ways to label it, but we'll call it relocation."

From outside, I hear a terrible commotion and gunshots. He grows quiet. There is a murderous scream. I do not want to know more. It is better not knowing.

I place my hand on him, "I am sorry for your loss."

I mean it too. I am sorry for all of us stuck in this human-sized hamster wheel where we live and die at whim.

"After he left, I changed, Mrs. Rechtschaffen. I could not protect Solomon. Plagued by nightmares, I drifted through my days and nights. My brother Bert got scared. He saw how I came undone. In reaction, he packed up his daughter, Orly, and sent her to Krakow. He could not stand the idea of the Nazis getting their hands on her. Orly leaving made me relive what happened to Solomon. I felt the loss the same way I felt the first time. Devastated, I no longer knew what was real and why was a nightmare."

I do not have adequate words to express how badly I feel for him. There is nothing that I can say to make it better, but I think allowing him to talk relieves some of his pressure.

"I don't think grief ever goes away. I think we just learn how to deal with it."

"My brother thinks not knowing what could happen to his daughter is worse. She is gone from his life and who knows if he will see her again. Who's to say who is right?"

"We left Galicia over twenty years ago to come here," I admit.

"Never did we consider going back. Beliefs change. The farm sounds idyllic now."

"Is Poland safer?"

He says and laughs ironically.

"Maybe?"

He sees it exactly as I do.

When someone else says what you are thinking, it is validating. When the hammer comes around, it wants big nails to pound. Aron tells me to be the small nail.

When the government generously funded cultural and athletic enrichment programs to the masses, no one objected to new decrees that did not apply to them. Last year, Jews were no longer allowed to be lawyers or judges. The court system transformed and there was no defense they could raise against the state's accusations. When Jewish children were no longer allowed to attend school, community clubs, and athletic enrichment, there were no objections. The government was passing out jobs for the unemployed. The unemployed were not going to defend their neighboring Jews. They wanted the jobs for themselves and needed them to feed their families. The government made it easy to ostracize the Jews. The absurd rules seem to affect the fringe, which made the abuse tolerable.

Earnest clears his throat, "I am sorry if I spoke too frankly."

"Come by the store on Tuesday. We need delivery help."

"Bless you."

"May Hashem bless us all."

Good family's lives are slipping away for no reason. Solomon's family chose to send Orly away. Can I send Manfred to Gittel in Holland? She is pregnant right now and he could be raised with them until we can get there. The Nazis will not let me leave. Exit visas are impossible to obtain. England closed its ports to Eastern Europeans until 1935.

******

That evening, Aron prepares me a strong cup of rum tea before bed. The headache above my left eye has not let up all day. Sleep comes slowly but deeply. I do not hear Manfred's barking coughs. I awake to Aron running to Manfred's crib. He screams my name and I turn on the shower to fill the bathroom with hot steam. Edde's son had croup last year. The steam from the shower juxtaposes with the cold night air to help open swollen lungs. Standing in my nightgown, I swaddle Manfred and rock him back and forth. Crying makes the coughing worse. Pleadingly, I look to Aron, "Sing to him, please? Start with Alenu."

Manfred lifts his head and turns to Aron. His lips relax and his mouth opens desperate for breath.

"Manfred's nose is cherry red. His keppe is warm but his wet cheeks are cool."

I walk to the door and Aron grabs my arm, "You're naked." I look down and see my nightgown is transparent, clinging to my breasts.

"You have to stand outside and wrap him up. The cold air will help him breathe. We need our coats."

Motorcycles in the distance alert us to the Nazis' omnipresence. Manfred gasps for cooler air, as I shiver in the night breeze.

"Marjem, I don't want you out here with the motorcycles. Go back inside and let me know when I can come back in." Within five minutes, the bathroom is filled with steam.

I close the door and head back to Aron and Manfred.

"This is going to be a long night, Marjem."

The next time we go outside, a Nazi Mercedes four-door sedan slithers down the street as a snake swims through water. My lungs contract. I do not want to move or attract any attention. I want to be back inside. My lungs contract. A second snake follows and the third one slows down as it passes before our doorstep. A window rolls down and an SS officer turns his head. His eyes tear through me. I feel naked. My heart stops. Closing my eyes, I pray away the Nazis. Manfred's struggle for breath wrestles my attention away from fear. I kiss Manfred. Aron and I repeat this process for the next several hours. Once his breathing eases, he drifts off to sleep in Aron's arms. The breeze from the open window is steady and pleasant. I awake to the smell of Aron making breakfast. Manfred is asleep beside me in the middle of the bed, surrounded by pillows. The sweet easy rise and fall of his chest is a testament to the rough night we all endured. A tired haze overwhelms my senses.

"He has the croup," I remark to Aron.

Aron reminds me, "Today is the eleventh and I need to make my deliveries."

"I know. You have to deliver more of those duvets for the Bavermans."

My mind cannot focus on the day ahead. Every morning, I awaken and ask myself what day it is and what must be completed. But I cannot seem to focus my mind enough to handle that basic task. Aron walks out of the room, leaving my breakfast on the table.

"We'll go to the pediatrician first, then you can head home with Manfred, and I'll do my errands. The store can remain closed today."

As we approach the doctor's office, I sense the tension in the air. Men rush past us, and a woman screams. Gunshots ring through the air. Six-pointed Jewish stars are painted in red, white, and yellow on the walls and wooden placards. The strokes are angry. An unusually large crowd mills in front of the center of the square.

"Aron, what are we going to do?"

"The stars are only on the Jewish owned businesses windows," whispers Aron. He takes my hand.

"We will be fine. Stay calm." Brown Shirts block the entrances to the square and fill the street corners. The courthouse, the cobbler, and the clinic are inaccessible. All owned by Jews.

"We need to go home."

I do not recognize my voice. Pointing to the right, I say, "Did you see those signs?"

Do not buy from Jews!

The Jews are our misfortune!

Aron places his hands on my shoulders and changes my direction.

"I cannot breathe," I whimper.

Small beads of sweat gather on my upper lip. I hold Manfred close and start to run. My heart pounds in my ears. I cannot swallow.

Running to keep up with me, Aron says, "Don't crush him, Marjem."

"I'm not!"

I yell back in shock and shame.

I loosen my grip but do not stop running.

Chapter 84
January 1934 Berlin, Germany
Aron Rechtschaffen

I am home earlier than expected. Sifting through the mail, I see a registered letter from France in care of Maurice Eisner. Our application is denied to France.

The VERBOTEN stamp glares angrily on the page. Tearing up the letter feels right. Marjem's still at the store. I heat some soup for dinner. She will smell the delicious soup and know immediately I will take the baby off her hands. She can sit down and put her feet up with a glass of wine.

She walks through the door, smiling from ear to ear. I place my hand on her cheek. She closes her eyes and leans into my palm. Manfred begins to jump up and down. I scoop him up and bring him to the bathroom to help him wash his hands and face in preparation for dinner.

"Aron, you're wonderful. It's in the small things that you do for me," says Marjem.

Manfred babbles about his day, and he is extremely excited about everything he is saying. Most of it comes out as gibberish. I understand what he is trying to say. It is the tone he uses. I place Manfred in his highchair. He begins to bang on the plate in anticipation of dinner. I hand him a boiled egg cut up in four, a piece of toast, and a bowl of chicken noodle soup with big slices of carrot and celery.

"Marjem, according to Manfred, you had an exciting day today."

Marjem smiles, "What did Manfred tell you?"

"He wanted you to tell me," I tease.

"One of the hens has a cleaning maid. The maid's sister works inside a high-level SS home. The hen won't say which maid because she enjoys the attention all the other hens give her, trying to guess and figure out who it is."

I ask, "Did you ever find out who?"

"No. They said their husbands were upset about something else. The state-sanctioned boycott against the Jews was not as popular as the Nazis hoped for. The Nazis believed anti-Semitism was much more pervasive than it appears to be."

Marjem is like a fly on the wall in the most important rooms. The information that she's privy to is exceptional.

"Sounds like good news to me."

I scoop up some toast that Manfred has pushed onto the floor. I'm glad to hear that anti-Semitism is not as palatable as the Nazis wish.

"I couldn't agree more, Aron. The Germans surprised the SS by defending the rights of Jews. Some Germans still conduct business in the 'Jew' stores."

"I hate that expression! I hear it all the time, Marjem."

Marjem says, "Unleashing the brown shirts intimidated the masses. The Nazis assumed people would not disregard a state decree. That is what one of the hens said. It was hard to contain my excitement. I'm happy people stood up for themselves and didn't let the brown shirts bully them."

"Marjem, you're right to feel that way."

"One official identified ten excellent candidates within the local brown shirt community. He said Himmler would be proud to save these lives."

"Marjem, what do you mean? Is she married to an SS officer?"

"Yes, these women do not mix with brown shirts or their wives at all. It is almost like a caste system. Brownshirts are feral. They hold no real power. Consider them weaponized pawns," says Marjem.

I regard her.

She is inside a communication network that no government knows exists. These wives complain and within the details are gems of information. One woman complains of relocation and Marjem hears of troop movements. Trucks filled with unmarked barrels means vital resources for future engagements. Marjem is my sexy, unassuming spy whose intrigue and capabilities are expansive. She keeps her composure under pressure. Her deep understanding of people is what makes her effective. She can read them and convince them of things they might not have considered before. She allows people space to compose their thoughts at the store. The store smells of freshly brewed tea and cake. I adore the radio Helena gave us. Marjem explained to me it is about atmosphere, creating a scene where people are comfortable. Our store is a destination where women can shop and socialize. There is a certain level of clientele that frequent our store, because running in the same circle as Helena elevates status.

"Marjem, why did he say he wanted to save brown shirt lives? Is there a split in the party?"

I do not want to push and make her explain how she faces their discrimination every day. I know she hates those women. Her station holds power. These vapid women have no idea she listens to every word they say. She communicates the information to me, and we relay everything we can to Maurice. Each nugget of information will come together. For now, we create a patchwork of facts to keep us one step ahead. To stay alive.

"Is Helena aware of how much these ladies talk about?"

"She said it's none of her business. Helena is smarter than them all combined. She does not pay attention to them, and they thirst for every glance she casts their way. She understands that I listen. I know when to keep my mouth shut. Most people like these women talk too much. Helena says, 'If you give them a platform, they'll be their own undoing.'"

"I'm glad you're on my side."

I reach for her hand and squeeze it. She laughs and gives me a loving shove. I make a face and she lands a big juicy kiss on my lips.

"Remember Chantal? That amazing swimmer from the south of France?"

"The one that married a young SS officer?"

"After she relocated to train in Germany, her coach promised her the Olympics. After she tore the ligaments in her shoulder, she had to drop out of the program. She is not German. The hens watch every move she makes. She is charismatic with a sensual accent. The Hens do not trust her. These stiff-as-a-board housefraus cannot compete. Anyway, her husband works in the broadcasting system. She said there was a lot of infighting within the party over a unified message."

"Marjem, he's talking about federalizing the radio broadcast station. There would no longer be any integrity in the message given to the people. The message would be controlled by the state."

"Her husband is the one who is to deliver the daily message to the citizens of Germany. He informs them about the state of the union. Her husband broadcasts messages of German superiority."

"How is he going to do that?"

"The broadcast will be public. To ensure all Germans know what direction the country is going in."

Chapter 85
February 1934 Berlin, Germany
Marjem Rechtschaffen

When I was nine years old, I got lost in the park. I walked away from my older brothers because I was mad about something. Self-righteous and inexperienced with the park, it did not take me long to lose my bearings.

Embarrassed by my naïveté, I did not call out for help. I was determined to get myself out of trouble. I was not wearing a watch and I did not know how long I had been missing.

At some point, I sat down beneath the shade of a tree.

When my anger stopped keeping me warm, I started to shiver. My eyes filled with tears. I had failed. When I heard my mother's shrill call, I could have jumped out of my skin. My siblings ran towards me from different directions.

My mother was busy juggling Gittel and Henie. When we all walked home together later, Maurice and François never took their hands off me. One of them was either holding my hand or resting theirs on my head. Being lost in the park did not end in tragedy.

When I struggle to resolve something in my life, the memory of the park comes back to me in my dreams. In the dream, I am left to wander in the forest until my clothes turn to tatters and my shoes no longer fit me. It is strange, I remember how the story ended, but in my dreams, I do not. It is that space between fiction and reality where my memories remain trapped.

When I first met Aron, he made me feel like a teenager. The air smelled sweet, every experience was new, even the sun shone brighter. I remember the first time he lifted me in the air and put me on a horse. He told me to hold onto his waist and lean into him. The movement of the horse brought me comfort. Once I was ready, he kicked the horse, and we took off into a fast gallop. My hat fell off my head. I lifted my face to the sky and closed my eyes. The faster the horse went, the more wicked and wild my laughter became. Aron gave me the space to let go. I do not have to be in control, and I do not have to have all the answers. All I ever must do is trust in him.

Chapter 86
March 1934 Berlin, Germany
Aron Rechtschaffen

Dear Walker,

I need to talk. The wildness in the streets of Berlin is ungodly. The brown shirts are degenerates who thrive on brutality. They used to target the homeless, the disenfranchised, and communists. Lately, they target Jews. The government is turning on the Jews. Young Jewish boys no longer attend school. Our teacher friends are unemployed. Different families in the neighborhood teach the children what they can. I don't know if this is sustainable. We might not have a choice. Marjem taught Manfred his letters and the beginning of his numbers.

He can sound out his words and he's so smart. Smarter than me, smarter than you. Marjem talks all the time about missing her father and wishing he could see the beautiful boy we have created. I believe he sees us from heaven. I don't know if she believes it. I know she wants to. Losing her father has not gotten any easier for her.

That's why I can't show her my genuine concern for our future in Berlin. The Nazis are a credible threat. Their hate is endless and their blood lust for Jews is enigmatic. I'm being shaken down every week by thugs who are no smarter than a bag of hammers. It makes me sick, and I'm alone in this misery. I can't complain to Marjem. Saying it out loud to you makes me feel better. I can't keep the panic inside of me anymore. How can I protect Manfred and Marjem? I remember our mother sitting with other women from the synagogue around the outside table. She sat there laughing, telling stories, probably sharing a lot of advice.

These women created a community within themselves and established unbreakable bonds. Marjem's made these kinds of friends in the sisterhood. Motherhood in modern Berlin has its challenges and her friends help. She found that in Jessica, Kira, Rosa, and a few others. She owes it to herself. To be vulnerable enough to accept the right kind of advice. I urge her to spend time with her friends whenever possible. Her friends don't visit the store as often as they used to. They are uncomfortable with a lot of our new clientele. The wives of the SS are our best customers. Their husbands are officers - highly educated and of superior stock in both mind and body. They consider themselves elite and the Nazis feel they are the best of what Germany has to offer. If that is not enough, there is another group of military elites.

Göring, your friend, and mine heads the Gestapo, which is more of an intelligence force. They use sabotage to control and overwhelm their enemies. I read about Göring, and I hear he is not an anti-Semite.

He was raised by a Jewish grandfather whom he loved; he has great respect for this man. He cherished the lifestyle he led as an aristocrat in Bavaria.

These women carry on conversations as if Marjem is not even in the room, like she's the help. The information discussed is *mundane. But not to all ears. Do these women know that we are Jewish? Some of her friends no longer attend the synagogue. She said she'll attend for the high holy days. I said one day at a time. We received a rejection letter from France. Marjem applied there six months ago, hoping we could use her brother's residency. I haven't told her the rejections yet, but she hasn't asked either. I'll have her apply to other places. Like I said, we have to get out of Germany before it's too late. The SA pressure people to comply during the state sanctioned boycott against Jewish businesses. Most Germans were not bothered by the decree and ignored it. Not all Germans are anti-Semitic. I do not know where this leaves us.*

Love, Aron

Chapter 87
April 1934 Berlin, Germany
Marjem Rechtschaffen

I greet Aron, overwhelmed with excitement.

"Aron, you'll never believe who is here? Maurice! He didn't tell me he was coming. The doorbell rang this afternoon and when I opened the door, I found him standing right in front of me."

"Where is he?" asks Aron.

"He's in the parlor with Herman."

Herman passes out cigars and Maurice pours generous shots of scotch. The two work together seamlessly. They act like they're thick as thieves.

Maurice says, "Brother, I'm here to visit you and kiss my beautiful nephew."

There's a sparkle in his eyes that wasn't there before. His life is filled with mystery. If I didn't know any better, I'd swear he's madly in love.

"We have all evening to enjoy ourselves. Maurice, how long will you be staying with us this time?" Aron asks.

Maurice considers the question and says, "I'd like to stay through the weekend. I have some business opportunities to attend to, but I would also like to spend some time with my family."

Aron says, "It's our pleasure to have you. Stay as long as you like. I haven't had a chance to tell you but the visa to France was rejected."

I walk into the kitchen to prepare roasted chicken and root vegetables. He never told me. Why didn't he tell me? I take a large sip of wine and digest the information. I'd rather prepare a delicious meal for my brother and my family than react to the bad information. In fact, preparing dinner saves me from overreacting.

Within half an hour, the house smells delicious. I return from the kitchen to join the men in lively conversation.

Maurice raises his glass in the air and says, "to the health and well-being of my beautiful family."

Manfred happily sits on his lap playing with a set of keys. The pile of exquisite and trendy French beauty magazines on the table says to me there was a woman involved in this selection. Herman adds, "L'chaim."

Maurice regales us with stories of beautiful Paris. He tells us about François and his new wife and child. He also shares about Gideon living in Belgium. He's been spending a lot of time there lately. I ask him if there happens to be a beautiful woman across the border that compels him to continue his travels. He smiles wickedly, blushes and says no more. We both talk about Mother, and we worry about her being a widow. Neither one of us can imagine how she feels but we want to make sure we stand by her.

"Maurice, there's a lot of things I don't ask you about."

I say, "We've always been a close family. There are a lot of us, but we were all raised to take care of one another. I know. I wish I could do more but being in Berlin makes it difficult for me to take care of her in Holland. At one point, I would've asked her to move in with us here."

Herman says, "Do you think she would be willing to do that?"

Aron says, "She should stay where she is. Holland is safer than Germany. Life in Holland doesn't resemble life here in Berlin."

Maurice adds, "I don't want her moving to Berlin. I want you guys to get the hell out."

Herman says, "Maurice, I agree with you. It is important to understand what your neighbors are thinking. The consensus is Adolf Hitler loves Germany. The pervasive starvation and poverty destroying his countrymen is upsetting."

Maurice says, "You're right, Herman. It's vital to understand the Volk's mentality."

Herman says, "My friend's son, Jeremy, disappeared during the night of the Long Knives. He'd risen to a remarkably high station under Rohm."

Maurice says, "Rohm was a well-known degenerate. I'm sorry to hear your friends' son got mixed up with those people."

He stops himself.

I know Maurice is averse to homosexuality, but he's more upset that stupid young men get taken advantage of.

"Was he murdered during the raid?"

"The Nazis eliminated all opposition. Hundreds of SA had their throats slit while Hitler, Göring, and Himmler attended high tea. If Jeremy were in the SS and not the SA, he would be alive today."

"German citizens," says Aron, "be wary. Adolf Hitler is a force who will kill anyone in his path."

The room goes silent, and everybody finishes their scotch. Maurice refills everyone's glass.

Maurice says, "When the problems of the world are too much, I check my gut and gauge how much I can bear. Sneaking into Germany was not difficult, but I suspect sneaking out will be."

Aron slaps his forehead.

"Marjem, now I understand what you told me the other day. I wish I would've figured it out earlier. Remember when you told me about the induction of ten brown shirts?"

"Yes," says Marjem.

"I'm still not following."

"Marjem, your contact was talking about the night of the Long Knives. Your contact knew about the murders before they happened. Those brown shirts didn't go to the resort that fateful weekend. I didn't put it together then but now it all makes sense."

Before Maurice leaves, he tells us not to worry. Good people like us are smart enough to know when it is no longer safe. As for now, we are probably safe.

"We're going to apply to Belgium and Holland tomorrow." Aron suggests this would be the time to prepare in case we had to leave without much notice.

Maurice agrees that would be a good idea.

Chapter 88
1934 Berlin, Germany
Herman

Together in the parlor sipping tea, Aron's presence soothes me. The week was difficult to get through and I'm depressed. "Aron, our world is teetering on a cliff. The veterans at the club can't avoid talking about it. Flashbacks from the beginning of the war plague my dreams. My son marched off and never returned."

Hitler promises to make Germany great again.

"I came to Berlin in the shadow of the night, after my Paps placed me on a train, to save me from conscription into the Russian army."

"Your story still saddens me."

"My brother Walker escaped the Russians in Poland and was drafted by Britain when he came of age. The skills he learned in the military offered him tremendous opportunities once he returned. He says he owes his success to Britain drafting him."

"Veterans understand that serving time for your country can mean different things to different people. If you're lucky to survive and not be destroyed by what you saw, or experienced, the training, discipline, and camaraderie are unmatched."

"Right now, the veterans support the established government because the government honors and protects them.

If president General von Hindenburg can't keep Adolf Hitler in line the world will have bigger problems to manage."

Adolf Hitler's work programs are employing an entire generation of men. Full-time employment can turn someone's life around. The latest newsreels show Hitler standing in front of thousands of men. They're digging ditches to create the fastest train in the world, and the Autobahn will be a legacy for Germany.

"These young men need a sense of purpose. They're the pioneers of a better Germany," I say.

"If Germany wants to transform itself beyond a class society, then every person must contribute to a better tomorrow. To create a better society, wages must increase so people can catch up financially to the economic class above."

"A world like that is where I want to live. Who doesn't want peace and harmony?"

The Nazis spread their ideas by installing affordable radios in every home and tenement building. Their concept of the Volk separates true Germans from outsiders. I sip the last of my tea.

"My friend Joseph keeps the radio on all day and all night. He thinks it shows commitment. Joseph is a proud member of the Nazi party."

I lean across to touch Aron's arm.

"Aron, Joseph can never know you are Jewish. My friends have no idea. You and Marjem, and your beautiful Manfred, will be eliminated in a world run by the Nazis."

Chapter 89
May 1934 Berlin, Germany
Aron Rechtschaffen

When I was seven, on the farm one morning, I saw something unrecognizable. Filled with dread, I ran to my father. He followed me back.

My father said, "You've done nothing wrong. Your body is warning you, telling you to stay away from death. It's the most primitive instinct we have. Death repels the living. Never forget this reaction, it could save you one day."

This morning, fists pound against my front door, leaving the frame splintered. Boorish men charge towards me, their calloused hands pawing and scratching at my face. Sweat drips from my forehead and stings my eyes. I am punched in the throat and blinded by hot, angry tears.

Gasping for air, I straighten my back to regain my balance. My neck snaps back and I'm thrown into my oak dining room table. Pain shatters my spine. My legs buckle and two men drag me from my sanctuary. Tripping over my feet, I can't stop moving forward. An older man barks orders.

How arrogant to think that I'd be spared.

My eyes search for Marjem.

Once I step on the bus I'll never return. I'll never touch my wife or my child again. The chaos in my head clears and I hear her. She's screaming my name and pounding her fists against our bedroom window. The window might shatter from her intensity.

Nothing can stop this moment from happening. I don't want her to draw their lascivious attention. The way these men leer, knowing she's bereft of my protection turns my stomach. The most beautiful woman I've ever known with hair that smells like honey, whose lips are shaped in a strawberry kiss, and whose body tastes like peaches and cream is slipping through my fingers.

A Nazi sneers, "Take a last look," and knocks me to the ground. Her figure blurs as my mouth fills with blood.

My body snaps back like a recoil from a shotgun. Gasping for air, I gag on a tooth. In a cloak of shame, I'm swept from my home at night like a criminal. I cannot stop what is happening. The stench of urine stings my eyes when I stumble down the narrow alley between the benches on the bus. Never get on the bus, I repeat to myself. My stomach twists with dread, my fingers cold and numb.

******

Plötzensee Prison is the destination. Surrounded by lakes, teeming with roaches, the bus stops and restarts at the front gate. Exhaust chokes the air with a toxic black cloud. My mouth gapes open even though I don't want to inhale. Moving as commanded, I follow the man in front of me and we step off the bus. I blink to clear my eyes. My life of little risk and no excitement didn't pay off. I still ended up here. I would rather be the person holding the gun than the one running from it.

Moving into a line, we shuffle along a cement floor to a room with high ceilings and white-washed walls. The smell of blood, metallic, old, and rusty, makes my nostrils flare, desperate for oxygen. My next breath is saturated with a cloying disinfectant.

I am reminded of the time Abba delivered a fawn in our stall in Poland. The smell of blood, iodine, and sweat overwhelmed my senses. There is no fresh air, no ventilation. Abba said life was a circle. I thought he meant one day I would retire to a small house near a lake. Instead, I ended up here, with meat hooks that line the walls at eye level.

I heard a story when I was a child about the Russians hanging men from their doors using these types of hooks.

Shaking the horrid imagery from my mind I see a second set of hooks line the lower rim of the ceiling where nooses and twine hang limp. If I never left the farm, this wouldn't be happening to me, but then I wouldn't have met my Marjem. The guards demand my attention. We form a line and strip down to our underwear. Prepping for delousing, men stand in soiled clothing. Eye contact is prohibitive. Brazen roaches scurry across the floor and over my toes. There is nowhere to escape.

"Thirty executions this month and they behead the condemned with an ax in the courtyard. Sometimes the buckets remain full for days," says one ghoulish man to another.

"There is an execution shed across the courtyard," a guard informs me. He snickers for emphasis. He is missing several teeth and his breath reeks of rotten fish. A man in front of me throws up, wipes his mouth with the back of his arm and stands up straight again. Hours pass and nothing happens. Throughout the day several men cross the courtyard, but none return. A man from the bus moves next to the window.

He witnesses executions.

"Someone must bear witness. These men will die, and their families will never know," says an old man no one regards.

His hands are gnarled and his lower lip quivers. He might be right. I walk around the room and stretch my legs. Walking past the windows, I glance outside. Two dull axes lean against a blood-soaked stump of wood. Prisoners shuffle through the courtyard and enter the shed. It is impossible to ignore the screams for mercy. My name's called. My body doesn't respond. It's not in my makeup to walk to my death. Two guards lift me up and usher me into another room. The judge looms before me and I stand on my own, determined to be my own man. A Gestapo spokesperson reads my charge: Carrying and distributing illegal tender. I have no defense. I'm tried and convicted of the illegal distribution of counterfeit goods. None of this is true. Jews have no rights. Adolf Hitler's *machtergreifung* is the prevailing law.

In typical Nazi justice, called *sondehonoredrgericht,* there is no opposition.

The judge leers down at me from his podium and says, "Do you find my judgment fair?"

"The trial is as it was set out to be," I reply.

I am oddly unafraid to stare him in the eyes. He's no better than me.

"That's a hostile answer," challenges the judge.

"I'm a quiet family man and I've lived in the great land of Germany since before the War," I say.

"We caught you during a Socialist sweep. Are you an intellectual? A socialist?"

"No. I am a landlord, a father, and a husband. I trade in ostrich feathers."

The Judge asks, "What if I say you could pay a fine and leave now?"

"I'll pay your fine. My wife and son need me."

The judge dismisses me. Guards lead me through the courtyard and past the shed. Flies swarm above the axe and stump. I heave and throw up.

I remember a time when Marjem and I were not far from here. We visited Wedding Beach in 1931. The lush forest was a beautiful backdrop to the lake where we swam, the clear water was cooled by glaciers. Marjem prepared a picnic for us, and we had too much sun. Closing my eyes, I bring my hands to my nose and try to smell her taut pink skin.

I will myself back into her arms and away from here.

Bars block me from the world I want to be a part of. Clearing away the noise around me, I try to compose a plan. What will I do if I am lucky enough to get out of here?

"Zieh dich an Juden und folgen Sie uns," barks a policeman. I dress and follow the officer. I walk out of the building and cross the courtyard. Still shoeless, my toes are cold and numb. I'm led to a small, dimly lit room. It's too warm.

The judge asks, "How are you able to own the building you have when you're an immigrant Jew?"

"I'm a Rechtschaffen and can trace my lineage to the 1600s. I came to Berlin and worked hard. When you work for yourself, no one can tell you when to go to sleep, when to eat, or when to stop."

"Where's Mozes Meijer Eisner?"

"He passed away in 1931."

"I'm impressed you'd rather pay a fine than sit in jail. Most men wouldn't have the means to do it. Others wouldn't want to spend the money, but you want to return to your family. I respect a family man. You shouldn't have been part of the sweep. You need to be careful. Stay out of trouble as best as you can but know this: someone is interested in your family."

Chapter 90
August 1934 Berlin, Germany
Marjem Rechtschaffen

Rosa's delicate touch releases the pent-up stress inside of me. My resolve crumbles as hot fat tears sear my face. Rosa allows me to wallow in my helpless misery. I can say the ugly things to her, and she won't judge me. I leave Rosa in my kitchen, while I wash off my face. Upon my return, she guides me to a chair with a slice of honey cake. While unpacking several bags of food she tends to a wailing kettle. My mouth salivates. I can't remember the last time I ate.

Through tears I whisper, "they took him after midnight. The Gestapo didn't give him time to dress. It was horrific. They pummeled our front door right off its hinges. The magnitude of their power sent me into shock. Large men filled the doorway wearing sharp uniforms and knee length boots. Their faces were clean-shaven yet they wore masks. One soldier in front of me wore a skull in the center of his cap."

Her arms surround me, but I can't feel them. All I feel is overwhelming horror. She chops onions, carrots, and celery and tosses them into a pan.

"I rushed to Manfred. I chose Manfred."

"Marjem, it sounds insane," says Rosa.

She breaks the chicken down into quarters and adds that to the first pan. While one hand deftly places the chicken into the oven the other hand flips the wooden chopping block over.

"He came home yesterday," I say.

"What a relief."

Rosa checks on the chicken soup and appears satisfied. She begins the cholent and adds garlic and paprika to soften the meat, then beans, tomatoes, barley, and the beef bones. The casserole dish overflows with warmed potatoes and turnips.

Rosa asks, "What was the charge?"

Her questions distract me.

"Incarcerated for illegal tender. The price of Reichsmarks changes daily. Aron says the charge was dropped."

"What will you do?" asks Rosa.

"What can we do? Once word gets out ..." I stop myself.

It is safer to say less. The Judge told Aron to remain out of trouble.

"The information's out, sweet girl. The people who care already know. The others are naïve," says Rosa with a sharp glare.

She removes the chicken and vegetables and tosses that into a large soup pot. She adds more water and sets it to simmer.

"Marjem, people would be foolish not to be nervous," she explains.

"No one wishes to get whatever it is you now have."

"We're targets of the Gestapo."

Heartache and exhaustion push all my panic aside. "Rosa, anger seems to have dried up the tears." She laughs.

We both like dark humor.

"Marjem, the Gestapo arrest Jews every day," she says with a wry grin. What she says makes sense.

"Did you hear about Rivka? People are talking. No one wants to make the same tragic mistake she made. Her cousin, Nachem, never cried out his name to alert her to his arrival at her front door. She heard thumping against her front door and assumed it was a drunk neighbor. Everyone is paranoid. She ignored the noise. The guilt of not opening her door to her blood will eat her alive."

"We can't judge. I don't know if I would've opened the door?"

"Nachem, the brilliant coach with the dark brooding eyes, a halo of black curls and thick eyebrows?"

"I've always admired his hair. I could run my fingers through his luscious locks for hours. When he mumbled in a hoarse voice, my knees weakened. At the beach one day, he asked me to take a stroll with him. I knew in my gut he would try to kiss me. He placed his heavy arms around my shoulders. Next to him, I transformed into the prettiest girl in the world. The kiss was everything I dreamed of. His lips tasted of salt and his tongue in my mouth felt wicked and grownup. I thought for sure we'd marry," laughs Rosa.

"You were what - fourteen?"

"I was envious. Everyone was crazy in love with him!"

"The Gestapo came for Nachem the other day and he ran."

"Of course, he did. It's what you do."

Rosa's eyes swell with tears.

"I didn't know," I say.

She leaves me with a fresh cup of tea and a slice of honey cake on my lap. There is more cake under a tea towel on the kitchen table. A delicious cholent bakes in the oven. A second pot simmers with chicken soup. When Aron awakens, I will feed him food that'll stick to his battered ribs and heal him.

Rosa's love transformed my apartment back to a livable place. The air is fresher. He'll get stronger, and we'll plan our next step. We can use this time strategically. I walk to the soup pot with a bowl to get a taste of the healing broth of my childhood.

Chapter 91
September 1934 Berlin, Germany
Aron Rechtschaffen

"Where is the missing money?" begs Marjem.

Her shrillness unsettles me. Acid rises in the back of my throat and my body hair stands on end. I've never kept a secret from her before and now I might've taken it too far. I don't know how to explain to her what I had to do to comply. In order to outsmart my adversary, I swallowed my pride.

"We aren't missing money."

A grain of sickness in my gut festers and the meal in my mouth tastes like chalk.

"Let's talk after dinner," I say.

The only way to keep this from her was to omit the money from the books. To be honest, I'm surprised I kept it a secret this long. Every week I manage one delivery entirely in cash. I use that cash to bribe the thugs.

Marjem concedes, "we'll discuss this after dinner." Uncertainty is discernible between us.

I take her hand in mine.

"Business is slow," I begin. Why am I starting with another lie? I just need to come clean and give her the bad news.

"Our friends, acquaintances, and congregants from the temple, won't enter the store."

Marjem recounts, "They're wise to be reluctant."

Marjem's pupils dilate, receiving every detail.

"Rosa, Karin, Kira, and Rochelle won't come. Herr Verlin visits. Ever since Nachem disappeared, Jessica has been spending time visiting Rivka."

"You miss them," says Aron.

"The inroads we've created with the hens, the officers, and the military don't reflect in our sales. The totals don't match," adds Marjem.

"Brown Shirts, SA, Nazis, the devil is know by many names. They serve one leader. Thugs extort us. These wolves travel in gangs, their teeth sharpened and poised for my throat. When the wolves howl, my neck grows slick with perspiration."

"I'm sorry," whispers Marjem.

She sits on my lap and pulls my head to her bosom.

"Were you harmed?"

It hurts to love her and our son this much.

We're powerless to change anything.

Chapter 92
October 1934 Berlin, Germany
Marjem Rechtschaffen

"How are you holding up?" asks Helena.

Within a heartbeat, she glides across the room. Her embrace is strong and compassionate. The clothes she wears hides her weight loss. Her summer trip through Paris and Vienna helped reduce her stress. Without a hair out of place, her red curls fall around her face. She wears an emerald-green silk scarf which matches her new silk dress.

"I haven't seen you in the store for far too long," I say.

Lately, we have handled her orders over the phone.

I change the sign from OPEN to CLOSED as Helena walks over to the pot of tea and helps herself. Our friendship is important to me. There's so much drama in the world and having her here feels right.

"It's good to lay eyes on you. Whenever you come in, I laugh, because the other ladies are afraid of you."

"Marjem, we're alike. We don't have use for many people, but we're not unkind. We trust family because that's blood. However, we understand that strangers can become more loyal than family," says Helena.

"You need to start protecting yourself better. Aron, too."

"Aron? He's a man of industry. He created a livelihood out of a pile of feathers and a fan."

My voice sounds high and tight.

Helena maintains, "He's impressive and caught the eye of a high-level logistics officer. My friend has taken an interest." Her tone changes. I start to sweat. The edges of my vision blur. This happens to me before I faint. My heartbeat throbs in my ears. Helena grabs my hand. She pushes a small piece of honey cake into my mouth.

"Chew, Marjem. Keep chewing."

Her tone softens.

"You need sugar." She pushes another piece into my mouth and the edges of my vision begin to sharpen again. My forehead is sweaty, and I know I've lost all color in my face.

"I will warn you in case I hear something important."

"Thank you."

Helena says, "Aron manages his business with discretion. If he remains valuable, he'll stay alive."

She places her hand on mine.

"Tears don't help. But you never know how long Aron's angel will have enough influence to keep him safe. All the Jews need to go. My friend tells me so."

"Helena...," I whisper.

"Hitler hates the Jews and wants them all dead. When my friend speaks this way, I pour him another glass of wine and smile. He keeps talking and I learn more about his plans. As his secrets unravel, I use this information."

She pulls her hand back not unkindly.

Helena's gaze is distant.

"I help whoever needs it the most. Once the wheels are in motion, I can't stop anything. None of us know the names of more than two contacts in the chain. You don't need me yet. You did a few months ago, and I solved that."

"I have money. I'll pay," I say.

"I know you'll pay. You've been paying for years. Some can't. Those who can, pay a little more for others," says Helena.

"What do I need to do?"

"Nothing now."

"What can I tell Aron?"

"The laws will change again. The Fuhrer won't let any Jew leave with money. They'll come for all your businesses. My friend has his eye on yours."

What's she saying? I'm speechless. Aron will never agree. He will say they are stealing the business right out from under our noses.

"I'm not sure what to say."

"I've said a lot. You need time," says Helena.

"I need time," I repeat numbly. She reaches out again.

"You know who I am, Marjem. If I take the store, no one will bother you any longer. We can put the pieces in place for your escape."

"Aron would consider Herman the right person to sign the business over to. I don't want to offend you. I'm indebted to you for your kindness and friendship."

Helene holds her hand up to stop me.

"Marjem, I take no offense. The government is stealing businesses away from hard-working people. There's nothing about this situation which makes sense or is in any way fair."

"Helena, what would you have me do?"

"I would have you sign over your business to me. My Nazi is more powerful than anyone who could protect Herman."

"I feel sick," I say.

"Nonetheless, Marjem, if Herman takes the business, he will be swept up and sent off to Dachau. For no other reason other than he is friendly to Jews," says Helena.

Manfred runs into the store, signaling Aron's imminent return from his deliveries. Ever since Aron's arrest, Manfred ties his internal rhythm to Aron's whereabouts.

"Nalena," squeals Manfred as he runs towards her for a hug. She closes her eyes and breathes deeply when he embraces her, a small smile on her lips.

'Nalena' is his version of Aunt Helena.

"Marjem, one step at a time. I will have the paperwork drawn up and we will never speak of it again."

She leaves moments before Aron comes into the store.

Haggard but happy, Aron kisses me deeply on the mouth. We close the store and go to the apartment. I start dinner. Manfred runs to Aron, and they fall to the floor laughing. As I stir the pot in the kitchen, my mind checks off a list of things I must accomplish. I will apply for a visa and go see my family in Holland. I will take the baby with me.

After dinner, when Manfred is asleep, I explain to Aron what Helena and I discussed.

In bed that night Aron confesses, "I'm on a list – the same list that takes men at night and sends them to the KZ. I won't return. There's no convincing anyone of my innocence. I can't escape Berlin, Marjem. I'm being watched. You will and you'll take Manfred."

He's a good man and his words come from the most protective place but when speaks to me, as if I'm a child, my immaturity mounts. It's counterintuitive. I won't argue.

"The Nazis know everything, Marjem. They have a detailed accounting of our finances. They know where we have applied for emigration. They know your mother lives in Holland. They don't appear to know anything about Maurice and François in Paris. I don't believe it was something they left out; it's a fact they know nothing about."

"Aron..." I am cold and dizzy.

"I won't make it out of Plötzensee again. The Judge told me as much. Your time has come, and you will take Manfred," demands Aron.

"I need fresh air," I gasp.

Aron drags me to the window and opens it. The League of German Girls parades up and down the street, practicing their formations; beautiful German girls with their brown vests and shining hair. When I was their age, we moved to Berlin to escape a Russian invasion in S Dobromyl.

Laughing at the absurdity, I burst into tears.

Chapter 93
November 1934 Berlin, Germany
Aron Rechtschaffen

Dear Cousin Karl,

I appreciate the last letter you sent, and we are both glad to hear about your wife giving birth to another beautiful boy. Marjem recently heard from Gerda. She couldn't be happier with her blossoming family in Long Island. Living close to the water suits her.

I would like you to open an application for them and file it under distress. As a single widow with a child her application will be considered priority. I will find my way out myself. They're my priority and I want them to be yours.

An associate of Marjem's has commissioned our store. Her friend is the girlfriend of an influential party member. She takes her slice off the top, no matter if the margins are there or not. There's no denying how tough this has become. The Nazis take whatever they want. The Nazi boyfriends' reputation protects our business. We're not interfered with anymore. Marjem's friend gives us an alternate sense of reality. Our friends don't visit the store anymore, which used to really break up her day. We don't blame them; it simply isn't safe.

I'm alive because someone else values my connections. When my usefulness wears out, I'll be shipped off to Dachau. The Germans intend to overtake the world. Today, I watched a military parade put on by the Nazis. My blood ran cold. Germans built more planes than any other country over the past two years. The military demonstration of might enraptured the citizens of Germany. I don't want to waste a moment. I have a life expectancy of three months, three weeks, maybe three days. I want to stand up for what is right; and living in a world that doesn't allow me to do the right thing is maddening. Save my wife and son.

Sincerely, Aron

Chapter 94
1935 Berlin, Germany
Herman

Berlin has been my home for nearly sixty years. It took meeting Marjem to fall in love with Monbijoupark. She requires me to commit to a daily exercise regime including an evening stroll with her. It relaxes her mind after a hectic day. Today I'm here to meet Gregory.

He claims, "The best way to motivate someone is to give them a goal to achieve. Something to strive for. Not something to run away from."

"Makes sense to me."

"Alexander, Burr, and I attended a Goebbels rally. His solution to all of Germany's woes is the extermination of the Jewish problem. Jews do not belong in German schools or the workforce. Those positions are stolen from proper Germans. People who will make German society better."

He informs me of every detail with gusto and idolatry. I must feign interest. When you do not respond properly, the wrong people notice. If my activities cause others to register my actions, I must revise what I am doing. Now is the time to blend.

"So, the Nazis identified a distinct pathway. They figured out what's required." Gregory slaps me on the back.

Good, he is happy.

He suggests, "First, we get rid of the Jews' sovereignty. We restrict their ability to intermarry with the Volk and cause further dilution of our valuable genetic map. Jews and Communists taint whatever they touch."

A young couple strolls by with a little boy. His father was wearing a military uniform. The child resembles Manfred. I grin at him, and he waves to me.

"I miss the club. After you mentioned how thrilling the rally was, I was envious. You call me next time, and I'll accompany you."

Gregory smiles at my revelation. He claps me on the back again.

"Herman, times are strange, and people are genuinely untrustworthy. Surround yourself with true Volk and praise the glory to come. Do not stick out."

"I don't intend to. Let us meet at Prater Gardens."

"Because it's my favorite biergarten?"

He chuckles at his quip.

"I'll pick you up before the next meeting. Burr, Joseph, and I always go together." I exhale.

These men are my friends, but the depth of their anti-Semitism disgusts me.

Chapter 95
August 1935 Berlin, Germany
Aron Rechtschaffen

Marjem packs two suitcases and ships them to Henie in Holland. Underneath a layer of silk blouses and scarves was our finest silver. The second suitcase held a fur coat and our Klimt painting. We understood it was a matter of time before the Nazis catalogued our possessions.

Marjem consulted Helena who suggested she send the suitcases from someone else's address. Helena thought that was a brilliant idea. Herman ships a suitcase every other week to Gittel and Henie. Off went our candlesticks, bedroom mirror, and wedding China. We agreed not to strip the house bare and make Manfred uncomfortable. Nightly I sew jewels into our red living room carpet. The carpet is vital to our escape.

"If I can't enjoy it, I'm not letting the Nazis get their hands on it," says Marjem.

She acts when others freeze.

"Marjem, don't let the brutality of the world darken your light."

"I'm harder now but it is necessary."

"Marjem, I fled from Perehinske and recreated myself in Berlin. When questioned by authority, I immediately show deference."

The starkness of the apartment depresses me. Marjem is not daunted. She cares for her possessions but surviving without clutter is emancipating. In the morning, I rouse Manfred. His sleepy body curls itself into my arms. I remove his pajamas and undershirt and put them in my drawer. While Marjem gets showers, I include her lingerie in the drawer next to Manfred's pajamas. Her scent persists as does Manfred's.

Chapter 96
September 1935 Paris, France
Maurice Eisner

Helena suggests Marjem apply for a visiting VISA to Holland; Marjem complies immediately.

Aron and Mariam move quickly in order to prepare for her escape. My sister's bravery inspires me. Aron's devotion to their success is evident by how he continues to push her. Their actions speak volumes.

François says, "Maurice, Hitler's in charge. It's our responsibility to get Marjem out of Berlin."

Heather immediately agrees.

"A woman will be brave and save her child before she thinks of saving herself. If that's how your sister thinks then that's how you appeal to her. She must refuse to accept limitations."

Heather is right.

The phone rings around eleven-thirty in the afternoon. Aron declares, "Maurice, I sent you my entire life. My wife makes me the man I am. My son Manfred is my greatest accomplishment."

His voice changes and his words are indecipherable.

"Stay safe and healthy until we're together again."

"I promise you there's nowhere else in the world they'll be safer." We share a few more words, and then Aron hangs up. My mother and my sister Henie walk into the room carrying a tray of teacups and cookies. Henie takes a cookie, and then a second one before she sits down. She turns to me and says, "Don't judge me - I'm a nervous eater."

My mother chuckles, "You come by that honestly. I have not stopped eating for an entire week. No amount of stretching or walking around the city could combat the amount of weight I've put on."

"Your vanity is refreshing," I say.

"Are we going to talk about what we're all thinking?" asks Henie.

"Your sister is coming today and she's bringing the baby. She is doing everything we are asking her to do. She is leaving her husband and her safety. I don't know if I could've been that strong."

"You did the same when you left Dobromyl," I say.

"Your Papa was impressed by Aron's gumption. He knew Aron would provide for and protect Marjem," says Mother. "One of your Papa's favorite stories about Aron is how he made money in the lumber trade."

"I don't think I've heard that story;" I say.

Mother explains, "Timber merchants need canvas bags to help sell and distribute their lumber. Jews have easy access to canvas bags. Timber merchants historically are anti-Semitic. Aron saw how he could navigate within both communities. He could sell discounted lumber to the Jews in return for an unlimited supply of canvas bags."

"How did he get access to the lumber yards? Jews never worked there," asked Henie.

"Aron looks like a good Polish lad. Tall and lean. He picks up languages effortlessly. He found his way in. My husband used to tell me it was all about timing. Being in the right place at the right time opened doors. A solid reputation can mean more than anything else. That is what gives you credibility. Aron saw an opportunity he could sell the extra canvas bags to the lumberyard, and he could sell the timber to the Jews."

"That's a man who will escape without notice." I say.

Mother continues, "Everyone benefited; his communication skills excelled, he worked long hours, and never turned down a shift. His work ethic earned him enough money to buy a horse. I remember your Papa saying, 'A horse is freedom - true freedom for a man.'"

Chapter 97
October 1935 Berlin, Germany
Marjem Rechtschaffen

The heightened tumult in the area inspires Helena's proposal. She advises me to apply for a travel authorization to Holland for Manfred and myself. Helena insists on return papers. Border patrol can be prickly, and we mustn't arouse any suspicion. I trace Arons' soft supple lips with my thumb, memorizing every crevice. His lips part and I kiss the love of my life goodbye.

Our lips linger barely touching. His breath is mine.

He whispers, "Do this for us."

His deep voice lacks depth and substance. It merely scratches the surface of sound. His face is red and swollen with sadness. He sucks in and I hear his heartbreak. I stand up straight and we kiss. He bites my lip when I pull away.

Growing up in Berlin makes travel abroad convenient. As a child I don't remember being captivated by the exquisite landscape. Consumed with myself or with my brothers and sisters we chatted away the hours in luxury. Henie, Gittel, and I would kick the seats in front of us when our parents weren't watching. Beyond our window the German countryside looks like a fairy tale backdrop of splendid gardens, parks, rivers, and castles. Did I see it this way as a child? Within thirty kilometers of Berlin suburban neighborhoods dominate. We've passed Brunswick and by Hanover, Manfred's already eaten both of our lunches.

He snuggles into me—fat and content; his exhaling breath smells sweet. When I caress his cheeks, he responds by looking right at me. I need instant gratification. Opening a window around Naturpark Honer Flaming releases an evergreen scent into the train compartment.

"Take a deep breath, baby, smell the forest."

I make an exaggerated breath in-and-out. I place my hand on his chest and feel his deep breath.

"What a good little boy you are."

Showing him my life through the safety of the train keeps the unease at bay.

My heart skips a beat when the train pulls into a station. My anchor is my husband. Out of habit, I turn to his absence, disconcerted. He calms me with a glance or a slight touch. I am used to him leading. I whisper to myself, small, simple commands to refocus my attention. Acknowledging the panic helps to control feeling overwhelmed. A bell signals and the doors close open and close. Preoccupied with the scenery, seats, tickets, and our snacks, the ride is pleasant. Manfred holds the tickets, which I am sure he'll tear or drop. Discouraging him is not how I parent; his desire to be a part of everything tugs at my heart.

"You're so proud of yourself, aren't you? Holding the tickets like a big boy."

Slapping the window in excitement, running deer capture Manfred's attention. In the late winter and early spring, a young moose can be spotted and turkeys, foxes, and deer all forage together. Manfred gathers his chubby legs underneath him, but keeps his eyes trained to the window.

"Manfred let me tell you about my father, Mozes. He loved visiting gardens, gardens of any kind - wide-open spaces where nature told a story in vivid color and texture. He could sit in a park and let the world around him melt away. One day he convinced my mother to walk through the gardens outside our windows, right now, instead of doing chores."

"Right now?" He asks.

"Yes, right now, look," I point.

"These are the Great Herrenhausen Gardens. I remember when he convinced Mother to visit these gardens instead of doing chores."

His eyes grow in delight.

"Mother enjoyed walking through expensive gardens with Papa side-by-side."

"I want to go," he demands as he slaps the window.

"He adored that this wonder was in his backyard. These gardens are magnificent - two cultures blended perfectly. The French flora is romantic. The German strictness of the stone paths encases the flowers and plants. His words whisper in my head. "These gardens represent wild untamed juxtaposed with rigidity. The pathways and statues trap the beauty."

His explanations echo in my mind.

"These gardens represent a beating heart. The heart is German, but the blood is French."

The conductor approaches to check our papers. Manfred distracts me from the conductor's attention, and I can't recall if he's already checked our papers. I am shocked at my carelessness. When will my memory return to what it was like before I got pregnant?

"Was ist der zweck ihrer weise?" (Why are you taking this trip?) asks the attendant.

"My Papa's sick," I responded.

"Wann werden sie wieder?" (How long will you stay there?") he inquires.

"We return in two weeks."

His eyes flash from me to Manfred, who is busy eating again. Manfred's cuteness softens the attendant's eyes. He punches holes in our tickets, in the shape of a smiley face for Manfred's pleasure.

He then places them in the seat above my head.

After lunch, I take Manfred to the bathroom to freshen up. As we return to our seats, dizziness overwhelms me. My stomach clenches and I rush us back to the bathroom. I must release my bowels. The indignity is manageable when I'm alone. The added pressure of taking care of Manfred is almost too much to bear. I rush to the toilet and smile through clenched teeth. The onslaught of nausea unsettles me. Holding Manfred's hand, I count backward from one hundred to one by threes. This distracts me until the soreness in my stomach subsides. I would like to crawl inside my bed with the windows open and shiver in the breeze. I close my eyes and imagine Aron telling me about his day. He maps out the neighborhood, explaining which streets are impassable and where a Jew can pass unseen. Manfred and I return to our seats.

We pass through Osnabruck, located between the Teutoburg Forest and the Wiehen Hills. During the economic depression in the 1920s, unemployment raged within the city limits and the population became overcrowded. The majestic landscape doesn't help the upcoming generation find work. There's no future for the young and industrious here. By Rheine, Manfred is hitting the glass window again in excitement. Forty kilometers left to go until we are free from Hitler. A train attendant walks towards me at an intense clip. My stomach lurches. I bite my inside cheek to gain composure. I'm running on pure adrenaline.

"Zeigen sie mir ihre papiere," (where are your papers?) demands the ticket taker.

He greedily snatches the papers from my hand. He scans them and walks to the back of the car without returning them to me. Manfred's eyes widen in fear. He feeds off my panic. Being a parent is reacting to a situation without your own concern in mind. Adjusting my reactions to protect my son is what matters. I turn my head and see that our ticket stubs, stuck in the back of my seat, are a different color. Six soldiers march down the aisle heading straight for us.

"Ihre papiere sind nicht gut. Sie mussen den," (your papers aren't in order, come with us) orders the German soldier in the front.

"Take your jacket, Manfred, and put it on. We're going to get off the train now," I say in defeat.

I want Manfred to remain calm. His mood can waver. I gather our possessions and put on Manfred's shoes. He needs his shoes.

"Ma taz?" (What's this?) asks Manfred.

"I don't know," I say.

The soldiers are in front of and behind us. We're led off the train like undesirables.

"Walk right in front of me, baby," I say to Manfred.

My palms sweat and strain against the leather handles of our luggage. Our escape is thwarted. Manfred's green pea eyes check my facial expression. Does he know I failed him? His cheeks are full and red. He is upset. His little face tells me he doesn't like what's happening. He lacks the control he wants. I want to comfort him, but I can't put his hand in mine.

My baby leads and I follow.

Passengers' eyes stare askance as not to share in our humiliation. There isn't a reason to scream or cry, no hero will come to help. Holding my head up high, clutching my suitcases and child, we're removed from the train and whisked off to the main passenger platform. My heartbeat quickens. On the platform, a guard instructs us to come inside the station. He opens the door and steps back. We walk towards another guard who stands behind a tall counter. A third guard checks my credentials against a printed list before him. Pictures of men, women and children that look like us line the wall. I wonder what happened to them?

What did they do to deserve this?

"The train is leaving without us, Mama," says Manfred.

"I know, baby. I know."

Chapter 98
November 1935 Berlin, Germany
Aron Rechtschaffen

The phone rings and my stomach drops.

"Where is she?" screams Henie.

Her voice hurts my ears. I pull the phone away, but I can still hear her.

"Aron, she never arrived!"

Gittel and Amalia argue in the background.

Gutted, my spine tingles.

"What do you mean? I put Marjem and Manfred on the train this morning."

Henie says something else but I don't comprehend. She sounds like she's underwater. What am I going to do?

"Aron, it's Maurice. Henie is talking to Mother."

"I have to find out what happened. I'll call you when I know more."

I hang up before he can respond. A fist squeezes my stomach. I wretch on the spot. I run through what I can make sense of. Her papers are legal.

I'm in the street, heading east towards Helena's apartment. The last time we were there was her Christmas party. Going to her house unannounced may be unwise. I reach her door and ring the bell. The chimes of wealth and privilege echo in my ear. Behind the thick oak door, a small door at eye-level opens and then closes. Muffled voices communicate and several locks open. An older woman with thick gray hair appears.

My voice fails and I stammer, "My apologies for coming unannounced. I seek ..."

The housemaid raises her gloved hand, "You can't be here. Take this basket."

She shoves a wicker basket into my arms, "There's a note from my lady telling you more. Do not do anything abruptly. Turn around and go home."

Before I can respond, she shuts the door. I rummage through the basket until I find the note: Meet me at Funkturm Berlin in one hour. Come alone. It is a good place to meet, a busy thoroughfare almost every commuter uses. She picks a time when thousands of commuters' hurry home for dinner. I cannot make myself go home. I go to our rendezvous and wait. I stand at one end of the street, and Helena appears before me. Tall and breath-taking, I notice her auburn hair. Marjem always said, "I trust Helena. She is a good person. She wears scandalous red lipstick and black leather gloves that reach her elbows. She's magnificent."

Hearing Marjem in my head comforts me. Helena is my only chance to find Marjem.

Helena approaches and says, "We'll talk while we walk. By the time I reach the end of the block, the conversation is over. It is not safe for me. Focus on someone else. I mean no disrespect. I must be careful. I don't know if they are watching me."

"I need to know if you can help me," I begin.

I have hundreds of questions on my mind.

"The Nazis removed Marjem and Manfred from the train in Reine. She is safe for now. A powerful associate of mine heard about your small business. He is interested in using your supply routes for his new installation project. I told Marjem this before she left. I am sure she told you. I thought she would be safe to escape to Holland, as my associates are only interested in you. I was wrong. For transparency, I am telling you things I would normally not share. He noticed Marjem applied to many countries to leave Germany. I knew she was leaving, forever. He must have suspected the same. He wants something he can hold over you." Helena explains. "Nothing more personal than your wife and child."

"I ... I ...will Marjem come home?" I stammer.

My throat is dry. I'm slick with sweat, like steamed fish. I must speak quickly. It is like a game I know I will lose with one wrong step. Pinching myself to regain control, I try again, but she interrupts me.

"You will meet him on the base next week. You aren't to speak about this to anyone," Helena says and then stops.

She opens her compact and checks her lipstick. I catch my breath. My body is flush with fever. Panting for air, I try to focus on my next words because they may be my last.

"Will she come back to me?"

I will give my life for Marjem and Manfred in a heartbeat. I want to growl and assert myself like a big black bear. I am nobody's pawn.

"Everything depends on you, Aron. If Marjem and Manfred return, then my friend owns you. You will fulfill the needs of my friend for his new military assignment and in return, you get your family back, but you will never leave Berlin. If you run now, then your life's your own and you can try to save Marjem."

"You have my store. Take whatever you want. Just give me back my Marjem. There is no question. Give them back to me," I say.

We are almost at the end of the block. I know my time is up.

"I'm sorry this happened."

She hesitates and is about to turn her head, "I never expected he'd notice she was on an outbound train today, but he has his ways. One day, Aron, I will tell Marjem it is time to go. If I can promise anything, I will not let Manfred perish here," Helena says as she steps off the curb and into the crowd.

Chapter 99
November 1935 Berlin, Germany
Helena

Marjem weeps, "I did everything right. I remained calm. It was almost easy."

I ring the excess water into the basin by the bed and smooth a cold cloth on her forehead.

Aron soothes her, "You did a wonderful job. You did everything right."

I say, "What happened to you was beyond your control."

"Helena, I never wanted to go without Aron," says Marjem.

"Please Marjem, don't speak. You must rest. You have a terrible fever and you have been trembling all night. Helena sent for her private doctor," says Aron.

The doorbell rings and Aron rushes from the room, returning with a short man carrying a leather bag.

"Am I going to be alright?" asks Marjem.

"Marjem, Dr. Butterman is my physician. He is Bavarian and served as a doctor during the war. Aron called me last night and told me about your fever."

Aron says, "Helena, I have never known Marjem to be sick a day in her life."

Dr. Butterman looks up.

"She is very dehydrated and exhausted."

I ask, "What is happening to her, Doctor?"

"The stress of the past forty-eight hours has been too much for her to handle. I've given her a B-12 shot and aspirin to reduce her fever."

"Is there anything else we can do for her?" asks Aron.

Doctor Butterman says, "There is something more going on here. I am not sure. You need to keep watch over her until the fever passes. I have a few more things to ask but we can do that in the other room and let her rest."

Aron follows the doctor out the door. Helena explains she has already paid him for his time, and he will return to make sure Marjem is alright.

"Aron, Aron, did I do it?" moans Marjem.

"You are here with me, Marjem. We are back in Berlin," I say.

Marjem pleads, "Aron, where are you?"

"Marjem, it's me! Helena. Aron is talking to the doctor."

I take another cold cloth and wipe the sweat from her face and neck.

"You have a terrible fever. You're dehydrated."

Marjem clutches her belly and throws up over the side of the bed. The retching continues and sounds painful.

"Where is my baby? What happened to the baby? In Holland, I had a doctor. Holland doesn't care that I'm Jewish." Marjem tosses and turns. She is growing agitated. Aron rushes in with the doctor.

"Marjem, what are you saying?" asks Aron.

He wants answers, but I do not know what to say.

"Manfred is safe and asleep in the other room."

"You mustn't worry. I brought a doctor here to take care of you." I repeat.

Marjem tries to throw up again but there is nothing left. Her body continues to convulse. All the color drains from Marjem's face.

"Don't leave me," she moans.

"No one is leaving you," I say.

"I tried," says Marjem.

Aron says, "You did everything right."

"Did it fall apart?" Marjem asks.

Aron says, "Nothing has fallen apart."

She opens her eyes in terror.

"I don't think I could've done anything differently," whispers Marjem. Her voice is growing weaker.

Dr. Butterman asks everyone to leave the room, but I linger. He turns to me and asks if blood makes me squeamish. I tell him no. The truth is, I have no idea. Marjem screams. She sits up in the bed and now her face is gray. Her eyes beg me to take away the pain. Blood spreads between her thighs. She screams again and clutches her stomach.

"No. No. Help me," says Marjem.

There is so much blood. To think, she almost made it out alive.

Aron rushes into the room and regards Marjem in disbelief.

"Aron. Leave," I say.

Dr. Butterman says, "Your wife is having a miscarriage."

He stops talking to us and focuses on Marjem.

"Helena, did you know she was pregnant?" asks Aron.

"No. I had no idea. She kept it a secret."

Dr. Butterman says, "Upon my initial examination, she must've been close to twelve weeks pregnant."

I walked over to Aron, and I put my hands on his shoulders. The gesture is familiar. Aron places a cold cloth on Marjem's forehead. Softly, he speaks to Marjem. Marjem confesses, "The Nazis won't let me leave."

"Hush now," he says.

She moans. He kisses her cheeks and wipes away her tears.

"Aron, how did you get here so fast? Aron, I did it. Manfred and I are safe. I dreamt we didn't make it across the border."

Dr. Butterman says, "She doesn't know what she is saying. Helena, we will be here for the day."

I think quickly about what needs to happen next.

"Aron, I will head home and pack a small bag. I will return with my housemaid Frau Wilma. She will take care of Manfred while I attend to Marjem."

"I can't ...."

"Aron, I will focus on Marjem. She will need time to recover. Women do not talk about these kinds of losses. We are raised to believe it is our fault, that our bodies are broken, useless vessels not worth compassion or respect. Miscarriage is a taboo topic. She will isolate herself. I will help her."

"Helena, thank you."

He appears lost and stunned.

"I will be back with Frau Wilma. We will bring some extra food from our larder. She will bake almond oatmeal cookies with Manfred and prepare our dinner. You need to work to keep everyone protected," I instruct.

"Helena ..."

"There is no need to worry. I know about your special eating habits. We will have fish tonight and tomorrow; Frau Wilma will go out and buy a chicken from the right place. We will make Jewish chicken noodle soup and get our girl back on her feet."

"Helena, she went through hell today," says Aron.

"Yes Aron, she went through hell, and she will come out. Marjem is the strongest person I have ever met." I admit.

Chapter 100
1936 Paris, France
Maurice Eisner

"Maurice, I worry" reveals François.

Uncertainty is a wealthy man's extravagance, our dad used to tell us. We're sitting around the kitchen table drinking wine. We just finished Heather's favourite dinner: creamy tomato basil soup and grilled cheese sandwiches.

"You never used to worry for me before, François."

I slap his back in jest and he rolls his eyes.

"The Swiss border is sticky right now. You're right. The access through Belgium is easier."

Heather snorts and François laughs outright, instantly breaking the tension. Heather stands up, grabs another bottle of wine from the counter and refills everyone's glasses. His point it's not lost on me. My travelling is more frequent and sometimes I get delayed upon my return. He used to ask me when he could expect my return. Lately he requests I simply show up unannounced at his front door.

Heather said, the one rule of subversion is to keep your loved ones in the dark. The two rule is if your family has questions about what you're doing then you're not doing it right.

Clearly, I'm not subversive enough. Laughing at my ineptitude I turn to my brother and kiss him on the cheek.

"François, I love you very much. It's wonderful how much you worry for me. Your time is better spent focused on protecting your beautiful family. I got Heather, here. As you say she's a handful."

I grab my lady by the waist and pull her closer to me dragging the chair with her.

Heather says, "on a recent radio broadcast the government raised the alert level."

Francois says, "The Nazi propaganda machinery relished Willem Gustoff's burial."

"They don't give a damn for him. He's a sacrificial lamb and they will use him like they use everybody else. They twisted his death into some big political parade."

She picks up her glass of wine, swirls it then places it back down.

Francois empties his glass and says, "I'm not convinced Hitler liked Gustoff. But the spectacle made it evident; Gustoff was a Nazi-loving bastard."

"The Swiss admired him," I say.

"He's an emblem of the Nazi effort. Hitler, Himmler, Göring, and Goebbels observed the service," notes Heather.

We sit quietly listening to the radio broadcast. The show continued and more propaganda overtook the radio waves. I turn off the radio in disgust.

"David Frankfurter assassination of Gustoff was an unprecedented act of nobility," declares Heather.

As her voice rises so does the flush that starts between her luscious bosoms and climbs up her neck. Redheads are so sexy especially when they're agitated.

"He's your age, François. He exposed Switzerland's hidden anti-Semitism."

Heather laughs and covers up her mouth quickly. She means no disrespect. It's the naïveté of the statement that tickles her. Heather places her hand on Francois' arm. She leans in and looks deeply into his eyes.

"Is their anti-Semitism a secret? There aren't any Jewish leaders in Switzerland, or inventors, or musicians? Does Switzerland strike you as the type of place to nurture a religious Jew?"

François eyebrows rise to his hairline.

"I'm not sure. We know the NSDAP is another face of Nazism."

"Do the Nazis offend the Swiss?" I ask.

I take off my jacket and loosen my tie. There's no reason to be formal, it feels like we're settling in for a good debate.

Heather reflects, "François, the Swiss like to say they are neutral. It is convenient. When lives are on the line, where you stand regarding the line matters."

I ask Heather, "Did you see Wolf?"

"Yes. He tangled himself up with that little Swiss treat Leandra."

François laughs.

"Of course, he did. What did her brother tell you?"

Heather says, "Hotel names."

François asks, "Why hotel names?"

Heather says, "We don't need to know. That is for my friend Simon. He'll take the information from there."

Dear Marjem,

I went to the movies last Sunday and the newsreel out of Germany left me breathless. Germany and Hitler are the main topics of every conversation. The French feel Hitler's influence is growing. They fear his fanaticism. The world is changing, and with Hitler's annexation of the Rhineland, where will it stop? France did not fight back. This made Maurice insane. He hates Hitler and how Germany has changed. He controls his rage, but he cannot remain still. He has been traveling more than usual back-and-forth to Holland and Belgium. Britain made a trite joke about not getting involved in the world's stage when Hitler was playing in their backyard. Maurice screamed and left the room with an open bottle of wine.

When we first arrived in Paris, I never felt alone with Maurice by my side. He bossed me around, but the truth is I liked it because he sounds like Ima. Paris is fantastic. The vibrant Jewish community has control of so many neighbourhoods here. People live an honest good life where they go to work, enjoy their families, and thrive amongst arts and architecture. The schools for the children cover a substantial curriculum. The children are bilingual in both French and Hebrew. Since Jews have lived here for centuries, the lifestyle is commonplace, it is neither religious nor restrictive. French cuisine is exceptional, especially the cheese. Every day for lunch I eat a baguette with cheese. My wife, Colette, makes me happy. We raise her daughter from her first marriage. Rosalie is a charming young lady who is complicated, brilliant, and mature beyond her years. Maurice confirmed I made the right decision about Colette. He said when you are lucky enough to find love you grab on and hold tight.

I am paralyzed with fear. I know you have more secrets, and I am sure those secrets are even more terrifying than what I imagine them to be. Whatever it is I can do, please tell me; I would do anything for you.

Love, François

Chapter 102
August 1936 Berlin, Germany
Marjem Rechtschaffen

Dear Henie,

Music streams in through the windows from the cafés and tea shops late into the night. Young European women from Paris, Holland, America, Denmark, and Belgium wear exquisite clothing in fashions we've never seen before. The blouses are fitted, in vibrant colors and with intricate detailing on the collars and sleeves. The skirts are long and tailored, cut to enhance a lady's beautiful shape. The skirts hug the hips and flare out like a bell below the knees. Hairstyles are short and fresh, yet undeniably feminine. Exposing the neck in a coquettish way is the secret to the allure. The stains of Nazism are temporarily scrubbed clean but it's like painting a wall in your home, if you don't use a primer coat the old and dingy color can seep through and ruin the whole new effect.

It's a wonder to visit Museum Island after Shabbat services again. You should see it. Entire neighborhoods congregate in Monbijoupark like the old days. The ladies from the synagogue are stationed in their prime locations. Aron and I move about Berlin like we used to. Manfred has never seen Berlin. A Berlin that is cultured and educated. Aron takes him everywhere. Manfred explores the park and finds the perfect secret spots for playing hide and seek. Aron teaches him to climb a tree. Within a few days, Manfred knows the park like the back of his hand. Before dinnertime Aron directs us to the latest evening concerts in the park. When the sun sets, the heat of the day is replaced with a gentle breeze. We eat out and socialize with old friends. Life is cherished again.

Krausnickstraße is happily buzzing. I visited Rennbahn Grunewald to watch our athletes' practice for the games. Through the freshly painted gates, the rich brown of the track surrounded by the vibrant greens of the manicured lawns reminds me of the gardens Papa had us visit all over Germany.

We eat Belgian waffles on Sunday mornings and wake up early before sunrise and walk around the city when it's quiet. Small pop-up bakeries and tea shops are everywhere. Even with all the walking I'm doing, the sinfully delicious onion boards from Oranienburger Straße are thickening my hips. Daily, Aron surprises Manfred and me with different cakes and pastries. His sweet tooth will be my undoing.

Last week, Helena gave me a second radio for our apartment. She already gave us one for the store. She insisted she needed it to have access to her programs while she came to visit. Aron understands the arrangement, but he also considers us quite blessed. We do not know any other Jews allowed to continue with their business the way we are. Most are simply squeezed out and are left to starve. She calls her profits her mad money, but we know she spends it to help good people like us.

The innovation in Germany makes me proud. The sophistication of the German Broadcasting Company enabled an Olympic broadcast to reach twenty-five viewing stations within Berlin alone and the broadcast was translated into twenty-eight different languages. Citizens can attend any event free of charge and there's additional short wave radio broadcast which can keep everyone up to date on the games and results. The Olympics increased tourism and helped the economy. This month alone, we made enough money to secure us for the next three months. The Italian national swimming team bought eight duvets. Aron watches whatever Olympic events he can during the day in between deliveries. Three months ago, we ordered extra fabric, feathers and expensive silk with intricate patterns. We made as many throw pillows and duvets as our machines could manage. I promised him our investment would pay off. I'm not a gambling woman but I believed the business would grow. These are times unlike any other. It feels good to be alive. I love you very much.

Love, Marjem

Chapter 103
August 1936 Berlin, Germany
Aron Rechtschaffen

A hundred thousand people surround me, electrified to witness Siegfried Eifrig running the Olympic flame down the Unter den Linden. We cheer alongside Germans, Jews, Europeans, and other Olympian-loving fans.

Marjem is flush with zeal. Manfred's mouth and eyes are wide open with every sense engaged.

Germany is free spirited and the undercover SS in plain clothes don't alert tourists to their oppressive oversight. Berlin's multiculturalism is heard in a bakeshop between a German and a Dutchman. In the early hours, before the sun is up, but once the birds have begun their morning song, Lithuanians and Serbians are collecting garbage and delivering packages. Young men argue in the way they do and there's no fear that the police will come and break it up. Not even good Germans want the attention of the police if they can avoid it. The sound of Polish brings my childhood back. The slang and jocularity make me light on my feet. My brain thinks in Polish, and my mouth can taste the words. I want someone to ask me for directions.

Walking out my front door, I hear men carousing down the street. Drinking pitchers of fresh beer on the terrace while eating soft pretzels with hot spicy mustard is a great way to start your Sunday. The Olympics have put most people on vacation from their regular jobs. Two weeks ago, the German Ministry of the Interior ordered a sweep of undesirables. Gypsies, communist and intellectuals disappeared. Lost in my thoughts, I find myself on Rennbahn Grunewald.

Two women adorned in hues of blue and purple rush in front of me. They speak fluid French punctuated with Dutch.

I suspect they're from Brussels. They dress like Henie. The short one is wearing a yellow skirt and glances inside her clutch purse.

I ask if they need assistance.

Yellow skirt shows me the address while her friend freshens her makeup with a mother of pearl compact mirror. I felt better turning them around. Beautiful girls with a terrible sense of direction aren't always safe.

"Let me walk you there," I say.

"It's on my way home."

She considers my offer. I reach into my pocket and remove a picture of my family. I pass it to her to prove that I'm a family man.

"It's simply not safe to let young women such as yourselves wander the streets."

Madeline and her sister step closer and she hands me back the picture.

"You're very nice."

She explained how her mother worried she'd run into the Nazis when we came to Berlin.

"Be conscientious because Nazis are all around you," I remind her.

"Berlin is beautiful, true, but Germany has changed a lot in a truly short amount of time."

"We heard Jews aren't liked here. Everyone knows. Jews aren't liked in a lot of places," admits Madeline.

"The Nazis bullied the Jewish children right out of school. He then fired the teachers and carded them off to work camps."

After the teachers disappeared, Socialists, journalists, political types disappeared next. Newspapers went out of print. Independent magazines with alternative opinions ceased to exist. The Nazis touch every aspect of life here in Germany. It's ruining what I grew up loving. Jewish lawyers can't represent their clients in court. Jewish doctors are forbidden to enter hospitals. You never know where evil lurks. I wish the girls a lovely evening.

Walking away, I turn down Friedrichstraße by the railroad tracks. As I walk along Luisenstraße, I head towards the bus stop. As the August sun beats down upon my back, I move into the shade and catch my breath in the muggy air.

The general sense of *gleichschaltungand* (overwhelming discomfort caused by others,) abates.

"Berlin feels different right now," says one man to another.

"The music is loud, the women are beautiful, and the entire world is watching us," says the other man.

They speak to one another with an ease that reflects their friendship.

"I hope it lasts."

"The Olympics saved lives, I'm sure."

"The abuse will continue, but today we can feel like regular people."

They stand together and laugh like teenage boys, attracting attention from any passer-byer, welcoming them into the conversation. The SS are listening and creating new lists for future arrests. A couple arrives at the stop holding hands.

Their fingers intertwined and oblivious to everyone around them. Two brown shirts, in full uniform, arrive, and the mood shifts.

The air is thinner, and it is harder to take a deep breath.

The bus arrives, I pardon myself for not walking in the sun, and I file into the bus with everyone else. The brownshirts stand in the front. A friend from the synagogue, Bert Walker, stands before me.

"I take this bus regularly for my deliveries," Bert says to me.

"Bert, the past week has been busy at the store," I add.

"My deliveries this month are all over the city. I want some time to enjoy the events," he confesses.

"Marjem is shipping duvets all over the world. She's having a hard time figuring out all the shipping costs."

Laughing he says, "These are good problems to have."

"True. What do you want to watch today?" I ask.

"Football, but that's not going to happen. I considered tennis. I want to blend into the crowd and be anonymous," confesses Bert.

We reach Olympischer Plaza and join the crowd; the energy is addictive.

A football game will be exciting. Unfortunately, Germany was eliminated in the quarterfinals. With nationalism soaring, most Germans threw support to Austria.

After the contested match between Austria and Peru, the Peruvians and Columbians left the Olympics. Reviewing my choices, I join a line for a cold lemonade.

Athletes are breaking Olympic and World records. Marjorie Gestring, a thirteen-year-old American girl, dove to the gold medal. A twelve-year-old Danish girl won bronze for the breaststroke. The biggest upset was the black Jesse Owens from the United States. He beat Germany's greatest long jumper; Lutz Lang. Goebbels wants to keep the loss a secret.

Such a disgrace in front of Hitler. Everyone was horrified. No one would know about this great upset unless they saw it with their own eyes.

Marjem waited for me just inside the front door.

"The radio broadcast shutdown without a warning. It scared me," said Marjem.

The results weren't broadcast. Visibly agitated, I realize how much calmer she has been during the Olympics.

It is important she remains calm and keeps her blood pressure down. Hitler loosening the reins on the Jews makes us all feel a little closer to normal.

"Everyone went outside to find out the results. I enjoyed gossiping in the street. It felt casual and unimportant. People theorizing felt salacious."

She rubs her belly.

"I'm sorry you worried."

She hasn't admitted to being pregnant yet.

The miscarriage spooked her. I'm allowing her the time to come back to herself. She was very happy when pregnant with Manfred. Her hair grew thick like a Mustang, her heart raced but her energy never waned.

I notice that she is sensitive to smell. She believes I don't notice these clues that are manifesting every day. It's not the right time and we certainly don't live in the right place but a brand-new life that comes from our love is a blessing.

Chapter 104
August 1936 Berlin, Germany
Marjem Rechtschaffen

Dear Henie,

I miss you, my Chana.
Without my three beautiful sisters' love and devotion, we would have lost Mama too when Papa died six years ago. Immersing Mama in your daily life ensures she will remain youthful and sharp. I would say more but it's been too long since I could see any of you.
Life during the Olympics was like being a teenager who missed curfew to kiss the bad boy. Living on adrenaline for as long as you can last. After the closing ceremonies, the confetti was swept away as were our freedoms and liberties. The plain suited disguises were replaced with full Nazi regalia. Life is back to a slow strangulation. This time we know what's ahead for us, if we don't leave.
Remember Elsa's dad, Dr.Gottielbaum? They followed Elsa to Palestine. She left in 1933 and is blissful. They live on a kibbutz with eleven other families. They sleep on the floor, eat together, and save water whenever possible. Elsa works

in their kitchen and says the oppressive heat makes her pant like a dog in the summertime. The air smells sweet, like almond trees. I would trade "almond-smelling air" and oppressive heat over another Berlin winter. Mr. Bremmerman is also headed for Palestine. His children left two years ago, and they had a baby. He is getting priority status to Palestine. He'll open a new school and teach.

Last, but certainly not least is Helena, the store and the continuing saga of the Hens.

Helena bought a radio for the store. The casual atmosphere lulled the Hens into chatting. The mission details for massive events are there for the taking, if you can catch the right clues. When the Hens bemoan some of their husbands' new assignments, they don't see the clues I can put together. These women are the biggest traders of their country's national secrets. Trying to outdo one another with possessions or their husband's relationships to Hitler.

Would you believe during the Olympics the Hens were jealous of tourists? They invaded their kingdom; my store, and unable to hold court here, they felt irrelevant. They aren't happy little sycophants any longer.

Factories formerly owned by friends are now run by the Nazis. Packed with secret merchandise and supplies for surreptitious means. Abandoned neighborhoods once teaming with immigrants are impassable due to the heavy presence of the police.

When my frustration mounts, I have full-blown arguments inside my head. I play both sides. To release the demons, I use exercise like a drug.

The exhaustion quells my agitation. I'm not sure if I'm being healthy but my legs are sculpted like a ballerina. I want you to be the first to know. Come June, Manfred will be a big brother.

I have been keeping it a secret, but life is short and there is no time for this kind of joyous secret.

Love,
Marjem

Chapter 105
June 1937 Antwerp, Belgium
Gideon Eisner

Dear Marjem,

Mazel Tov on the birth of Rudolph Nathan! May he bring your health, wealth, and happiness. Happy birthday to your Manfred. I bet he questioned every limitation put in front of him. They are all bumps and bruises.

Keeping our business viable in the shambles of an economy is a challenge. Who can afford to board and preserve fine furs for the summer when work and food are sparse.

My wife Laura makes pretty clothing; she's an accomplished seamstress. Mending and patching don't begin to encompass her true skill set. We diversified and Laura runs the shop. She mentors local young girls through the Secours Rouge Belgique. Tailoring is a great skill to master. The SRB appreciated her dedication to the underprivileged. Her access proved invaluable.

I reached out to Maurice. Antwerpen is a second home for him and his lovely Heather. Belgium remains neutral on the global stage, but neutrality is unsustainable. If Hitler wants the Jews of Belgium, Belgium will hand over their Jews. A year ago, the king declared Belgium would never get involved in another world war in Europe.

Hitler is a tyrant. He will destroy everything ancient, beautiful, or historic if he cannot lay claim to it. He knows exactly what he is doing. He is a psychopath and can convince others he is sympathetic because he feigns compassion. He works hard to never let down his guard. He feels misunderstood. He craves the company of others who will mirror his actions. His unfulfilled dream to find others who reflect his own beliefs will transform his rage into monstrous terror.

We know how hard it is for you to be there. We pray for you every night and wait for better news to come. Stay strong, my beautiful sister.

Love, Gideon

Chapter 106
September 1937 Berlin, Germany
Marjem Rechtschaffen

"Palestine offers opportunities for Jews, Marjem," says Helena.

She lays her palms on her skirt and straightens a particularly stubborn crease and other invisible wrinkles. After she clears her throat, she sips her tea.

"The Judentagung upset many people. The larger the grouping, the more noticeable the anti-semitic it becomes. Which reminds me, I brought you something."

She reaches into a pouch and raises a bottle of schnapps.

"Can I add some to your tea?"

I inquire as I unwrap the paper before hearing her answer.

"You are exceptionally generous. I want you to have this for later," says Helena.

"Helena, if I have learned anything - later is never promised. Let us fill our cups with a little tea and a lot of that extra flavor you just unwrapped." We agree.

She begins, "Eichmann and Hagen cajoled peasants to revolt against the Jews. That's what *my friend* says. Germans

439

want only the Volk to live here. The Jews must leave. Their wealth and property must remain within the German borders. The Nazis want the rich to pay for the peasants to leave."

She pauses, studying my face.

"Marjem, are you alright?"

I say, "The Nazis can have it all. Take everything."

Helena says, "I made my mother some potato and leek soup. When I brought it to her, I noticed her hands trembling. She has deep furrows between her eyebrows. My mother was the most beautiful woman I have ever known, and she could mask her age like a magician."

Her eyes filled with tears.

"And now?"

"She's grown complacent. She's lost the will to drag a brush through her hair and put lipstick on."

"Helena, I don't know what to say."

"Marjem, I put myself in great danger being your friend. I started because I like your strength. I continued because I saw how intelligent you are. Then, I recognized a way to save you."

"I don't think we will survive here much longer."

"Marjem, I have eyes everywhere. Aron is safe. The business is good. Do you have enough money?"

"Yes."

I cover my face in my hands. I am trying to hold myself together. I know how much Helena hates tears.

"Marjem, what have you done to your fingers? Your cuticles are unacceptable. Marjem, go get some gloves."

She is right, I would never let myself go like this before...

"I need to control my anxiety. Helena, you have protected the business, and you have saved our livelihood. Without you, they would have taken everything away from us and we still wouldn't be able to leave."

"Marjem, my plans are in motion: paperwork, entry visas, and passports, but if he figures out what I have done, he will kill me."

"Helena, I didn't know."

"No matter how well I cook, dance, make myself pretty for and have sex with him, none of it will matter...," she trails off.

"If you get caught."

"If I get caught," says Helena.

"Patience is not a virtue of a pregnant woman. You are so beautiful; Aryan beautiful. Big breasts, bouncy blonde hair, evergreen eyes, and a big bottom. Your beauty will help you escape. For now, I am focusing on Manfred. You are close to giving birth. Having a baby in transit is not optimal for anybody involved," says Helena with finality.

Chapter 107
March 1930 Berlin, Germany
Manfred Rechtschaffen

The baby consumes Ima's attention.

She relishes curiosity and never tempers the countless questions I have about how things work, or why we must do something one way and not another.

We're heading to the bank today, which is an important chore. She runs the deliveries, and she monitors the books.

After we leave the bank, she holds a large white envelope in her gloved hand. She takes the envelope and folds it over once and places it inside her purse. She pats her purse and says, "deep, deep."

She takes a second white envelope and folds it in half.

This time she hands it to me.

"Don't let go of this envelope, Manfred. It is important," she says.

"All right, Mama."

"I need to know you can follow simple instructions when you might not understand the importance."

"I can do that for you, Mama."

"Good. A big brother always thinks about how to protect his baby brother."

Her voice softens.

"Tell me what you know about Rudy."

"Rudy can't put his socks on yet. He wears his shirt and sweater backwards. He doesn't like the feel of the scratchy tag against the back of his skin. I can comfort Rudy when he wakes up abruptly. He likes carrots but not green beans. Cherries are his favorite fruit, but peaches are easier to eat. In fact, apples are his true favorite. He's clumsy and will always spill something. He davens even louder than he speaks, but he hates loud noises."

"You know quality things, one day, I may not be around. You will be Rudy's champion. He will need you to guide him through the world."

She will not meet my eyes as she keeps walking forward.

I do not want to tell her how frightened I am. Why wouldn't she be around to take care of me? I want to ask but do not.

My panic overwhelms me, and I start to cry.

"Manfred, this is important. Recognize what is happening around you. There may come a time when you will have to take care of Rudy."

I do not understand the expression in her eyes. I wipe my tears away. She didn't acknowledge that I'm upset.

She used to care when I cried.

"Where are you going?"

"I'm not going anywhere," she pauses.

"It's very important to me that I know you will always protect baby Rudy."

I want to say, who is going to protect me? Why are you not worried about me? I am so mad at Rudy right now and it is not his fault, it is hers.

"I will always protect Rudy," I say.

She grabs me around the shoulders and pulls me in for a hug. She smells good.

Her hair shines like the sun streaming through the windows at sunrise, "I am the voice in your head, and I am a voice in your heart."

She takes her hand and places it upon my chest. The heat of her hand warms my body. I am proud of how well she takes care of herself.

"If you come across a situation and you do not know what to do, stop. Take a moment and pause. Consider before acting. Ask yourself, is this a good situation for me? Am I doing this for myself or am I doing this for another reason? Would my Mama be proud of what I am about to do? If you consider these questions, you will have more success in your life than failure."

I hold on tight to my envelope. I understand the importance – this is a test. I want to learn how to cook eggs, stay up all night and protect Rudy. She wants me to hold onto an envelope and show her I can focus and listen.

My mother knew she was running out of time, but I never felt her unending panic.

My parents' lives were threatened daily. I didn't know we could cease to exist in an instant. In the months leading up to our escape from Berlin my mother instilled as much knowledge as she could. She said it's more important to listen than to speak. Be keenly aware of what is going on around you and who the players in the room are.

She said there's always an advantage to be had.

Chapter 108
October 1937 Berlin, Germany
Manfred Rechtschaffen

Trucks and cars pass our home at night; their headlights create dancing shadows on my wall.

I hear Abba outside my door, and I join him in the hallway.

He looks messy and unattended after he runs his hand through his thick hair.

With a weighted sigh, he says, "go back to sleep, Manny. It's late and you need rest."

The skin beneath his eyes is brown and jaundiced, like that stubborn old bruise I had on my knee after I fell down on the sidewalk. I'm agitated and I don't know how to tell him.

He wants to teach me how to be a man, steer a carriage, shoot a rifle, and drink a beer.

Our time together is running out.

Clutching the neck of the baseball bat, our weapon to fight off the Nazis, he tells me stories about Ima.

Some stories are silly, and others are private.

They both dreamt that a good life in Berlin is the secret key to the kingdom. The future is unclear, and any decision not definitive drives Ima crazy.

"If I die, cover your eyes and shield Ima."

He shares his mistakes, the ones he couldn't control, and the ones I could've. These secrets are the catalyst for me walking away from childhood.

Control became the most important thing to me.

Control over my thoughts, actions and speech. Abba has none, and I need to get some.

As the sun rose, Abba tired, open and honest, answered every question I came up with.

Why is Rudy able to sleep through the din of the motorcycles?

Why does my fear and anger wash me in sweat?

Ima says Rudy will depend on me one day. Ima taught me to read and write. I can bathe and put him down for a nap without issue. His slumber is deep and the gurgling sound he makes means he's at peace.

I placed my head on Abba's lap and he stroked my hair.

Years later, I am a father of three beautiful boys. I remember this moment. It never occurred to me as a child how ineffectual his baseball bat would be against a Nazis rifle. Jail changed a once upbeat and light-hearted spirit into an omnipresent dark man. He sees difficulty before opportunity. To me, in those years living in Berlin, Abba was immortal—a Jewish man, which the government could not disappear.

Chapter 109
March 1938 Berlin, Germany
Marjem Rechtschaffen

I'm sitting at the kitchen table with a newspaper open in front of me. Seeing the words in print makes the unreal believable.

Aron says, "After the Anschluss in Austria...."

I interrupt, "Maurice's letter could only say so much.

The phone call last week at the store gave me a little bit more. Helena showed me pictures that her friend showed her in confidence.

"Jewish people have a long history of living and loving Germany. Generations of Jews have prospered. The history for Jews in Austria is not as great or as extensive. They now stand with the Nazis. Maurice listened to Kurt Schuschnigg, the Austrian Chancellor, deliver an address on the radio. He tried to withstand the Austrian Nazis but failed."

We read in the paper the handover of power was peaceful and many lives were saved during the bloodless coup.

The paper didn't use the word cool but that's what it was.

"Maurice wrote Jewish owned property, businesses and vehicles were surrendered to the Nazis."

Aron circles behind me and places his hands on my shoulders.

"Marjem, stop winding yourself up."

He massages the right side of my neck while I rest my left ear against my shoulder.

While pushing down my right shoulder, the stretch elongates my neck and releases pressure.

"Maurice told me the military parade rolled over Vienna with soldiers and tanks consuming the boulevard. Hundreds of billowing flags hung from every building and windowsill. Exhilaration and wonder vibrated from the stands erected for the event when bombers flew low to the ground."

"Marjem, I would've been terrified. German stormtroopers guarded the Austrian workers to ensure they never stop working. Remember when Maurice said something about staying up at that party for over two days in celebration? That's what he was talking about."

"It makes me sick. Good people at the mercy of evil. They turn coercion into their precision weapon of distinction."

Aron walks over and sits down next to me.

"We knew about the Germans in Austria almost six months ago. The Hens discussed the new Centre for Jewish Emigration in Vienna."

The information in the right hands could save lives. Helena never divulges anything directly; she simply enables the larger conversation; providing trigger comments to propel the Hens to one up each other with their pillow talk.

"Austria is tossing away their Jews. Whole neighborhoods are evacuating."

"Nothing good will come from this, Aron. It's crass. Money for visas."

"What else did she say, Marjem?"

"A Jew is lucky if she can hold onto her coat. The Nazis take whatever they want. They use underfed German Shepherds to terrorize children. On command, the beasts sink their teeth into Jewish flesh."

"The latest summons from the government requires us to report assets over five thousand Reichsmarks."

Aron wants to report for the both of us. The work orders from Helena's friend keep us occupied. Shipping dozens of high-end duvets, goose-feather pillows, and wool blankets to Vienna. Hindsight makes the pieces fall into place. Helena's friend ran logistics for the Anschluss.

"Marjem, we need to speak to Maurice. We have a large shipment headed to Krakow in six months."

"Aron, what if we close the store?"

"Marjem, the store is the only thing keeping us alive."

Chapter 110
March 1938 Berlin, Germany
Helena

I awake with a staggering headache. The sunshine seeps through my blackout curtains. Dressed in my powder blue morning coat and slippers I pick up the phone and cancel my plans for the day. Frau Wilma greets me when I enter the kitchen; she's preparing my breakfast.

"You resemble last night's leftovers." Frau Wilma isn't as funny as she thinks.

"Buttered toast, a hard-boiled egg, and a cup of tea. I'll be in the salon by the window." My tone lacks kindness but she doesn't care either way. Tough as nails and constantly overstepping her post, she's judgemental but takes great care of me.

The salon is my favorite room in my apartment. Overstuffed couches, antique tables, and a set of Marie Antoinette lamps gifted to me years ago. My oak wooden breakfront is filled with porcelain animals like bears, birds and cats. The glass shelves and hidden lights showcase my treasures. In my parlor I remain hidden behind a curtain with a perfect bird eyes view of the world outside.

The captivating outdoors is picturesque from my perch.

"You're a voyeur," says Frau Wilma.

The backyards are shared across many neighbors. I raise my eyebrow and open the morning paper. I have no intention of reading with this headache. I wrestle with the newspaper for dramatic effect. Opening the window allows a cool breeze to waft across the room.

A dog whistle outside assaults my ears. People gather and gossip. Children electrified by the excitement find purpose in running around in circles. The boorish boys across the street upset the neighbors. I move the cool cloth across my forehead to find a cooler section.

A mother in her early thirties, rail-thin, wears a threadbare apron with a faded pattern of flowers. She carries a wicker basket large enough to carry four regular loads of wash. Her tight bun strains against her face. She removes sundried clothing from the laundry line. An elderly woman opens her front door and yells, "Animals!"

A plump older woman responds, "Listen to the commotion out there. Every day it's something new."

Another woman says, "We don't know what's happening."

The thin woman grimaces and continues to pick her wash off the line. Several boys run towards her: blonde-haired boys wearing ironed Hitler youth uniforms.

The tallest boy says, "The SA needs our help. We're hunting a Jew."

She reaches out and grabs his arm.

"You're not a hunter. Go inside the house."

He pushes her away. She falls backward onto the ground. He does not reach out to catch her. Only a disgusting child would allow their mother to fall to the ground.

His face is unkind; she puts her head in her hands.

The child says, "I'm on official business. If you try to stop me, I will report you."

The police troll the streets at night. Gunshots fire randomly. Aren't Germans worn down by the constant disruption? Another dog whistle blows, and a young brown shirt runs into the thin woman's backyard.

Even in my home, I cannot escape the terror.

"Wilma, bring me my medicine, I have a migraine."

Rubbing cocaine across my gums will alleviate it.

My doctor says It's harder to find my medicine lately.

"Thank you, Wilma."

"My pleasure, Miss."

Hitler prefers mass distribution of synthetic concoctions over natural supplements like morphine, cocaine, heroin, and opium. The government is concerned they will lose control of the people if they're addicted to drugs. My friend met doctors and reviewed the science of addiction. The extreme cases strip people of their ability to think, reason, love and even recuperate.

Last week, my friend handed me a beautiful box of chocolates. We each ate two. When I went for the third he told me I'd had enough. My mood soured. He listened to the radio program while I pouted.

Thirty minutes later, we attended an after-hours private night club. We drank, we laughed, we celebrated life, like a teenager until three in the morning.

We came home dancing and then we collapsed. Two days passed and Frau Wilma was furious.

My friend explains this is a new aid the Nazis created for society. It is fast-acting, fills you with energy and delight, and can keep you awake when you need to keep working. He told me it was synthetic crystal methamphetamine.

The energy rush was superb, but the hangover was far too brutal for my precious bones.

"Frau, bring me a Cocaine-Cola, my stomach is sore."

I glance out the window one last time before I return to bed.

While asleep I reminisce on better times, standing in the sun, carelessly laughing with my hair caressing my bare shoulders. We had a summer cottage by a lake, as did my best friend Jonathan's parents.

Johnny and I spent every summer together.

The summer I turned sixteen our mutual competitive streak took us over. We raced across the lake, and I beat him. I stood on his shoulders and pretended to stand on the podium, thanking everyone for coming to our race.

We were silly and young.

As I slid down his body, I felt every inch of his taut, tanned flesh. His chest against mine, my legs slippery against his. His thick, black lashes framed his dusky blue eyes. Thick black curly hair crowns his face like a boy king. Lake water drips off his skin. Holding my face in his hands, he gently brushes my lips with his. He drags me closer and I kiss him harder. His scent makes my body buzz.

In my dreams, his hands never stop touching me.

Our passion burns like a newly struck match.

When I come home my mother takes my hand and brings me into the closet. She closes the door behind her and speaks quietly and decisively.

"Helena, you are spending too much time with Jonathan. It was fine when you were ten, but now it's bordering on inappropriate."

"What's inappropriate about Johnny?"

"Nothing. He is a good boy. He comes from a wonderful family but let us not be naïve," then she whispers, "you won't marry a Jew."

Shocked by her narrow-mindedness, I'm rendered speechless.

On a hot, lazy July afternoon, we head to the lake for a swim. After half an hour, he slips his arms around my waist like an octopus tentacle. Pulling me closer, his fingertips roam my ribs and his thumbs extend close to my breasts. He kisses my neck and buries his nose in my tangled wet hair. He moves as if he has all the time in the world. His hands, unafraid.

He knows exactly what he wants.

"Close your eyes." He growls.

He holds me harder and presses me up against a rock, leaving me nowhere else to go but forward and into him. He slides his thick muscular thigh between my legs.

This time when he holds me, he rubs his thumbs over my breast, nipples.

Greedy for him, wrap my legs around his waist.

Chapter 111
April 1938 Perehinske, Galicia
Naftali Herzl

Dear Aron and Marjem,

Mazal Tov on the birth of your second son, Rudolph! Children are a gift. The wonderment in a child's eyes makes me hope for a better world. Slow down when you can. Cherish the smallest changes in the boys.

One day, a child wants nothing more than you. In a blink of an eye, a child's needs change. The urge to pull away is natural and necessary but it hurts.

A parent understands the constant care taken to protect their children. Carving out a path for survival left me sleepless.

After Walter left for London, the headaches began. After the draft they worsened. Your mother prepared Tree-Tea by the carafe. Each night, I drank two cups. I slept without dreams. My body awoke feeling thick and slow. Once he returned from the war, the headaches stopped.

Your mother and I drink tea nightly because our children are growing up under an occupation. You lack rights and sovereignty. Your family appreciates how you teach the boys to respect our faith in a world that is disrespectful. That makes your love brave.

We cannot avoid the discussions in the marketplace, on the street, and in every club and store.

The Polish state is not any better. They don't want the Jews to return to Poland either. It's shocking. Over the past fifty years, millions of Jews left Poland and emigrated all over Europe, to escape pogroms or conscription by the Russians, the Polish, and the Ukrainians. Germanic outward antagonism towards the Jewish people forced the Polish authority to embrace their version of anti-Semitism. They don't want any Jews to return to Poland.

The Polish Ministry of Internal Affairs mandated an endorsement stamp on every citizen's passport.

By denying the stamps to Jews who live outside of Poland, the government squeezed out their own Jews.

Meanwhile, Jews, Ukrainians, and Polish townsfolk grow tired of the Polish government's exorbitant taxes. Townsfolk no longer accept the government ripping their sons from their mothers' breasts for an unsupported war effort no one supports.

The path for most people is difficult. Without the ability to educate, raising your station in life is impossible.

Get yourself to Holland. Holland is splendid. Where the sunsets fill the sky with pinks and purples, my eyes drink in the majesty. The colors bleed together until they touch the water. Lulled to sleep by the ebb and flow of the sea, would be a great replacement for Tree-Tea.

Love, Abba

Chapter 112
May 1938 Berlin, Germany
Manfred Rechtschaffen

My best friend Daniel says his parents went out for milk and never returned.

At first his aunt Sarah was frantic searching for her sister discovering clues as to their whereabouts.

A week later she stopped looking.

The following week Daniel moved away with his aunt to Poland. When she says, goodbye, her lips pulled across her teeth. Ima told me to watch people's expressions more than listen to their words.

Experiencing the trauma in small stages made it more palatable for me while forging my resistance. It's the individuals who didn't break who taught me the most. After the raids, Families disappeared, and confiscated homes and warehouses became the norm.

Chapter 113
June 1938 Berlin, Germany
Aron Rechtschaffen

Someone covers a discarded body of a murdered man with hastily applied newspapers. I can't shake off the vision. Before I slip my key into the lock, I take a few deep breaths. Calmness flows through me when I turn the key.

Marjem plays on the rug with both Manfred and Rudy-bear. Instead of washing my hands after a long day. I sit down hard on the couch sending magazines onto the floor in Rudy's delight.

Pouting I say, "I've outlived my usefulness."

"Aron, not to me."

She brings me a warm cloth to wipe my hands with.

"Always with cleanliness, Marjem?" I mock her.

I meet her eyes with candor.

"My connections are perishing."

"Our Jewish contacts are dead or in Dachau."

"Marjem, that's harsh. Our backs are up against the wall."

"Helena wants Rudy to be older and more controllable."

"We're lucky that she cares," I say.

"Sometimes I forget myself, and I confide in Helena. She makes my days exciting in an empty, non-threatening way. The dynamics have changed since we first met. "She needs our business to expand. She needs to save enough to run. We stay alive because of her."

"She takes her life into her hands every time she intervenes and saves a Jew."

Chapter 114
June 1938 Berlin, Germany
Manfred Rechtschaffen

My parents' whispering echoes through the apartment. Ima repeats, "Why was he arrested?"

Her shrillness picks at my stomach.

"Do they need a reason?" questions Abba.

They dissect each other's responses to figure out why this happened.

Finally Abba concludes, "He was sloppy and made mistakes."

Ima says, "You manage to stay out of their view. That is your strength,"

"I can't show thugs respect without bile rising in my throat."

"He'll kill thousands. Tens of thousands if he starts a war."

"The Hens gossip as though Hitler's domination of Europe is a foregone conclusion."

"What else would they do?"

"Their upwardly mobile husbands receive the best postings which tend to be outside of Berlin. The wives never accompany them. The older Hens enjoy the peace, while the younger ones weep from loneliness."

"I guarantee you, Marjem, the Hens are better off staying home. These postings are ill-equipped for the finer sex."

"Helena says Vienna is the brightest feather in Hitler's cap."

"It's the truth."

"Helena says we can't leave right now."

"They'll drag me away. I can't die in a boxcar, Marjem."

He lowers his voice.

"The men from the synagogue who met in secret held shiva for Aleks Herschmann. He is the latest cautionary tale. The Nazis hauled his beaten body into a field and shot him in the head. His wife found him in the field behind the rail yard."

"Baruch Hashem," says Ima.

I scream into my pillow under my duvet. I hate his words. Boxcar. Drag. Death? There is a secret network of Jews? Don't they pray? Why don't they help and fight?

Abba says, "when your mind is racing, it's hard to slow it down and listen."

My mother says Germans love Hitler more than they like Jews. Abba says their small-minded leader makes their decisions for them. That's why Jews are not small-minded, they want to make all their own decisions for themselves.

Abba says, "What are we waiting for?"

"Helena says Rudy is too small. It will be difficult to keep quiet."

The Gestapo arrest parents and leave their children behind. Tonight, when the motorcycles pass us, I wonder who'll be unlucky tonight.

The overwhelming sensation of helplessness plagued me. I didn't want to be weak, but I wasn't sure yet how to be strong.

Chapter 115
July 1938 Berlin, Germany
Marjem Rechtschaffen

Aron starts my day by bringing me a cup of tea. It's a small gesture coated in affection. The day in front of me at the consulate was going to test my patience, tenderness was crucial.

Passing through the first stage of inspection, a hairy, overweight soldier leers at me. His penetrating gaze makes me feel guilty. I ignore his advance, wishing another woman will distract him further. That's terribly unkind but I've reached a point where I need to protect myself.

A day standing still in the heat causes my ankles to swell.

My friend Avery suggested bringing an extra umbrella. Unofficial taxes are laid upon many women where officials take a pretty umbrella, a leather purse, or even a fur coat. The dark side of me considers dressing in seasons past fashions in order to rid myself of unwanted possessions.

After security, the blue card I receive directs me to the second floor. Without warning, a new payment was demanded in order to continue. Once my receipt is stamped, a new line leads me to a fingerprint station.

My goal is the yellow card and a trip to the third floor. My friend Avery suggested this is where I'll hand over the umbrella. Waiting for my picture to be taken, I went over every step to solidify that nothing could be denied to me.

My temporary ID validates my return to the first floor. The green card grants me access to a separate room. Women wait in a queue. The clock on the wall says three-twenty-six p.m. My day began at nine-fifteen a.m. Panicked and exhausted, some women openly offer bribes to officials if they're willing to ignore the clock for another five or ten minutes. Some accept bribes. The Embassy closes its doors at four p.m.

This line moves quickly, but not fast enough. At three-forty-nine p.m. There are eleven people in front of me, and we're all going to run out of time. Women like me can spend our entire days in his ineffectual lines. It's a Sisyphean task. The Chilean Embassy line is different from the German Consulate. I bring the children with me in the hopes the sight of a baby will manipulate the heartstrings of an otherwise unkind officer. After six hours, I leave empty-handed. I'll try the French Embassy tomorrow. I will wear a nice hat.

"My sister picked up her new identification card last week," says one woman to another.

Her buxom stout friend with a tiny waist responds, "You mean Sarah?"

"Her current identity is Sarah Sarah. Can you imagine the foolishness?"

She laughs out loud. Easy laughter on the boardwalk outside of a Consulate is risky.

"Why Sarah?"

"She was the spouse of Abraham, the original Jew," Iinterject. Both ladies consider my reply.

The stout one asks, "Why are they changing men's middle names to Israel?"

I had not heard they were doing this.

Her companion murmurs, "Each page of the permit bears the letter J. Jews now stand out at the borders and fake paperwork is much harder to come by nowadays."

"Germans proclaim the left ear of a Jew is monstrous."

I touch my ear. My ears are small and pixie-like.

I have nicer ears than any German.

"It's dehumanizing," an older woman asserts, using her cane to emphasize her point.

Chapter 116
August 1938 Rozniatow, Poland
Naftali Herzl

Dear Aron and Marjem,

I am mailing you a card. Germans open letters from Poland and either suppress or throw them aside. Postcards get through unchecked. Who would be stupid enough to say something private on a postcard that anyone could read? War. War. War. That's all anybody or talk about.

Your mother and I have lived a great life with two beautiful sons who found love and made their own families. Everybody is healthy and alive and prosperous at the end of the day everything that we wanted we had. If the Russians haul us off to Siberia, we don't have the strength to fight. I set up a hidden cellar, near your favourite tree. The spot is sufficient for six individuals. We will take Bubbe Etel and Zaydeh Hersch and whomever else we can. Don't come back to Poland. Going backward is not what you need to do. My dream for you is to call America your home. I need you to take your family away from Europe. Make me proud and get as far away from home as you can.

Love, Abba

Chapter 117
September 1938 Berlin, Germany
Aron Rechtschaffen

Herman and Marjem are dancing in the kitchen, howling in laughter with the radio on.

"Herman got us a chicken. I roasted it with onions and garlic. I'm already working on a stock for tomorrow's lunch."

Manfred says, "We're having turnips and yams and glazed carrots. Doesn't the kitchen smell wonderful, Abba?"

Herman regards Marjem with delight.

"I gave her the elements. The majesty is in her cooking expertise."

He turns to Manfred and says, "head upstairs to my kitchen and grab the two bottles of wine I left on the counter."

Manny adores Herman and responds to his needs.

Herman loves Manny as much as I do.

When Manny returns, we sit down together to share dinner. After a glass of wine, we began a delicious feast accented by Herman's buttery rolls and red wine.

The meal feels decadent and well deserved. Manny eats his weight in glazed carrots. Rudy licks mashes yams off his fingers. Herman tells anecdotes from his youth.

"This wine is special. The day I married my beautiful wife my father gifted me a case of wine amongst other things. He said life has obstacles, but anything is manageable when you're surrounded by great people. Drink with people you love, reminisce about the better times and dream of the future happiness to come. Each sip is a blessing from me to you."

He raises his glass to Aron.

"For you, son, L'Chiam. To life."

"That's lovely, Herman."

Marjem walks over and touches his arm, then sips from her glass.

"It's smooth and light for a red wine."

Herman says this wine is from France. They know how to nurture the grapes.

"Manfred, go run upstairs and grab the Wildberry Salzburger Nockeri in the cake box in my kitchen."

He stands and takes Marjem's arm.

"Let us move into the parlor and open the second bottle."

Manfred carries in a large cake box tied with string and places it gently on the table.

"These desserts look plain but taste luxurious. When I visited the shop, the baker was trying a new recipe."

"My mouth is watering," laughs Manfred.

We finish the second bottle of wine and eat Wildberry Salzburger Nockerl. After dessert, Marjem puts Rudy to bed. Once Manfred falls asleep on the lounge, I put him to bed. Through the window, the streetlamp casts a warm glow over Marjem. I'm grateful for her, and proud of our family. I kiss my wife on the lips. Touching her is like the sun warming your face on a beautiful new day.

Returning to Herman after placing Manfred to bed with a stack of hollow apologies, we find him asleep in his favorite chair.

Marjem turns to me and asks if we should bother waking him up.

If we don't move him now, his back will be murderous tomorrow and he calls for rain which makes his knees ache.

I walk over to Herman.

Every step feels like I'm walking in quick dry cement.

My mind flashes to the farm standing beside Abba.

His voice echoes in my head, "Aron, it's a natural instinct to recoil from death."

Gasping for air after being punched, I say to Marjem, "Herman is dead."

Chapter 118
November 1938 Berlin, Germany
Manfred Rechtschaffen

Ima screams, "They're trying to get inside. How do we keep them from getting inside?"

Abba leaps from the bed in one single movement.

Ima grab some of her clothes and dresses quickly.

"Manfred, run to baby Rudy," he shouts.

He's never yelled at me before.

"Marjem, go to the children. Close their door. Don't open it for anybody," demands Abba.

I run to my room and check on baby Rudy. How can he still be sleeping? With the doorbell ringing nonstop, he will awaken soon. I go to the dresser and pick out an outfit for him. I collect extra clothes and put them in my satchel. I run around in small circles in the center of my room.

My mind cannot settle. I go to the window and see the morning sky streaked in orange and yellow. When police and brownshirts fill the street, I crouch down underneath the windowsill. My spine tingles and my back arches, willing me to look outside. Being prepared allows me to tackle new problems. Ima opens my door and Nazis shout loud enough in clipped German to be hears from the street below.

"Don't answer the door," demands Abba from the kitchen.

"Ima?"

When the Gestapo came for Abba, Nazi beasts tore the hinges off the door frame.

This time they ring the bell. It seems ridiculous.

Our neighbours obey and sleepwalk without their coats stumbling into the street. Rifles are pointed at children. Mr. Wiesenburg runs down the street without his hat.

Ima's eyes plead with me. There's no reason to. Her lips relax and her entire face softens for just a moment.

"I don't want to go outside either," she mumbles.

Abba, from the hallway, says, "we stay here."

Why would anyone go outside under their own accord? The authorities aren't here to help us, they're here to kill us. My parents walk over to the crib.

"Ima, I want to scream."

"Please don't," she begs.

"I won't," I promise.

Quietly, she says, "Aron, they are throwing cement blocks through windows."

"All the windows..." whispers Papa.

"Our window?" I ask.

"We can fix windows," he says. Ima holds me so close our breathing synchronizes.

"Better than bones," she whispers.

"Are they coming for Abba?" I ask.

He leaves the room and goes to the front door.

Ima crawls on her hands and knees across the door, waiting for his return.

"The Nazis are here for everyone."

Goosebumps cover my body. Her tone is laced with defeat, Abba makes an unintelligent noise. My mind can't grasp what he is doing in the other room, it bugs me.

He grunts and sighs.

A truck barrels down the street filled with another group of brown shirts.

"Ima, what are they doing?"

"Manfred, who can say?"

Is she telling the truth? Abba screams and runs into the room wearing his winter galoshes.

He twitches the curtain aside and gasps.

"Marjem, those are flamethrowers! They will torch everything. Marjem, get the bag and basket for the baby. Do not wake him yet. Let us not have him distract us until we have to move."

Men move three abreast through the streets.

A huge blast shakes the ground beneath me. The windows rattle in their frames.

Flames light up the street and men run in all directions.

"Ima?"

"The synagogue is on fire."

His voice has no life. He sounds tired like after the night he was up taking care of the baby when the baby had a fever. The next morning even coffee couldn't wake up his voice.

"Are they going to set us on fire?"

"If they set the business on fire, we had to be ready to run."

Ima packs up a light bag for Rudy.

Down below, men and women run as a raging fire licks their heels. Soldiers fire their rifles without hesitation.

The men drop to the ground. A woman, running behind them, is shot in the chest. Her head snaps back and forth. Vomit rises in my throat. Ima tries to shield me, but it's too late. Rudy cries out.

"I'll make him a bottle," I say.

Abba stands behind Ima, who is rocking baby Rudy in her arms. Abba's tears surprise me.

He says, "What a great idea."

We'll stay and feed the baby.

As the world falls apart outside our window, we wrap ourselves around the needs of the baby. Abba closes the curtains as the street fills with flames.

Ima fills me with confidence.

"We'll wait. It's chaos out there. Broken glass, screaming people, we'll stay."

"The ringing stops," he says.

"We'll keep the lights off."

The fire in the street illuminates the entire apartment.

"There are fire marshals in the street."

He shoves the breakfront in front of the door. Moving the furniture obscures the chaos.

"We'll escape through the back door."

"Aron, did the Nazis break our windows? We can't escape through the back door."

"No, we'll use the inner courtyard. I left a fire ladder there in case."

"Where did you get the ladder?"

"From the Nazi military base."

"When?"

He says, "Two weeks ago. Frederick, my man at the front gate, the one to whom I gave the duvet last month, gave it to me. He said I would need it."

"Someone told him?" She's incensed.

"Marjem, I didn't understand at the time...."

"There are good people out there!"

"The fire down the street engulfs the synagogue. How can we save the Torahs and prayer books?" Abba says to himself.

"Life is more important than a Torah," says Ima.

Abba never left his tallis and tefillin at the synagogue. Other prominent men in the congregation do.

He suspects this action breeds familiarity. These men claim the synagogue as their own. Abba says his tallis and tefillin belong at home. A man returns home every night.

Home is the first place to worship Hashem. You wrap your head, heart, and arm in your tallis and tefillin with the rising sun. His tefillin wrapped in a blue velvet bag. His Ima stitched his Hebrew name in golden thread on the bag. He's told me more than once, "When I die, Take the silver off my tallis and put it on yours."

Within a few hours, the synagogue burns to the ground. Ima soothes baby Rudy back asleep. I check on him. He's too tall for the crib. He outgrew it overnight. The railing is below his waist. My parents haven't not fixed it yet. Ima made me responsible for Rudy-bear.

"Manfred, go lie down. You need your rest."

Watching Rudy sleep makes me drowsy.

He says, "If he sleeps through this horror, it's better."

My eyes burn. I hang on each word they say, but sleep takes over and I don't remember when I stopped listening.

"The Nazis demands are a clarion call."

He stops speaking. Men are loaded into cattle wagons. One woman throws herself down on top of her son.

"He is only nine," she screams.

"Please, leave him with me. He is all I have left. His father fought for Germany in the War.

"Where is his father now?" sneers the SS man in black.

"The Gestapo took him three months ago."

"He's dead. You can join him."

The Nazi shoots her between her eyes. My parents talk and I remain motionless. I don't want to open my eyes anymore. Ima's arms are around me.

Abba's hands open and close around the neck of the base-ball bat. The explosions rattle the windows.

The riot rages on.

Abba says, "Berlin is on fire tonight. If our synagogue is aflame, all synagogues all over Germany are burning."

"What are we going to do?" I ask.

"The Nazis planned tonight, and we won't take part. Going outside means death. Their destruction won't be ours. I'll leave early in the morning."

She can't mask her emotions right now. When her lower jaw stiffens, she's upset. When her lips are soft and pouty, she's tranquil. Those moments are fleeting and usually involve the baby. She bites her bottom lip when she's thinking about something, not her fingernails.

Adults try to hide the truth; it complicates an over-complicated world. The street goes dark.

"What's happening?" asks Ima.

"What time is it, Aron?"

"It's three o'clock in the morning."

Kristalnacht, the night of Broken Glass, defined my parents as brave in the face of monstrous evil.

The possibility that we wouldn't survive never crossed my seven-year-old mind.

Only now, as an adult, can I begin to process blood curdling screeching, incinerating buildings, glass shattering, and the suffocating smell of burning paper.

As gunshots and terror ravaged our neighborhood; my fathers' refusal to leave the apartment that night saved us. I remember lying on the floor with my chin in my hands. We were glued to the radio, listening to a report.

An impoverished Jew murdered a high-level Nazi official. At the time no one understood the price the Jews would pay for one man's act of retribution. As a child the brutality was so extensive, I couldn't understand the complexity. This damning psychological experience it's not something I could've come back from if I understood what was happening at the time.

Chapter 119
November 1938 NYC, New York
Karl Eisner

My dear Marjem,

I read the papers and prayed for my eyes to betray me. Kristallnacht made my blood boil. I am surprised by the political display of might targeting a minority.

Blood lust at that level isn't great. Adolf Hitler cast himself as the emperor of barbarians. He gained the support of the masses. On November 9th, their devotion went up in flames. The newsreels feature Hitler's military procession through Vienna. Unbeknownst to the filmmaker, innocent souls willingly plunged to their deaths from their apartment windows.

I sought an affidavit to back your entire family. It cost six hundred dollars.

My business will guarantee you employment.

My friend Bernie, from Holland, brought his sister to America. Bernie is proud to have his sister here. She sits next to him with a sweet, open smile. She wants a husband. My friend Paulie from Belgium brought his brother over last week. A friend of mine in the synagogue suggested you buy your way out. According to my friend Jay, the Nazis don't want German funds leaving the country. Relinquish the property and money for your freedom.

The choice is simple.

New York City remains vibrant and a constant scene. Lights and noise are all around us. The department stores close at suppertime, unlike public libraries that stay open late. People commute into the city on buses and trains. There is shift work in warehouses, hotels, factories, and drugstores. The city has five boroughs, but Manhattan is the most developed. Immigrants start in Queens, Brooklyn, and Staten Island and once successful, they move into Manhattan, while others head north to "the suburbs," and buy large houses and drive cars.

Jobs are everywhere. There are service workers, tradespeople, and professionals.

Public school is available to every child. No one drops out to work in a field. They will experience college and become doctors or teachers.

Immigrants arrive at different ports along the East Coast. In the early 1900s, passenger liners from Russia docked in Boston, Massachusetts. In 1895, a passenger liner from Liverpool, England docked in Chicago, Illinois. I docked in New York. When you arrive, no matter where you land, we will get you to New York.

Receiving your letters is important. Please do not stop writing - it is my only way of making sure you are alright.

With great love and respect,

Uncle Karl Eisner

Chapter 120
November 1938 Berlin, Germany
Manfred Rechtschaffen

Mama sweeps jagged shards of broken glass into small manageable piles into the dustbin. The wastebasket overflows with debris from the night before. She won't let me help her. Other children are emptying trash cans and being useful. My hands itch without something to do.

Abba says, "we have lived through a pogrom, Marjem. I never thought that kind of violence would come here."

"My father said he saw the aftermath of pogroms. That's why we left Dobromyl. He's seen neighborhoods wiped off the face of the earth."

"The Germans were organized; their actions were swiftly executed."

I keep replaying last night in my mind.

Ima continues to clean the store and sends Rudy and me back inside.

She says, "Abba will be back with some wood to replace the windows in the store. He must report to the local government offices and file a damage report. He will return as soon as he can. If you need me, I am downstairs. I love you, Manfred."

She kisses the top of my head and kisses Rudy on both cheeks, "you too baby."

We play by the window, and I pull the thick curtains back enough to peek outside. Adults huddle and whisper.

I open the window because the hushed conversation isn't audible through a closed window. Babies cry in mothers' arms and the mood is dour. I hear the word "shock" over and over again. Ima mentioned people being in shock.

She says when something becomes too difficult to manage the body shuts down.

The enormity of last night's destruction is too close to fully understand. The final impact is yet to come. Rudy plays with his wooden blocks, and I stand by the window.

His crafted wooden tower crashed all over the floor and the sound startled me.

I scream. His big brown eyes grow wide, then he cries.

I hate his tears. Hugging him helps stop his tears and makes me feel better for causing them in the first place. The adults downstairs have answers.

"Being angry at you isn't fair," I say.

He picks up his blocks and places them back in the box.

We decide to sneak downstairs together to check on Ima. I take Rudys' hand in mine, and I am struck by the softness and pudgy quality of his sweet little fingers.

There is no strength in these little hands.

He is defenseless and small, but he is smart, and he listens well. I take him all over the apartment building and show him my secret hiding spots; my favorite is a loose brick which I can slide out from the wall. Inside my safe is a cloth containing a special coin, a toy soldier, a book of matches, and a candle.

Rudy's eyes grow wide at the discovery of my treasure.
"My hiding place is a secret." Rudy nods.
You're my best friend and my favorite person in the world.
I'm here to take care of you. Rudy hands me his pacifier. He
points to the brick in the wall. He wants me to add the pac-
ifier to my most cherished possessions.
It breaks my heart. I want him to hold on to being a baby.
My brother chose me today over his own comfort.

*At six years old, it upset me when my brother gave up his
baby toy. I understood at the time he was choosing an alli-
ance with me over his needs. I didn't comprehend, at the
time, how our childhood ended that day.*

Chapter 121
January 1939 Perehinske, Poland
Naftali Herzl

Dear Aron and Marjem,

In the morning, your mother wakes and sits outside watching the local girls walk to school, relishing their innocent laughter.

Being surrounded by children elevates her spirits. We discuss how life repeats itself, from generation to generation. We dream about your sons and the future we want for them. There's nothing we can say that will solve your problems. I don't think we will rest again properly till we know you're out of Germany.

We know how smart you are and if there's anyone, they can figure out a workable plan, it's you.

Love, Abba

Chapter 122
March 1939 Berlin, Germany
Aron Rechtschaffen

My chest contracts, bile rises in my throat, and my vision is blurred. I rub my thighs to ease the muscle spasms. Marjem rushes towards me, "Run. Run. Don't let them take you!"
I dash into our room and snatch my coat and boots. I'm out of the window, like a high jumper, faster than the last time I practiced. I'd rather scrape my back on the side of the building than have my foot hanging over the edge.
My overgrown hair blows into my eyes.
My regular barber immigrated to Chile. Lately, no barber is willing to cut the hair of a Jew.
Men thrust towards their death, are loaded onto the bus; they're defeated faces energize me. The Nazis won't put me on the death bus tonight. Inside my home, the Gestapo interrogates Marjem.
I hear their anger through the walls. Once they leave, she removes the boys from the hole in the closet and feeds them. While she's in the kitchen I imagine her warming the food on the stove top and placing the baby back in the highchair.

Manny will help get the food prepared with her. They relate to each other without words; he can read her emotions. When the boys race into our bedroom after dinner, my heart skips a beat.

Deep agony consumes me. I miss my family.

Marjem embraces Manny while holding Rudy.

Manny laughs at something Marjem says.

There's peace in our bedroom. She created that for them. In the midst of the tornado that consumes our lives she provides comfort and reassurance. This was my second chance, and I evaded the Nazis. I won't get a third.

I'm not entitled to endanger my family. Motorcycles shred down the boulevard. I leave after the second set of motorcycles pass our home.

Chapter 123
April 1939 Berlin, Germany
Marjem Rechtschaffen

Helena attempts to harden me.

Preparation for today is important.

She assures me, "Marjem, the children will be secure. I will take Manfred and Rudy out of Berlin myself if I have to."

"Helena, I can never compensate you."

I cast my eyes downward. She doesn't appreciate wild displays of emotion.

I'm a refined woman who runs a thriving business in Berlin. Yet when I'm in her presence I'm no better than a youthful teenager.

"You're sharp and clever about life. Rising above the misery is a testament to your character. Trappings like wealth and material possessions mean nothing. You know what is superficial."

"Helena, I'm suffocating."

I hand her my wristwatch, a few rings, and a sable fur hat. She pushes them back at me with both hands up.

"There's no need, Marjem."

"These soft black leather gloves are for the children. Take my silver candelabra. I couldn't bear for the Nazis to have it."

She continues to rub my back soothingly.

"Each volunteer I know owns two links in the chain. It's effective because no one carries too much burden. If anybody is caught and interrogated, they would only be able to identify two others in the network. Everyone is appropriately paranoid. Some have been captured; while others have mysteriously disappeared."

I wipe my eyes and my skin is sore.

"I'm grateful for many things, Helena."

"I will take them out of the city. They will walk to Holland from Duisburg. You'll need the rings and the watch more than I will."

I place them deep in my pocket.

"What do I do now?"

"Stay alive? Motherhood wasn't my destiny. I save the innocent. Each child I help is mine. The time will come when I'll outlive my usefulness."

"Don't diminish yourself," I declare forcefully.

She laughs and I can see the back of her throat.

"He's not as clever as he thinks he is. The signs will be there and then I'll disappear and take an orphan with me."

"Where will you go?"

"America? Paris? Canada? I can't say."

"You are a genuine friend, Marjem."

"In another lifetime, we would've been inseparable."

"I love you, Helena."

She hugs me once more and with a sigh and sends me away from her so we can focus on the business of saving my children.

"Madame Strausburg is a wonderful woman. We have worked together since 1932. She knows the train schedules in Berlin, another link in the chain. Her surveillance controls the transportation of children. Madame Strausburg will take your boys on the first leg of their journey. Once she has them, I will alert the Jewish refugee committee for children."

The first time Helena entered my store, she brought homemade lemon bars which were the color of sunshine. I wiped my hands clean on my work apron as she locked the door. Madame Strausburg approached Rudolph with a lemon bar and introduced herself to Manfred. Helena took her silk handkerchief from her purse and wiped Rudy's face clean. Her tenderness caught me off guard. After that first introduction, Madame Strausburg visited often. Within a few weeks the children were calling her Auntie. She spoke to them eye-to-eye, earning their trust. Helena chose well for my children. Madame Strausburg's strength and kindness will save them.

Chapter 124
May 1939 Berlin, Germany
Manfred Rechtschaffen

I remember how Shabbat used to be.

The preparation for Shabbat dinner took up the entire afternoon. Ima closed the store early and started preparations by eleven in the morning.

Cooking relaxed everyone. The house was filled with music. When Ima cooked, she crooned. The buttery scent of sauteed onions, celery, and garlic made her tone fuller.

"Where are my carrots?"

"Over here," I called back.

We lock eyes and chuckle.

Her smile spreads across her face.

"Help me roll the matzoh balls, Manfred."

I dry my hands off and stand beside her. Shabbat began with a prayer over the candles, wine, and challah. Our challah is baked with raisins the way Abba ate it back in Dobromyl. The menu includes smoked fish, soup, and roasted chicken with potatoes and green beans. Tonight, she cooks an entire fish in a salt bake. The fish's eyes looked sad, a sadness I forgot once I licked my fingers.

My families escape from Nazi Berlin began that night. A knock on the door tore my family apart. Ima understood with certainty the Nazis were hunting down Abba.

Poised she fed the devils strudel while Abba climbed out the bedroom window to escape with his life. Tonight's Shabbat is peculiar. Ima isn't singing and Abba doesn't play his records.

"Judenlager! Stop!"

A shot rings out. Someone screams.

"Gestapo."

She freezes and runs from the room.

"Run," she screams.

Shaking her head back-and-forth, she seems to remember something. Ima runs to Rudy in the highchair.

The fury of her movement startles me. Rudy, sensing tension, cries out. Ima caresses his cheek, and he forgets to cry. His agitation melts away. My heart pushes against my rib cage. She swiftly places him in my arms.

I take him to the closet in the bedroom and tell him a story.

"One day on Noah's Ark, Noah didn't feed the lions before he fed himself. By the time he got to the lions, the male lion was so hungry he bit Noah's leg. Noah, permanently damaged, walked with a limp; a constant reminder of his selfishness."

The sounds of the Nazis invade as I place Rudy inside the hole. Their voices feel too close.

"This teaches us to always feed animals and babies before yourself. They're too young to realize the food is coming."

I fasten the false store and sit back next to Rudy.

"You must take care of those you love. Especially when you are wiser."

Abba won't save us.

He's nowhere in sight.

Ima speaks in perfect German. The nasty men disrespect her with their impatience.

I want to be big and strong and rip their faces apart.

I hate the Nazis.

I hate the Nazis.

I repeat the words in my mind until they no longer have meaning.

Abba taught me how to climb out the windows. I jump first.

Ima passes Rudy to me. Then she would follow.

Chapter 125
May 1939 Berlin, Germany
Aron Rechtschaffen

The Gestapo are pounding on the door.

The Judge warned me. I'll either end up in a forgotten boxcar or a relocation camp.

His exact words were, "No one returns."

Abba explains our lineage has survived generations of persecution. Our adaptability to the whims of life's design allows us to navigate through impervious obstacles.

We're sharper in the long run.

My partner is stronger than anyone else, I know. A halo of shiny blonde hair and a heart-shaped face comes into focus. My lips whisper my love to her. This was the plan. The children are alone in the apartment waiting on Helena. My world walks towards me and we promise not to speak. In case I'm being watched, I don't want to put her in danger.

A motorcade is upon me before I step off the curb. I'm paralyzed from head to toe. The motorcycles pass, but the truck stops. My heart pounds inside my throat and I forget how to swallow. Panic courses through me.

These barbarians dressed in soldiers' uniforms invade the street. Another truck arrives. Soldiers fill the interchange. These monsters desire to tear me away from my family. My father whispers in my head, "Walk away, Aron." I push the voice away. Marjem is trapped in the bank. If I stay, they'll arrest me, and I'll never be reunited with my sons. Waiting means certain doom. How can I provide for them if I'm dead? What is my legacy then?

As a Nazi dismounts his motorcycle, his eyes meet mine. His black pupils are wide open obscuring his pale blue eyes. I blink away an invisible piece of dust. He tilts his head to the left, and I dig my thumbnail into the flesh of my palm. Spots form before my eyes.

My father's words ring true in my mind.

"Walk away. The only way to have a future is to leave."

He said these exact words when he put me on the train over ten years ago. The strongest walk away, because they have nothing to prove.

The Nazi bastard approaches me, and a commotion erupts behind him. When he turns, I slip away and am absorbed into the street traffic. Removing my hat and coat alters my outward appearance. The gentle breeze cools me off. Poised enough to not run, every step emboldens me.

Nazis bark orders, and my heart beats in syncopation to their jackboots against the cobblestones.

Chapter 126
May 1939 Berlin, Germany
Manfred Rechtschaffen

"Inhale and exhale," I repeat under my breath to Rudy.
I coax him to repeat it with me. Rudy mouths the words
soundlessly. Ima prepared honey-soaked handkerchiefs for
us to smell inside the closet. I offer him a handkerchief.
"Rudy, the handkerchief cuts the stale smell in the air."
He smiles weakly and inhales. I check my wristwatch, a gift
from uncle Maurice. A man needs to know the time.
"Rudy, I'd be scared if I was alone."
Flushed with relief, my confession absolves me. Disbelief
washes across his face. He squeezes my hand.
Having him next to me helps. Ima is fighting for us; she's
doing the hard work because that's her job. She never backs
down. She's the strongest person I know. Marching boots
and angry orders fill the air.
The mood appears to have shifted.
"Rudy, Ima never capitulates. She won't give up."
My fear becomes white hot anger. The Nazis are vultures
and we're defenceless bait. I want to break something - or
set the entire apartment on fire. Rage makes me impulsive,

and the explosion feels righteous. Pinching myself hard on the thigh brings me relief. The voices quiet themselves.

It's cramped. Rudy stands and stretches. A dish shatters and someone yells. Rudy dives for my lap.

He whimpers and I beg him to breathe with me. Placing my hand on his chest, he mirrors my gesture. Breathe with me, I say again. We can cry later all we want but for now we can only breathe. The last time I cried, Ima scolded me. Explaining that only babies cry and that men need to control their feelings. I'm not sure if I can. I'll make sure Rudy gets the chance to cry.

He can cry for both of us. He can be a baby for as long as he wants.

"I'm here," whispers Ima near the closet.

"Stay here until the guards leave."

I listen at the false door.

"This doesn't have to be unpleasant. I've made a fresh strudel. My specialty. How about you officers sit down and eat some strudel while I collect the paperwork."

Chairs shuffle and drawers open and close. Their heinous accusations make me sick.

I find myself opening the secret door.

"You were summoned," sighs the Gestapo officer.

Their anger deflates. Why does she feed them our strudel? Her strudel is better than any bakery: the icing is bright and sweet with lemon and vanilla overtones. The inside is soft with ribbons of cinnamon infused butter.

She feeds them our food, and they steal our lives. There is laughter without delight. The chortles sound villainous. My guts twist and grind to their demonic dark laughter. Her hospitality quells their rage. They aren't yelling at her anymore. Nazis pick away at Jews like meat on a carcass until there's nothing left. No school. They eliminated teachers. No hospitals. They eliminated doctors. New rules are posted every day. Walk here, don't walk there, buy from this store even if you boycotted it last week.

Why is the park off-limits? Every restriction makes another neighbor disappear. Ima's tone has a curious inflection.

One voice emerges.

"You don't belong here. You're not even German."

A gruff voice insists.

"You must report for relocation. The Furor wants the building."

Ima says, "Here's the certificate."

One man declares, "We've reassigned your residence. Relocation to the east for you and the boys."

Rudy snuggles up next to me. I place his hand on my chest again.

"Feel my breath. Close your eyes and imagine a cloudless blue sky. We sit on a fluffy blanket on the sand. Waves of blue and green crash on the shore. Mist soaks our skin. We assemble a red kite to fly. The air is salty, and our hair stiffens in the breeze. Can you see it?"

The soldiers go and the building exhales. Rudy bites his fingers and I take his palm in mine to stop himself. Plump and soft, his fingers are sticky. I count to one hundred, first in German and then in Hebrew. It distracts me. I reach for Ima's handkerchief. I count to one hundred again.

Ima reaches out for me.

She clutches my thigh, "come out and let me love you." Like a corks release from a champagne bottle, I burst in happiness. We clamber out and climb on top of her.

Rudy squeals and grabs her cheeks with his little hands.

She laughs and the terror drifts elsewhere. Staying in this moment is all I want. When she kisses me goodnight, she whispers, "all I wanted was you. I was happy with just you, but we knew you needed more - someone of your own to care for. We gave you Rudy. Make sure to always take care of him."

Even as a child, I recognized monsters are real and sometimes disguised themselves as men. They bring wherever they go.

Chapter 127
May 1939 Berlin, Germany
Marjem Rechtschaffen

The Gestapo interrupts our dinner, demanding Aron's whereabouts. I give them the documentation they want, but they don't really care.

They're there to make us nervous and see what they can get away with, with no one coming to help. I prattle as my love runs away to save his life.

I spin a narrative of plausible lies.

The evening from here can go in a myriad of directions.

They make themselves comfortable at my dining room table. Standing there empty handed makes me vulnerable.

One bastard notes the smell of fresh "Jew-Cake."

I serve them my strudel and pray my good cooking will soften them. I wish I had time to get them a sprinkle of rat poisoning disguised as powdered sugar.

When I open the door to the secret hiding place, my spirits crumble. We have to get away from here. This is no way to live. Rudy sucks his thumb while Manfred strokes his hair. They are defenseless. The three of us return to eat dinner.

While eating, I rub Manfred and Rudy's legs and arms. I cannot stop touching them.

Between bites, I kiss their faces. The peacefulness here, in this moment, fills the holes in my chest left by Aron's exit. Before bed, I change my bed linens. Fresh, clean sheets are an uncomplicated pleasure. Making my bed gives me a moment of normalcy. I climb into the shower and wash away the hideous evening. The hammering of water between my shoulders beats back my trepidation.

The steam from the bathroom smells of lavender and honey. While I bathe my mind drifts. Mother cautioned me to trust my gut. Without a moment of hesitation, my mother walked away from her life. Dread consumes me when history repeats itself. Generations of parents across races and religions send children elsewhere.

Why can't we keep our babies close? All Jews share this tale in their lineage.

How did Naftali and Tzizel send Aron away at thirteen? How did they do it after they sent Walker away to England? What convinced them that Berlin was the right choice for Aron?

How did Tzizel go on, constantly frightened for her children?

Unresolved doubt must have plagued her. A parent is accountable.

When does a parent recognize when they're not enough?

When must I rely upon them to show their own strength, intelligence, and will?

My mother, Amalia, left Holland and followed Mozes to Dobromyl. Bubbe Etel and Rabbi Tzvi Rechtschaffen allowed their youngest daughter, Tzizel, to leave Rozniatow. We left Dobromyl as a family and ran from the Russians. Tomorrow I will escape from Germany and run to Holland.

I dry off and climb into my bed. My sheets reveal a lifelong history - the exhilaration of my marriage and the joys and struggles of parenthood. I chose Aron.

We made Manfred, lost a child, and made Rudolph.

Sacred love shaped our lives. Tonight, I will sleep alone.

I take a deep breath, the kind you take before you jump off a bluff into the blue water. I made peace with my decision. Others will criticize. The toughest decisions are the loneliest. Manfred will never forgive me for lying to him.

The resentment will fester into a lifelong wound. I own it. I am a liar. My plan means their survival.

They will live because I chose them over myself.

Chapter 128
May 1939 Berlin, Germany
Manfred Rechtschaffen

"Manfred, I'm running to the bank. Madame Strausburg is on her way over." Ima speaks quickly while her face remains calm.

"Alright," I say to Ima.

"Protect Rudy until I'm back," she demands.

The intensity concerns me. She holds my face in her gentle hands.

"I love you Manfred."

"I love you too."

She snaps her black leather clutch bag closed. The one with the hidden compartment behind the zipper.

She hasn't used that clutch for years. It's not particularly big but the secret compartment is priceless.

She meticulously puts on her white leather gloves.

She used to wear those whenever she went out with my father. She claimed there's nowhere fancy enough to wear them anymore.

"Last night I dreamt of you. Abba and I willed you into the world with all our love. Abba found me in Berlin and made me an Ima. We made two perfect children."

I touch her warm tears and dry them. She chokes.

She kisses me one last time straight on the lips. Within a heartbeat she walks out the door.

Papa left us, now Mama. A torrent of tears builds up behind my eyes. I cannot unleash these feelings in front of Rudy. We curl up and fall asleep in my bed waiting on Madame Straisburg. The whispers I've overheard for years come rushing back to me.

Maybe knowing all I do now is worse? The monsters in my nightmares are real. They want to kill me and my family.

Someone unlocks our front door.

I run to the closet with a half-asleep Rudy.

We close the false door just as our front door opens.

Trembling in silence, my hand covers Rudy's mouth.

"Don't cry," I whisper to Rudy.

The click-click of a woman's high heels dance across the flat.

I climb on top of him and try to shield him. The closet door opens, and my scream catches in my throat.

"It's me, sweet boys. Madame Strausburg."

Rudy sobs overtired and ravenous.

"Manfred, you are ready to go?"

She asks Rudy, "Can you find your boots?"

Rudy races into the hall. I take hold of her; does she know my parents are gone? Rudy throws his coat on the floor, runs in a circle, and puts it on while his back is to it. Outside the building, I look at Madame and see her mouth trembling. We walk in silence as the wind whirls around the taller buildings. Rudy's ears are sensitive to wind; he's prone to earaches. Rudy clutches Madame's palm.

Mama's words echo inside of me, "Madame Strausburg is trustworthy."

Last week Madame brought us to her home. My mother said it was important to know my whereabouts in the city. She was preparing for today.

Madame Strausburgs block is familiar, yet the scenery is foreboding. My heart races and I'm sure everyone in the street can hear it. Being outside means we're vulnerable. She doesn't look scared.

Maybe she should be? Madame's strides instill confidence. I tell her that I'm scared and she stops, looks me right in the eyes. Overwhelmed and filled with shame, I'm shocked I admitted to my weakness so easily. I want to run and hide. "You should be scared," she says.

"The world is a mess and you're floating around in the middle of it."

She stops speaking. I hug her tightly. Rudy hugs her too.

"No one tells me what is happening and it's happening to me." I look at my brother, "and to him."

"Not knowing is easier. You should believe me because I have a lot of experience. I'll take children out of Berlin as often as I can. You're all leaving for the same reason. If you don't know the monsters are out there it's easier for adults to shuffle you around and keep you hidden."

"Tell me more; I hate surprises."

Madame says, "There is no time for me to explain it all to you. Your Mama loves you. You are a piece of her heart. When you are together, she is strong. When you are apart, her heart does not beat properly..."

"Will she be alright?" I ask.

"Once you are reunited, her heart will heal. Until then, protect yourself and Rudy."

"Rudy is part of my heart and I'll never leave him."

Chapter 129
April 1939 Berlin, Germany
Marjem Rechtschaffen

Religion doesn't control my Papa's life.

He earned prosperity and position through arduous work. Gregarious and a whiz with numbers, he actualized his dreams. He dropped out of school and learns every three started out in the middle of Galicia, built a pipeline and solid business until he moved to Berlin and worked as an advisor in a bank. After I graduated, I joined Papa working at the bank. In celebration, Mother baked a strawberry shortcake, taking exquisite love to measure each ingredient, and the result was impeccable. Papa commended her creation.

In a black pinstripe suit and bowtie, his grin caused his big rosy cheeks to glow.

Last night, I chose my outfit with great care. My shoes have a strong heel and fit comfortably with rain boots. My coat is light, but incredibly warm.

Wrapping myself in the jade scarf Henie bought me on her honeymoon in Paris. She told me the story several times.

"In Paris, a painter uses the Seine as his backdrop. Hand-painted scarves captured the frivolity of Paris. He painted the

Eiffel Tower with a ballerina soaring through the air. The dancer's tutu is the exact hue of your eyes."

Henie Eisner 1938

I channel Henie's energy.
One foot in front of the other brings me closer to the bank and Aron. By 1939, not many Jews live in Berlin.
Living here comes with many costs. We wear our smiles like masks pretending we're impervious to Nazi hostility.
Gunshots ring out. People react in slow motion.
My legs slip out from underneath me. Dizzy from the buzzing in my ears I clutch my heart. I look at my hand and there's no

blood. There's no pain, I wasn't shot. This must be what paranoia looks like.

Did I imagine the entire thing? Sobs fill the air. I didn't imagine it. I can see the bank and Aron down the street. Rushing towards him, I almost leap into his arms. When his breath touches my collar, I am keenly aware of our surroundings. His whisper is lost in the breeze. With a deep breath, I enter the bank and announce myself. A teller approaches, with a cup of water in her hand, her lips pulled tightly across her face. Her eyes betray her intent.

"Please come upstairs, Mrs. Rechtschaffen. We have paperwork for you to sign. There is a form for the withdrawal transaction."

Not one word she says registers in my mind. Her lips strain against the tops of her teeth when she tries to smile. I excuse myself to the powder room.

When I am out of her sight, I stop.

Slick with sweat, I concentrate on my path back to the door.

How many steps to Aron?

My hands stiffen and my fingers clench inside my gloves. My spine sizzles. They would arrest me here. I cannot stay here. Freedom lies outside the bank.

But Aron is not on the sidewalk.

When I call his name, he always responds, but not now.

I forget myself for a moment and spin around.

Then I recall we agreed that if we could not find each other, we would take the Spandau line towards Zehlendorf.

I turn towards the rail station and concentrate on walking normally.

Chapter 130
May 1939 Berlin, Germany
Madame Strarsburg

"You mustn't be fearful; your mother anticipated this moment. In fact, she's been preparing for this moment since before Rudy was born. When you are reunited in Holland, forgive her for any of her lies or deception."

"Madame Strasburg, I'll be brave. I promised my mother," Manfred says with as much conviction as a six-year-old can muster. Such a big albatross to carry on such little shoulders ravishes my heart.

Their passage will be astonishing.

"Your mother said you were ready for an adventure."

"Is that why she left without us?"

His question pierces my resolve. I can't confess to a truth that is not my own. Aron's back was up against the wall. Was hers? The plan was for her to return from the bank and pick up the children at my apartment.

Something went wrong. A child can't conceptualize the magnitude of a parent's dreams for them.

"Manfred, she made an impossible decision; to shield you and your brother. Your mother chose freedom. Her foresight will save you all."

The three of us eat breakfast. Manfred doesn't want to eat. Coaxing him through breakfast is harder than I imagined. Rudy eats my pancakes and oatmeal with gusto.

"We will reunite in Holland," Manfred says.

His words ring hollow. After we finish breakfast, we'll head over to the train station.

"Can we stay here?" His question is fair.

I wish I could say yes because I don't want to reject him. They've been through so much and they have no idea what's around the corner. I could take them away somewhere special and make them my own.

Helena and I have discussed this before. There will come a time when we can no longer save innocent lives and we'll have to run. That time is not upon us yet.

There are still plenty of children that can be saved. Marjem will get out and Aron is industrious enough to slip away unseen.

"Step one: A woman will approach and ask me a question. If she asks the right question, then she will be the one to take you on the first step of your journey."

"Has Mama met her?"

"No. It's better this way."

The details are too complex for him to understand.

The amount of stress would break most, but Marjem prepared him as best she could. He tends to his brother's needs like a parent. His attention is honed in on every movement his brother makes. The baby hasn't said a word since he's been in my presence. Young children do this sometimes. They lose their voices when under great trauma. I speak to Rudy quietly as I wipe sticky jam from his face and fingers.

"He likes the sound of your voice."

"I miss the sound of his," I reply.

"Manfred today is a fresh start. Only push forward. Never look back."

"You sound like her." We laugh.

How nice to forget for a second...

"That is the point, sweet boy. Parents want to protect their children and their innocence."

"Do you think they miss me?"

"Yes, Manfred. It is hard to grasp the full picture. Life is wonderful and wild. Faith helps when there are no answers. Hope allows me to sleep when the nights are too dark."

"Remember, Manfred, your parents refused the Gestapo. They bravely walked away."

She looks me in the eye again.

"Do you need me to carry Rudy?"

"He's not heavy for me."

We approach the train station.

Manfred mutters, "Don't leave us."

I squeeze his hand and quicken my pace. A soldier at the corner has a gun on his hip. Pretending not to notice, I slow down. Manny's hands grow slick with sweat.

"Do you know who's taking us?" He asks.

"Yes," I mumble.

We sit down on an iron framed bench; I pull Rudy onto my lap. I've grown to adore Marjem's children, sending them off into the network is terrifying. I inspect each passing person, wondering who is coming for them.

"The world has brave people. Mama says that."

I place my hand on his thigh.

"I've known your Mama for a long time."

"My parents refused the Gestapo. They bravely walked away." Manfred repeats after me.

A young man sits down next to me. I hold my breath and wait to see what happens next.

He checks his watch and runs his hands through his hair.

I turn to Manfred and shake my head, no and whisper, "It's not him."

The man gets up when the next trolley comes into the station. After the trolley leaves, a woman nods at me.

My hand tightens around his.

A woman sits next to me.

"Did I miss the trolley?"

"Yes. The trolleys are on a schedule. Another one will arrive within fifteen minutes. The line for tickets isn't long; you have enough time."

"I purchased my ticket on Tuesday. I should be fine."

That's exactly what I needed to hear. I squeeze his thigh and nod my head yes. The interaction is smooth and clean.

"It is time," I say under my breath.

"You can do this, Manfred. Listen to the woman and do not ask too many questions. Be invisible until you are in Holland."

He rises and takes Rudy. When the next train pulls into the station, she says goodbye and takes Marjem's boys.

Chapter 131
May 1939 Berlin, Germany
Marjem Rechtschaffen

Helena introduced me to a unique tea shop; a members only club for high end clientele.

The first time she brought me here was after I lost the baby in my failed attempt to escape to Holland in 1934.

It was a difficult time. My heart knew I was nearly three months pregnant, but my mind couldn't accept the enormity of what was happening. Berlin's incisors were trained on the Jews. Aron insisted I attempt an escape to Holland with Manfred. I did everything in my power to give us a better life, but Manfred and I were removed from the train. When I returned home, I lost hope.

Helena picked up on my despair. She never said anything straight out, but I knew she understood.

The elusive victory wasn't within my grasp that day.

A row of brick apartment buildings line the street. The money on this block is old, and most likely Austrian in origin. The nicer buildings have gardens in both the front and the back of the buildings. I wouldn't find anyone from my synagogue within a stone's throw of this neighborhood in 1929 let alone 1939. Small specialty shops occupy the bottom floor of every building. The one I'm headed to today is my refuge from the storm.

The way Aron tore a hole in the wall of our closet to protect the children, Helena's friend Herr Diane Fortune crafted a sanctuary for Jewish women to escape and regroup in a posh Berlin suburb on their way out of Berlin.

Herr Diane Fortune is compassionate and insightful. She cares for her disabled son, Anthony, a beautiful boy with dark black hair and mocha-coloured eyes. Her husband, Phillip, a foreman in a warehouse, lost his leg in the war. Most people looked the other way when they saw him, as he reminded them of what they lost in the war.

After he returned from the war his job wasn't waiting for him. While he was away at war, his wife opened up a tea shop out of their home to help support their child. Without any other prospects, Philip taught himself to bake and turned Diane's tea shop into a delicious bakery.

Their son is mute, and his hands don't work properly. Phillip took the time and taught Anthony how to bake bread and danishes.

When Phillip died from complications from the war, Anthony took over the baking. Anthony listens to the orders, prepares them, and delivers hot carafes of water to each table. He's disciplined, attentive, and his explosive smile nurtures your soul.

Herr Diane Fortune jokes that in another life she was the daughter of a great concert violinist. A violinist who could fill theaters if only there were enough people around him to appreciate the music. He moved his family to the capital of Poland in order to further his career. There's more money in repairing instruments than playing them. His repair business flourished. Herr Diane plays the violin. She studied in Poland as a child. Rumor has it she is a prodigy. The family left Warsaw at the bequest of a great instructor here in Berlin. Helena said she played for years until she met Phillip.

Today Diane welcomes me with the warmth of a mother. She moves me to a quiet table at the side of the shop and serves me a fresh cherry danish.

The monogrammed linen embroidered tablecloths make the room elegant. Each table's linens feature a different letter of the alphabet. Small oriental rugs adorn the floors. Mismatched Bavarian teacups and saucers enhance the eclectic charm.

The teacups are relics of extinguished empires. Each one is a fragment of art.

"I made you some peppermint tea to calm your nerves. I don't expect to see Helena today, but I will let her know that I saw you."

She leaves a small carafe of steaming water and a tea strainer filled with her famous peppermint tea.

She squeezes my shoulder, and her kindness almost dissolves my resolve. After finishing my danish, I wipe my lips and remove the rest of my lipstick.

Using my hand mirror and my compact, I reapply my face powder and even out the flush on my skin. The reapplied lipstick brightens my face. With a cordial nod to Herr Diane, I tap my teacup with my index finger.

She returns with another small pot of boiling water. As the tea steeps, my mind clears.

Helena's words ring in my head, "Marjem, get up and get going."

Chapter 132
April 1939 Oranienburger, Germany
Aron Rechtschaffen

Outside of Oranienburger, a pleasant town on the banks of the Havel River, I hitchhike a ride in the rear of a truck. The driver offers, "I can take you as far as Neuruppin."
I thank him with a nod and join the others in the rear of the truck. Good people exist everywhere.
Vanilla fills my nostrils. Anglers use vanilla to conceal the cloying fish gut stink, impenetrable to soap and water. Their unrestrained laughter brings me back to my childhood. Once while Walker chased a hen for hours; our faces ached from howling with laughter. The tempo of their prattle reminds me of an uncomplicated youth.
A stout man with a mustache and a pig nose says, "I spent the summer running a canoe service. The hours were merciless, but the money was easy. The guards drink beers until they're sloppy."
"The stories they tell make my skin crawl."
His companion, a tall skinny guy replies, "the prison brings good jobs to locals."

The pig man says, "We owe a lot to Hitler. With mouths to feed, Hitler kept his promises. After the war, Havel suffered because an entire generation of men never returned."

Their conversation repels me. Bile rises in my throat thinking about the audacity they have, to thank murderous beasts like Hitler, for raising their station in life. I tilt my head back and close my eyes.

The skinny one says, "The prison ruined the forests, which used to be my favorite place to be. As a kid I played tree tag with my brother. I would leap from low branches to big rocks and never touch the ground. If you touched the ground, you immediately lost the game. We'd try to hunt rabbits and we'd climb trees to gaze at colored eggs waiting to be hatched in the springtime. My mother taught us how to trap rabbits. We ate delicious rabbit stew. While neighbors struggled to pay for food, we sold pelts and Mother made gloves and hats."

"My uncle killed squirrels with a slingshot."

He spoke at length about how much he respected his uncle. I realize both men grew up fatherless, raised by their mothers. As long as a child is nurtured, they'll thrive. Even though they both love Hitler, they abhorred what he did to their beloved forest.

"The forest is a burial ground. Birds don't nest here anymore."

The pig-faced one says, "The stench is intolerable."

I wish they would stop talking.

"We know why it smells. How many Jews do you think are buried there?"

"A wretched Jew tried to bury himself with leaves. Can you even imagine?"

Their laughter deprecates the stupid Jew who tried to bury himself. The Nazis abhor the Jews. The guards in the camps are merely disgusted by the Jews.

Perhaps it's the conditions in which they work, or they don't respect the people inside the camps because criminals deserve what they get.

The camps are filled with good people who've done nothing wrong.

"Jews ruin everything. We lost the war because of them."

"Most of them are cocaine addicts. That's what my dad says."

The anglers, established anti-Semitics, weren't ideal company. Hitler built camps outside of Berlin and required these camps to stay a secret.

"Never approach an abandoned boxcar in the forest."

"Why?"

"Boxcars are packed with dead Jews. You'll see rotten corpses clutching suitcases."

Wretched images roll around in my mind. Sitting beside them ruined any potential appetite I could've had.

I felt peace in the back of the truck until I listened.

The anglers leave at Oranienburger.

Relief overwhelms me. A man and his son move to the back. The boy is Manfred's age.

He has red hair and freckles.

The boy asks, "Why didn't we take the train?"

The prison receives box cars filled with people at the railway station.

The higher land of Kremmen, a picturesque town surrounded by verdant, rolling greens makes me forget the anglers. Marjem and I would have retired somewhere like here. I'd build us a middle German-style house with timber framing.

We'd lay by the lake in the blistering July sun. The lazy shores of Ruppiner Lake remind me how much I love living by the water.

Now that I've left Berlin, I'm never gonna live far away from water ever again. I have to make sure to tell Marjem that. My next destination is the lighthouse.

From the lighthouse, I will steal a boat and piece my family back together again in Holland.

Chapter 133
Berlin, Germany
Marjem Rechtschaffen

To my satisfaction, the train arrives, and it's not over-crowded. Aron told me eye contact is easy to avoid when you sit next to a window.

Cataloging the advice he's given me provides my mind enough distraction to combat the presence of soldiers. They swarm the platform beside the train. I'm frozen in place.

"Survivors don't panic," I whisper.

Helena would say, "you can't give up without even trying." Hearing her voice in my head makes me less lonely.

One woman with thinning dull brown hair turns to her friend and says, "Gibt es einen verräter in den zug. Ruhe bewahren? Die türen bleiben geschlossen." (Is there a traitor on the train? Keep calm, we must remain calm.)

The woman to my right snarls, "Juden machen uns alle verruckt" (Jews drive us all crazy!).

I remind myself again and again to not pull the emergency handle in order to escape. When my breathing becomes labored, I squeeze my thighs together and feel the cold blade strapped against my inner thigh.

Another thoughtful gift from Helena.

The mouse responds, "Sie alle toten!" (Kill them all!)

My upper lip trembles. To control the spontaneous tremors in my hands, I bite my tongue hard. Her friend replies in kind. They continue their vicious conversation, and I struggle to conceal my agitation.

Reapplying my makeup will keep my hands occupied.

I rub off my lipstick and hear the jackboots before I see them. Soldiers barrel down the aisle, headed straight for me.

The last time this happened, I tried escaping with Manfred and a baby inside of me. We never made it out of Germany.

My unborn baby girl died. I shut out the pain. I'm a guest in my own life, and I'm losing sense of myself.

Two soldiers drag a woman by her hair – like holding a cat by the skin behind their collar.

Her lips are crushed and bloodied. Her lipstick stains her skin as if she was slapped across the face. Her eyes reveal acceptance of her fate. She won't make it out of this situation alive.

The doors of the train open and close.

I can identify the catch and release of the metal bolts inside the train door. Police step onto the platform side-by-side and drag her like an afterthought.

A man hollers himself sick at the soldiers.

"Nehmen sie nicht ihren! Sie ist unschuldig. Sie niche weib." (Do not take her! She is innocent. You do not know.) Will his words save her life? "Niche sie!" (Not her!).

A single shot ends his red-faced screams.

Her body collapses to the ground before the second shot fires, killing the man.

The doors open and close. A man clears his throat. Conversations restart as if in unison.

Some passengers stand, gather their packages, and exit the train. As the clicking of the Nazi's jackboots echoes in the distance, I decide to wait a little longer.

My bones vibrate from shock and fear.

Chapter 134
April 1939
Manfred Rechtschaffen

Nazi soldiers fill the aisles. Nathalie's tense palm betrays her tranquil facade. She's petite with brown hair and freckles. Madame Strausburg and Nathalie, I repeat the names of the women who helped me when the fear gets too big. Mother told me to name my fear, then conquer it. She said monsters aren't real and if humans act like animals there's nothing scarier than that.

I attempt to catch her gaze. She won't look at me.

Nathalie mutters, "follow me."

We leave the yellow and red trains behind. I learned nothing on that ride. Wherever I go, on a train, a trolley or even a chore, my parents taught me about the world around me. No one's teaching me now.

My father said these trains are the fastest in the world; he wishes he could appreciate Hitlers astute modernizations, but his murderous hatred of the Jewish people makes the appreciation nearly impossible.

The neighborhood reminds me of home with big shady trees. An indistinct apartment building is our destination.

Climbing one flight of stairs we enter a three-bedroom apartment. Adults mill around us. Nathalie walks away. We stay by the door. Other children sit on the floor talking to one another. I sit on the couch and lay Rudy on top of me. A woman with a gold wedding band hands me a dish of porridge. Rudy and I eat two bowls.

When I awake, Rudy is on the floor with a bowl of hard-boiled eggs between his legs. My stomach rumbles. He removes a hard-boiled egg from his bowl and hands it to me. The porridge woman smiles at Rudy.

"He is very young," she says.

"He's good. He won't cause any problems."

I'm always on the defensive when it comes to my brother. I can't read her expression. Rudy places an egg in his pocket.

"Here is a plate for your eggs and rye bread. I don't want your brother placing eggs in his pocket."

She laughs at her joke. Adults do that when they're trying to put you at ease.

Children leave and new ones arrive. A man shaves his beard, and his curly brown hair litters the kitchen floor. We eat more porridge. No one talks to us.

A blonde woman enters the apartment. She has a black eye and a torn dress. The porridge woman walks into a bedroom with her. The blonde reappears as a brunette.

We eat stew for dinner.

The next morning, the brunette approaches. Her name is Sophia.

She says, "We'll leave after you freshen up in the washroom."

Chapter 135
May 1939
Marjem Rechtschaffen

Solomon Fikotzki is a mathematician and high school teacher. He Tutor children from his large oak dining room table since the Nazis eliminated his position. Students, parents, and friends adore him. The SA arrested him in the middle of the night and shipped him off to Dachau.

The dead have it easy because their suffering is finite.

Martha, his wife, wears an open wound that won't mend itself. She lives every day missing him, remembering the better days. Despite her pain she chooses life.

She's adapting to her tragedy and hasn't shut down. Martha Fikotzki married Solomon at eighteen. He said he fell in love with her nose. He couldn't imagine how anybody could breathe with a nose so smart. That's just the tip of the iceberg with those two, they tease each other, and their laughter is based on substantial love.

When the Nazis took Solomon, she poured herself into serving others. She'll help anyone in need without considering the personal consequences. She uses her radio and her access to foreign language periodicals to help others plan their exit. The rain makes the air heavy, almost cloying. Martha's neighborhood is unrecognizable.

Unattended fences and overgrown bushes offer easy shelter, allowing plenty of places to hide.

Martha's backdoor is a ten-minute walk from the terminal. Climbing up her wooden back stairs, I take off my gloves and knock on the green door.

My protector wears a smock and slippers. Framed in graying brown coils, Martha emotes warmth.

She pulls me into a hug and lifts me off the ground and deposits me in an overstuffed chair worn soft by memories and time. Her strength never wavers, and her voice doesn't tremble.

"Is Aron here?" I ask as Martha flutters around the kitchen. She says no and her tenderness melts my reserve.

"Do you think..."

Martha interrupts, "He's too smart, Marjem. Don't try to fix this problem. You'll make it worse."

Her tone is harsh, but she doesn't criticize to be judgemental.

She states the facts as she sees them, and it's based upon years of personal observation.

I tell her the entire story.

"I got him out alive, Martha. He escaped through our bedroom window while I fed the bastards my strudel. We were to rendezvous at the bank. I saw him before I went in, but when I came back out he was gone."

Martha takes my arm, leads me to her bedroom, and guides me to sit on the bed.

"Brave lady. Now sleep."

We are in Monbijoupark.
The children sit beside me on our plush picnic blanket.

The blanket is lined in short green and red fringe. Manfred jumps up to run and Rudy struggles to tie his shoes. Manfred runs back and throws Rudy over his right shoulder. I tilt my head up into the sunshine and warm my face. I drift off and doze for a moment. The sun brings me peace. My babies chase each other and laugh with unbridled joy. The wind picks up and small gray clouds appear in the sky. The azure sky muddles. Within a handful of minutes there is lightning and thunder. Like a greyhound, I'm fast on my feet, chasing after my children, when the sky brightens like the inside of the sun. Manfred is within my grasp. I'm blinded. I shriek without noise with severed vocal cords.

I awake the next day and Martha is pleased.
"You look much better today. But Aron is not here."
"That makes sense. It was unsensible to help."

Chapter 136
May 1939 Holland
Manfred Rechtschaffen

When insecurity creeps in, my stomach churns like meat being put through a butcher's grinder to make sausage.

Our escape, although planned by my mother, doesn't bring me any security.

Madame Strausberg promised our reward is a new life together where we will be free and not afraid every day.

Right now, we're not together, we're not free and I'm afraid every minute.

Her words to me are as meaningful as a handful of dirt.

Sophie, our caregiver, looks deceptively young with a face full of freckles. Mumbling under her breath at a constant rate is oddly comforting. An unforeseen force alerts Sophie. She doesn't verbalize her concerns, but she changes our direction. She walks with a significant limp which is greatly exaggerated when she picks up the pace. I sense her discomfort and see beads of sweat collecting on her brow. I see her mumble to herself. She's counting the steps it's going to take her to get to the next destination. This action distracts her mind from the pain. I've seen Herman do this sometimes when he's pulled his back out and he's having difficulty walking down the stairs or across the hall. Sophie explains, when this nonsense is over, she's going to open up her own bakery.

She loves to bake cookies. Running through the ingredients needed for her favorite shortbread with candied cherries, absorbs my mind.

Momentarily I forget to be afraid until she whispers, "we must be mindful and remember to be quiet. Fading into the shadows is where the children are safest right now."

"Rudy's tired; he needs rest," I say.

Empathy softens her face revealing small fine wrinkles gathering at the corners of her eyes that disappear into her hair.

She says, "I'd like to laugh about something, relax and laugh in a way that makes my sides hurt."

"I don't know if I've ever laughed that way before."

Sophie considers. She and her sister one day laughed themselves silly. Sophie confesses she doesn't even remember what it was that made them laugh that hard. They almost peed in their pants. Shocked by her immodesty, the outrageous story is exactly what I needed at this moment.

I want to do crazy wild things with my brother one day. I look over at my baby brother and hope for a future filled with laughter.

Sophie says, "No one will bother you in the barn. Hay will keep you warm at night when the sun sets, and the air grows cold. Stay inside. A man will come, and he will have a wagon. He knows where to find you; he's done this type of exchange before. Stay inside the barn."

"Yes, ma'am."

"Repeat what I said." I repeat her instructions back to her. The words taste strange in my mouth.

"Half-a-kilometer down the road is a brown barn. Look for a broken window on the top floor."

She hands me two bundles with bread, blankets, and matches.

"Thank you."

"Remain alert," she demands.

Sophie walks away without another word. They all walk away. Abba, Ima, Madame Strausburg, Nathalie, Sophia. If we disappear on this road, no one will ever know. Rudy's overwrought. His eyes are soft hazel, like a sea of mossy green. He needs me to carry him.

I've never been inside a barn and neither has Rudy.

It smells terrible, like wet animal hair. Rudy inspects every wall, corner, and beam he determines is important. Afterward we stretch and do jumping jacks.

We play, eat, and nap. I make a bed in the hay placing one blanket on the hay and another on top of Rudy. I call it a blanket sandwich.

"A blanket sandwich is an ultimate luxury. It is way better than clean sheets and one blanket."

Rudy giggles at my silly explanation.

"Have you ever slept outside?"

He looks at me and nods. We cozy up to each other in the hay and stare into the night sky through the hole in the roof. Rudy nuzzles his nose into my neck, which is exactly what I need. On the third day I've run out of games for the two of us to play. Our food resources are diminishing. Rudy eats a full meal and I eat half. Hunger distracts me from my anger. Rudy needs security. Abba and Ima denied this to me, and I won't do the same. I don't want to call them Ima and Abba anymore. I'm going to refer to them as Mama and Papa. It sounds less childish, less Jewish and more American. When Mama left us, Rudy stopped talking. She took his words with her.

Rudy jumps to the sound of a braying horse. A man approaches. Through a splintered hole in the wall of the barn, we watch him approach. He's the same size as my father but he has a beard. Men in Berlin have clean shaven faces or a simple mustache. He wears a full beard.

He calls himself Bart and he hands us cheese and pumpernickel bread. Pumpernickel bread travels well, Ima says, because it doesn't get stale before it's finished. My shoulders relax and my spine tingles in a pleasant way. My defeated eyelids throb. Having an adult with us makes me feel better. A numb buzzing rolls over my body.

Closing my eyes and not being afraid feels good.

He laughs kindly at Rudy's appetite. Watching him eat makes me happy too. I take one bite and put the rest in my pocket. I don't know when we'll get more food.

The cart moves through the night. The worn wooden wheels find every divot in the dirt road. Five long planks of wood run across the floor of the cart. Four planks fashion the sides to prevent hay from tumbling out. Small splinters surround the nail heads. I describe the knots in the wood on the sides of the wagon. We identify small faces and animals in the cracks and shadows. We gaze up at the sky.

"Rudy, the sun rises in the east and sets in the west. When we follow the sunlight, we are heading west. At night, we use the stars as our guide."

We continue westward as the sunlight travels across the sky.

Bart tells us, "We are going around the center of Dortman. I was invited to a wedding in the Old Synagogue. The sanctuary seats over a thousand congregants."

Listening to his story is fascinating. The time he spends detailing the food makes my stomach rumble. I take another bite of cheese and savor the sweet creaminess.

Bart hands us a bottle of milk. My eyes drink it in. Rudy's little hands can barely grasp the sides. I help him sip the milk. After I take a sip, I help Rudy drink more. With full bellies I let the drowsiness take over. Bart tells us about the wedding party, how pretty the bride looked and how drunk he got that day with good friends.

He begins to describe his friends and I enjoy listening to his story. It's different than any other story I've ever heard and even though I savor every word as sleep takes over.

Shouting wakes me. I cover Rudy's mouth with my hand and roll over him. His face presses into my chest. I shift, allowing his nose to rest inside my armpit.

"Da ist nichts," suggests Bart. (There is nothing there) Rudy stiffens beneath me.

The German officer snickers, "Wirklich?" (Really?)

The hay obscures my view of the soldiers, making the whole situation scarier.

Rudy shifts his pinned leg. Hashem, please protect us. Bart kicks the wagon, and the horses squeal. A bayonet pierces the hay and grazes Rudy's plump thigh.

I pray soundlessly in his ear, "Shema Yiseoel Adonai Elahanu Adonai Ehad," and shove a crimson bandana into Rudy's mouth before his scream escapes.

Chapter 137
May 1939
Marjem Rechtschaffen

"Wash up, put on a fresh face, and join me in the kitchen," instructs Martha.

"Today, we allow hope to seep back in."

"Apfelstrudel."

Nostalgic tears moisten my eyes.

Her kitchen smells like my mother's; honey, butter, cinnamon, and apples. The level of commotion reminds me of growing up with six siblings. Her home is a waypoint for those struggling to slip away from Western Berlin.

"Marjem, stop those tears," she says sternly.

"Marjem, be relentless. Start anew."

Desperate choices, desperate times.

Outsiders do not understand. Modesty in Judaism is a basic tenet. Women cover their hair because their hair, signifying beauty, is meant to be cherished only by their husbands.

Out of respect, men won't look women directly in the eyes. Hassidic Jews trim their beards with Solomon's shears. They pray for mercy with wet cheeks. They cut their payas. Their hair litters Martha's kitchen floor. People arrive here to be reborn before they escape. Others tuck in their tefillin and remove their black hats to adapt.

The plan to escape is different for each person. My plan involves a man with a blue handkerchief.

"In the most perilous of conditions, this man eases discomfort. He loves attractive blondes."

Martha's good with people and what motivates them.

"He's a typical German man. The kind who wants other men's wives as much as his own."

The next morning, I head for the train station and kiss Martha goodbye.

"Be fierce. Live a remarkable and cheerful life. Laugh in Hitler's face and raise those beautiful boys to have cherished families of their own."

Chapter 138
May 1939
Marjem Rechtschaffen

Twenty minutes into the journey, the train doors open and close. Two SS officers flank a towering blonde-haired man in a proper-tailored overcoat.

The blonde's air of superiority suffocates the rest of us. An officer takes notice of me.

Uninterested in his assessing gaze, I rebuff his approach with my book, a useful tool to hide my eyes behind.

To steady myself, I repeat 'blow out the candles, smell the flowers.

"It's so hot," the blonde man announces.

I glance up and his welcoming smile catches my eye. He pulls out a blue handkerchief. The police proceed down the aisle unaware that he stopped.

"Edvard, come sit with us. I have new stories to share. We play new hunting games with Jews. Sit, we'll tell you all about it!"

The taller officer laughs at the smaller pig-nosed man's joke.

Vomit rises in my throat. The flush inside my stomach grows. I fixate on my breathing to even out my heartbeat. In a low voice, Edvard says to me, "I'll tell you where to go." Turning back to the officers, he says, "What? You love to talk!"

The banter continues, but he takes a seat across the aisle from me. I wait, wild and desperate. Mass travel is convenient and a great place to hide in plain sight. The guards with Edvard are all I care about.

After they exit the train, I'll feel better. Before they step off the train, one catches my eye and winks. Edvard remains seated and doesn't acknowledge the sleazy gesture.

"Three more stops. Visit Evelyn Roselle on Edelweiss. She bakes the best cakes."

I almost miss the instructions in his hushed tones.

A crowd of Hitler Youth enter. They pick over every morsel of space the way teenagers do, chattering like monkeys. I try to concentrate on Edvard's words: Evelyn Roselle, three stops. Shouting interrupts my daydreaming.

"Halt, sir!"

Edward is gone, but the officers are back.

The air evaporates around me. I'm numb around the fringes and voices echo back and forth, as if I am in a cave. I grip the seat in front of me to brace my fall. My heartbeat fills my eardrums. Pain pierces my ribs and spreads through me like a crimson stain on a white rug. My breasts are slick with sweat.

A short man asks, "Are you alright?"

He's worried, not inconvenienced. The dizziness subsides. Shocked, I caress the seat. I have not fallen. I pull myself together.

"I'm sorry, I'm a little thirsty."

"Frauline, the officers make everyone anxious. My wifes' nerves get the best of her too," he adds.

"You are kind."

Another man chimes in: "My wife's on edge around the soldiers and our son is in the SS. The uniforms are bright, but women seem especially affected by them."

******

The man with the blue handkerchief is gone. The crisp wind on the platform blinds me. Bell Shaped tears strain my cheeks and ruin my makeup. Anyone within whispering distance can hear my heightened heart rate.

A woman stands before a weathered door.

"I'm Frau Roselle."

Motionless, I wonder if she addressed me.

"Don't stand there." I step forward.

She touches my face.

"You're stunning."

The way she ogles me is creepy. My mind is blank. How did Frau Roselle recognize me?

"Go into the kitchen. Wash your hands. The trolley is filthy."

I follow her directions like a child, afraid to place a foot wrong.

"Stop acting like a fugitive," she says behind me. I jump.

"You're wound up tight, aren't you?" She laughs at her joke.

"I'm Marjem."

I'm led to the kitchen. Once inside she pushes me into a smaller room off the kitchen, and I brace for what comes next. Her mood shifts, and her expression changes.

Leaning in, she says, "You're safe."

She grabs a stool and motions for me to sit down. A hot cup of tea warms my hands and brings me to tears. This is unlike me. I'm not a crier. She laughs at me again while she picks something out of her teeth with a toothpick.

"I can't place the expression on your face. Tell me quickly what you're thinking. Don't lie. I'll know."

"The injustice and hatred I've faced daily has made me cry like a baby."

She laughs louder and I cry harder. It feels like a vicious game, but my tears are drying up and I'm gaining my composure again.

"You're soft. That is your problem to fix. Many women come here feeling all different kinds of ways. I don't care why. What I do care about is making sure they cleave here battle ready and hard. The Nazis will tear you to shreds for sport. That can't happen. Not because I care about you. I can't have them coming after me and my husband."

"Did you see the German soldiers' kitchen behind my bakery?"

I blanch. "I didn't."

"My husband runs it. You come from money."

She grabs the meaty part of my arm. I gasp.

"I don't thank you for helping me."

"Don't thank me yet," she says with a wry smile.

She twirls in a circle with her arms outstretched and her chin in the air.

"This is all mine."

"You are fortunate to have your own business."

"My mother died when I was five. Papa never remarried. He made me work at the bakery from the time I could reach the counter. I made rolls and churned butter, learnt my math, and handled the register. Even after I burned my leg at eleven, he made me love our business, and he ensured my independence."

"Financial independence for a woman is rare. What a gift," I say.

"Many young women and mothers come through my bakery. To gain their trust, I tell them my story. If I tell them mine, they share theirs."

"Makes sense."

"The Gestapo raid apartments. They take men and boys. They never return. Did that happen to you?"

"My husband and I walked away from the Gestapo."

"Good for you. I wanted children, but I'm not cute. You're young and stunning," she chides.

"My choices for a husband were old, crippled, or dirty and without manners. My father made sure I didn't need a man to eat."

"A smart man," I say, and I mean it.

Frau Roselle inquires, "What did your Papa do for you?"

"He made me work hard in school. I enjoyed getting great grades. I was smarter than any boy in my class. Germany educates everyone, and I took full advantage of all services possible. I worked until I got pregnant."

"Even after you got married?"

"Yes, I was proud of my job. Perhaps, upon reflection, I didn't show enough humility. My sister Henie was prettier and funnier. She stole the spotlight whenever she entered a room. My older brothers, all good men, made my Papa proud, but I was his favorite, and the whole family recognized it."

Flashbacks distract me until Frau Roselle speaks again.

"You're interesting, but the nervous version of you gets distracted."

She slaps my back and moves me to sit straight.

"Tell me more about you."

"My mother is in Holland with my two sisters and younger brother. Two years ago, Papa died. He meant the world to me. I feel untethered to the earth, more than orphaned without him."

Frau Roselle nods.

"It never stops hurting. I miss Papa every day. Herman relying on me helped. We married within a month."

"He anchors you," I reply.

"Yes, he does. We're happy. He cares for me and wants my happiness. During the War, he saw first-hand how desperate men treat one another. Depravity transforms people. Good people turn vile when hardship becomes depression."

"Not everyone."

"My husband said the country is changing. Hitlers' vision means a certain war."

She snorts at my expression, then stands up and moves to the stove to heat the kettle.

"My husband can feed men with few resources. He converts my leftovers into stews and soups. Those men eat well, and they love my husband."

"Loyalty is everything."

"Most people are dullards."

She says with an eagle-eyed glare.

"True," I say.

"We don't care about God," explains Frau Roselle.

"Instincts, I trust. Good people vouched for you. I will help because I can."

We sit and drink more tea.

She laughs and says, "No one suspects us. My husband feeds wayward travelers. These poor souls, like you, come to my bakery to escape Germany."

"Your plan is the ultimate deception."

"We live small, and we keep to ourselves. Power can shift at any moment. Be the small nail when the hammer comes by. Be mindful of your environment. Everyone smells fear — it's sour and sickly," says Frau Roselle.

"It's true. Fear smells like limes, green onions, and vinegar."
"Living by instinct is the smartest way to survive. You've made it this far. Paranoia is a tricky, whimsical bird. Here, we see things differently than the city folk of Berlin. The German plan is almost complete. We have seen the transports. We appreciate how far and wide Hitler's armies have spread. Hitler wants the world."
She wants to talk, share her suspicions.
"Poland is next, I am sure. Names have been added to lists to prepare for mass deportation. Good people will die. Hitler will take Holland, Belgium, and France. Pick somewhere else. You'll be alright as a blonde with big boobs. Use the love you have for your boys and push until they're back in your arms. Anger is fuel," she instructs.
"Now rest. There is a cot behind the stove. You sleep in the kitchen; it is warm. I get up early to start the bread," finishes Frau Roselle.

******

I dreamt that Manfred and I were in a park. He was flying a kite and Aron was running behind him.
I joined their chase, but I couldn't catch them.
Manfred transformed into Rudy and the sky went black.

******

In the morning, Frau Roselle works me hard. She is an intuitive baker cursed with swollen knuckles and twisted fingers. Frau's husband Willem enters the kitchen. Frau Roselle stands beside him.
"The soldiers are fresh. Stay away from the soup kitchen."
She chooses not to notice his wandering eyes, as he leers at my bosom. I'm self-conscious like a teenager.

After he leaves, she rolls her eyes.

"German men are pathetic. They find themselves irresistible."

She hands me a biscuit.

"Thank you," I say with fresh tears blurring my eyes.

There is nothing more to say.

Chapter 139
May 1939
Aron Rechtschaffen

A boy named Paul sits next to me in the back of the truck.
He opens his satchel and removes a loaf of warm rye bread.
"Thank you for your hospitality," I say.
"Caraway seeds are my favorite. My mother made the best rye bread."
I responded, "My wife bakes the best honey cake in Germany." He laughs.
"I prefer honey cake. Mother made that for festivals."
The common ground of food is protected. He tells me how chicken is by far the most impressive protein because you can change the taste depending on what side you serve it with. He would never turn down a delicious roast beef, but roast beef is not as versatile as chicken. Children's opinions are filled with delight. We eat in silence. Paul's tall with round shoulders. He reminds me of a puppy - all paws.
His knuckles overwhelm his long, slender fingers.
When the truck stops, he says, "a farmer lost control of his cows." Other vehicles pass us going south towards Berlin.

"Must be another Nazi transport," declares a stout man with a thick black beard.

"What are they moving?" questions the mustached man.

"My brother lives by the sea," declares a man.

"He has arms the size of tree trunks. He transfers barrels off the freighters and stacks them six high. Filled with petrol and oil. Camouflage tarps cover the stockpiled barrels."

"The Nazis' purloin our farmland to stockpile provisions. They steal pigs and chickens from small farms and grill them."

"The soldiers target farms run by widows. Women are more afraid of rape than stolen poultry and pork," says the stocky man.

"Transportation of Nazi supplies was impossible given the current roads. In May, they reworked the infrastructure and paved many roadways. Smooth roads created higher trade value which brought more jobs and opportunity. The refinery where my papa worked hired a third shift of laborers. The problem that arose was the laborers weren't local, and there wasn't enough housing for them all," says Paul.

Paul's comment illuminates a broader perspective, beyond the prison camps - Hitler is working refineries to capacity.

"Papa told me they move sleeping bags, blankets, and even machine guns."

Lost in his minutia, the truck jerks forward.

"The cows must have passed," I remark in delight.

I wipe my lip with a handkerchief.

"My father claimed an admired man always carries a nice handkerchief."

"I agree."

He adds, "My mother embroidered handkerchiefs for my Papa."

He shows me one.

"This was her favorite. She made this for him when pregnant with me."

"It's lovely."

He refolds the handkerchief carefully and tucks it back in his pocket.

"The Nazis set up depots along the eastern border of Germany. Papa complained how he changed our beautiful countryside. Hitler built warehouses along the waterways. Papa saw troops on the trains all the time."

Children mimic the language their parents use, and that's how you realize the real truth that's going on.

They're oblivious to repercussions.

Paul cannot grasp the high-level picture.

"You're smart."

"I quit school to help Mama at home. Walking was a chore for her because she had polio. All the boys in the local Hitler youth receive free bicycles. Papa wanted me to have a bicycle to help out mama."

Paul laughs, "But conscription wasn't my preference. I won't fight for Hitler," he asserts.

"Where are you headed?"

"To my uncle."

Paul suggests I join him in Güstrow. His uncle can bring me to Rostock.

"There are five lakes that feed into Güstrow. The canal is straightforward to negotiate."

"Adventure builds character," I declare.

"Mama is Jewish… *was* Jewish. The Nazis killed her. We assumed she would be safe. When the Gestapo came for Papa, Mama fainted," says Paul.

The familiar story out of Paul's mouth is heartbreaking.

"The Gestapo didn't expect Mama to collapse and die. Papa screamed in horror. I stood still and did nothing."

He didn't meet my eyes.

"You're so young to handle such trauma. These monsters unleash more than a grown man can bear."

"They shipped Papa off to Dachau."

"I'm sorry."

Paul asks, "Who did they take from you?"

Chapter 140
May 1939
Manfred Rechtschaffen

We followed Emma, our new escort, in silence.

She explains, "I'm taking you to a man's house. He helps children like you. His name is Charlie."

I repeat to myself, Emma then Charlie. Emma speaks to somebody and glances back at us like a second thought. When she catches my eye, she smiles nervously, and I don't believe her. Real smiles make women prettier; her smile is unsettling.

We walk into Charlie's house, and I turn to Emma and say, "Thank you for taking care of us."

She leaves us without a goodbye. Reviewing the caregivers helps me track time. I'm not sad because I never got to know her. Nathalie kept us safe on the train.

Sophia got us to the barn. Bart in the wagon and Madame Strausberg were the only ones who cared about us.

He says, "I bet you boys love eggs."

"We do," I declare.

Buttery eggs and onions remind me of Mama. The sizzle drives me crazy. The one-armed man cooks us eggs, potatoes, and onions.

Mama always kept me full. Whenever I detect food, my stomach clenches. Cramps throb on the left-hand side of my body underneath my rib cage.

He adds bacon to his plate. "Eat!" he commands.

His abruptness scares Rudy.

"We're going to be okay. We're tough."

Rudy and I eat from the same fork. Contact soothes him.

I place my palm on his thigh and he visibly relaxes.

His breathing slows down, but we keep shoveling food into our mouths.

"There is no reason to rush. We have plenty of time," offers the one-armed man.

"The fat lady got mad. She took our plates away because we ate too slow. Ever since then we eat fast," I explained.

"Eat slow, Rudy. You don't want stomach aches," says Charlie. He nods towards my brother.

"Why doesn't he communicate?"

"He has nothing to add," I answer.

The old man chuckles. His one arm does not upset me.

"I scare the little ones until I show them my medals." Charlie places a box in Rudy's lap.

"Open the box when you are ready," he says to Rudy.

Rudy nods in confirmation. He opens the box. It contains a treasure trove of medals, coins, and maps.

Rudy empties the box on the table. Charlie unfolds a map and shows Rudy where we are.

"My name is Charlie Anderson. What is your name?" he says to Rudy.

Rudy doesn't respond. If he answered, it would be a miracle.

"This medal is for bravery," says Charlie.

"I'm a veteran. In battle, I saved my lieutenant. I returned to a parade. A pretty girl liked me enough to get married. We had a son. His name is Henrik."

I survey the room and walk over to a photo of a beautiful girl.

"That was my wife when she was seventeen-years-old," says Charlie.

He stands beside me as we admire the picture.

"Mama had pictures in silver frames on our mantles at home."

"It is nice to look upon the faces you love," replies Charlie. Charlie's photos are not in silver frames. His are simple. The photographs tell the story of a single boy growing up in Germany. Charlie is silent. He stands before a picture of a Nazi.

"My son is SS. He speaks many languages and is strong. After his mother died, I did my best. People do not pay attention to the aged. The crippled and infirm are unseen. A one-armed man can never hug. My son needed more. The Nazis gave him what he coveted." says Charlie.

"Are we safe?"

"He won't return. Nazis are not welcome. Hitler's vision for a better Germany is not mine. Germany broke my body apart. A person can lose their sanity."

Charlie picks up a medal.

"This medal didn't put food on our plates or keep us warm in the cold. My small farm did. I worked the land when I came back from the war. With one arm, I made a life for Henrik and me. He was clean, cherished, and rested."

"My Mama and Papa didn't allow the Gestapo to take them away."

"You come from very brave individuals."

"Thank you."

"I raised him to be a good boy, but he was gullible. His new friends wore brilliant uniforms. They carried sidearms. A parent cannot compete with that. He enlisted. I begged him not to go and he refused."

"If he came back, would you absolve him?"

"I don't know. He has done evil things," says Charlie.

He sighs.

"You will remain here for a few days. I have a friend who will smuggle you and your brother closer to Dalheim,"

"We will live if we make it to Dalheim," I tell Charlie.

"You have a legitimate chance at freedom," says Charlie.

"Mrs. Strausburg promised," I told Charlie.

"Promises are sacred."

Chapter 141
April 1939 Rostock, Germany
Aron Rechtschaffen

Rostock smells of saltwater, sunshine, and fish. Mixed aromas bring me back to my teenage years when I never grew tired. Here, mornings begin by observing the sunrise over the various vessels. Deck crews are hard at work before others have awakened. Engines on the larger ships emit a persistent hum. Other ships pull up their anchors.

The call of the sea controls the dock.

At lunch, I walk barefoot in the sand. Hot sand collects between my toes. Touching the earth with my bare feet connects me to the world. The squalls of the gulls mark the passage of time. The sea has its own lifestyle; the ebb and flow of the waves bookend my days.

Deliveries are regular making it lively but not frenetic.

The scarcity of a military presence invigorates me.

A lovely woman in a golden yellow shirt stands beside a vendor selling fish on skewers. Their teamwork is a coordinated dance. He greases the skewers, and she stirs the fire. When he disturbs her, she rolls her eyes in reply. He secures the money and greets customers. She seasons the fish with salt and pepper from six or seven inches in the air. The fish lies on a bed of sliced lemons. Lemons prevent the fish from adhering to the grill.

The fish is flaky and succulent. I lick my fingers clean, and my lips burn from the sea salt and lemon.

One stall sells buttered poppy seed rolls with small pieces of sausage. I walk farther and find two sisters in their thirties running another stall, with a line down the pier. They sell boiled eggs with chopped liver spread on hot rye bread.

My kind of food. My eyes follow the line to its end, and I join the queue. A mother and her daughter, about ten, are standing in line.

"Do you think I'll like Copenhagen?" asks a young girl with red curls.

She has a round face and windburned cheeks.

"Will they like me?"

Her eyes fill with tears, and I see the sadness growing in her mother's face.

"Who cares. It's you and me against the world."

She holds her daughter close and strokes her back.

"Let us get some sandwiches. I don't know when we'll eat again."

"Yes, Mama," says the little girl.

She teaches her daughter to trust and love, to rely on her, and know her love has no limits. Marjem is that kind of mother. Not in her words, but in her actions. The way she protects and teaches Manfred. Everything he knows is because of her. The mother and daughter talk to each other as if no one else exists. It's a blessing for the mother and child to stay together. A large ship leaves the dock. Another one arrives. Men move towards the food stalls. The smell of body odor is strong. I overhear one man speaking to another.

"Travel across the sea is fast and simple. You can grab work with my brother-in-law."

He's lucky to have an opportunity handed to him like that.

"That sounds great," says the other man.

Relief washes over his face.

He didn't have a plan, now he does.

"Do you have papers?" Relief is replaced with uncertainty.

We move forward in the queue.

"My papers are valid." He's lucky.

"The women in Copenhagen are outstanding."

Jeers the smaller of the two men.

"You won't stand a chance. Danes are tall, proud people. Beautiful with ruddy cheeks."

I continue to eavesdrop.

More ships arrive at the docks. Throngs of men, women, and children fill the empty spaces left in this thriving port. I dive into the rye bread sandwich and relish the oily liver paste coating my tongue and teeth. My satisfaction runs deep, in a primal child-like way, and reminds me of all I am missing: Przemyśl; my mother's ever-present love, Marjem's buttery blonde hair falling in her face when she laughs. Rudy's sleep sounds, and Manfred's soul food eyes. Living under duress weighed upon me for so long, my mind moves faster than my body. The load I carry is far away. I will work my way across the sea. Small boats have a crew of two to three men. There are luxury taxis, fishing boats, and small cargo vessels. Two officials stand in front of me.

"You need papers. Show us your papers."

The three men behind me reach into their pockets and hand over their papers. I don't have valid papers.

"The Gestapo pulled me over and took my papers," the tallest man explains.

"I was with my friend. He shocked the Gestapo. He took off. They chased my friend. I went in the opposite direction."

The officials nod as he is talking. One spits on the floor.

"I would've done the same thing."

"A few weeks ago, they found him and shot him. They still have my papers, though."

I clear my throat.

"I'm great at knots, if you need a crewman."

We speak and within five minutes he hires me. Once the boat leaves the port, the passengers relax. I find work sweeping floors.

A woman with corn-coloured hair speaks.

"We're fortunate to be on a ship to Denmark. The farther we can get from Hitler, the better."

A woman with a mole near her lip says, "Danes hate the Germans."

A few members of the crowd mumble but I can't decipher anything clearly.

The blonde continues, "When we arrive at the dock, no one will stop you. The Danes know why people run from across the sea."

"You have taken this trip before?" asks a tall man with a thick mustache.

"Yes." Says the blonde woman.

A stout man with graying temples stands beside a small girl. She has big brown eyes and short brown hair. He hands her morsels of food, and she eats quietly.

He shivers and rewraps her tattered jacket to warm her in the sea breeze. The woman with the mole clears her throat, "Denmark is wonderful."

The little brown-haired girl looks at her father. She opens her mouth and closes it. Her father picks her up, and she rests her head on his shoulder. After whispering in her ear, her body collapses into his. He hums. I lean in and close my eyes. My mouth opens and I draw in a breath.

I recognize his tune. The Kaddish. Mourners say the Kaddish to show God that despite the loss in their life they still praise God. The song belongs to the living.

Does anyone else recognize the tune?

Two other men close their eyes. A grey-haired lady catches my glance. Her mouth curves upward.

In the crisp air, the captain's bell rings clear.

He announces, "We will dock in ten minutes. Gather your belongings and small children. Leave nothing behind."

My chapped lips taste like freedom.

Chapter 142
April 1939
Manfred Rechtschaffen

Our guardian angel is a railroad laborer named Otis Daniels. He's big with skinny hands covered in scrapes and welts. He smuggles us like contraband across Germany, wedged between crates carrying black market goods. Otis Daniels speaks with his mouth full of food.

He spits and curses. Most importantly, he doesn't ask me any personal questions. He talks to me but doesn't care if I remain silent.

Otis starts talking and once he gets going, his words spill out like a Shabbat wine stain, overwhelming Ima's fine white tablecloth.

"Go to New York City. Remember that. Leave Europe. Start a new life with your baby brother. If they ask, and they will, what do you say?" he prompts.

"America. New York City with my baby brother. My name is Manfred Rechtschaffen, and I can spell it too," I say.

"You're an impressive little big man. You'll handle New York just fine. I can see it in your eyes. You're going to be a man who knows his value. Everything about New York City moves quickly; the people, cars, buses, bikes, and even underground trolleys! People work throughout the day and night. They walk fast and talk faster. I cobbled together several jobs, bus driver, fireman and delivery man. Finding work is easy if you're willing. It's called shift work, which isn't reliable but gives me the chance to live without a lot of obligations. Teachers and firemen live next-door to butchers, bakers and a shoe repairman. The city has its own personality. Churches, synagogues, bowling alleys, men's clubs, tea shops the list goes on and on. Cafes are accessible all night."

He stops himself and pats me on the head.

"Your eyes are as big as saucers."

Otis Daniels suggests I close my eyes and take a nap.

He promises to keep talking if I try.

"In twenty-seven, I joined a jazz band."

He asserts with a toothy grin. His voice is robust but whimsical. I could listen to him for hours.

He'd be great on the radio. The world he describes would swallow me up.

Abba knows how to make everything smaller.

He would say to me, "life is messy and don't judge yourself too harshly. Surround yourself with people that care about you."

"If you see my Papa, will you help him?" I ask.

"Of course. If I can help a family, that's aces," he replies. His hands are in fists and his thumbs stick straight up.

I don't know what "aces" means, but I like how it sounds in my mouth. He shows me how to position my hands and we practice a few times. I mold Rudy's little hands into the same position.

His vocabulary is vibrant and pictorial. He mentions he once was a teacher. He taught poor kids, children who had to work for the family instead of going to school and getting educated.

"What did you teach?" I ask hoping to keep him talking for as long as possible.

His easy cadence matches his soothing voice. The rumble in my chest caused by the vibration of his voice is pleasant.

"Languages: German, English, and French."

"That's a lot," I say.

He likes being a teacher. The classroom antics he describes are unimaginable to me. I told him I had never been to school. He told me about Kraków. A beautiful city with magnificent architecture and proud people who are smart and cultured. The Nazis took his brother-in-law away. "You know it goes, he's Jewish. A fate worse than death." His skin puckers and deep grooves between his eyebrows appear. His expression is a cross between guilt, sadness, and dismay. An expression every caregiver wore in one capacity or another when shuffling us away from Berlin to Duisburg.

Madame Strausburg was sad when Mama never made it back from the bank. Nathalie pitied Rudy and was spooked on the train. Sophia's abandonment on the dirt road surprised me. My mother never would've paid for this kind of treatment. Emma was running from something with her newly dyed hair and we simply tagged along for the exchange. Charlie worried but he used his medals to make Rudy and I feel better. His wrinkles fused into a permanent scowl; bothered immeasurably by Rudy's silence.

He didn't blame me like the others did. Herman would've liked Charlie. Same with Papa. They both would've liked Otis Daniels too.

"It's true," I confess.

He speaks to me like a man speaks to a boy but not in a "looking-down" kind of way.

Otis, Charlie and Herman are similar. I'm more inclined to listen when people speak to me this way. I never knew there was a difference before.

Now I realize it's all about communication. How you treat people and how they treat you matters more than possessions, political beliefs, and wealth.

In Kraków, Jewish children ran wild in the streets because most of their fathers had disappeared. Unfortunately, many Germans didn't mind Jews disappearing.

Otis Daniel said it is nasty, but it's true. He said he did his part to teach the children. His reward was in imprisonment for two weeks.

"Sometimes when the jails get overcrowded, you get released early. I had this lady friend, a real bearcat. The guards loved her; beautiful. When she came around to see me, they treated me better. She brought the boy's soup. She knew how to fill in a skirt and an aching belly in need of good wholesome home cooking. Short, temperamental, and smart, she used her beauty to make everyone crazy. Underestimated she held her tongue when necessary and never missed when a hint was dropped. At seventeen she traveled all over the country with a backpack. I've been told, she's won every argument she was in, whether she was right or not."

"What is her name?"

"Greta Michelle Beaulieu."

She is as sexy as her name implies. She got me in trouble with a local Eggman. It was downhill from there.

When I got sprung from jail, I left town. No one needs that kind of trouble. If I had the chance I would do it all again. She used to paint, naked, on giant murals in her apartment.

Drop clothes strewn across the floor. As Otis weaves his tales, Rudy falls asleep.

"He needs rest."

Before Rudy was born, I slept wonderfully.

I'd never heard a gunshot before. I knew soldiers existed, but I didn't know secret police took children from their homes.

There was no discussion of evacuations or neighbors disappearing. Staying awake at night, listening to my parents' plans, was preferable to the uncertainty of not knowing. Otis grabs some newspapers and crumples them up. He stuffs them in a burlap sack. He covers the makeshift mat with a wool blanket he pulls out from his rucksack. He takes Rudy from me and lays him down.

He removes his jacket and wraps it around Rudy.

"What if she's dead?" I whisper.

Rudy stirs. I move to his side. Otis doesn't know us.

He stood up for his sister and innocent children that didn't belong to him. I'd like to imagine him standing up for us. He tosses me a fruit.

"What is this?"

"A tangerine."

Otis explains how it's filled with vitamins, and how you peel it, eat it, and if there're pits you are to spit them out. "When Rudy eats a piece, bite it in half first, and then give him the rest. Sometimes the skin inside the tangerine is hard to shred when you don't have the right teeth."

He peels another tangerine and hands it to Rudy. He holds it in front of him like a Hanukkah present. I take a bite. Sweet juice explodes in my mouth. I want the taste to last.

"Rudy, this is delicious."

I take a bite of the next segment and then hand the rest to Rudy. Rudy hands me his tangerine. He moves his hands around in circles. Rudy and I eat two tangerines. Otis opens the train car doors, and the German countryside rolls by.

"You've seen wild things for such a young boy. Do you think you're going to remember everything you saw?"

"There is plenty I wish to forget."

"No doubt," he says.

"However right now I wish to remember every moment. Fresh air blowing on my face, eating a tangerine with my brother, and feeling safe. This is how I want to remember our journey."

Chapter 143
April 1939
Marjem Rechtschaffen

The Baudouin Tower overlooks the tranquil countryside where Holland, Germany, and Belgium converge.

Nestled in thick greenery a system of serpentine footpaths run throughout the woodlands. I'm a breath away from freedom once I cross the border at Trois Bornes.

The border between Holland and Germany is being monitored, my guide Gloria says. It's better to cross into Belgium. She reminds me to stick to the goal. Get out of Germany. Once in Belgium access to Holland is easier. I look around at the forest and everything is dark and ominous. Aron would be in his element. He grew up in Przemyśl, a district of timber merchants, with a childhood spent in exploration beneath a luscious canopy of foliage.

Gloria executes the uneven terrain of roots and rocks nimbly. Every step is a tenuous battle for me. A hollowed log catches on my boot and I lose my balance. I draw blood from my lip trying to suppress a scream. Landing clumsily, my feet scramble to regain composure. I roll my ankle, tearing something within. Gloria says we should slow down now.

"Cross when you can't see your hands in front of your face."

Simple, easy directions that I can wrap my mind around.

"Will you come with me?"

"No. This is for you. Take the path of least resistance."

My mother's face flashes before me. She'd say I did things the hard way. I wasted years being annoyed by her.

I mistook her advice as criticism, and her concern as disrespect. In realty, she admired me the entire time.

My mother is strong and fierce; an impressive role model who believes in love. She left security in Holland for an unknown world in Dobromyl.

My parents' mutual ambition then propelled them to Berlin. Like links in a chain, we are better together.

Many strong women got me to where I am now. Helena changed my life. Her elegance under pressure taught me a lot. When fear becomes insurmountable, I channel her. She says, "Marjem, pull yourself together, wipe off your lipstick, and apply a fresh face."

I pinch my cheeks and slap my face, brushing terror aside like the dirt on my clothes.

Martha adjusted my mindset. She paved the way for others to alter their destiny. She led me to Frau Roselle, who called me privileged, took my clothes, and possessed an inner grit unimaginable to women like *The Hens.*

Gloria taught me to be smart about my surroundings, stick to my plan, and stay focused.

Tonight's sunset will be my last German memory. My journey is composed of small steps. From the bank to a tea shop to a friend's arms. I followed a blue handkerchief that led me to a bakery. I hid on a farm and found a new role model.

Countless German citizens helped me to escape my country. I'm grateful to all.

A twig snaps. I crawl on the ground and find the wooden fence just as Gloria said I would.

The worn slats are no match for me. I claw through the dirt until my fingers feel frostbitten. When my bosom rests upon Belgian soil I'm flooded with renewed energy and the pressure to be better.

Covered in sweat, I shake from the chills and the adrenaline. I put this pressure on myself. Everything slows down and my heartbeat thumps in my head like a train screeching through the forest at top speed.

Bursting into a run, I chase the shadows of Aron and my boys. My feet pound the earth and I pick up speed.

Aron comes into focus.

He yells into a vacuum. "Don't stop until you get to the barn. The babies are in the barn."

Chapter 144
April 1939
Manfred Rechtschaffen

The ground is cold and unforgiving under my swollen feet. My body throbs. My discomfort is visible, but Rudy doesn't understand it.

The pain reminds me I am an orphan. I'm alive.

Rudy is alive. I did my job.

There was a lady in the house, where we met the blonde with the black eye, who walked into a room blonde and came out a brunette. She praised God before she ate her meals. I lost faith in my God when Papa was arrested. Rudy is asleep inside my coat, his fists in his mouth. Unwrapping Rudy from inside my coat, I prop him up on hay in the dimmest corner of a barn. A pail filled with rainwater will be sufficient for washing. Foraging for food takes focus. Dusk is the optimal time to steal food.

A fast-moving child can be mistaken for a shadow.

A cramp stabs the left side of my body.

To assuage the ball of misery, I stretch.

A soldier approaches. The trooper is not part of my plan. Sharp in his fresh clean uniform, he is well-fed, warm, and lost. I stand tall.

Papa's voice takes over, *I spent my life preparing you. Look him right in the eye. You're meant for more than these beasts will ever witness. Ima refused the Gestapo.*

She didn't shrink in fear.

Believing that my family will reunite invigorates me.

The soldier interrupts my pep talk.

"Where is Dalheim station?"

Papa voice murmurs *Act casual. Strength breeds trust.*

He is lost.

I see the train depot is down the hill. I point westward.

The soldier releases a held breath and turns away.

Extreme hunger feels like an athletic cramp in your stomach. The ache, like a compass, leads me to a nearby house. I see an open windowsill with checkered red and white curtains. Her house smells of supper. My adrenaline is pumping. Three fresh loaves of bread are on the sill. Inside the kitchen is a mother and two boys.

I hide below the windowsill and wait. My head pops up and I see that her back is to the window. She turns and ducks down. Did I stare too long at the bread? When I pop up again, two loaves remain and a bottle of milk.

I dash back to Rudy with not a drop of milk spilt.

His expectant face makes the panic worth it.

"Rudy, we're in Dalheim."

His small body trembles in my arms.

"Now we eat fresh bread and milk."

I hand him the bottle and he takes a sip.

"Drink more, but don't drink fast," I instruct.

I rip off another piece of bread and hand it over to Rudy. Sweet milk drips from the sides of my mouth.

Rudy touches the milk on my face.

"Madame Strasburg said, if we made it to Dalheim, we'd see Mama and Papa again. Tomorrow could be that day."

Chapter 145
Trois Barnes, Belgium
Marjem Rechtschaffen

"...She requires sleep. She's exhausted."

"Hush, we're uncertain..."

My eyes can't focus. I open my mouth and I'm speechless.

I close my eyes again.

"Noorah, she's opening her eyes again."

My throat is parched like a dead husk.

The cold water coats my cracked tongue.

"Can you hear us?"

The lights are bright.

Hot tears run down the sides of my face.

"Noorah, she has been comatose for three days."

Someone pats my hand and speaks slowly, in heavily accented German, "I'm Elyse. Do you recognize where you are?"

"No," I whisper.

Joyous laughter erupts.

My body shakes when the coughing begins.

"You passed out in my barn. We're here to help."

"Please. Please!" I tried so hard to get this far.

"We wish to help you locate your family."
The women speak. Their tone is urgent. I ask for help. I'm
in Trois Barnes. North is Holland.
"I want to be in Holland. My sons are there."
"Holland is not far away," says Noorah.
"Your sons. Quelle supreme."
She lifts a bowl and removes the lid.
"You survived."
She takes a spoon and fills it with golden stock. I see bits of
celery, onions, and carrots - the Jewish trifecta.
I digest the aroma. My lips sweep across the spoon. Warmth
fills my mouth and spreads through my chest.

Chapter 146
1939
Manfred Rechtschaffen

The silver haired girl finds us in the barn. She acts more like a mother than a teenager. We keep quiet and move quickly. She tries to take the baby from me, but no one takes care of him better than I do. Her name is Cecile.

She winds us through a few streets masterfully passing near but never approaching the train station.

Rudy is exhausted and can barely hold up his head. Looking for shelter, hoping for reprieve and never getting it. Open to the possibilities, hope takes over.

The pavement beneath my feet turns to a dusty path climbing over gnarled roots. I see the woods before me and pick up my pace. Every few minutes, she halts ensuring we're keeping up.

"I'm bringing you to Mr. Cohen. Repeat his name to me."

"Mr. Cohen," I say and I almost trip over my feet.

"He helps children," she says into the wind.

"We are very lucky that he will help us."

"I want you to follow me and do everything I do."

The forest surrounds me as darkness looms. I see faces in the trunks of the trees. My shoulders are fused together in tension. The moon is weak.

Cecile wipes her palms on her thighs.

"This is the best time to move. Most people are at home eating dinner." she says in an urgent tone.

"Wait for a second," I say and put Rudy down.

She stops and looks puzzled.

"Rudy, climb up," I instruct, and he wraps his hands around my neck, and I grab his legs.

We have grown so close; he's always climbing up on me or snuggling close when we sleep. As we run, I hum.

He kisses my head.

"We can't be on the main path."

She moves us across the grass until even that runs sparse.

"From here forward, stay as close to the ground as possible. I haven't seen many people since we left the town."

We come upon a fence, which we climb over. She helps Rudy before I can object.

"We're parallel to the train tracks now."

Cecile looks as tall as a mountain.

"Mr. Cohen will meet you on the other side. The other side is Holland. There is a house that stands bravely against Fascism. You're leaving Germany now."

I listen to her words, and they sink in. We did it.

"Where am I supposed to go?" I ask.

"You have to climb over this hill and then run through the trees. Keep low to the ground and don't stop running until you see a house. No matter what you hear, don't stop for anything," she instructs.

Her strange silver hair glows in the pale moonlight. Rudy is shivering but it's not cold. He might sense my terror.

"When?"

"When I tell you, we're going to use the noise of the trains to cover any sounds you make," she says.

"Get ready Rudy. We're going to run, and I need you to hold onto me with all your strength. Don't let go of me," I say.

"Have the baby wrap himself around your chest. Button up your jacket and use that to bind the baby to you."

We wait.

I'll run like the wind, be as fast as a kite. I have protected him the entire time. I kept my promise.

Gunshots pierce the silence.

"Where there are rifles, there are soldiers," she whispers under her breath.

The ground beneath us begins to shake.

Her reaction makes me nervous. She checks her watch and looks at us again.

"Soldiers are coming, get down!" she says.

We hear the soldiers and their horses before we see them. The soldiers rush past us and then stop. Two men argue with each other in German. A third man arrives yelling. One man takes off and the other two pursue him. I hear a roar in the distance and see smoke. I start to sweat. What if Rudy slips from my grasp?

"Grab your hands together behind my neck and don't let go."

My heart skips a beat, and I can't swallow. My fear and exhilaration makes my whole body pulsate.

Clutching my baby brother to me, I feel his heartbeat change and match mine.

The ground trembles as the train roars louder.

"Run! Now!" she commands.

I stand up and my knees shake. She points me in the direction of freedom. I look behind me and see shadows of soldiers. My back tingles with fear.

I start to run, and I can't feel the ground. I want to scream and make myself run faster. I hold Rudy close, and we are up and over the hill. We sprint through the trees. Branches slap and tear at my skin as I go full speed.

Rudy buries his face in my chest. My ankles twist and turn on roots, but I don't stop. I run through the trees, as instructed, and see a small field.

Blinded by tears, nothing comes into focus. I don't know when I am supposed to stop. I keep running and crying until I run right into a man.

Chapter 147
April 1939
Marjem Rechtschaffen

"The Germans will kill everyone!" I scream.

My eyes snap open in terror. My mouth is moving faster than my mind.

"Are they here for me?" I sit straight up.

"Did they find me?"

Someone places their hand on my arm soothingly.

The gentle touch works miracles. I lay back down.

Sweat covers my arms and back.

"Doctor, her heart rate is climbing."

The aide moves closer. The lights are bright. I see kind eyes.

Several sets of hands touch me reassuringly.

A man in a white coat sits on my bed.

"You are safe."

"Am I safe?"

The words taste like cherries in my mouth, plump, firm and sweet.

"Yes. Do you know what year we are in?"

The nurses' faces come into focus. Such young pretty girls.

"1939."

"Do you know where you are?"

"No."

"You're in a ward in Trois Barnes, Belgium."

Belgium isn't Holland. I remember making that distinct choice.

"Where am I?"

"A hospital. How do you feel?"

"Tired."

"Your shoes reveal an adventure, Marjem. I'm giving you medication to relax you."

"Why?"

"Your body needs to heal," says the doctor.

My throat closes. I choke for air. "I cannot ..."

Two nurses step closer.

One says, "take a moment, Marjem."

My vision blurs. Rubbing my eyes doesn't help.

"Where are my children?" I shout into a tunnel.

My entire body is on fire, vanishing from the inside out. People swirl around me. A warm sensation makes me dull and foggy. My arms tangle themselves up.

I soak my pillow in tears. In defeat, I sleep.

******

I want to break everything around me. Smashing a saucer against the walls, the noise of porcelain shattering satisfies me. I holler at people inside my head. Mistakes were made. Questions stay unanswered. We weren't able to wait any longer. Helena and I examined the contingencies. Helena paid off more bribes than I could ever afford. Germany tore my family apart. My dreams blew up in my face. None of it was my fault. I was unable to control a thing. Trauma changed me. Made me sharper at the edges. My anger is a precision instrument I must utilize for my own survival. There is no rescue coming.

I struggle to escape this place. I must find my children and Aron. Heavy and bloated, my legs drag beneath me.

The seams on my shoes burst free. I stomp my feet to recover sensation. My fingers splay to grasp the walls. My heart pounds in my rib cage. It might rupture. My mouth fills with saliva, no words have time to form. As my head drops forward, I brace for impact.

******

Awake, I drown in my tears. My wrists strain against the bed rails. An old mother's face, lined around her mouth and eyes, appears.

"A nun found you in the street. Unconscious. You are in a hospital. Exhaustion has made you hysterical."

She wipes my forehead with a cool cloth.

It feels wonderful.

"No choice. I had to..."

Tears flow.

"He didn't wait for me."

"You survived. What you needed you found. Bravery, arrogance, luck? Whatever it was, you pulled it out of yourself," says the nurse.

"I have a sister in Holland."

"That's wonderful news! We'll get word to her," says the nurse. Again, the cool cloth strokes my brow.

I feel a pinch and my mind wanders to a field of lilac blossoms with canary yellow puffs in the center.

The color reminds me of artificial Easter eggs. Springtime in Holland produces extraordinary colors and flowers.

Crusty mud covers my boots. The rain left the air humid. I am withered and wish I were able to have a small cup of hot tea with lemon.

Chapter 148
April 1939 Amsterdam, Holland
Aron Rechtschaffen

The small room has several piles of stacked paper, a typewriter, and a telephone. A bare lightbulb swings from a cord attached to the ceiling. A wastepaper basket overflows with crumpled up paper. A tidy looking man approaches. His face is fixed in a grimace.

"I have to be mindful," declares the Chief.

"My job is to protect Dutchmen. Holland is ill-equipped for the inflow of exiles from Germany. I am not a cruel man; I am in an unthinkable situation as impending doom streams across our shores."

His face softens; power can convert a simpleton into a scoundrel. Insecurities that beleaguered them since childhood mutate lesser men into masochists.

The Judge and the Chief are two sides of the same coin. Power is a tool not a weapon.

"The Gestapo came for my son and bribed him with a bicycle. They wanted him to leave with them and abandon his baby brother. Imagine a six-year-old boy refusing the

Gestapo? He impresses me every day and I want the chance to see what he becomes."

"What happened next?"

He leans forward in his chair. Eager.

"They came for me, and I hid. Marjem, my wife, distracted the Nazi guards by serving them apple strudel. My wife is beautiful. Aryan blonde with green eyes. Their egos were easily manipulated, and I slipped out the back window and down the fire escape."

It doesn't feel good to be saved by your wife, but I'd rather manage the guilt and be alive. The Chief confronts me.

"Is that a fact?"

He rummages through some papers on his desk and stamps a few others. The silence terrifies me.

"My wife's family is from here. I want to reconcile my family. Work and be helpful while we await our affidavit from America."

"Hitler is not God. One person cannot rule who lives or dies."

Another man walks in and places a gray folder up on his desk. The chief regards the information inside. He has a huge responsibility to the people of Holland.

"I am not inhumane," he says to himself.

Opening a drawer, he removes what looks like headache powder. exhaustion registers on his face.

"Unsanctioned entry is illicit." I remain silent.

He opens up a folder and moves a few papers around. He checks his watch against the clock on the wall.

"Your arrest is unnecessary."

"Thank you, sir."

My hands involuntarily clap. He looks up from his paper and licks his lips.

"It appears you chose the scenic route from Denmark."

His mocking tone implies familiarity. My heart no longer races. As my pent-up fear dissipates, a small laugh escapes my lips.

"Be careful the DNP (Dutch Nazi Party) party members are growing in rank. The younger more restless members erupt into fights with Jews. What would you have me do? What if I make a mistake that I can't undo?"

Ironically, I suggest, "Let me go?"

"You have bigger obstacles than you think. On the wire, we heard that ex-pat Marjem Rechtschaffen was admitted to a hospital in Belgium."

"What?" I choke, stunned.

Small bright lights fill my vision, and my body goes numb. Before I fall, he helps me into a chair.

"I can tell by your reaction who she is."

His expression changes, and compassion fills his eyes.

He explains the situation has to be delicately managed.

After Kristallnacht, the Dutch government feared what Hitler might do if he came after them. They got nervous. They wanted to close their borders to the needy and that's not the Holland I know and love. He gives me the address of the hospital and opens up an investigation on behalf of Manny and Rudy.

"We all disappeared," I murmured to myself.

He uncuffs me and motions for me to follow him, past cells stuffed with men awaiting their faith. We walk into another room and on the table is cake.

He walks over to the coffee and pours two cups. He hands me one.

"Thank you," I say.

He empties his wallet on the table.

"Find your wife and sons. Live a wonderful life and spit on Hitler's grave."

The Chief walks out the door. I drink two more cups of coffee and most of the cake. The rest, I put in my pocket. Together, Marjem and I will reunite our family.

Chapter 149
April 1939 The Hague, Holland
Manfred Rechtschaffen

The women at the refugee board are slim. A brunette with pink lips walks past us. She flashes me a grin.

"How handsome are you, young man?"

In a flurry of perfume and talcum powder, my nose itches. She touches my cheek. Everything else around me is vivid and cold, but not her hands. They are smooth and warm. I stand up. Rudy parrots me.

"Sweet lambs, you're safe with us. We'll find your Mama and Papa."

Rudy mouths, "Ima?"

I shake my head, "She's not here yet."

His hopeful eyes fade like a birthday candle blown out too soon.

She offers Rudy a bottle of milk. I can smell the cream. The gracious lady hands me a glass. She tells us to bathe and put on clean clothes.

The nurse reassures me.

"Take your time. Use the bin by the door. Knock on the door when you're ready."

We haven't taken a bath by ourselves ever. I try to remember what my mother does. Rudy is a forgiving audience. I check the water to make sure it won't burn Rudy. I take off my clothes and he tears off his.

We race for the bath. He climbs in first. When the water rises over his shoulders, he looks small. Lathering up in soapy bubbles reminds me of home. Rudy farts.

We giggle. Rudy freezes. Afraid we've caused too much commotion; we stare at the door.

Our silliness makes us laugh harder.

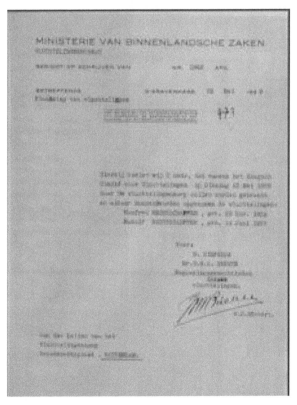

Document of the arrival in Holland

Chapter 150
May 1939 The Hague, Holland
Amalia Eisner

Maurice finally described the raging antisemitism in Germany which forced Marjem and the boys to escape with merely the clothes on their backs.

Their hardship provided a roadmap of what's to come for Poland. Once they murder, deport, and enslave the men and boys, they neutralize that dog from having unnecessary children, Poles, the rest will support the growing German army.

Even though Germans like the Netherlands, we must remain vigilant.

Mozes kept us one step ahead. We absorbed the hardship and provided a wonderful childhood for our children. Marjem faced a certain death, without running, but not the others.

I grab Gittel on the arm.

"What did you find out?"

Maurice interrupts, "Beneden-Heijplaat has the boys. The director transported them from another refugee facility, but Beneden-Heijplaat isn't equipped for children."

Gittel sings, "the boys have been found."

Henie says, "they outsmarted the Nazis."

"Where are they now, Maurice?" I ask.

"In Rotterdam," replies Henie.

Maurice adds, "Mother, there are a lot of lost children. At least they're protected in Holland."

Henie croons, "Marjem's children are alive."

"Baruch Hashem. God is good," I say.

"Amen," prays Maurice.

"Gittel, you have the biggest home. We'll use your address for an official inquiry," instructs Henie.

Maurice declares, "Those brave boys will live long and wonderful lives."

I rise, determined.

"Maurice let's go. I want my babies. Not one more minute will pass without those boys knowing they're loved."

Amalia, 1940

Chapter 151
May 1939 Belgium
Aron Rechtschaffen

Entering the emergency room, I'm engulfed in chaos. My eyes don't know where to land. I know I don't want to be here but the emergency room is the easiest way into the hospital undetected. The sky is blue, the weather is clear without a chance of rain. I'm filled with vigour and hope.

"Pedestrians versus a motorcycle, I need someone here." calls a doctor carrying a young boy in his arms. Right outside the hospital."

Violently torn from my reverie I'm accosted by puddles of blood on the floor and a sickening metallic smell.

Unfazed by the stains coating the boy's shirt, hands, and arms. The doctor works with precision. He nimbly removes the boy's clothes and leaves them in a forgotten heap on the floor. I move through the chaos. A nurse sprays iodine on the boy's chest. I see a forgotten shoe on the floor. The laces were still tied.

A woman runs through the emergency room doors shouting, "He ran him over!" As two assistants and another doctor approach, I make eye contact with one nurse. Stupid move, Aron. You're a landless man without papers. Be discreet.

"He isn't breathing," states another nurse flatly.

"I didn't see him," pleads a man.

"I backed up and his bike lurched forward." His head was in his hands. "I didn't mean to harm him."

A police officer arrives and plants his hands upon the frantic man. Another police officer comes in, and the incident escalates. I cannot get mixed up with the police. Doctors bark numbers while nurses run around carrying tubing and small glass medical vials. An empty gurney sits by the wall.

I walk through a set of swinging doors and I can no longer hear the desperate cries of the mother of the broken boy. Saying her name out loud, knowing in my bones she is close, makes my heart race. I move past another nurse. I turn the gurney down one corridor and into another.

"We need a gurney over here," shouts a nurse. "Hey, you–"

I stop.

"Of course, how can I help?"

A fellow has passed out. Looking down, I take my arms and clasp them around the man's chest under his arms.

The nurse counts, "one, two, three..." and we lift him onto the gurney.

Another man steps forward and puts his stethoscope in his ears.

While they are busy with the man, I take a stairwell that brings me to the second floor. A man exits a closet with rags and a small dolly. I open the closet and take a smock, gloves, a bucket on wheels, and a mop.

A perfect disguise. I locate Psychiatry. She is on the north side of the building.

Chapter 152
May 1939 Belgium
Marjem Rechtschaffen

"Good afternoon, Marjem. You look refreshed," says a woman in a yellow sweater. I hear voices that I don't recognize. The words aren't clear. If I stay completely still will they know that I can hear them? They ask me what my name is. But a moment ago they called me by my name. I'm confused.

"I have a headache." I don't recognize my voice. One woman with soft hands and skinny long fingers takes my blood pressure.

"Marjem, let us move you to the outdoor atrium. You need fresh air. Sun on your face will heal you. The sedatives we gave you are extraordinarily strong. When you came here, you were hysterical."

"Heavy," I say. I can barely open my eyes.

"Let's get you out of bed."

I wear a blue night robe draped over my shoulders. My feet are in slippers and strange knee socks. People line the hallways in gurneys and chairs. She wheels me towards the sunshine. My eyes sting from the glare of the sun.

The woman in the yellow sweater leaves me by a window. The green grass reminds me of Manfred running along the hills of Monbijou Park. A fat fluffy squirrel leaps from limb to limb on a gigantic oak tree. Aron loves squirrels. I turn to tell him, but he is not here. I grab the armrest of the wheelchair. Is this how I'm going to end up? I escaped Berlin to lose my family?

I dared to dream crazy, like my parents before us. My blood matters. I need my blood all around me.

My heart races against my chest, but my panic remains in check. Remarkable. The friction of my palms against my thighs awakens me. I pinch my thighs. Harder. Pricks of pain shoot up my fingers; pain I understand. My life is not finished. I have more to give. Blood rushes to my cheeks. I am not cold, and my mind starts to clear.

A man comes up behind me. He pushes me across the room. I see a deck of cards on the table. Two people play gin rummy. Aron loves card games. When I was in labor with the boys we played for hours. The cards distracted me from the contractions.

Two new nurses administer medication. A doctor records notes in his charts. An elderly woman in the corner falls asleep. A young volunteer announces dinner is available in an hour. My stomach rumbles. I cannot remember the last time I ate. Someone takes control of my wheelchair and guides me down the hall.

"Are we headed for the cafeteria?" I ask.

A man clears his throat.

"I haven't eaten in a long time," I say.

"I have an appetite. It must be a sign that I am feeling better."

"I sure hope so," says the man in a grave tone.

My heart stops. That voice. I practically scream.

Twisting backwards I nearly fall out of the chair.

"How? How? When?" I stammer.

He places his palm on my neck. He came for me.

He gives me back my hope.

"Can you stand?"

Aron places a jacket around my shoulders and hands me a pair of men's rubber galoshes.

"Put the galoshes on over those socks. Hand me the slippers. You must walk!" he insists.

"I will."

"My love, walk strong," Aron begs.

The emergency room is chaotic.

"I'll wheel you as far as I can and then you have to stand."

He explains this again to me as if I don't understand. I do. I know what to do. We pass screaming patients in blood-soaked clothing.

"We're almost there, Marjem."

Aron's voice sounds reassured and impassioned. Counting in my head to calm my breathing, I know everything is about to change.

"Good starts happening right now," I say.

Harnessing my energy, the next moment will be a jump-off. I rub my numb thighs willing them to hold me up.

"Stand now," he commands.

"I have you. Lean into me. I will hold you forever. I promise I'll never let go again."

Tears raced down my cheeks running away from the pain that released them.

"I believed it was over for me."

We walk away deliberately, this time hand-in-hand towards freedom. Aron opens a car door. My adrenaline fades. He runs around the other side and slides into the driver's seat.

"I found you," he says.

He pulls me across the seat and into his arms. Our bodies touch. I'm electrified. He devours my mouth.

Chapter 153
September 1939 Holland
Manfred Rechtschaffen

Life in Holland is remarkable. We dine, laugh, and experience everything as a family. We live with my Aunt Gittel and Uncle Daniel. Rudy and I share a bed in our cousin Olivia's room. Uncle Daniel supports us while Papa secures employment. Tomorrow, he starts in a tailor shop. Mama devotes her days watching Rudy and Olivia. At night, she completes small sewing projects for extra revenue. We live around homes that are beautifully decorated on the outside with small shrubs and flower boxes in every window. Tall windows nearly five feet high show off meticulous craftsmanship and luxurious couches and crystal chandeliers.

Houses have small front gardens and ample backyards. Young boys deliver newspapers to everyone's homes in the morning from their bicycles. The shops are open, and people go about their lives. Cafés, theatres, and movie houses are open to everyone, and curfews don't exist. I attend school with Henie's sons Jonathan and Marcus. I have never had a formal education before. Teachers let me absorb and ask nothing in return. They pity me, the super skinny little boy with a strained face. The Dutch children take school for granted. Boys act out, and the girls chatter.

Students laugh amid a lecture.

They misuse their chance to learn, and their disrespect angers me. Anger brings nightmares to plague me. Rudy makes all the rest of it slip away. He un-haunts me.

In Holland, our household has multiplied. We're our own wolfpack. We each add value. Aunt Gittel welcomed us into her home. Uncle Daniel connected my parents to work. Aunt Henie is teaching me Dutch by reading magazines.

Aunt Cyla is married to Uncle Art who is an auctioneer with a deep, booming voice that makes me feel safe.

Cousins, large and small, loud, and quiet, run around the living room and knock themselves into couches with thuds and groans.

Aunt Gittel says, "Boys, don't break the furniture. Take a snack and don't ruin your appetite."

She turns on the light next to the couch and places a dish of peanuts and raisins on the table.

"Yes, Mama," says Marcus.

He doesn't call her Ima. Using "Ima" feels babyish; something I would have said a lifetime ago.

Grabbing two crackers and placing one in my pocket for Rudy, I remember he forgets to eat when he plays.

"It's marvellous to watch you eat," says Aunt Henie, snorting.

"I was always ravenous, but I kept Rudy clean, warm, and well-fed," I insist.

Aunt Henie looks at Mama with pity. Aunt Gittel places her palms on Mama's shoulders. The conversation halts. Uncle Art walks over and communicates silently with Aunt Cyla. They don't include anyone else in their exchange.

"You're remarkable," breathes Mama.

Her face is proud and sad at the same time.

"Mama told me you escaped from Berlin by yourself," says Jonathan, bouncing up and down next to me.

"Shut up," shouts Marcus.

"Mama told us not to talk about that!"

He rushes towards his brother.

"We had help," I admit.

Their sharp tones agitate me. Their quarrel is pointless. Too many eyes, too many people are concentrating on me.

"Were you shot at?" asks Marcus.

"Marcus, we don't ask those kinds of questions. Leave it in the past," demands Aunt Henie.

"We don't discuss this in front of your Aunt Marjem and Uncle Aron."

"Sorry, Mama," says Marcus.

Satisfied she has made her point; she walks into the kitchen.

Jonathan leans in and whispers, "Were you terrified?"

I nod, speechless.

"Did you sleep outside?" asks Marcus.

"Yes, we slept in a shed for two nights."

"Were you scared?" asks Marcus.

"Yes. When a Nazi soldier in one town asked me for directions to the train terminal, I practically peed in my pants."

"Just listening to what you're saying makes me nauseous," says Marcus with a shiver.

They wrestle with each other while I lose myself in memories. Around every corner, someone kept guiding us towards freedom. Our journey made me believe in the certainty of God. God exists.

He watched over Rudy and me. Religion will not define my life. My loyalty to God will.

Gittel's daughter, Olivia, charges into the living room, pulling Rudy along with her. He is squealing with joy. We laugh at their silliness. Olivia sings and Rudy mimics her.

Their joy reverberates through the walls.

Uncle Daniel walks in with my Bubbe Amalia.

Bubbe says, "Are my girls in the kitchen?"

"They're baking a chocolate cake to celebrate life," I say.

"Is Aron back?" Uncle Daniel asks.

Aunt Gittel walks in and answers Daniel, "He finished work late. He's in the shower."

"I'll make tea," says Bubbe Amalia.

She heads back into the kitchen and Uncle Daniel follows her. Papa arrives in fresh clothes, sits down, turns to me, and says, "Today was a good day."

"Every day is a great day," I say.

"Agreed," says Papa.

The family starts to assemble around the table. There is not enough room. No one is bothered. My Aunt Gittel brings out Mama's silver candelabra to light the holiday lights.

"Marjem, your silver candelabra guided your family back to us," says Aunt Gittel.

"Mama put a small piece of herself in the candelabra," I share.

"She had to make it here to put it back together."

My parents are quiet. Everyone is. I made it awkward. Henie carries a platter of bagels, chopped liver, herring, celery, and carrots. I take a bagel and put half away in my pocket for Rudy. Uncle David carries in two cake boxes.

We have a joyful holiday celebration. I'm surrounded by everyone I love.

Bubbe says, "Aron, do the honors and consecrate our wine and challah? Tonight, is our Rosh Hashanah."

Papa declares, "Tonight, we celebrate for everyone who is unable, for the lost souls taken from us too soon, for the children without parents and the parents who have buried their children. Tonight, we praise Hashem."

When Mama walked away from the Gestapo, Rudy stopped talking. I thought she took his words away with her, to keep her company and God made us chase her to get the words back. The moment he saw Mama, he spoke.

Chapter 154
September 1939 London, UK
Walker Rechtschaffen

As a pilot, my view from the clouds kept me innocent of the horror I created. The military transformed me. Through death and gloom, I found purpose. Hitler is the devil. He destroys everything. The murderous rage he instills might consume me. There is no changing my mind. I addressed my old lieutenant colonel. He snickered. He did not understand. I went to the paint store and bought the exact color required. Late into the night, I crafted my plan. When Rosie awoke the next morning, I kissed her lips and wished her a wonderful day.

"Rosie, I'm going to enlist."

"Walker, you're mad to enlist in the military at your age. This is not your war."

"It's my war. It's everyone's war."

Rosie says, "War is for the inexperienced and hungry. I won't let you die. They won't let you fly."

"Let the enrollment office tell me."

My uniform from the war still fits me. I walk to the front door. Rosie follows me and screams.

"You can't wear that; you cannot leave this house!"

I knew what I was doing.

"What are you trying to prove?" I'm not sure.

My religion is personal. But when the devil tries to crush the Jews, I must stand up. Being a Jew cannot be private any longer. The evils in the world are everyone's problems.

The horror stories on the radio are real. Rosie pleads with me, "Walker, I understand your feelings. But your methods?"

Enlisting filled me with pride. The British military is a tremendous institution. They teach youth how to serve their country. The equipment is top-notch. My best friends are veterans. By the time I approach the front of the enlistment line, I'm aware of the snickering and general displeasure.

I recognize the enlistment officer as a Lieutenant Flight Commander.

He takes one look at me and erupts in raucous laughter.

"We need you. An inspiration to these young boys. Come with me."

In my commander's office, I removed my jacket. These men have never seen a tallis before. I wear one over my commissioned dress uniform. On the front and back, I painted a crude canary yellow star of David. In the middle of each star, I wrote, Jude. The edges of the letters bleed into each other. The effect is horrific.

The lieutenants superior enters the office.

"Where's the crazy Jew everybody's talking about?"

I stand up and salute my superior. He looks over my file. "Sargent Rechtschaffen, you're not the optimal age for enlistment. Your military career was excellent. What can you add?"

"Experience, sir."

"How can we use you? You put me in, and I'll kill every Jew hating Nazi I find."

Another officer enters and salutes his superior.

I swear, "In the name of the Queen and the name of Jews, sir."

Chapter 155
September 1939 The Hague, Holland
Manfred Rechtschaffen

Loud sirens blare from the radio. German forces invaded Poland and dropped incendiary bombs from the sky. The unprovoked attack occurred without a formal declaration of war. In response, Prime Minister Neville Chamberlain of Britain declared war with Germany. Aunt Henie and Bubbe cry.

"I had hope. I never stopped believing. Here we stand unharmed," Papa acknowledges. Tears streamed down his cheeks. He looks relieved.

"Hope can mask reality," says Uncle Daniel.

"Aspiration can make you weak." Uncle Daniel rings his hands. His eyes dart back and forth with uncertainty.

A violent wind rustles the leaf-laden branches on the trees. The sky turns gloomy, and a crack of thunder follows. Branches sway until they practically snap.

The leaves cannot contain the moisture coming from the sky. The drops grow larger, and the wind keeps howling until the rain is blowing sideways. We rush to close the windows before the water soaks the floor.

Aunt Gittel says, "The Polish will resist the Germans. Every merchant, peasant, and farmer will grab their rifles to stand up for their land."

What she doesnt know is once the Germans come for you there is nowhere to hide. My dad tore a hole in the wall and bloodied himself to save our lives. Others hide in between walls, in cupboards, attics, floorboards, and storage spaces. Mother told father the search for Jews hiding in Berlin intensifies. Citizens are turning each other in.

"The Germans want Warsaw. After they seize the capital, the rest of Poland will fall," says Daniel.

Papa mourns, "I could've taken my parents and left them in Denmark."

Aunt Henie says, "No. Never look back."

"Marjem." Papa's voice is defeated as he sits down in the armchair and runs his fingers through his hair.

He hangs his head in defeat. Mama walks over and kisses him on top of the head. The gesture is childish. Papa exhales, and he leans back into the couch.

After dinner, the adults put their children into pajamas. Olivia and Rudy go to bed after dinner, but Jonathan and Marcus fall asleep first. I remain quiet and try to blend into the background. Uncle David takes Bubbe Amalia home. Aunt Henie and Uncle Daniel put on their coats and say goodbye when the phone rings. The ring sounds alarming. Aunt Henie freezes.

"Any call this late at night cannot be good," says Aunt Gittel. Uncle Daniel answers. "Hello. Who is this?"

He covers the mouthpiece and murmurs, "It's Francois."

Mama exhales. Aunt Henie carries Jonathan and Marcus upstairs. When Aunt Henie comes down the stairs without the boys, I know they are going to stay the night. Uncle Maurice takes the phone, "What happened? What does that mean?"

I want to sit with Mama, but I cannot draw attention to myself.

"Is everything gone?"

Papa covers his eyes with one hand. Mama moves behind him and places her hands on his shoulders. We wait.

I have done that before. I can keep quiet for hours, even days if I must. Mama takes the phone.

"Francois, my love. It's Marjem." Papa is stoic.

"Yes, Mother is here." She listens.

"How far? … it's too soon … makes sense."

The conversation wraps up and we all wait.

"The news is grim; the great rabbis were shot by firing squad. All synagogues, large and small, were burned to the ground," says Maurice.

Gittel says, "I'm sure they must've thought it was the Russians. I doubt they ever suspected it was Germans."

Papa says, "My childhood on the farm began each day with the dulcet tones of Abba davening. His devotion brought him comfort. He knew his place within Hashem's universe. His belief that Hashem would protect him made me want to believe. I felt closer to Hashem in Poland."

"As did I," says Mama.

"I was closest to God when I prayed beside Papa under his tallis. When I could sit beside him and pray, there was nowhere else I wanted to be. That's why I have had a hard time going to a synagogue since he died. I entangled my devotion to my papa with my love of religion. How can I pray without him?"

Mama's feelings are raw and written all over her face.

"Armies of barbarians thirsting to kill Jews. Did the sirens warn the people in time? What about the children who played behind the temple on Żydowska Street?"

I could not recognize the sounds emanating from Papa.

It was grief and rage and pain all mixed into sound.

"You played there as a child?" David asks.

"The synagogue is the moral and actual center of the town."

Bile rises in my mouth. I want to go to bed.

I do not want to hear anymore.

Maurice pours an amber liquid into a large shot glass. "Drink this…" Papa drinks.

Maurice refills his glass and says, "Drink again."

Papa listens as a child listens to their parents. Bubbe Amalia walks into the kitchen and returns a few minutes later with a tray of tea.

"Abba installed a bell in the Administration building. As a defense measure," weeps Papa.

"Aron…" Bubbe Amalia tries to give him a cup of tea, but he ignores it as Maurice continues.

"Przemyśl fell tonight to the Germans. They fought valiantly. Many Jews perished. The Germans were better equipped than the Poles or Jews. They dropped bombs. François said the San River is the divide between German and Russian occupation."

"My Przemyśl grew wheat on earth the color of oil. Fruits and spices like thyme, rosemary, and mint added fragrance to the air. The San River created hills and lowlands abundant with purple, yellow, and pink wildflowers. Waterways meant endless fishing."

Bubbe Amalia says, "Then that is how your Pennsylvania will remain. Tell your children about Beautiful outdoor markets with bushels of apples and peaches bigger than your fists. Let them love Poland the way you do. They will only know the Poland that you create for them. Choose your words carefully. The vivid imagery you craft will be their narratives. Talk about those you love. Don't hold love inside."

Chapter 156
December 1939 The Hague, Holland
Aron Rechtschaffen

Dear Walker,

Address all correspondence to my sister-in-law Gittel's in Holland. The boys enjoy their cousins. I do not need friends because the family around us seems to multiply all the time. Marjem's sisters live beautifully in Holland. Maurice and François are in France. Marjem's brothers Gideon and David are close by in Belgium. Our family is safe from Hitler. You are safe, and I am safe, but for everybody else in Poland, I cannot say the same. Britain opened a path for you towards life, family, and purpose. Living in Holland is restoring us. Marjem's steadier. She is closer to who she was before the Nazi occupation. Berlin, in my remembrances, holds wonder and passion. Hitler cannot take that from me. I won. My Marjem will regenerate. Manfred will forget. Rudy won't remember Przemyśl, Perehinski, Rozniatow, Dobromyl, Berlin, Holland: all these places live within me. We honor them through our survival.

Love, Aron

Chapter 157
January 1940 Perehinske, Galicia
Naftali Herzl

Dear Aron,

Four months ago, the battle of Przemyśl lasted for three bloody days. As you know, our ring of fortresses stretches across forty-five kilometers of enchanted countryside, a bulwark against Russia.

The Germans wanted the defensive position.

Every able-bodied Jew fought off the invasion. Bluma, Shalom, Shimson, Zacharia and Binyamin defended their homes and families. Those that couldn't fight, ran from their burning homes.

Those not beaten or deported hid in their cellars. Other souls walked for days in their stocking feet before they returned. Thugs broke your grandfather's arm, cracked his ribs, and bruised his face.

He succumbed to his injuries four months later and once he perished, Shalom needed me. I saw him as a young boy in desperate need. Together, we chose a plain pine box. While your uncles Zacharia and Binyamin guarded your grandfather's soul, as the Torah prescribes, your uncle Shimson placed white sheets over his body on the floor and prayed over him. Aunt Bluma and your Grandmother Etel covered every mirror, and we all tore our clothes.

Your mother wept with her brothers and sisters. His death left a gaping hole in my world.

Staring at a pine box, knowing the person you love is inside, is the most incongruous feeling you'll ever experience. The love you carry in your heart is alive but the person who the love belongs to is gone. What remains, their body, is merely the vessel that houses the spirit that you miss.

Bubbe Etel wouldn't sleep in the house after that. She moved in with Aunt Bluma. Her brother Shalom held the shiva in the Rechtschaffen Synagogue.

Rabbis from as far as Lviv attended. I laid my hand on his wooden casket; hard and raw; nothing like the man inside. The air smelled like apples by his graveside. Fluffy white clouds filled the gray sky. As the Jewish tradition dictates, each family member takes a handful of dirt and lays it upon his casket. My hands with cold black earth. I bring it to my face, blow a kiss and then toss the earth onto his grave. I thank him.

Dirt from the graveside is still underneath my fingernails. I cannot bear to wash away this last connection to him.

Nothing feels real. His death shook my belief system.

You made him proud. You outsmarted the Nazis.

He said another generation will live on and keep the Rechtschaffen name alive. Your mother has a lingering cough and cannot catch her breath. She doesn't have a fever, but her body aches.

We frequently take short walks, then she soaks her feet in Epsom salts and lavender oil.

The doctor offered her a tonic and a prescription for rest. She taught me how to make her famous Tree Tea.

Bubbe Etel said my version is a sin. Your mother found this funny.

Please write back as soon as you can. Your letters mean everything to us. Stay safe.

Baruch Habah,
Abba

Chapter 158
January 1940 The Hague, Holland
Marjem Rechtschaffen

Early in the morning when the fog rolls in there's a sense of peace in the world. The heavenly clouds blanket the earth while she slumbers. I hear lesser birds chirping in the thick greeting of the day. He speaks to his mate and his offspring join in the early morning banter.

The bird calls last for hours until a distinct siren call from the male alerts his mate to food. He has a crimson crown and a brown forehead with a thin black stripe of feathers. His underbelly is fluffy white with slate-gray legs and his mate has the same shade of white on her crown. Small like sparrows, these birds spend most of their time at the top of tall trees. The male darts before my eyes.

Their feeding ritual begins when the father gathers the seed and delivers it to the mouth of his mate. After she's eaten, he flies away. She gathers her babies, and all three eat the remaining food. Every day the ritual is the same. The sameness of the morning heals me.

My nature is to plan; the more difficult the situation the calmer I become. When my anxiety is insurmountable, I compartmentalize away the shame of my mental weakness. Once the immediate danger in Berlin abated, I disintegrated.

Aron glued me back together. Spending time with my sisters and family allows them to reinforce me, the way gold foil paint can strengthen and bind cracks in a porcelain vase or teacup.

My sister Gittel is our angel. She moved us into her nest without a second thought.

The building is narrow, and the rooms are small. We're packed in like sardines immersed in love, laughter, and joy. I can't imagine myself anywhere else.

We're waiting to move forward and unwilling to go back. The four of us occupy Gittel's daughter's bedroom.

Pink walls with butterflies and rainbows surround me. The streets of The Hauge are serene and joyous. Manfred sees wagons full of young toddlers in groups of six to eight on their way to parks and nursery schools. Every morning, Gittel navigates our little wolf pack and brings them to school. When Gittel returns from dropping the children off at school, Henie, Cyla, and Mom are with her. Mom heads straight for the kitchen with a basket of eggs. Cyla follows her to brew us all coffee. Henie tides up the house to help with the mess created by four extra bodies.

Gittel says, "Marjem, each day the sun rises. You can count on that. You will learn how to live again."

I can't remember my dreams, but nightly I wake up dripping in sweat. In my nightmares, I'm screaming.

In the morning, my hands are sore because I sleep with them in fists. The only one rushing me to get better is myself. Being the best version of myself showed me how very capable I am in the most adverse conditions. Henie says, it will take time to unwind. I'm impatient.

We sit together around a table not big enough for all of us. I explain to Gittel, "lying to Manfred was the worst thing I've ever done. He'll never forgive me, and he won't forget. Breaking his trust is irreparable."

"Children don't understand the complexity of the decisions we have to make in order to exist because they shouldn't have to," says Cyla.

Mom demands, "You lied to save your children's lives. Stop feeling guilty. It's nonsense."

Being separated from Manfred and Rudy changed my dependency on them.

I'm sick when they're out of sight. The only time I can stand it is when I'm asleep.

I sleep whenever I possibly can. I've been frightened into paralysis.

The terror of the unknown: of what could be - what if - what is; it can't end you.

Gittel says, "The Hague is a beautiful place. You'll join the hard-working small-business owners and keep your children with ours. Between yours, mine, Henie's, and Cyla's; it's like us all over again."

"Holland, like Berlin, has culture, museums, nightclubs, and expansive parks. Your children can be doctors, teachers, even diamond cutters," boasts my mom.

Her tone brings me back nearly twenty years.

We left Dobromyl for Berlin. Mom credited dad for the vision and bravery. Here she stands, without him for nearly a decade, preserving despite her fears.

She spearheaded our lives beyond Dobromyl into Berlin as much as my father. Henie crushes me in an adoring hug.

"Welcome back to civilization," says Gittel.

"Berlin served its purpose. Coming back to your people makes the most sense. You can't be stripped of your citizenship here."

Henie says, "The Dutch don't consider being a Jew a crime."

Chapter 159
March 1940 London, UK
Walker Rechtschaffen

Dear Aron,

A wedding carriage passed before me at dawn. A youthful couple ran up a flight of stairs into the courthouse to pick up their marriage certificate.

Her white rose bouquet hung from her hands as she gazed at her intended. She wore a white satin wedding gown with translucent sleeves.

Her father followed the couple, clad in a sophisticated black suit and black top hat. Her mother was wrapped in a fitted black dress. Her fox stole and splendid high heels reminded me of Ima. Their rejoicing was contagious.

My children play on the living room carpet while listening to the radio. Rosie sits beside Pearla.

The radio broadcasts our commander Winston Churchill. He proclaims that Adolf Hitler will attack Holland and Belgium. Churchill maintains that despite his declaration of neutrality, Adolf Hitler wants the world. Making it to Holland was a phenomenal accomplishment, but Hitler will consume the entire European continent. Emigrate to America. They refused your petition for migration to Britain, but there's a loophole to America.

With an eventual destination outside of Britain, the UK can be your layover.

Let us possess the audacity to trust you will get into America. Haven't we suffered enough misery?

Let us threaten to spell out our bliss. Holland is free and neutral. Appreciate the cabarets, galleries, and music. Drink spirits. Watch your sons grow up.

Take a breather, understand what you overcame, and state your next step. In the interim, take your boys to the temple on Shabbos. Bounce Rudy on your knee and attend to Manfred. Sing "Adon Olam," at the Bimah.

Hold on to prosperity. You're overdue.

My family sends our love to you.

Love, Walker

Chapter 160
May 1940 Paris, France
Maurice Eisner

I washed wine glasses at the Cafe de Flore. Just outside the Saint-Germain-des-Prés Metro station, the cafe-life immersed me in local society. Sebastian, an occasional dishwasher, taught me quick French lingo. Around the corner is the Church of Saint-Germain-des-Prés, a small choir rehearses daily for the Sunday service. The church reminds me of home.

It is incongruous. Stained glass is too extravagant for Dobromyl. The sanctuary is splendid. It is a sense of quiet I cannot discover anywhere else in Paris. Jesus, their salvation, is portrayed as cared for or abused on every wall of the church. Like the predicament of Jews.

We are tortured because we are directed to worship a God that others claim is wrong.

I met Heather Martine at the church. She navigates through the capital using footbridges. She taught me to detect patterns even in the cadence of traffic. To notice an inflection in someone's speech, or the tempo of a gesture. We devise elaborate fantasies about strangers. On the Pont de la

Concorde, Heather kisses me. After running across the Pont de Arts during torrential rainfall, I avow my affection. She laughs until she cries.

"Mon chere, I won't marry again," she explains, and we never speak of it again.

For years, my body betrayed me, and she changed me. It tied me to her forever. I treasure her but she was not mine to claim. She recognized the fellow I would become before I knew. Tonight, we share a carafe of wine at a street cafe.

"Heather, do you keep a list of every soul you've smuggled?"

"The day I stop saving people, I'll stop recording. There are youngsters, parents, and siblings to reunite."

"Aren't you worried they will confiscate the list?"

"Maurice, mon chere, fear doesn't stop me from anything."

I kiss her hand and take a long slow sip of wine.

"I must take a trip to the Somme valley next week, Maurice. The Germans attacked. My sister needs me."

"I will join you?"

"Sweet, homme, no. You are needed here. Margeaux will have a package ready in two days."

"I'll have François handle it," I answer haltingly.

"No, Margeaux is practically ready to fly solo. I want you there one more time to make sure she's set," explains Heather.

She puts her hand on my thigh. I can feel the long, graceful fingers.

"Did you meet the new paper man? He comes with great references from Orin," I ask.

"Yes, he'll do. Widower. He is eager. I need a few more young girls like Margeaux and a few older ones that will not interest the German soldiers. We moved more children this month than we ever have before."

"It's true."

"When it gets hard, I list the names of the people I helped. I can name everyone."

François enters the cafe. He tips his hat to Heather, who smiles.

"François, mon amour, ça va bien?"

"Oui, merci. Heather," answers François.

Our conversation moves to wine, Heather's favorite topic. As with every conversation, it then shifts to war and politics.

I explain, "The war escalated faster than any of us guessed. When Germany conquered Poland, the British called up two million men."

"The British are honest folk. They're smart and stoic," says François.

"I love the Brits," she says.

"They're tough when they need to be, tougher when it's not needed."

"How do you mean?" asks François.

"Mon petit enfant, they jump into war to defend the underdogs. They ration food and fight for morality."

"Heather, our sister Marjem has a brother-in-law named Walker who lives there," explains François.

"Brits stand taller in the face of adversity. They instituted food rationing to avoid severe shortages of sugar, butter, and bacon. They use a ration booklet."

Paul says with horror, "They ration bacon?"

I look at François and laugh.

Heather snorts. "Women love bacon too!"

"If the British believe they can overthrow Hitler, why should they regulate their resources?" asks Paul.

"They aren't stupid," says Orin, the weekend night chef. He joins our circle and drags another table over to make more seats available.

"The British prepare thoughtfully."

François says, "I have never been more terrified of a man."

I declare, "Fear is the body's way of sending you in another direction."

"Fear tells me I'm alive," counters Heather.

I regard her and refill her wine.

"Marjem is changed. The darkness almost swallowed her whole. She stared evil in the face and lived through years of depravity. She is more courageous than any of us."

"I agree," says Heather.

"I suspect Marjem won't be safe for long."

Our family had a reprieve and we're luckier than most. The reunion in Holland healed wounds opened since my father died. Paul explains how Britains' been supervising the North Sea. In reprisal, Germany classified Britain's ships as battleships. It's causing complications for the transport of youngsters out of Germany. English passenger ships laden with Jewish refugees and orphans aren't protected on the seas. Francois understands that Denmark is a critical gateway to Norway. Norway is an excellent staging ground for Hitler's continued war effort with its superior Air Force. The Danes were pretentious. To uphold the soundness of Copenhagen, the onslaught was a fait accompli.

Heather maintains, "Dutch border troops' operations have multiplied. It's become impenetrable."

Our friend Wolf says the same. The Germans can infiltrate Scandinavia whenever they require. Volunteering my life to shield the faceless is easy, but I am daunted by the obligation. Delivering my family to safety will ruin me. I cannot fail. My next maneuver is to re-enter Holland.

Informer are everywhere. Partisans are working overtime. Alliances tested by undercover Nazis are harsh on loyal volunteers. Decent people collapse under the pressure. The network emphasizes the attack on Holland is forthcoming. The Nazis equate appeasement with frailty.

We need the Dutch to join the fight.

François and Maurice 1947

Chapter 161
May 1940 The Hague, Holland
Manfred Rechtschaffen

Living at Aunt Gittel's is incredible.

Endless laughter fills our evenings when my aunts cook together in the kitchen. Our Shabbat dinners were like this before the Nazis took our lives away. We eat rich food and honey cake for dessert.

Bubbe Amalia says, "Listening to my girls in the kitchen takes me back a lifetime. Remembering my younger, stronger self-invigorates me."

I tell her, "I was reminded of Mama making Shabbat with honey cake and a silver candelabra."

"Honey cake is the finest dessert. That's a terrific memory. Keep it. You can replace an unpleasant memory with the recollection of us spending Shabbat together, experiencing Holland and breathing free. Home is anywhere your family is. Home is love and safety and support. I am your home. Holland is your home."

She hugs me and smells like talcum powder and roses.

"Bubbe, is that how it works?"

"Yes. Listen to me. One day you will explain this to Rudy. Your mind can hold a distinct number of recollections. Each new memory is filed into your memory box inside your mind. Dreadful memories take up more space."

"I had no idea."

"Your mind only has a small section free for images. If you have more pleasant memories, they force out the rotten ones."

"Bubbe, I enjoy having a big family. Wherever I turn, there are people taking care of me."

"Manny, your journey matured you. Wouldn't you agree?"

"I'm not anxious about the dark anymore."

"How wonderful!" says Bubbe.

Father walks into the room.

"Rudy and I walked down a country road. We found a barn with a broken roof in the loft and made a sanctuary." Papa paces.

"I told you hay is soft," whispers Papa.

"Every man should have that knowledge."

Bubbe says, "How was the night sky?"

Papa continues to pace and run his hands through his hair. If he keeps doing that his hair will fall out and then he will look more like Otis from the train.

"The night sky has more stars than I could count. We saw them through the hole in the roof on the second night. Rudy and I shared our warmth."

"Abba, I imagined we were on your childhood farm lying beside you."

"The night sky is magnificent," said Papa.

His voice sounds weak like someone is squeezing his throat, but his eyes shine bright with pride.

"Rudy never went without food. I'm proud of that."

"You should be proud. You hold that inside your heart forever. He is alive today because of you," says Bubbe.

"Rudy didn't talk the entire time." I mutter.

Papa and Bubbe take notice of me.

"After Papa fled through a window and hid at the train station, the next morning, Mama left through the front door and Rudy stopped talking. She stole his words. It sounds crazy when I say it out loud."

Bubbe pulls me onto her lap and whispers, "This memory can be forgotten once you fill up your memory chest with wonderful fresh ones."

"You've seen things I cannot imagine. We took away your innocence and I can't give it back to you."

I want to tell him more, but I don't think he can take it. One day when I am older, he will be ready to hear about the tall, thin man on a train. Or the one-armed man with war medals. They helped us.

Papa turns to Bubbe and explains that last month, Mother applied to the Bolivian embassy. She stood in line for four hours. He says admirably how she never stops.

She doesn't give in.

Bubbe says, "My Marjem will confront the devil and dismiss him. She's resilient like bamboo."

Papa tells Bubbe we've applied to the Dominican Republic, Palestine, even Shanghai. But Palestine is no longer accepting Jewish refugees. Since the war effort, Britain can no longer divert funds to support the mass exodus of refugees into Palestine.

He wants to move us to America. He has a cousin, Uncle Karl from Przemyśl who owns a textile store in Manhattan, New York.

"The Dutch can't see what is coming. Is that what you're saying?"

"Yes. The Dutch are collecting names of the Jewish people in the neighborhood. In Berlin, we didn't wake up one morning with the entire world turned upside down. We lived a good life. Meticulously, our civil rights were stripped away. I recall in 1930 a special telephone book in Berlin. The telephone book only listed Jews. Your Mama thought it was a very convenient idea. Her friend, Helena, the key to your departure, understood the evil intentions."

"That was seven years ago," Bubbe says in disbelief.

"In hindsight, I see it. Hitler started collecting information before he was in control. He segregated individuals by race, religion, and political beliefs. He registered and eliminated undesirables in 1933. The stubborn ones perished," says the Papa.

Bubbe is upset. Papa should stop.

"We're leaving on Thursday."

That's in three days. "We're traveling to Liverpool. From there we will sail across the Atlantic on a passenger ship."

Chapter 162
June 1, 1940, Holland Docks
Manfred Rechtschaffen

Mama hugs Bubbe and keeps her close.

"Once we're in New York, Cousin Karl and I will write up the paperwork to send for you and David."

He used to be called Majer Kalman, but Karl sounds like an American.

Mama's voice shakes like a shutter in a hurricane.

Mama stands there motionless.

I am told that when something ends something new and wonderful has the chance to begin.

However, the heartache on my mother's face is not something she's going to get over anytime soon.

Bubbe takes Mama's face in her hands and kisses her right on the mouth.

"You are my heart."

Tears stream down Mama's face. Naming her pain won't make it go away. She can't hide it or run away from it.

She's never looked so sad.

Bubbe caresses are heavy with devotion. She turns to Papa, "I chose well. You escaped. You all survived."

She pats his face.

"I love you," he says to Bubbe.

He takes her face in his hands and kisses her on the lips.

"I love you dearly."

"Don't blame Hashem for the heartache," says Bubbe.

She kisses each eyelid on Mama's face.

"Don't worry about us," she takes Uncle David's arm in hers.

"I am going to look after Mother. Even if I must harness her to my back and walk her to France myself," adds David.

Both Maurice and François endorse his plan. We all laugh. The laughter rings empty, but it appears appropriate to pretend. David kisses the baby. He hugs me.

"I love you, Uncle David. Take care of Bubbe," I say importantly.

Bubbe Amalia kisses Rudy and hugs me. She holds me for some time.

She says, "I didn't like your father when I first met him because he took away my beautiful daughter. But I have grown to love him, and I consider him as precious to me as any of my own children. He is brave and strong and will protect you in your new home."

She makes steady eye contact with Rudy and I.

She holds both our hands and kisses them.

"The two of you can handle whatever life throws at you. Never live in fear. When the uncertainty of life catches you off guard, and it will, pour your love and your life into each other's hands."

Chapter 163
June 1940 The Hague, Holland
Henie Eisner

Dear Marjem,

Nine days after you left, on May 10th, the Germans ravaged the Hague airfield. They attacked from the sky, and Holland didn't stand a chance. Their superior military decimated us. On that very same day my husband brought my babies to work with him at The Hague airfield.

The children were excited to help their father at work. During breakfast, they barely tasted their pancakes when they gobbled them down. Before they left that morning, I kissed them all smack on the lips. Marjem, my partner in life, is gone. Everything I loved and made from my own body was stolen from me. How did you survive in the belly of the beast? Hitler took my life. My husband was adaptable, sympathetic, and patient. My heart has been torn from my body. I can't figure out how to move forward. During the Shiva, Maurice's friend Wolf appeared. Bedraggled, he said, you have to turn on the light and face fear. I told him; all Holland holds for me are ghosts. Together, we crossed the border under the cloak of night. Hand in hand, we walked away from Holland and embraced France. Wolf deposited me in Marseilles.

The water heals and I need to disappear. I'm no good for anybody right now. Wolf explained more about his work in France. He transports wounded souls across borders. Did you know that Maurice publishes a paper in Yiddish? It's his act of rebellion. He communicates with other Jews and entices them to act. Be better and do more for those in need. Complacency isn't justified. I see why all able-bodied Jews must fight. Hashem demands a better world. For now, the beachfront of Marseilles helps. Solitude helps. Wet sand under my feet helps. The ocean goes on forever. This is enough.

Yours forever,

Henie

Chapter 164
August 1940 Liverpool, England
Manfred Rechtschaffen

Papa promises, "Liverpool, England is our last stop before America. Once we arrive in New York, we'll be free."
I trust him - he's never given me a reason not to.
His bright hazel eyes are sincere.
Papa has the same eyes as Rudy; I never made that connection before. People's eyes and mouths reveal a lot. Encountering many strangers in a brief time enabled me to sharpen my skills in detection quickly.

New York 1942

Twitches and tics betray the unskilled liars. Some people worked hard to gain our trust; others didn't bother. Ensuring Rudy's safety has been my singular focus.

"You've grown in extraordinary ways. I never imagined what I would miss."

He's right. In group conversations the adults listen for my point of view.

I'm still my Papa's son, but I don't feel like his child any longer. My love for him hasn't changed, nor my devotion, but I don't rely on him the same way I did in Berlin.

In Holland, Aunt Gittel's home seemed like a palace.

For nine months, we ate whatever we sought, attended school collectively, and fell asleep with sore stomachs from late night laughter. Aunt Gittel is my favorite. Mama is the most comfortable around her, and that draws me to her. She looks past the commotion, identifies the root of the problem, and solves it.

There's no big fuss, no debate, just results. My mother tells me to take notice and learn from her.

Aunt Cyla, Mama's oldest sister, is most like Grandma Amalia. Quiet, watchful, invariably with a book in hand, she's unnecessarily stuffy according to Mama.

She cares too much about tablecloths, matching fine dishes, projecting her wealth, and standing through her possessions. She's the complete opposite to Mamas' younger sister Aunt Henie. Aunt Henie plays on the floor with me and her sons. When we play ball in the park, she doesn't care if we return with muddy shoes. Mama isn't playful and silly, but she loves that about Henie. Each sisters' home is a wonderful place to grow and learn. I am part of something bigger here. A household and a feeling I never knew existed. Giving it up was devastating.

"Do you notice that Mama sleeps a lot more now? More than she ever did in Berlin."

I hope Papa has seen this change as well.

"Leaving Holland was exceedingly painful for her. We lost years struggling to stay alive. Her escape took a toll on her no one expected."

He clears his throat.

"Berlin gave us the best of everything until it didn't."

I squeeze his hand in mine because I'm proud of the decisions he made. Hitler didn't get us.

Rudy fusses and Papa moves swiftly. Our discussion is instantly over. I wish we had more time. He dresses Rudy and prepares waffles. We play jacks and examine pictures. I read the local news report out loud. It's a simple way for Papa and I practiced our English.

A few hours later, once Rudy is rubbing his eyes, Papa places Rudy next to Mama in their bed for a mid-morning nap, and we set out for the waterfront.

The one-on-one time with my Papa by the waterfront, with smells of saltwater, fish heads, and sweat, quiets my unease about being in England. Attending school for the first time in Holland was thrilling.

I didn't speak the language, but it didn't matter. I relished every new experience that came my way. My cousins made it easy. I fell in with that crowd effortlessly. I don't attend school in Liverpool; we're not supposed to be here for very long. England is merely a stopping point between Holland and America.

I don't know what to expect out of New York. We don't have a big family there for me to get lost inside of the way we did in Holland.

Mama says when you go to a new place you get to recreate yourself. No one knows your past. You become whoever you want to be. You make your own truth because you can control your own history. What kind of person do I want to be in New York? Am I the kid who escaped the Nazis and dragged his brother across the black forest to freedom? Perhaps I will keep it all a secret and be an immigrant from Holland?

My Papa checks his watch. In another hour we're meeting up with Mama and Rudy for lunch. My heart beats quicker, frightened this moment will slip away.

"We slept in a barn for two nights. Rudy and I saw colors in the sky we've never seen before. Through a crack in the roof, I counted stars until I ran out of numbers. A woman moved us from one checkpoint to another. I guess she was afraid she'd be caught because she abandoned us on a dirt road. I've never been in that type of situation before, where whatever happened was up to me. We could've walked off and never been heard from again. I thought about Rudy and how I was all that he had in the world. After the terror passed, I found hope. You told me to believe in myself. I spotted the barn, and I protected Rudy. His joy became my consolation."

"Your adventures," Papa draws in a bloated pause, "changed you."

His tone is flat, and I sense what he feels.

Without looking at his eyes, I can't know his truth. I'm transformed. It's not his fault.

"Can I tell you more?"

He nods and stories pour out of me.

Will my confessions unburden me? I can't make him feel better.

"A decent man smuggled us in a wagon loaded with hay. It was hopeless to get comfortable. The wheels, worn down by time, struck every divot on the dirt road. Several soldiers approached and one plunged a bayonet into the hay. It slashed Rudy's thigh. To stifle his wail, I shoved mama's red scarf into his mouth."

Papa's hands tremble. He pulls me towards him. Giving in and being held feels good.

"Remembering is draining," I admit.

"The funny thing about time, Manny, is that memories fail. When you suffer afterward, you can't recall the intensity. Once you persevere, your limits are expanded. Pain triggers growth. Manny, your shock is your own, but your pain will crush your mother. She cannot help you. Choose me. Share the bitterness with me."

******

Days later, the waterfront is all turbulence and excitement. It's the morning of our departure, and I can't eat.

Young families, older women, and abandoned children mill about. Papa carries Rudy in one arm and a suitcase in the other. He carries another duffle bag strapped to his back. It is bigger than me. The red carpet is inside.

Trucks arrive at the dock. One stops near us.

The driver and his companion hop out and adjust strange belts around their waists.

They unload crisp white linens, blankets, pillows, and mattresses. Loud sirens announce a medical transport.

They sort through the sick and wounded in a makeshift triage. Mama points to a sign I can't read. The pit of my stomach tingles. The sensation fills my belly and runs up my arms and down my legs. I'm out of my depth, navigating blindly. Before we left Berlin, I didn't know this feeling existed. Its recurrence now plagues me.

An untethered horse races down the dock without a rider.

The absurdity of the situation is joyous.

"Someone thought they could take their horse on the ship with them. She is a beautiful horse. It's a shame to leave her behind."

Papa's tentacles expand and contract with us like an octopus. The tempo in the air picks up like Korsakov's Flight of the Bumblebee. The sea of people moves like a swarm. The lines are endless.

When we stop, I put my suitcases down but never take my eyes off them. Mama's eyes flash in fear until Papa pats the duffle bag and nods.

This seems to help her.

When he delivers us to the final registration checkpoint, Mama's eyes fill with tears.

"It's happening," Mama whispers.

Our passenger ship used to be a luxury vessel. Cabins on higher floors are more extravagant than others. Fancy people dressed in ball gowns and tuxedos once waltzed where mattresses now line the floor. Royalty gambled in the rooms now used for birthing babies and taking care of newborns. The incongruity works in my mixed- up head. We spend our days on the ship in exploration.

We practice English and learn how to say our names slowly and clearly.

"If we can spell our names," Papa says, "America won't take them away. We are Rechtschaffens. We have been for centuries. The soil beneath our feet does not define us. Our name means something. Righteous. Honest. Right Thinking."

Nights on the top deck under the stars feel hopeful.

Lightning ignites a dark, brooding cloud that lights up as if struck by Hashem's drumstick. When the rain pours down, Mama laughs. Others flee, but not Mama.

She stands and says, "Raise your hands to the sky and let us wash away Berlin. We hold Holland and Poland in our hearts. They are our strength. Our secret weapon against the world's hatred. Let us leave the misery of Germany behind. May we never talk about it again."

She takes my hand.

"Don't lose your innocence, Manfred. I cannot alter what has transpired, but against the odds, we persevered."

The night before we dock, I have trouble settling to sleep.

Mama and I whisper until sunrise.

She tells me, "Nothing in life is given. Talent with hard work only goes so far. Everything in life is for the taking. You 're smart, smarter than most and with an honorable backbone. Education in America will make you wealthy. Wealth alters destiny."

Shaping the path for Rudy won't be hard.

Relying on him strengthens me.

He saved me, proving I don't need anyone but Rudy. The sun burns high in the sky, and our vessel approaches the dock. Rudy fidgets. I pull him to my side and get him to focus on basic exercises. Jumping jacks, running in place, hands the sky hands to your toes. He's vibrating with nervous energy.

Mama scolds Rudy, "If you don't settle down, they won't allow you into America."

In response, his face flushes, and his lips shape into a scowl.

Why must she ruin this moment?

Rudy's eyes fill with tears.

He's had enough harshness to last a lifetime.

I'll protect his innocence.

Faking a cough shifts Rudy's attention.

He looks up and points.

"The green lady. We are here. I see the lady!"

New York, 1950

Manhattan Quilt and Bedding store, New York 1945

Chapter 165
January 1974 NYC, New York
Rudy Rechtschaffen

Ronni clutches our newborn like a Mama Bear. Her name is Candace Melody; we'll call her "Candi," for short.

Her square-shaped face is framed in soft wisps of brown hair. Candi's long spindly fingers wrap around Ronni's index finger as she sleeps in her arms.

Her mouth sits in a swollen pout as if stung by a bee.

My beautiful baby girl is twenty-one inches long, eight pounds, four ounces.

A team of doctors wear neutral expressions as they approach us. Ronni shifts uneasily in the maternity bed as a nurse gingerly removes Candi from her arms.

I step across the room and pick up her newly emptied hand. Dr. Schwartz delivers bad news in a clinical and dissociated style.

"Dr. Rechtschaffen, Mrs. Rechtschaffen, your daughter has an intestinal blockage. The prognosis is fatal if we don't operate."

His words are lost in the crest of a tidal wave. I collapse into the armchair beside Ronni.

A surgeon steps forward and references a chart. Another doctor presents a set of x-rays.

My brother, Manfred, steps forward and asks Dr. Schwartz, "What are the odds?"

"I won't know until I'm in there," reports the surgeon impersonally.

I plead with the surgeon to save Candi.

Adrenaline courses through my veins.

My brother stands before me, but I can't hear him over my heart pounding in my eardrums. Ronni holds our daughter again and kisses her apple sized cheeks.

"Hashem, hear my pledge: I'll name her Amalia Rona, for My Grandmother who perished at the hands of Hitler. Rona for song, as my Grandfather Naftali loved the sound of the congregation singing together. I will pray every day for the rest of my life if you save my daughter."

Rudolph standing in front of family store, New York

Chapter 166
August 1985 NYC, New York
Candi Rechtschaffen

My father, Dr. Rudolph N. Rechtscaffen, is many things: a scholar, a teacher, a mathematician, a physicist, and a reliable man.

New York, 1980

Rudolph N. Rechtschaffen's development of static analysis of processor performance has made it possible to categorize delays in processing and to assess how improvements affect each category, so that alternatives in processor design can be studied independently for effects on different aspects of performance.

Just like his forefathers - Rebbe Rechtschaffen, Naftali Herzl, and my grandfather Aron - my dad's circadian rhythms obligated him to rise with the sun, sharp and ready to pray to Hashem.

After his morning prayers, my dad buys a dozen bagels, a container of TempTee cream cheese, and one six-ounce package of smoked lox from Bagel Power, our local bagel shop in the Golden Horseshoe shopping center.

Rudolph and Ronni

Just like his forefathers - Rebbe Rechtschaffen, Naftali Herzl, and my grandfather Aron - my dad's circadian rhythms obligated him to rise with the sun, sharp and ready to pray to Hashem.

After his morning prayers, my dad buys a dozen bagels, a container of TempTee cream cheese, and one six-ounce package of smoked lox from Bagel Power, our local bagel shop in the Golden Horseshoe shopping center.

Dad's usual Sunday morning breakfast wakeup ritual begins when he whistles up the stairs, "Now hear this, now hear this, get it while it's hot."

My dad, a mountain of a man, has gray hair, hazel eyes, and a soft, clean shaven face.

Mama comes down the stairs in her lime-green robe and slippers. I've already toasted her bagel for her. She'll only eat a half the bagel, but she'll pile an entire bagel's worth of lox onto it. Dad teases her about this every week. I like the consistency.

My brother Tommy can be heard rumbling upstairs, shaking the house. He stumbles down the stairs in his typical teenage fashion.

Daddy eats two garlic bagels, Tommy eats two onion bagels, and I eat one plain bagel.

On the weekends before the Jewish holidays, Dad takes us to the lower East Side of Manhattan, the heart of the Jewish diaspora, to shop for our supplies.

The Lower East Side is a part of my heritage. None of my friends in Scarsdale are first generation American.

Their Jewish traditions aren't the same as mine.

Dad prepares us for the holidays the way his family did. Walking along the intersection of DeLancey and Grand is like walking back in time through my own history.

Dad's Jewish-American refugee experience during the 1940s and 1950s became my foundational reference.

Through his eyes I see Kossar Bialy, Guss the Pickle Man, Rabinowitz Judaica bookstore, Kedem Winery, Streitz Matza, and Gertle's Bakery. Dad and Uncle Manny grew up on East 91st and Columbus Avenue above the family's bedding store, Manhattan Quilt and Bedding.

My grandparents purchased the store and apartment one year after moving to America in August 1940.

They didn't need a generation to achieve success; they managed to do it in one year, through hard work, bravery, and very little food or sleep.

My family piles into the Golden Bird, our white Impala station wagon with wooden side panels. Inside the car with the windows closed, the air smells of dad's Brylcreem and Irish Spring soap. Within fifteen minutes, we're off the Hutchinson River Parkway and onto the Cross County Expressway. Westchester slides away and we enter the Bronx. Tommy is listening to his walk-man and playing a handheld baseball game. Dad's taking the 3rd Avenue bridge today.

Mama quips, "Ru, I see we're taking the scenic route."

He smiles. They both grew up in the city and are the definition of sarcastic New Yorkers. We take the rickety metal swing bridge across the Harlem River. I feel the weight of the car bounce on the suspended bridge.

My stomach rises into my throat, like on a roller coaster. Dad has several secret routes into the city. We cross the bridge and stop at a red light. Instinctively, we lock our car doors. In Westchester, we drive all day with unlocked doors, but there we don't see homeless men walking in between cars to clean windshields for money.

Dad's lip curls and Mama wraps her arms around her purse in her lap. The homeless man approaches the car behind us. Dad instructs us to look away. What is he afraid I'll see? His fear of the homeless scares me more than the homeless man does. The light turns green, and we drive away.

Clusters of tall red-brick apartment buildings with black-ened windows and abandoned floors roll past my window. Their walls are covered with graffiti and obscenities. The playgrounds in the inner courtyard have missing or broken swings. I see a slide but no seesaws.

There aren't any paddle tennis courts and the basketball courts lack nets. It looks nothing like the IBM club in Armonk that we visit twice a month.

Litter blows across the faded hopscotch board and the wire trash cans remain empty.

Tommy leans over and says, "See how lucky we are? You work hard in school, and then you can raise your family the way we live in Scarsdale."

Dad snarks, "Anyone can live on Park Avenue..."

Tommy replies, "If you want to live on 150th street!"

Mom and Dad laugh in response, but I don't like what Dad's implying.

He'd never choose to live in any of these red brick buildings. My dad grew up in the city with people all around him, and he didn't like it.

He craved vast green spaces where he could walk, play with us, and breathe in peace. Dad doesn't enjoy the general conversation. He likes to speak but he's not particularly interested in other people's opinions.

That makes talking in the car difficult. His way of controlling the situation is to keep us singing.

Dad leads us in religious Gospels, Jewish prayers, and American classics like "Take Me Out to the Ballgame," the Columbia University Fight song, and "Yabba Dabba Dabba."

Mom and I sing full-throated while Tommy mumbles along.

Tommy asks, "Are Uncle Manny and Aunt Pamela coming today?"

Dad says, "We might run into Manny at the Rabinowitz bookstore."

Mom says, "It will be good to see them. We haven't seen them since Tommy's bar mitzvah."

"Pamela won't be there today. She's very far along in her pregnancy. A third son to be a great blessing," Dad states.

"Rudy, Pamela desperately wants a daughter as sweet as Candi," says mom.

I glow from the warmth inside my chest.

My mother loves me so much and she doesn't hide it, ever.

I love being the prized child in my mother's eyes.

All conversation ceases when dad begins to sing the Columbia University fight song.

"Roar lions roar, the alma mater on the Hudson Valley, fight on, for victory evermore!"

Tom joins in and their combined voices raise the hair on my arms. Mom turns to me and smiles.

The red and white sign of Kossar Bialy can be seen half a mile away. My stomach rumbles in anticipation. You can't buy bialys at home. They're a Lower East Side delicacy.

Entering the world of Kossar Bialy is a special treat.

I love being alone with my daddy. He's the smartest man in the entire world.

His booming voice is melodic like a Chazzan.

His full lips and his smile are magnetic. His demeanor and mannerisms change when he speaks Yiddish.

He's in an element unlike anywhere else in the world.

The warm smell of flour and baked bread excites my senses.

Three men dressed all in white, with starched aprons, stand behind the counter. They fill countless brown paper bags effortlessly with bialys leaving customers satisfied.

The hum off the industrial-sized oven is the perfect background to the chirpy customer banter.

The combination of sounds lulls my brain into a haze. White subway tiles cover the walls of the small store.

One wall features thirty or forty black-and-white photographs of Eastern European Jewish families over multiple generations. Daddy says those families could be ours. Trespassing through their private family diary consumes my entire focus. One photograph has a chuppah made of sunflowers. Another shows men dancing with Torahs, a third with families smiling and mountains in the background.

The clothing is different, but the loving smiles are familiar. Dad orders an onion board, a large cigar Bialy for Tommy, a small cigar Bialy for me, and a dozen Bialys to take home for the week. Mama doesn't want one, it's too much bread for her. She's holding out to get a falafel later.

We walk back to the car, and dad places his palm on the top of my head. His touch is loving. We deliver the two warm bags of Bialys to Mom. Tommy jumps out of the car and joins Dad. Mom unrolls the car window and reminds dad, "don't forget a small jar of half sours for me."

Dad smiles, and says, "yes, dear."

I like the way he speaks to her. It's not an afterthought. Two simple words filled with love and devotion.

Daddy hates half-sour pickles. He considers them a big waste of time, but mom doesn't like the full sour pickles. The sourness upsets her stomach. Dad's going to order a jar full of sour pickles, which marinates in the brine liquid for nearly three months, and a small container of pickled peppers. If Pesach wasn't around the corner, he'd buy a jar of sauerkraut.

Guss also features pickled sweet red peppers, tomatoes, pickled cucumbers, half sours, and three-quarter sour pickles. Retail stores on the lower side have a metal gate that pulls down from the top and locks at the bottom with a padlock.

This security measure is used to deter break-ins.

The cold metal gate is Guss the Pickle Man's front door. His shop is smaller than our two-car garage at home.

Once the gate is up, his entire store can be accessed from the street. The front of the store is lined with five-foot-tall gray rubber garbage cans filled to the brim with pickles in the brines. The seasoning contains garlic, vinegar, salt, coriander seed, mustard seed, and black peppercorn.

Guss is a stout man at five-foot-six. His messy gray hair is overgrown and hangs over the tops of his ears. His wire frame glasses enlarge his eyes. He looks like Mr. Magoo.

His white undershirt and button-down short sleeve shirt are clean but worn through. He's sweet looking with a round face, a flat nose, and small lips that disappear when he smiles. Guss personally addresses each and every customer. No one waits without a pickle in hand. Other men serve the customers, but Guss establishes and maintains the relationship. His easy banter immediately disarms.

When he approaches dad, I'm not surprised he remembers him.

"Doctor. Doctor. Good to see you," says Guss.

Dad's shoulders drop. He smiles warmly at an old friend.

"It's great to be here," says dad, offering his hand in friendship. Guss shakes it heartedly.

He then takes a piece of waxed paper with a full sour pickle and hands that to dad.

Dad nods and says thank you.

"She'll have a full sour and so will my son."

Inside his simple one-story tenement store is a small counter and a portable cash register. Large glass bottles line one of the three walls. My grandparents knew the original Guss the Pickle Man.

He emigrated from Poland around 1905.

This neighborhood, a bastion for displaced Jewish business-men, became known as the pickle district.

His family spent generations using their old-world talents to succeed. Our next stop is Gertle's Bakery at fifty-three Hester Street.

Passover is a special holiday in our house. I love the Sedar my Papa performs. The rituals harken back to centuries past. The food is limited, and my digestive system cannot take seven days of matzo.

In order to make their food more palatable my dad buys a different cake for dessert every night, including a lemon roll, a strawberry roll, the chocolate seven-layer cake, honey cake, apple strudel cake, marble cake, coconut lemon seven layers cake, and sponge cake.

My favorite part of Gertle's bakery has nothing to do with cake. The mechanism the cashier uses to tie the cake boxes fascinates me. A large spool of twine the size of my friend Jenny Ross is secured by a metal dowel fastened to a spinning tray. The twine is fed through a series of hooks and tracks suspended above the customers, allowing it to spool through the store above the customer's heads without getting in anyone's way.

The cashier lifts her hand into the air, clasps the thread, and ties the cake box within a second.

As mom heads into Economy Candy with Tommy to buy two pounds of dried apricots, my dad and I head into Rabinowitz Judaica bookstore. Rabinowitz Judaica bookstore doesn't look like the Barnes and Noble on Central Avenue. The bookshelves are metallic and industrial, not over-polished mahogany wood.

Customers don't linger in the store. There isn't a private reading nook set up with colorful bright area rugs and over-stuffed leather chairs.

Stacks and stacks of leather-bound texts line shelves as far as the eye can see. Dad is happy here.

Every holiday my Dad buys one book.

He says, "historically the Jews believe in educating themselves to the highest level imaginable."

After he purchases a book, he then writes either my name or my brothers on the title page.

"I will take care of your education. When I die, you take all the books with your name in it, and then you allow Tommy to take all the books with his name."

His sentiment would be sweet if it wasn't so brutally morbid. Our next stop is the Kedem Winery. Owned by the Hertzog brothers. They brought their Slovakia and winemaking talents to America. Back in Poland, Jews didn't have easy access to fresh grape-based wine.

They drank mead, honey, and raisin dry wine.

The Hertzogs came upon Concorde grapes which grew in abundance in New York state. Fairly inexpensive, they use the Concorde grapes as the base of their juice and wine company. They opened a store with a basement big enough to hold jumbo wine casks used to ferment the juice. Dad explains that the sidewalk is stained purple because of the discarded mash from the wine preparation. Dad buys two bottles of grape juice, one for each Sedar, and one bottle of wine. The last stop of the day is the Streit's Matzo Factory. The store is under the street on the basement level. It's smaller than our two-door garage at home. The dank room sweats as the large ovens bake thousands of matzahs a day in preparation for Pesach. Every store we visit is a cash business. Nothing has a price tag, and everything is negotiable. It's a different way of living, and a wonderful tradition to be part of.

Dad shares his secret world with us.

He gives us the keys to his kingdom. With pride he holds onto my mother's hand.

We're home within twenty-five minutes. We unpack the car and set up the new television set dad haggled over in Yiddish and bought on a whim.

He's proud because he got a good deal and supported the community he cares about the most. We've had a great family day. Mom heads upstairs to call her friend.

Tommy finishes some last-minute homework and I join my Dad in the family room.

"Candi, let's watch a quintessential Quincy episode."

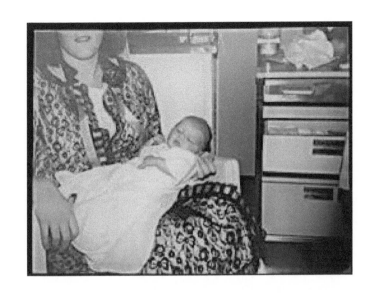

AFTERMATH

1928
Yudah Rechtschaffen 1867 - 1928 emigrated from Rozniatow with his wife and children to Argentina.

1931
Mozes Maijer Eisner 1869 - 1931
Retired in The Hague, Holland and died in Holland surrounded by his loving family.

1940
May 10, 1940 - The German invasion of Holland. Daniel Cohn (husband of Henie Eisner) and their two sons were killed during the invasion of Holland.

1942
Rebbe Tzvi Hersch Rechtschaffen 1890 - 1942
In his fifties he fought bravely during The Battle for Przemyśl. He later died from complications of the beating. He is buried in Rozniatow. He was survived at the time by his ten children, innumerable grandchildren, and his wife Etel.

Bluma Rechtschaffen 1900 - 1942 and her family were deported and killed in the Belzec concentration camp.

Cyla Eisner (dates unknown) was deported to Westerbork transit camp before she was killed in Auschwitz.

David Eisner 1914 - 1942 was deported to Westerbork transit camp before he was murdered in Auschwitz.

Etel Rechtschaffen 1880 - 1942 was murdered with a gunshot to the back of her neck and was buried in a mass grave in Grochowce Forest.

1943
Amalia Verbelte Eisner 1875 - 1943 was deported to Westerbork transit camp before she was killed in Auschwitz.

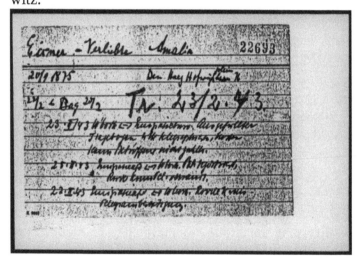

Gittel Eisner 1909 -1943 was deported to Westerbork and was killed at Auschwitz. She was survived by her daughter who confined the family line in Holland and eventually America.

Shalom Rechtschaffen 1902 - 1943 and his family never made it to Israel fulfilling his Zionist dream. His family were deported and killed in Belzec concentration camp during the total annihilation of Rozniatow at the hands of the Nazis.

Shimshon Rechtschaffen 1903 - 1943 was murdered during the battle of Przemysl.

1944

Maurice Eisner 1894 - 1944 became a Partisan fighter for the French underground. He smuggled out countless women and children and was captured in 1944 in a sweep of remaining Jews who still lived in France. There is a plaque dedicated to these fighters of France in Paris where his name is etched in memory and honor.

1971

Aron Rechtschaffen 1901 - 1971 Immigrated to New York in 1940. Worked with Karl Eisner for one year and bought his own store in 1942 called Manhattan Quilt and Bedding. They were proud members of the Congregation Kehilath Jeshurun. He lived to see one grandson each born from both of his sons.

1981

Marjem Eisner 1905 - 1981 Immigrated with her family to New York in 1940. She ran their store and enrolled her children in Ramaz Jewish Day School. She lived long enough to meet four out of five of her grandchildren.

1985

Henie Eisner Cohn disappeared with her older brother François to Marseille, France after her husband and children perished. She subsequently immigrated to America, remarried, and passed away in the 1980s.

1987

Karl Eisner (1898 - 1987) immigrated to New York in 1910 and married Bertha Dicker, a schoolteacher, and had children. He maintained a close relationship with Aron, Marjem, Manfred, and Rudolph Rechtschaffen.

1998

Rudolph N. Rechtschaffen 1936 - 1998 married Ronni Fink and raised his two children in Scarsdale, New York. An inventor for IBM, a physicist, a mathematician, and a statistician. He received an undergraduate degree from Columbia University, a Master's degree from Princeton University, and his Ph.D. from New York University. His proudest moment was my brother becoming a doctor. His second proudest moment was my graduation from Barnard College in 1996.

2007

Yaakov Rechtschaffen 1922 - 2007 immigrated to Australia. All Rechtschaffen in Australia are from this line. The last names include Rechtschaffer, Rechtschaffery, Rechtschaffner.

2022

Manfred Rechtschaffen 1932 - 2022 Survived and prospered in New York City. Manfred went on to become a rabbi and serve in the Vietnam war as a chaplain. Upon his return, he became a financial mastermind and created the Rechtschaffen group. He is survived by three doting sons, Alan, Andrew, and Eric, and nine grandchildren. He was exceedingly proud that each of his sons graduated from Ramaz and all of his grandchildren are either enrolled or graduates themselves.

He is survived by my brother Dr. Thomas Rechtschaffen, myself, Candace Rechtschaffen-Gillhoolley, our mom Ronni Jil Rechtschaffen, and his five grandchildren, Nathaniel, Ronin, Jessica, Autumn, and Zachary.

INDEX